Jefferson's
America

Jefferson's America

THE PRESIDENT,

THE PURCHASE,

AND THE EXPLORERS

WHO TRANSFORMED

A NATION

Julie M. Fenster

CROWN PUBLISHERS
NEW YORK

Published in the United States by Crown, an imprint of the Crown Publishing Group, a division of Penguin Random House LLC, New York.
crownpublishing.com

CROWN is a registered trademark and the Crown colophon is a trademark of Penguin Random House LLC.

Library of Congress Cataloging-in-Publication Data
Names: Fenster, Julie M., author.
Title: Jefferson's America : the President, the purchase, and the explorers who transformed a nation / by Julie M. Fenster.
Description: New York : Crown, 2016.
Identifiers: LCCN 2015041160 | ISBN 9780307956484 (hardback)
Subjects: LCSH: West (U.S.)—Discovery and exploration. | Louisiana Purchase. | Lewis and Clark Expedition (1804–1806) | United States—Territorial expansion. | Jefferson, Thomas, 1743–1826. | Explorers—West (U.S.)—History—19th century. | West (U.S.)—History—To 1848. | BISAC: HISTORY / United States / 19th Century. | BIOGRAPHY & AUTOBIOGRAPHY / Adventurers & Explorers. | BIOGRAPHY & AUTOBIOGRAPHY / Presidents & Heads of State.
Classification: LCC F592 .F46 2016 | DDC 973.4/6092—dc23
LC record available at http://lccn.loc.gov/2015041160

ISBN 978-0-307-95648-4
eBook ISBN 978-0-307-95654-5

Printed in the United States of America

Maps by David Lindroth, Inc.
Jacket design and illustration by Nick Misani
Jacket portrait: Rembrandt Peale, Thomas Jefferson, 1805, oil on linen, 28 x 23½ in., 1867.306, New-York Historical Society, Photography © New-York Historical Society

10 9 8 7 6 5 4 3 2 1

First Edition

To the memory of my
Aunt Roses
(Lynn Berk),
whose spirit of adventure never failed

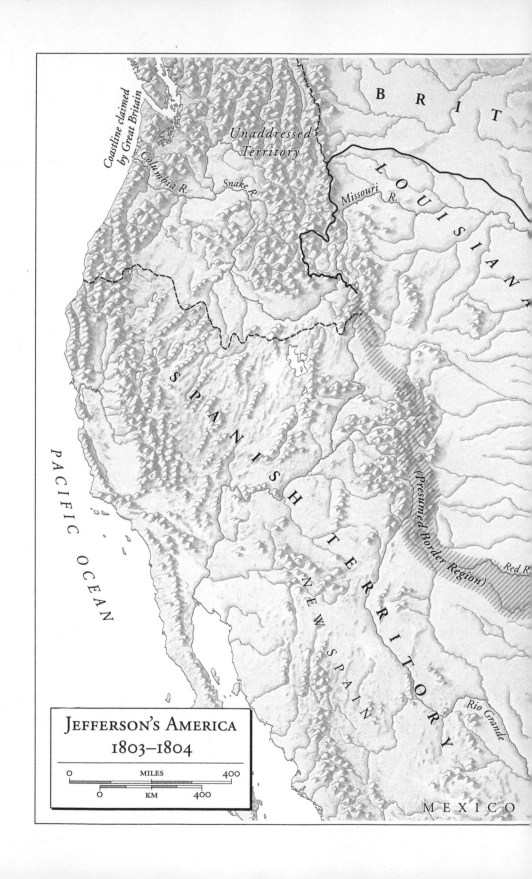

Coastline claimed by Great Britain

Unaddressed Territory

B R I T

L O U I S I A N A

Columbia R.

Snake R.

Missouri R.

S P A N I S H   T E R R I T O R Y

(Presumed Border Region)

Red R.

PACIFIC OCEAN

N E W   S P A I N

Rio Grande

JEFFERSON'S AMERICA
1803–1804

| 0 | MILES | 400 |

| 0 | KM | 400 |

MEXICO

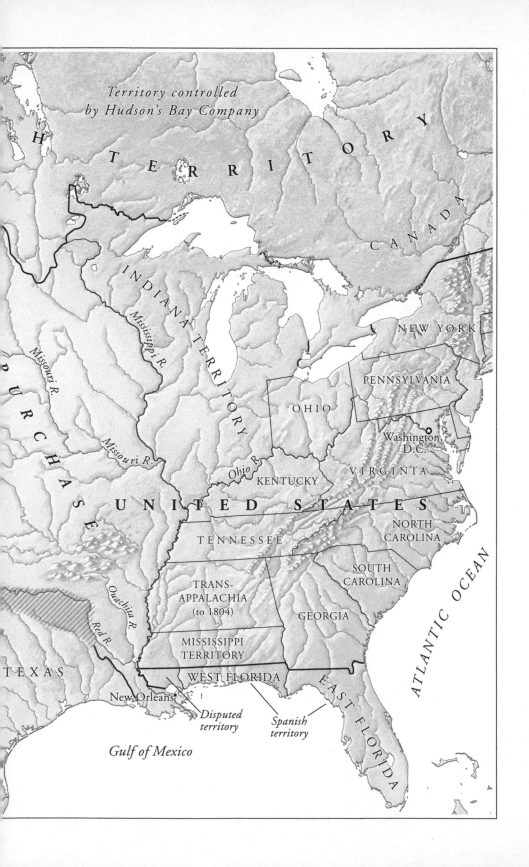

Territory controlled
by Hudson's Bay Company

H

TERRITORY

CANADA

INDIANA TERRITORY

Mississippi R.

Missouri R.

PURCHASE

Missouri R.

NEW YORK

PENNSYLVANIA

OHIO

Washington
D.C.

Ohio R.

KENTUCKY

VIRGINIA

UNITED STATES

NORTH
CAROLINA

TENNESSEE

SOUTH
CAROLINA

Ouachita R.

TRANS-
APPALACHIA
(to 1804)

GEORGIA

Red R.

MISSISSIPPI
TERRITORY

ATLANTIC OCEAN

TEXAS

WEST FLORIDA

New Orleans

Disputed
territory

Spanish
territory

EAST FLORIDA

Gulf of Mexico

Contents

Introduction

John James Audubon, the ornithologist and painter, left his family at home in Ohio in October of 1820 and traveled in a slight state of desperation to New Orleans, a well-worn city newly vibrant and very rich. As he sat on a flatboat heading downriver, he gazed at the birdlife on the water. When he couldn't do that, he liked to look at his billfold. It was stuffed, in lieu of money, with letters of recommendation from powerful people in the North. He fingered the letters, reread them, and even copied them one by one into his diary. At thirty-six, Audubon may have been gripped by a compulsion to draw wild birds, but he was headed to New Orleans to make money painting humans, preferably free-spending ones. He chose a city that was chock full of them.

The fact that New Orleans's prosperity soared so steeply after 1803, when the city was acquired by the United States in the Louisiana Purchase, was anything but coincidence. The Spanish, who owned Louisiana up to 1801, had clamped down on the slave trade for long spans. They also enforced laws granting significant rights to those already living under slavery. Once the Americans were in charge, though, the law favored slave owners and the traders who shipped slaves in by the hundreds. If only in monetary terms, the price of labor dropped. New Orleans was soon clogged to the walls with cotton. Like an old bon vivant with money to burn, it was the latest favorite of a whole swarm of fortune seekers. Some worked even more quickly than others: a pickpocket made off with Audubon's billfold on the second day the artist was in town.

Audubon had the grace to spare some pity for the thief, who had plucked a nice, plump wallet only to end up with a bunch of letters. Those letters, however, had been Audubon's treasure. For days afterward, his spirits were "very low," but they perked up when an acquaintance wrote a new letter of introduction, giving him entrée to the resident he most wanted to meet—a naturalist who had once been very famous.

As Audubon wrote in his diary, it was "a letter to Doctor Hunter, whom I wished to see to procure the Information I so much Need about the Red River."

Dr. George Hunter had actually seen only about twenty-five miles of the thirteen-hundred-mile Red River. In 1804, President Thomas Jefferson had arranged Hunter's role in the exploration of a section of the Lower Mississippi's western tributaries, including a short run on the Red River. Afterward, he included Hunter's exploits in a special report to Congress; it was immediately published in book form, finding wide readership.

In April of 1821, Audubon made his way to Hunters Mills, the collection of small factories that Hunter owned, either outright or in partnerships. The fact that Hunter was rich suggested to Audubon that he might need a portrait. So it was that Audubon's assistant, a teenage friend of the family from Ohio, accompanied him to Hunters Mills, lugging a portfolio of Audubon's artwork. "Low in funds,"

Audubon wrote, starting his description of the day. "Travelled as far as Dr. *Hunter* the renowned *Man* of Jefferson—We Came on him rather unaware.

"The good Man Was Pissing," Audubon continued. "We Waited and I gave him My Letter. . . ." After that, the interview faltered. It came to a complete halt if Audubon asked Hunter to describe the Red River. Nor did the old adventurer want a portrait. "This *Physician* May have been a Great *Doctor formerly*," Audubon wrote, "but Now deprived of all that I Call Mind I found it *Necessary* to leave [him] to his Mill's Drudgery—."

Something stinging or just sad bound together the contrast that Audubon drew between the explorer that he anticipated and a vague sixty-five-year-old making water in the yard. Yet for all of his disdain, tinged as it was with sarcasm, he gave Hunter a title that fit: "the renowned *Man* of Jefferson." When Hunter was exploring rivers for Jefferson in the newly acquired Louisiana Territory, leading an expedition with Mississippi's William Dunbar, he did his job gathering information on the terrain and the local residents. Even in the midst of the celebrated trip, Hunter might not have looked like a hero at first glance, if that was what a "*Man* of Jefferson" was supposed to be. He shot himself by mistake. He designed a boat for the trip that didn't float, and he was so interested in money that Jefferson secretly warned Dunbar not to let him spend all his time looking for gold mines.

Hunter earned his title "Man of Jefferson" not by doing everything right, but by going west when the president asked. He was one of eight people that Jefferson either hand-selected or oversaw as leaders of expeditions to explore the Louisiana Territory. The range in their ages reflected a search for leaders that was sometimes desperate and a spirit that was surprisingly rare. Meriwether Lewis, whom Jefferson had already sent to trace the Missouri River and a northwest route to the Pacific, was twenty-nine when he left. William Clark, Lewis's choice for a cocaptain, was thirty-three. Hunter was fifty when Jefferson called on him, a wholesale chemist with a busy family in Philadelphia. Dunbar, his comrade, was even older. Jefferson sought men whose curiosity overcame any sense of complacency. The desperate desire to look over the horizon didn't prevail with others whom Jefferson asked, and there were said to be many: comfortable easterners expert in science or navigation who turned down the chance to endure months of hard labor with dangers as sly as malaria and as sudden as the strike of a water moccasin.

Jefferson had in mind a very special combination of characteristics when he chose his explorers. He succinctly described the ideal as "a person who to courage, prudence, habits & health adapted to the woods, & some familiarity with the Indian character, joins a perfect knowledge of botany, natural history, mineralogy & astronomy." He then added gloomily that no such person existed in America. He'd looked. Making it especially difficult was the fact that American colleges had yet to offer courses in the pure sciences, such as geology, or in the social sciences, such as geography. Making it even more challenging, according to Secretary of War Henry Dearborn, was the money-maddened atmosphere of the United States circa 1803. Dearborn was assisting the president in seeking men for the expeditions. In the rare cases in which a person might be interested or even expert in science, Dearborn was told during the search, their study goes "just so far as it may be subservient to this all devouring passion of gain." Jefferson initially wanted only scientists or geographers, but he was forced to broaden his criteria after a growing list of refusals. Peter Custis, who ultimately made the trip to the Red River for Jefferson, was a medical student. Thomas Freeman, the leader of that expedition, was a surveyor. For all different reasons, they decided to go west for the president. For one dominant reason, he snapped them up when he could.

The explorers were Jefferson's other army. Wherever he sent them, the American flag followed. Yet they could go on the march without naming an adversary, a critical point at a time when the

United States was locked in hair-trigger tension with one European power in particular. The enemy that was innately and relentlessly hated by early Americans was Spain. For millions of Protestants, the cause was carried in the name proudly given by Spain's subjects to their monarch: "His Catholic Majesty." Many Americans, especially in the New England states, were not only virulently anti-Catholic, but fixated on Spanish persecution of Protestants in South America a century before; they had no intention of allowing any such measures to take hold in their new country. Merchants in the middle states resented Spanish control of the Mississippi, already a critical trade route. In what was then the western frontier of Kentucky and the Mississippi Territory, Americans lived close enough to the Spanish to distrust them on geographical grounds: bad neighbors continually bickering over a fence.

The fact that the Jefferson administration is best known for the Louisiana Purchase of 1803 and not for the disastrous War of Louisiana—a war that was soberly expected, but never occurred—is the result of a diplomatic attitude that reflected Jefferson personally. His emissaries, Robert Livingston and James Monroe, had taken the initiative overseas to negotiate the Purchase from Louisiana's short-term owners, the French. It was Jefferson's job to wrest it from the Spanish, who had been there for generations. The Spanish in the region were perfectly right to be angry. After the Purchase, the tension along the border between the two nations was real, mostly because no border existed. The French sold Louisiana and intentionally left the detail of drawing boundaries to the new owners. For that very reason, after the Purchase, the president urgently focused on the exploration of the more southerly region now occupied by the states of Louisiana, Arkansas, and Oklahoma.

To say that Jefferson responded to the new territory in a personal way would be an understatement. "Louisiana is the President's favorite Topic on all occasions," reported the British ambassador in 1804. "He introduced it as usual, when I made him a Visit on his return [to Washington] from his Estate in Virginia." The previous British ambassador, who had remained in Washington, was far less patient with Jefferson's effusiveness, informing the Home Office that the Louisiana Purchase "has elevated the president beyond Imagination in his own Opinion." Calling Jefferson "the vainest of men" in relation to Louisiana, the ex-ambassador then accused him of hogging all of the credit for the transaction.

Vain or not, Jefferson built his strategy for shaping the West on a truth. Right from the start and without having to think about it, the president made his name and Louisiana practically synonymous. If American voters noticed, it was politics. When foreign ambassadors noticed, it was diplomacy. His greatest problem, though, was giving that truth of his own making a strength that America didn't then possess. If Louisiana as a concept was too important for Jefferson to share, it was also too dangerous as an expanse to leave alone. Before anyone else, Jefferson entrusted the future of the American West to those varied *Men* of Jefferson who explored it for him.

One

—————

IN PLAY

Early in 1790, North America's two superpowers were arming themselves for all-out war while their respective allies across Europe fell
into line for what promised to be stupendous carnage. Ships of the
line were summoned to their home ports. Supplies were ordered and
cannon made ready. Tens of thousands of men and more than a few
women from Spain and Great Britain, Prussia, France, and Holland
would die, but their lives wouldn't be lost for nothing. The coming
war would decide once and for all which nation—Spain or Great
Britain—held the right of entry into a village of two dozen houses
on a small island along the Pacific coast in what is now Western
Canada.

The village became known among the Europeans as "Nootka."
It was occupied by the Nuu-chah-nulth Indians, who were amenable
to visitors from either nation. The Nuu-chah-nulth enjoyed a stable
society, although there were persistent reports that they practiced

cannibalism. Such accounts have been denied by their descendants; one explanation was that the Nuu-chah-nulth thought that it was the Europeans, indeed, who were the cannibals, and the Indians only offered a baked arm or leg, or worse, as a form of hospitality. More important, in terms of international relations, the Nuu-chah-nulth could supply otter pelts, newly valuable in European trade with China.

The English claimed possession of Nootka, because their explorer, Captain James Cook, had been the first European to visit there, in 1778. The Spanish claimed it, because *their* explorer, Vasco Núñez de Balboa, had been the first European in the Western Hemisphere to encounter the shores of the Pacific Ocean—albeit four thousand miles to the south and 277 years before. According to a treaty current in 1513 among exploring nations, that moment accorded Spain legal right to all of the land along eastern Pacific waters, from the tip of South America to the top of North America. Including Nootka. Because of the otter pelts, a rich theater of commerce was opening in Nootka in 1790 and both nations wanted to control it, but no one in diplomatic circles missed the more telling point. Britain was challenging Spain's claim to possess most of two continents on no firmer pretext than the fact that one of its sea captains had crashed out of a jungle one day in 1513 and stepped onto a beachfront in Panama.

While the majority of wars throughout history have been regarded as the result of failed diplomacy, foreign ministers at the end of the eighteenth century had different expectations. In fact, the profession of the diplomat was turned upside down. Maneuvering into the best wars was the art form for chief diplomats of the era, notably Talleyrand in France, Godoy in Spain, and Grenville in Britain. With all that was at stake, the move toward all-out war between Spain and Britain escalated during the first part of 1790 until the European owner of Nootka, the little village with the odd-smelling fires, was perceived as nothing less than the tacit overlord of the entire Western Hemisphere.

The British needed to find out how the Americans would ally themselves in the coming war, but they had no ambassador in the United States. Seven years after the end of the Revolutionary War, His Majesty's government still wouldn't stoop so low as to officially recognize its former colonists. Momentarily stumped, the British decided to send an alert, smooth-talking insider who was aware of the needs and nuances of British policy at the highest level—a diplomat in all but name. The man who was chosen, George Beckwith, was a military officer then serving as an aide to the governor of Canada. The only complication was that since he lacked diplomatic credentials, he couldn't hope to be received by the secretary of state. From the British point of view, however, that was just an added benefit.

At the time, the secretary of state was Thomas Jefferson. His distrust of the British was such common knowledge that an Anglophilic U.S. congressman warned his colleagues that the secretary of state "cannot be confided in" with information from London.

Working in the nation's temporary capital of Philadelphia, Jefferson was no happier than that congressman with President Washington's choice of secretary of state. He felt constrained at every turn, "shut up in the four walls of an office," as he later put it, "the sun ever excluded." For the first time in his life, Jefferson wasn't in charge; President Washington was. And he had coworkers who were on his level or straining to be just a little above it—notably Alexander Hamilton, the secretary of the treasury. Leadership at the State Department was a position well suited to Jefferson's conviction that the primary function of federal government was foreign affairs, but in practice he spent much of his time brooding over the outrages, real or perceived, perpetrated against him by Hamilton. Nonetheless, arriving at the State Department headquarters on High Street every morning, Jefferson duly presided over his staff of five employees: four clerks and a messenger.

When Beckwith finally traveled to Philadelphia for high-level meetings on Nootka, he bypassed the State Department on High Street entirely and continued on to Walnut Street, where he conferred with Hamilton on the impending war. So it was that the secretary of state with his four clerks, plus a messenger, sat inside those annoying walls of his office, keeping still and waiting for the secretary of the treasury to parry with America's greatest enemy—or ally. It is no wonder that Jefferson's frequent letters of resignation reflected his most impassioned writing in Philadelphia. Deliberate, as usual, and a politician to the core, Jefferson stoically worked through his friend President Washington, who spoke for Hamilton, who spoke for Beckwith, who spoke for the British Foreign Office in the newly evolved mechanism of Anglo-American statecraft. Of particular interest to Jefferson was the fact that the future of his continent's western territories had, surprisingly enough, suddenly come into play in the Nootka affair.

In the officially unofficial discussions with Hamilton, Beckwith disclosed that Britain was seriously considering seizing all of Spain's possessions in the New World. According to Beckwith, Britain would then free Spanish possessions in Central and South America as independent republics, but keep the North American tracts for itself. This would include Florida (which was divided into east and west sections then) and the Louisiana Territory, giving London control of the Mississippi River and New Orleans. Britain would also, incidentally, absorb Nootka.

In leaking this possibility to Hamilton, Beckwith was testing whether the United States would object to Britain's goal or, perhaps, embrace it. Hamilton was initially receptive. Spain had alienated the United States with a recently enforced policy forbidding American commerce on the Mississippi River. Reversing Spain's policy concerning the river was one of Jefferson's top priorities at

State, and the British promised that if they seized Louisiana, they would indeed lift the banishment of Americans on the Mississippi River. Surprisingly, though, Jefferson didn't welcome any switch in the West. Although the United States was an infant nation and an exhausted one in terms of war, Jefferson was determined to protect the Louisiana Territory, without even the remotest expectation of ownership.

Jefferson prepared a long memo on the subject, arguing that Britain's presence in the American West would leave the United States completely encircled, both on land and through Britain's dominance on the sea. According to Jefferson's foreign policy, the West protected the United States more effectively than any army, but only in the hands of the right foreign government. In the memorandum, which he titled "Considerations on Louisiana," he described Spain and England—each of which then controlled large expanses in North America—as "two neighbors balancing each other." He tentatively accepted that status. In fact, he found comfort in it. Rejecting the prospect of a single power dominating all of America's borders, he feared that any war between England and Spain would prompt one to invade the North American possessions of the other, notably by bringing Britain into Louisiana, disrupting the balance of America's neighbors.

Jefferson's conclusion was that Hamilton should tell Beckwith that the United States would "view with extreme uneasiness any attempts of either power to seize the possessions of the other on our frontier." Hamilton conveyed as much in the next meeting with the British official, which Jefferson was actually allowed to attend. For the time being, Britain set aside the proposed conquest.

The preparations for the Nootka war continued to sweep forward. And then, in 1792, Spain unexpectedly approached Great Britain, suggesting that the two nations should not fight one another—on the contrary, they should coexist in Nootka. The reason given for avoiding war over the little village was that the two powers would be

better off joining forces—against France. The horrors of the French
Revolution, especially in toppling the heads of aristocrats and roy-
als, had changed the priorities in many monarchal governments at
the time, though not enough to dissuade a strong nation—which
Spain purported to be—from protecting its empire.

Spain and Britain each sent emissaries to the Nuu-chah-nulths'
village to work out a permanent compromise. Their four-month negotiation was almost absurdly convivial, a battle of escalating hospitality. It was the last time either nation bothered with the place, and
yet Nootka had changed the future of the North American West.

In the Nootka affair, the United States voiced its first claim to
influence European ambitions in North America. Jefferson's maneuverings were a demonstration of strength, a very early seed of
what would become the Monroe Doctrine thirty-three years later.
But the Spanish had a doctrine, too, albeit an unwritten one, believing that they possessed by tradition or law or plain inevitability all
of the territory south of the Canada border from the Pacific Ocean
east to the Appalachians. The Spanish envisioned the eventual pro-
gression of their culture from Mexico and the Caribbean into the
open spaces of the American West—that is, the Mexican North. In
1792, Jefferson's stance in the Nootka affair had given the United
States something new, however: the presumption of influence over
the region. It was a victory he wouldn't forget.

Nootka also foretold more widely of Spanish defeat. The late
monarch Carlos III had presided over a formidable empire. At his
death in 1788, Spain was well situated, but his son and successor,
Carlos IV, faced the first test of his reign with Nootka. He funked
his chance. Even if the conclusion of the Nootka affair had all the
elements of peace and reason, it was seen as a tremor of weakness
on the part of Spain. Jefferson recognized it. So did Spain's own officials in North America, particularly those in the territorial capital
of New Orleans and its satellites, Natchez and St. Louis. The Spanish crown may have blinked, but that only made the men on the

job, the ones controlling Madrid's claims in North America, more adamant than ever.

Natchez, 268 miles north of New Orleans by water, served a middle range of the Mississippi and the territory to the east. St. Louis, 1,180 miles farther north, administered what the Spanish knew of the Upper Mississippi, and lands to the west. Both answered to the governor-general of Louisiana, who was based in New Orleans. Starting in 1791, that influential post was filled by Francisco Luis Héctor, barón de Carondelet. At forty-four, he was a former military officer with far-reaching ambitions for New Orleans. Arriving four years after a fire had tragically, but conveniently, erased much of the old city, he worked enthusiastically to rebuild it as a fully modernized trade center, the economic powerhouse of the West.

If Carondelet hadn't been under orders to allow Americans to operate businesses in the city proper, he wouldn't have had any use at all for them. His subordinates, working in distant locales, were more flexible or at least more resigned. Zenón Trudeau, the amiable lieutenant governor based in tiny St. Louis, did little to discourage the stray Americans who made their way to his region, trusting that they would eventually be naturalized into loyal Spanish subjects. Manuel Gayoso de Lemos, Natchez's lieutenant governor, also encouraged individual Americans in his district, even as he involved himself in serpentine schemes against the United States as a whole. But Carondelet was incorrigible—if not as a governor, then as a watchdog. He perceived the midsection of the continent in four sections, each of which existed to protect Mexico, Spain's treasure house, from American encroachment. First came Texas, then Louisiana, then the Mississippi River Valley, then Trans-Appalachia. If Carondelet had his way, all four would be scrubbed clean of Yankees.

Carondelet had a problem, though, and so did His Catholic Majesty: the open secret was that Spain didn't have the money or the population to fulfill its territories. Its presence was especially lacking in the upper section of the Louisiana Territory, bisected by the Missouri River. According to statistics gathered by Lieutenant Governor Trudeau, the 400 million acres of Upper Louisiana was home to just 2,665 Spanish subjects in 1795: "Whites, Free Mulattoes, Free Negroes, Mulatto Slaves and Negro Slaves." Nearly all of them lived along the Mississippi River, with a few dozen in the hamlet of St. Charles, twenty miles up the Missouri River.

Carondelet was aware that he needed to populate the Louisiana Territory in order to protect it, but he was adamant that he wanted only Europeans, mainly Catholics, and specifically ones who could love and respect a monarch. He didn't want Americans, regarding them as "ferocious men who know neither law nor subjection." He wasn't entirely wrong about that, since he was speaking specifically of the ones who were first into the Trans-Appalachian West. Many Americans along the East Coast would have agreed with him; the first westerners were a rascally and often treacherous lot. But that changed quickly as the population of the Trans-Appalachian West grew into the hundreds of thousands in the 1790s.

The migrants who struck out to the western edges of Trans-Appalachia were not looking for new rights, as were their ancestors. They were fleeing the country that offered more rights than any other on earth. A war had no sooner been fought for that cause than the exodus to the west began, bringing into question just what the cause had been. Only a few months after the peace treaty finalized the Revolutionary War, Washington himself was on his way west to Ohio looking for property. First in war, first in peace, and first in line at the Ohio land office, he bought his share of tracts, having once summed up the prevailing attitude in a letter: "Any Person," he wrote, "who neglects the present opportunity of hunting out good Lands & in some measure Marking & distinguishing them for his own 'in order to keep others from settling them,' will never regain it." Americans with political ties far less staunch than those of General Washington poured into Trans-Appalachia and straggled into regions in Spanish possession, east and west of the Mississippi.

Although Americans were forbidden by the Spanish from settling in Louisiana and from using the Mississippi River (except with permission), Lieutenant Governor Trudeau was more generous in his attitude—and far more desperate to populate his region. He tried to convince Barón de Carondelet not to think of every instance of American immigration as a "hostile incursion," but without success. Carondelet saw only the worst in the American character, or at least he had an accurate impression of just a small sampling of it:

> A little bit of corn, gunpowder and balls suffices them, a house formed from the trunks of trees serves them as shelter; their corn crop finished, they raise camp and then go further inland, always fleeing from any subordination and law.

Teasing the Americans across the Mississippi was easy for the Spanish. Driving Jefferson and other American diplomats into fits of frustration must have come naturally, too, since they did it for years, and could have gone on doing so in perpetuity. The basis of Spain's dominance was benign stagnation, a workable system over the course of generations. From one corner of the vast Louisiana Territory to another, the empire depended on the ability, gleaned from desperation, of local governors who played for time without population or wealth or military might. The Spanish finally met their match, though, in the form of a shaggy-faced hunter named Jacques d'Eglise. In October 1792, d'Eglise paddled down the Lower Missouri River and trudged into St. Louis. With the information he delivered, a new front opened for the Spanish in America, and they saw clearly just how embarrassed their position had become.

———

D'EGLISE WAS A Spanish subject despite his French name. He told Lieutenant Governor Trudeau that he had traveled twenty-one hundred miles to the north and west on the Missouri River. At first, Trudeau seemed to classify d'Eglise with animal life, describing him as "an ignorant man who made no observations and who hardly knows how to speak his own French language." Later, Trudeau allowed that d'Eglise probably did know how to speak his own language, but that he was "from a province of France of such a peculiar [dialect] that nobody can understand it." Trudeau couldn't resist adding that he still thought d'Eglise was "simple." He shouldn't have been quite so quick to make that judgment known; for the moment, the simpleton was smarter than anyone else in St. Louis.

Traveling alone up the Missouri River, d'Eglise had been seeking undiscovered hunting grounds or, even better, Indian nations that had yet to open trade with Europeans or Americans. What he found was astounding to him and all who heard about his journey later. In what is now central North Dakota, he came upon a highly active cluster of villages. They were at the center of, in Trudeau's words, "a nation about which there was some knowledge under the name of Mandan, but to which no one had ever gone in this direction and by this river."

The Mandan Indians and their neighbors, living in permanent domed houses behind the safety of stockade fences, seemed "like Europeans" to d'Eglise. They had lighter complexions than nearby tribes, such as the Sioux, and some had light-colored hair. D'Eglise estimated the population at four to five thousand; more recent estimates set a figure about half that size, but it was by far the biggest Native settlement to the north or west of St. Louis (and, in fact, it was at least twice as big as St. Louis itself). With large fields of corn, beans, peas, and oats, the people of the villages variously grew vegetables and hunted; they also traded with other tribes that were less productive, and apparently almost all of them were. Mandan commerce grew into a major operation: the economic powerhouse of the West, indeed. Colin G. Calloway has written that "Assiniboines, Crees, Ojibwes, Crows, Blackfeet, Flatheads, Nez Perces, Shoshones, Cheyennes, Arapahoes, Kiowas, Kiowa Apaches, Pawnees, Poncas, and various Sioux bands all visited the Upper Missouri villages, either regularly or intermittently." Then the Europeans arrived.

When d'Eglise walked into the Mandan villages in 1791, the first surprise was that he was welcomed. He might just as easily have been killed on sight, but the Mandans were accommodating to most visitors. D'Eglise then wasted his time by describing to the Mandans "the advantages that would come to them from the commercial dealings he was about to establish with them."

If anyone could judge commercial dealings, it was the Mandans. D'Eglise started to realize that fact when they showed him the array of goods they had for trade, starting with horses, the standard valuable of the Native American economy in the West. Even Indian slaves were available for sale. The Mandans and their neighbors could also offer English manufactured goods of every type, including teapots and snuffboxes, but notably they stocked a full line of guns and ammunition. D'Eglise was told that they had an active trade with the English, who had a settlement that was quite close by the standards of the West—accessible in only two weeks. D'Eglise was particularly taken aback when he was shown leather goods from the Rio Grande area two thousand miles to the south—"they have saddles and bridles in Mexican style for their horses," he marveled to Lieutenant Governor Trudeau. "They have furs of the finest sort and in abundance." Apparently, the Mandans were connected in trade with everyone on the better part of two continents—except for the Spanish in St. Louis.

D'Eglise's report struck Lieutenant Governor Trudeau and other Spanish officials like a lightning bolt. The English, without an army or diplomacy, had brought their mercantilism deep into Spain's territory. Letters followed, back and forth from St. Louis to

New Orleans and then on to either Madrid or San Ildefonso, Spain, where Charles IV's summer home was located.

Before d'Eglise, the Spanish who were administering the frontier had come to the sensible conclusion that without money or soldiers or people in abundance, a territory can't be controlled. It can only be *held*, and rather gently. D'Eglise gave the Spanish, especially Trudeau, a fourth means of securing territory. Exploration could assert control, because accurate information was another basis of power.

Without delay, Trudeau launched a trading company to explore the Missouri River. Its earliest expeditions learned very quickly that d'Eglise had enjoyed a kind of beginner's luck. In his first voyage along the Missouri River, he had slipped past Indian nations that proved difficult or dangerous for later travelers. Despite the fact that d'Eglise didn't keep a journal, didn't collect samples, and probably never looked twice at an unusual flower unless he thought it might buy something from him, he moved among the Indians with more sensitivity than many of those who followed. Traders and travelers could easily disrupt trade and elicit trouble from one or another of the tribes—or cause trouble between whole nations.

Joseph Garreau, a trader who accompanied d'Eglise on his second journey, left an example of the damage that could be done by a crude interloper. He stopped at a Sahnish village and never went any farther. D'Eglise continued on without him. Garreau, having borrowed sixteen hundred pesos' worth of merchandise on credit to use in trade for peltry, spent it instead for "improper uses," according to d'Eglise. As one of his contemporaries explained, the nations along the Missouri varied widely in their attitudes toward carnal relations. Within several, though, it was reported that "husbands, fathers and brothers are importunate with the white men who visit them, to make free with their wives, daughters and sisters, particularly those who are most youthful and pretty; and in consideration thereof accept a few baubles or toys. Indeed both the girls and married women

are so . . . easy and accessible that there are few of them whose fa-
vours cannot be bought with a little vermillion or blue ribbon."

After about eighteen months, Garreau couldn't return to
St. Louis, because he had nothing to show for all the merchandise
that he'd borrowed for his trip. During the same span, the Sahnish village wouldn't trade its pelts to the Spanish, since they were
already receiving from Garreau everything that Spain had to offer.
Garreau left a debacle in his wake, but he wasn't entirely unique in
that respect. Misguided European Americans who looked on accommodating tribes as a vacation from their own cultural strictures
caused problems, yet they continued to arrive, as one disapproving
explorer wrote, "running at full speed, like escaped horses, in Venus'
country." For explorers in the West, the attraction to hardship had
to be stronger than anything, except for the resistance to ease in
societies dramatically different from the one left behind.

While further exploration of Upper Louisiana stalled in disarray,
two men arrived separately in Philadelphia in 1792 hoping to follow
the Missouri River west from St. Louis. Neither had any knowledge
of the Mandan villages or of d'Eglise's trip to them, but one of the
two, André Michaux, was an experienced investigator who caught
the attention of Thomas Jefferson.

Michaux had grown up on a farm in Versailles, near the royal
preserve outside Paris. Learning botany from local authorities,
he was nothing if not driven, and despite his humble origins, he
planned and completed a series of complex research trips. Gaining
sponsors, he traveled farther and farther through Europe and Asia
Minor, focusing on the study of trees. At age thirty-nine, his reputation was such that he was appointed by the French government to
make botanical surveys in the Western Hemisphere. After completing a heroic trip to the shores of Hudson Bay, Michaux began to
plan a trip west, as far as possible on the Missouri River. He had all
of the requisites for exploration: field experience, knowledge of botany, and physical stamina. A vivid personality didn't hurt, certainly

not in the very first step, because he needed someone to underwrite his trip to the West. Michaux soon found, however, that rich Americans were far less enthusiastic than their European counterparts in regard to both science and to spending money on science with no hope of a return. He eventually found his way to one of the exceptions: Thomas Jefferson.

Jefferson wasn't in a position to express an official interest in exploration west of the Mississippi; it was foreign territory in unfriendly hands. Nonetheless, as secretary of state, he placed a high priority on the Louisiana Territory. On meeting Michaux, he was intrigued both by the visitor's plan to find the source of the Missouri and, no doubt, by his background.

With Jefferson's active assistance, Michaux received the endorsement of the American Philosophical Society, and the promise of $5,000 on completion of a trip all the way to the Pacific Ocean. The APS, cofounded by Benjamin Franklin fifty years before, was a private club, dedicated to spearheading intellectual thought. At that time, "philosophical" had a different meaning than it does today; it referred to rational knowledge and especially, in common use, to the pure sciences. At a time when U.S. colleges had yet to fully embrace chemistry, biology, astronomy, zoology, or anthropology, the APS encouraged those few Americans with an interest in such sciences. It was based in Philadelphia, where Jefferson took full advantage of his membership and enthusiastically attended APS meetings.

The APS raised a small advance to help Michaux, while continuing the promise of more, once he had finished his journey west.

The second hopeful to land in Philadelphia looking for the chance to chase the Missouri's source had, in comparison to Michaux, no qualifications. In terms of field experience, he'd never traveled anywhere, except in his native Wales, and then mostly along country lanes. Knowledge of natural science: he was a twenty-two-year-old part-time clergyman. Stamina: untested, as was everything else about him. Even in Philadelphia, John Evans was a greenhorn—and Philadelphia was a long way from the wilds of the Missouri River.

Evans had arrived in America all alone, on a mission that had nothing at all to do with scientific exploration. His quest was the legendary tribe of Welsh Indians. The Welsh Indians were said to be descended from a hero named Madoc—who was said to have traveled to America in the twelfth century. The most compelling evidence of their existence came from a minister originally from Wales, who claimed he'd been captured by Indians in North Carolina around 1740; just as they were on the verge of burning him alive, he said some sort of farewell to himself in his native tongue. The Indians responded in Welsh and after a happy reunion, of sorts, the execution was canceled.

The legend intrigued many people of a romantic nature in Britain, and so it was that one of them stepped forward with loud fanfare to search for the tribe. Fanfare is all that there was, however. When he bowed out at the last minute, John Evans impulsively took his place and set sail across the Atlantic.

In Philadelphia, Evans was looking for sponsorship money at the same time as Michaux. But while Michaux was jotting a splendid entry in his journal—*"Ma proposition ayant été acceptée, j'ay donné à M. Jefferson, secretaire d'Etat, les Conditions auxquels je suis dispose à entreprendre ce voyage"**—Evans was making a cold call on one of Philadelphia's many enclaves of Welsh immigrants. He did his best to make a patriotic argument for a stipend, but when he was finished, he was bluntly informed that they'd already sent someone to look for the Welsh Indians. Regardless of whether that was true, or just a ready answer for a callow young man, Evans failed to win a single sponsor in Philadelphia. Quitting the city in March 1793, he made his way west anyway, without help.

---

* "My proposition having been accepted, I gave Mr. Jefferson, the Secretary of State, the conditions under which I would undertake this journey."

Michaux also left for the West early in 1793. By that time, Jefferson may have begun to doubt him. Although he had written letters to raise funds for Michaux, he only gave $12.50 of his own money to the effort. Moreover, when a neighbor from Virginia, eighteen-year-old Meriwether Lewis, wrote to Jefferson and "warmly sollicited" permission to accompany the Michaux expedition, he was flatly turned down.

Indeed, Michaux never even made it as far as St. Louis. On his way to seek the Missouri's source and a route to the ocean beyond, he was sidetracked to Kentucky, where he was instrumental in a French plan to conquer Spanish Florida—and, perhaps, Louisiana. The trip to discover a water route to the Pacific would have to wait; a revolution was rising.

The fact that Michaux had so many adventures from which to choose reflects just how unsettled Trans-Appalachia was during the 1790s. A robust person could barely stop there without being invited to conquer it. The French plot for the Floridas and Louisiana was being overseen by a diplomatic official, the plenipotentiary Edmund Genêt. He was authorized by his superiors in France to raise an army, which would attack Spanish possessions from a base in Kentucky. The head of Genêt's military force, a man who was accorded the title "Major General of the Independent and Revolutionary Legion of the Mississippi," was George Rogers Clark.

Clark had once held a different title: Major General of the Kentucky Militia of the Continental Army of the United States. Storming British strongholds in Indiana and Illinois early in the Revolutionary War, he'd been a national hero just when the American side was starved for them. An acquaintance described him then:

> Col. Clark was nature's favorite, in his person as well as
> his mind. He was large and athletic, capable of enduring
> much—yet formed with such noble symmetry and manly
> beauty, that he combined much grace and elegance together

with great firmness of character. He was grave and digni-
fied in his deportment, agreeable and affable with his soldiers when relaxed from duty, but in a crisis, when the fate
of a campaign was at stake or the lives of his brave warriors
were in danger he became stern and severe. His appearance
in these perils indicated without language to these men that
every soldier must do his duty.

Clark spent his own money outfitting his militia and he took a
physical beating during his successful campaigns for the American
cause. In 1793, though, ten years after the war ended, he had yet to
be repaid for his expenditures and was reduced to shuffling among
his siblings for care. His older brother, Jonathan, a Virginia legisla-
tor, continually pressed his case with the authorities there and in
Philadelphia, to little avail.

George Clark's problem was summarized by historian James
Fisher, "On the basis of his success in 1778–1779, Clark had assumed that he was the pivotal personality in the West." During the
war, he was just that. Fifteen years later, though, few others saw
Clark the way he saw himself, which is a predicament for anyone
when it becomes an obsession. The number of believers was, if anything, only dwindling.

First among those who did look on Clark as the once and future
"pivotal personality in the West" was his little brother, William. For
him and by him, George's heroism was kept buffed through all the
years. William, also serving as an army officer, took responsibility
for the organization of George's claims on the regional level. At the
age of forty-one, though, George Rogers Clark had his own plan
to recoup his losses—all of them. He was raring for new conquest,
if only someone would call on him. Disavowing the United States
in favor of the opportunity to return to glory, he had even tried to
interest the Spanish in several ventures.

Jefferson felt as tenderly toward George Rogers Clark as for the members of his own family. He had known Clark as a toddler, nine years his junior; their families both lived for a long time near Charlottesville and they socialized frequently. In adulthood, Jefferson moved toward statesmanship and Clark toward the military from his new base in Kentucky, but they always remained loyal to each other. Jefferson, as secretary of state, was aware of Clark's seditious forays with the Spanish, attributing them to disappointment "grown morbid." He also knew that Clark had taken to drink. He wrote to a mutual friend, Harry Innes, the federal district court judge in Kentucky, saying of Clark:

> I know the greatness of his mind, and am the more mortified at the cause which obscures it. Had not this unhappily taken place there was nothing he might not have hoped; could it be surmounted, his lost ground might yet be recovered. No man alive rated him higher than I did, and would again, were he to become again what I knew him.

Unbeknownst to Jefferson, Judge Innes was even more involved with Spanish intrigues than was Clark. But then, the same could have been said of a whole cadre of officials in Kentucky, including its U.S. representative John Brown and (most notoriously) its military commander, General James Wilkinson. That was Kentucky in the 1790s—swarming with conspiracies. Even in 1792, when it was rushed into statehood, its future was still up for grabs. Spanish, French, American, Independent—any status might have awaited Kentucky. Clark, attaching himself to Genêt late in that year, was no great American patriot for his action, but he was trying with pathetic desperation to find his way in a state full of shadows.

Genêt's scheme was uncovered and it exploded in scandal. Clark was yet again disgraced and rumors spread that he would be arrested. He wasn't, but his problems continued. He wouldn't stop reaching, despite the fact that with every new attempt, his reputation suffered yet another blow. William Clark watched his brother descend and continually tried to prop him up, to the extent that a young man could.

When the plot to found a new French empire in Kentucky disintegrated, Genêt and Michaux both quietly left the state. The American Philosophical Society just as quietly marked the expedition to the Missouri River "failed." Michaux retired to a tree nursery business that he owned in South Carolina.

John Evans, the tortoise to Michaux's hare, was still moving west slowly, arriving in St. Louis before the end of 1793. While he was there, he enthusiastically repeated the story of the Welsh Indians and expressed his belief that they almost certainly must be living along the Missouri River. He had heard of the Paduca Indians of the Northern Plains and thought the name sounded something like "Madoc." The logic of his conclusion was tenuous enough, but sadly, even his supposition was faulty. There were no Paduca Indians. It was a name rather sloppily attached to any number of tribes, especially Plains Apaches and later, to Comanches. It could also be given erroneously to any party of Indians that was otherwise hard to identify.

When Lieutenant Governor Trudeau heard about the Welsh Indians, he issued an arrest warrant for John Evans.

It never occurred to Trudeau that a person could actually believe in anything as preposterous as Welsh Indians. He considered Evans's story an overly imaginative British plot to place a spy along the Missouri River. That being a military offense, there was no trial and no sentence. Evans was simply locked in a cell in a jailhouse in St. Louis, entirely at the mercy of the lieutenant governor.

The best hope for proceeding with the exploration of the West was shut up in four walls. Moreover, as 1794 began, the best hope for promoting it wasn't.

Two

THE MAN IN THE FARMING COAT

At the end of 1793, Thomas Jefferson left his post as secretary of state, sending one last, truly final letter of resignation to President Washington, who sent back a reply, thanking him kindly, expressing his understanding, and then asking him again if he wanted to stay a little longer.

He didn't. Even after Jefferson arrived home at Monticello, he continued to be disturbed by his firsthand experience with American government as it grew into reality out of a stack of praiseworthy documents. His reversion to the farming life didn't take long, and by spring he was able to write a letter to President Washington that didn't make reference to Alexander Hamilton even once. It was just a docile message from one farmer to another, discussing land use and crop rotation: "First year, wheat," Jefferson wrote. "Second, corn, potatoes, peas; third, rye or wheat, according to circumstances; fourth and fifth, clover . . ."

If Jefferson felt unloved and ultimately exhausted after years away from home, the land at Monticello was in much the same shape. Jefferson described the condition of his fields as "wretched," telling Washington, "abandonment of them to the ravages of overseers, has brought on them a degree of degradation far beyond what I had expected." During his first few months at home, Jefferson discussed his theories of crop rotation endlessly in letters and also in conversation. His neighbors tired of the very phrase.

Jefferson was a contradictory character in most respects, but one facet was consistent in every light. Jefferson needed his land, that particular land at Monticello. He could have lived without his house had it burned down or needed to be rebuilt. He might even have enjoyed the chance to correct his mistakes, especially the ones that only he noticed. If, however, he had ever been forced to sell Monticello outright, there would have been nothing to replace it and nothing left under his feet.

At the age of twenty-four in 1767, Jefferson had already inherited landholdings that totaled nearly 2,000 acres, but the little mountain and its surroundings, a tract of 683 acres, gave him the sense of home he'd never quite had before. As he wrote later, it was "a hill 500 f. [feet] perpendicularly high. On the east side, it breaks down abruptly to the base." To the north, the property followed the Rivanna River. In the northwest, it overlooked the town of Charlottesville, three miles distant. Due west, the hilltop took in three valleys and the Blue Ridge Mountains, twenty-five miles away. To the south, it looked to the Ragged Mountains, which were just that, jutting up into points. Jefferson's mountain featured slopes and natural meadows, but the crown and great patches of the rest were covered in hardwood forests when he first started hiking there.

The most obvious attraction was the view, which seemed to first-timers to be only of the surrounding lands and distant ranges. Jefferson never tired of those vistas, but he especially liked to look into the air above the land and, even more, to look *down* on the very sky to which others looked up. Writing to Mrs. Maria Cosway, an artist friend in Paris, he composed a rhetorical argument to tempt her into visiting America; he knew she would never make the trip, but to show her why he, likewise, couldn't remain in Europe, he described the place where he lived:

> Our own dear Monticello; where has nature spread so rich a mantle under the eye? Mountains, forest, rocks, rivers. With what majesty do we there ride above the storms! How sublime to look down into the workhouse of nature, to see her clouds, hail, snow, rain, thunder, all fabricated at our feet! And the glorious sun, when rising as if out of a distant water, just gilding the tops of the mountains, and giving life to all nature!

Jefferson thought in the long term about Monticello, continually experimenting with ways to take care of his tracts there and elsewhere. That idea contradicted the commonplace attitude in an era when land was expected to take care of Americans; farmers used a tract for a few years and then found more land somewhere else, or let fields lie fallow for five or ten years. Without those farming techniques, there wouldn't have been quite so many people rushing west, past the Appalachians.

Unlike other farmers in the late 1700s, Jefferson had no intention of letting his fields dry up, blow away, or wash out. For the first time in a long time, though, books offered no answers for him; he couldn't ask anyone either. If he wanted to know his land, he had to walk it, look at it, give it time, look at it again, and try to know what it was communicating. Before long, he "knew the name of every tree, and just which one was dead or missing," as Edmund Bacon, manager of the estate, recalled. Monticello is best known for the house, which Jefferson designed. First, though, it was the land that designed him with the patience to be in something for the long term.

Jefferson liked to inform his friends that he had returned to farming with "an ardour which I scarcely knew in my youth." He explained to his friend President Washington that "instead of writing ten or twelve letters a day, which I have been in the habit of doing as a thing in course, I put off answering my letters now, farmer-like, till a rainy day, and then find them sometimes postponed by other necessary occupations." He was happy to point out that, far from being locked inside the four walls of an office, he spent his days traveling from farm to farm and field to field on horseback. Jefferson described himself personally plowing fields and bringing in the hay, the hottest and dustiest job on a farm. At night, so he said, he was usually too tired from the outdoors and its exertions even to pick up a book. He boasted to his friends of wearing a "farming coat" with his riding overalls—the perfect picture of the rustic man.

While Albemarle County was not as prickly as Philadelphia had been, neighboring farmers were openly skeptical of Jefferson's theories on agriculture, just as he was outright disdainful of theirs. Jefferson was an adamant proponent of the live fence, rarely seen in the United States. Where his neighbors installed wooden fences around their fields to protect them from animals, Jefferson looked for a plant that would provide the same barrier. After considering a few possibilities, he planted neat rows of peach trees between his fields at Monticello. He seemed to be at his happiest planting trees, especially ones that would give him something to eat with heavy cream in midsummer. Peach trees were bushy enough for the purpose, and they grew quickly.

In one sense, though, the timing of Jefferson's retreat was unfortunate. In 1795, two years after Jefferson left office, his successor as secretary of state, Thomas Pinckney, presided over America's first diplomatic coup. He extracted from Spain the Treaty of San

Lorenzo, a triumph that allowed, among other things, for free navigation of the Mississippi River by Americans. He also convinced the Spanish to recognize American sovereignty over Trans-Appalachia. The man in the farming coat had once been the guiding hand of those same negotiations, but Pinckney pressed the American case at the right moment, when Spain was exhausted from its losing involvement in the French Revolution. The diplomatic victories, especially the one that opened the Mississippi, were celebrated like another Fourth of July, with speeches and fireworks in town squares throughout the United States.

Along the river, from New Orleans to Natchez to St. Louis, Spanish residents were crestfallen. Many felt that their long-term efforts to control the Mississippi Valley had been "annulled," according to the Spanish historian Miguel Goméz del Campillo. The vision fostered there by Carondelet and many others for a conservative and stable society in the Spanish vein would be thenceforth under pressure, if not outright attack. It was, in Carondelet's view, like trying to build a quaint village adjacent to a shantytown slum. Gayoso, the lieutenant governor of Natchez, had his own dilemma with the treaty; he was expected to surrender his seat in Natchez to the Yankees.

All along the Lower Mississippi River, the Spanish turned as slowly as possible to their new obligation, under the Treaty of San Lorenzo, to survey the 31st parallel (a line marked on modern maps by the northern edge of much of the Florida Panhandle). Once that was done, there would be a border, and with a border, another nation would be leaning against Spanish America's doorstep.

In the meantime, glumly awaiting the Americans, the Spanish along the Lower Mississippi continued to provide the government for Natchez and other sections of their stillborn empire to the east. Barón de Carondelet could hardly contain his disappointment over losing the chance to absorb it. "In conformity with the Treaty," he wrote to his superior in Madrid, "it [is] not in my power any longer to restrain the eruption of the people from the American States, who are approaching and are going to establish themselves on the eastern bank of the Mississippi. . . . Your Excellency will see himself obliged to take beforehand the most active measures to oppose the introduction of those restless people, who are a sort of determined bandits, armed with rifles, who frequently cross the Mississippi in numbers." He recognized a strain in the American character that did indeed reject government, whether American or Spanish. There were those for whom rights did not come from law or even from "their Creator," as described by Jefferson in the Declaration of Independence. Full and true independence was derived from just one thing: land. Seeking that sole connection where it was abundant, early Americans were drawing ever nearer, to the disgust of Carondelet.

Lieutenant Governor Trudeau in St. Louis was among the few Spanish officials who accepted the new treaty and even embraced it as an opportunity. He petitioned the government in New Orleans to emphasize Upper Louisiana in lieu of Trans-Appalachia by building a string of forts along the Missouri River. That would offer one form of resistance to invasion from the north, where the British loomed. The plan to build a network of forts didn't materialize (only one was constructed), but Trudeau wasn't finished trying to scoop up the lost Spanish zeal for Trans-Appalachia.

With the permission of Carondelet, Trudeau offered "the award of 3,000 pesos to the first who should arrive at the South Sea."* As part of the new impetus, the trading company that had been organized in the wake of d'Eglise's reports was revived and immediately sought men to carry out that forgotten aim: to follow the Missouri River to its source and then, by water or land, to the ocean beyond.

At about the same time, Lieutenant Governor Trudeau took his own trip, east across the Mississippi River, to pay a visit to a colorful

---

* Since the time of Balboa, the Spanish used the name "South Sea" for nearly the entire Pacific Ocean; the "North Sea" was in the vicinity of Alaska.

American judge named George Turner in Illinois. Over the course of their conversation, Trudeau mentioned John Evans, probably as an example of all that he had to forbear: spies disguised as Welshmen pretending to look for distant relatives in unexplored territory.

Judge Turner had met Evans when the eager young traveler passed through Illinois, and he'd been impressed, recommending him so highly that Trudeau returned to St. Louis and set the Welshman free, after two years' incarceration. Upon his release, Evans fairly burst back upon his main goal, cheerfully joining the Spanish voyage to find the source of the Missouri River. He was back on his way west again, and so were the Spanish. No expense was spared for the new expedition, which included four boats stuffed with goods to be used as presents for the Indian nations en route. The Omahas were to receive the first boatload, the Sioux the second, and the Mandans the third. The fourth was to be reserved for Indians in the Rocky Mountains. The flotilla was a veritable department store making its way upriver, and to say that it was irresistible was also to say that it was doomed.

The first major stop was the Omaha (U-Mo'n-Ho'n) settlement of Big Village, on the west side of the Missouri, a few miles from the influx of the Sioux River. About one thousand Omahas lived in Big Village under their charismatic yet absolutist chief Oa-schin-ga-sa-bae, known as "Blackbird," who was said to live more luxuriously than any other person in North America. Europeans compared his lifestyle to that of an Arabian potentate. Blackbird had servants whose sole job it was to lightly massage his legs as he slept, using a specific technique that kept him from being awakened. When they weren't available, his military commanders vied for the chance to fill in.

Blackbird had not inherited his chiefdom; he'd assumed it. A former medicine man, he generally maintained peace throughout the surrounding region—either because he could be a cunning diplomat or because he was an expert in the use of poison. On one occasion, he invited sixty other chiefs to a banquet and then after dinner put a damper on the whole evening by announcing that the Great Spirit had just informed him that the guests would all be dead by morning. They were, but it couldn't have been a total surprise to Blackbird, since he was the one who put the arsenic in the food. Stories such as that indicated the reputation of Blackbird. His people loved him and his rivals feared him, and he instinctively knew how to meld the two emotions in others; he certainly understood the Europeans, even as they began to encroach on his river. As long as Blackbird was chief of the Omahas, the British and Spanish empires vied with everyone else to honor his undeniable power along the river he'd made his own.

Blackbird duly received his allotted boatload of merchandise from the Spanish expedition, but when he heard about the other three, he wanted those too. Negotiations were protracted and tense. The Spanish gave him far more than his original share, even while they sought to gain his permission to establish a fort named for King Charles IV near Big Village. To finalize the deal, they attempted to bribe Blackbird with a solid silver medal. It proved to be a misstep. The medal was not merely symbolic: it was spiritual, or had that capacity in bringing other powers and energies into the new relationship between the Spanish and the Omaha. In addition, the manner in which it was proffered and then accepted was as important as the object itself to Blackbird, the lord of the Missouri River. Soon afterward, a Spanish boat was seen paddling as quickly as possible back to St. Louis to get another medal—of solid gold.

For Indian nations in the Louisiana Territory's contended regions, the last quarter of the eighteenth century was a pinnacle, especially in relations with European Americans. Because Indian allies were crucial in the administration of territory, as well as in the development of trade, European nations competed to prove who could treat each nation or tribe with the most respect. The French were the most successful, the Spanish the most generous. The British varied, although they were the most innovative, creating, for example, biannual conclaves in towns such as Prairie du Chien, to which thousands of Indian leaders were invited, mostly for merriment. The most obvious method by which alliances were cultivated was through giving "presents." That was the word used, and while the goods bestowed were indeed gifts in the usual sense of a thoughtfully selected item, they had other connotations as well. Acceptance of a present, especially a flag or a medal, indicated a certain understanding, even a contract.

The goods were also given in lieu of fees for what amounted to business licenses on tribal lands. It would be wrong to consider "presents" in the late eighteenth century and on the Northern Plains as a paternalistic gesture on the part of the Europeans. They were in no position to be paternalistic, because they were not then the ones in control of the situation.

By summer 1795, with the Spanish explorers mired down at Big Village, working to keep Blackbird on friendly terms—and to avoid his dinner invitations—John Evans received orders to leave the main corps behind and continue northward. The expedition leader, a Scot named John MacKay, considered him "a virtuous young man of promising talents, undaunted Courage and perseverance." Spanish officials, in turn, including Carondelet and Trudeau, recognized that Evans offered their best hope for a successful expedition to the West and prepared instructions that were forwarded to him at the Spanish encampment, duly christened Fort Charles, near Big Village. (One of the indications that the lower part of the Missouri River was becoming more organized according to European sensibilities was the quantity of important letters that could be sent reliably along the route, in the care of independent traders.)

The orders and advisories given to Evans were remarkably similar to those that Jefferson wrote for Michaux, although the Spanish would not have been aware of the American document. The very first clause listed the extensive natural, astronomical, geographical, botanical, zoological, and general scientific data expected of Evans, along with specific facets of the sociology of every Indian nation to be encountered. The next clause, not surprisingly, advised what Evans should do when he ran out of ink. The directions continued with further suggestions, orders, and advice. According to the overall plan, Evans was to receive a load of goods from a Spanish trader who was thought to have stopped either in the Mandan villages or another Indian outpost along the way.

In January 1796, Evans set out with about a half-dozen men. "The river," as he described it later, "has its own way and rushed impetuously through mountains and hills." He was describing the Badlands of what is now South Dakota. Two months later, he reached the Mandan villages, where he found that members of a British trading company had recently constructed a fort—on Spanish territory. What he didn't find, though, was any sign of the Spanish trader who was supposed to resupply him for the balance of his trip. In the meantime, Evans took the initiative to capture the fort for Spain. Only twenty-five years old, a civilian and practically alone, he removed the five traders inside, lowered the British flag, and raised the Spanish one. The fact that he was himself a British subject didn't stop him from acting on his conviction that Spain controlled all European interests in the region.

Drifting loyalties were a part of life in the Louisiana Territory. When a good Briton or Frenchman, and sometimes an American, arrived in the West, patriotism turned a fresh page—and sometimes a whole stack of them. Opportunism was the order of the day, as though one could choose where one was born—or, at least, for whom one would die. Across the Mississippi, a man such as Evans could tear down a flag that had once been his own, simply because he had decided for himself that it didn't belong. That was a powerful reason, just in itself, to travel a half a world away from the kings and the courts and the great diplomats of Europe.

Several of the British traders were remarkably kind to Evans—as though they were abiding his rule as much out of pity as anything else. One of them, noticing that Evans had very little food, sent chocolate and sugar. Another, a well-known trader on the Canadian side named Big John McDonnell, sent a selection of English magazines. He also sent Evans a geography book: "for your amusement." Considering that Evans's current address was terra incognita, it was a witty gift. When Evans maintained Spanish authority at the post for more than six months, though, Big John lost patience and told one of his traders, the villainous René Jusseaume, to adjudicate.

Jusseaume's favored style of debate was assassination, according to Evans. He wrote that on three occasions, the Mandans interceded to save him from Jusseaume's plots. Ultimately, Jusseaume was banished from the villages, but by that time, Evans had decided on his own to leave, realizing that he could neither travel farther up the Missouri nor continue to hold the fort any longer. Living on the largesse of the Mandans, he desperately needed new supplies and presents, neither of which were anywhere to be found. But for the missed intercept with the Spanish trader, he could have started west. Instead, Evans was forced to go in the disappointed direction, south and east to the port of St. Louis.

Evans reported to Trudeau about his trip and left his own hand-drawn map of the Missouri River region. After recuperating, he traveled to New Orleans, where the governor-general wanted to discuss plans for him to lead further expeditions—Evans, the former prisoner of the Spanish crown, was even given a room in the governor's mansion. By then, though, his health was declining, precipitated or advanced by heavy drinking after his return. Evans died in a dissipated state in New Orleans; suicide was suspected. He wasn't the only explorer of his era to fall victim to that fate, trying to hold the long reach of the western horizon in the pocket of a city suit.

Evans had proved himself the most stalwart of the Spanish explorers, undertaking a journey of intent from which he couldn't quit—and didn't, until the lack of supplies made it impossible to continue. Long after his original reason for leaving Wales had dropped away, he had pressed on, to the end of every ability. Evans embodied the primary characteristic of the explorers who would follow him soon enough: he was hungrier than all those he left behind to see the New World of his generation—the American West.

NOT LONG BEFORE Evans left St. Louis for the last time, heading south, one of the men who would eventually take his place in the exploration of Louisiana arrived from the east. "Came into the Town of St. Louis, on the Spanish side," wrote Dr. George Hunter, referring to the newly differentiated Spanish (western) side of the Mississippi River. Hunter, the *Man* of Jefferson" in Audubon's description, paddled from the American side to St. Louis in a canoe. "Here," Dr. Hunter continued in his diary, "we also paid our respects to the Commandant [Trudeau] & were politely received; & desired to go & visit any part of the Country we chose." Hunter, a Scot who made his home in Philadelphia, was a rare tourist for his day. He had traveled west with a friend, just to have a look at Trans-Appalachia and maybe the Mississippi River. After seeing it for himself, he planned to return to Philadelphia.

Lieutenant Governor Trudeau had no sooner met Hunter than he offered him one thousand acres. "Wherever we liked," Hunter marveled. Smiling at the two Americans, at least of one whom had a Scottish accent, Trudeau was a lot more charming than he'd been to Evans, the quixotic Welshman. But Hunter was wealthy by the standard of the frontier, and he spoke its language; he knew land in tracts and hungered to speculate in them.

At forty-five years old, Hunter had taken it upon himself to go west in 1796. His wife, Phoebe, had relatives in Kentucky, although she never felt the slightest motivation to visit them herself. Instead,

George was the one who used her family as an excuse to make a tour. The areas he visited were still on the cusp of American settlement; they may not have been totally unexplored, but they weren't comfortable for casual travel, either.

After riding on horseback from Philadelphia to Pittsburgh, Hunter and his friend, a man named Atkinson, bought a flatboat, pausing in the thrill of the moment to christen it the *Illinois*. Very few people named their flatboats—they were one-way vessels, barely able to ply through a current upstream and typically sold for scrap downstream. More auspiciously, Hunter and Atkinson fitted out the *Illinois*, hired a crew of three men and started down the Ohio River. At the time, a private boat with a crew constituted first-class travel on the river. The luxury, such as it was, didn't last long. In a region of drifters, work on a boat was easy to find and even easier to leave behind. Following a frontier tradition, two of the crewmen soon jumped ship. Hunter and Atkinson had no choice but to take over as deckhands.

Hunter was undaunted. An animated tourist, he delighted in everything from the howl of wolves in the distance to the sight of boats from the west, piled high with furs. Spotting another vessel on the river, manned by Indians from Illinois, he crowded the rail of his boat for a good look. He wanted to see everything of the West. Or almost everything:

> I examined them with my spyglass & found them all quite naked except an handkerchief tied round their heads & a breathclout round their middles; as we approached their boat they perceived my Glass & immediately two of them lifted up their breechclout & stuck out their bare Posteriors.

Along the Ohio River, Hunter passed "Lands of Gen. Washington on the Virginia side now advertised for sale." The tracts had been described in ads in Philadelphia papers and Hunter had taken care to remember the location of the plots. The first president, then finishing his second term, was making good on his intention to profit from the frontier. Along the trip, Hunter continually made notes on land and whether it was for sale, with his own comments on its worth.

Disembarking at Louisville, the river town founded by George Rogers Clark during his heyday with the army, Hunter and Atkinson sold the *Illinois* and took to their horses for the rest of the journey.

At the same time that Hunter was in Louisville, the town was home to yet a new plot to separate Trans-Appalachia from the United States. Barón de Carondelet himself was the instigator, the New Orleans governor-general hoping to obviate the Treaty of San Lorenzo by taking over the American states of Kentucky and Tennessee. It was so unlikely a hope that even the ever open-minded and open-handed American general James Wilkinson advised that it couldn't be done. Carondelet wanted to go ahead with his plan, anyway, and thanks to a purported one hundred thousand dollars in support from Madrid, Wilkinson was convinced to be willing. The first payment was made through an intermediary, Wilkinson's assistant, Philip Nolan. The drop was made, clumsily, in a barrel of sugar in Louisville—a crossroads in the summer of 1796 of Spain's complex dream for the West and Hunter's far simpler one.

Aside from occasional missteps on the way west, including the triple disaster of losing his horse . . . at night . . . in a swamp, Hunter was a good frontiersman and always a resilient one. Sometime after he and his horse managed to reunite, his trip took him all the way to the Mississippi River, as part of his determination to see "the farthest of our settlements." And then, once he was there, he decided suddenly to cross the river—an inclination that wouldn't have surprised Barón de Carondelet one bit. Hunter made the trip after dinner one night and was presented to Lieutenant Governor Trudeau the same evening.

As their interview wore on, Trudeau embellished his original offer, dangling a premium of ten thousand acres if Hunter brought more settlers from Pennsylvania. Hunter may have been tempted, but it was early to start speculating in Louisiana land, particularly since it lay in foreign territory. He returned to Philadelphia as one of the very few Americans at that time to have been as far as St. Louis.

Thomas Jefferson was also heading to Philadelphia, preparing to leave his beloved Monticello behind. After two years at home, he had started talking about politics again, and after three, he was the vice president–elect of the country. Jefferson's change in attitude was conspicuous, especially in light of his description of his last stint in public service as "everything I hate" and of life at Monticello as "everything I love." Both of those opinions had tempered to some degree.

At Monticello, Jefferson's deliberations on crop rotation had been sound, but the concomitant *will* was flawed. In the first two years, the yield in almost all his crops was weak, especially his cash crop, wheat; he was losing money on farm operations. And his live fence was dead. The peach trees, members of one of the weaker arbor species, hadn't held back any animals, who, when they weren't trampling the fence, were eating it. The ancients, as Newton quoted them, divided the art of getting things done "in a twofold respect." There was the rational and then the practical. In the fields of Monticello, the practical had proved to be less sleek and satisfying than the rational. Bogged down in yet another mass of frustrations—for all the beauty of the setting—Jefferson was caught again, trying to carry a good plan through the twisting course of actuality. The land sent him back into government with the perspective to finish his first plan, and at Monticello he opted to rent out most of his land as the rotation plan withered away.

The truth, of course, is that Jefferson was not a working farmer, for all of his delight in the term. To compare him to a small selection of other Virginia farmers, his friends George Washington and James Madison were both far more successful. Where he argued that he was never home enough to maintain the viability of his farms, they were both away as much as he was, with no particular detriment to their operations. They each experimented a little in agriculture; they were not complacent, but neither had his ambition to perfect farming in bold strokes. Nor did they have quite his disarmed love for land. Jefferson saw instead every bud, and felt, by his own description, affection.

Jefferson assumed the office of vice president, awarded to him because he had been runner-up in the presidential election of 1796. He didn't like the winning candidate, John Adams, for president, but then, he hadn't liked him as vice president under Washington. One of the primary jobs of the vice president is presiding over U.S. Senate sessions; many who have held the office left that chore to others, but Adams and Jefferson both actively fulfilled their duties in harnessing the Senate's daily activities. Jefferson thought that Adams was inconsistent and sometimes capricious in his pronouncements. The new vice president determined to do better, spending his first months in office conducting legal research on precedents in American parliamentary procedure, of which there were not many. (Jefferson's study not only gave him something to do in Philadelphia; it eventually became a book used ever since as a standard reference in the Senate.)

As vice president, uncomfortably biding his time in the Adams presidency, Jefferson was working in Philadelphia again, because the federal city of Washington wasn't ready to serve as the seat of the American government. In fact, building had barely started after a contentious process of surveying it over hill and swamp in the District of Columbia, according to the design of Pierre L'Enfant. The Frenchman had long since withdrawn, however, arguing that the actual layout wasn't at all according to his design—especially after the principal surveyor, Andrew Ellicott, assumed increasing responsibility. Ellicott, a Pennsylvanian with ties to Maryland, was an influential mathematician, astronomer, and mapmaker, who had risen to the rank of major during the Revolutionary War. He was an active member of the APS, but instead of pursuing a career in academia, as might be expected, he chose to remain loosely attached to the government, where his three areas of expertise led him naturally to the pursuit on which they overlapped: surveying. To his credit, he made bold strokes of progress laying out the new city. A political animal at heart, he also cultivated friendships, nurtured feuds, and nimbly navigated the issues of the day. In reality and in spirit, Ellicott was the first Washingtonian.

Ellicott had been recommended by both Jefferson and Washington to finish the layout of the capital, but eventually he had his own problems with the board of commissioners in charge of the project. He left the job, as had L'Enfant before him. Jefferson tried to take an active role in the plans, with his innate interest in design and the shaping of land, but the process of creating the capital on a ten-year schedule resulted mostly in bitter squabbling. Qualified surveyors weren't anxious to enter the brawl, further contributing to the troubled process.

Ellicott's former position was ultimately filled by a surveyor named Thomas Freeman. Even though Jefferson was not closely involved with the appointment, he probably looked over Freeman's letters of recommendation. One credited Freeman with "much knowledge in surveying, and all the branches of the Mathematics."

Born and raised in Ireland, Freeman arrived in the United States in 1784. He had been well educated, soon gaining a reputation along the East Coast as a highly capable land surveyor, an accolade that made him a busy man. As the new nation expanded, frontier surveying was a crucial field—and it would also develop a pool of men trained in the practical skills of exploration.

Surveying—matching maps to land or vice versa—required a diverse cross-section of skills. First, one needed academic training in math, astronomy, celestial navigation, geology, and, of course, geography. On a human level, a frontier surveyor needed a strong sense of diplomacy and sound judgment, in order to resolve disputes with settlers, who tended to argue unendingly with newly arrived surveyors. A frontier surveyor had to be hardy, able to survive in the deepest part of the backwoods for weeks or even months at a time. On a daily basis, the job typically found a surveyor and his crew crashing through brambles, swamps, ravines, and all other natural barriers in the effort to mark that most unnatural of all features, a perfectly straight and invisible line. Delicate brass instruments attached the position of celestial bodies to those invisible lines. Hardest of all in the lot of the frontier surveyor was the absolute certainty that in his wake, fortunes would be made in land speculation. Hometowns would be born and new arrivals would settle into the comfort of secure tracts, but by then, the surveyor who made it all possible would have moved on to the next crag.

Freeman dedicated himself to the profession, and all the potential he saw in it. Remaining single, he accepted long-term assignments all around the country, laying out major roads or defining borders for new towns and counties. Until later in his life, he didn't have a home address. Compared to the overachieving members of the APS, to which he did not belong, Freeman may have been a journeyman in science, but he was single-minded in his ambition to become the best in his field. His personality was as much a factor in his progress as his skill. His mind was organized by numbers and the mathematics in which he placed his trust. They could be a home, too, with their own welcoming serenity.

Around his friends, Freeman was friendly and humorous in a corny way: a polite gentleman, an uncle to all. He was also principled, even righteous, at work and away from it. On a job laying out the path of a road in Tennessee, he wrote to his boss, an army general, about his coworkers:

> Mr. Strother is yet with me, and I shall detain him as long
> as I can. I cannot live alone, and you know that even the

old adage, 'Want of company, welcome trumpery,'* will not apply to our acquaintance, Mr. O____e, for his is too trashy even for trumpery, What a life a savage lives! How far removed are we? What trash, what worthless worms are all!

Bound only to the job at hand, Freeman managed to bring the cursed survey in the national capital close to completion in 1796. Writing to President Washington, he then requested assignment to the showcase surveying job of the era: the new border between Spanish Florida and U.S. territory. To mark the 31st parallel on the land, the United States and Spain were each to appoint two leaders for a surveying party. Ellicott had already been appointed as one of the surveyors for the Americans. Freeman was still a long shot for the second appointment, even as the chief surveyor of the national capital. He didn't have connections, at least not ones on par with those of someone like Ellicott.

Freeman and Ellicott hadn't worked directly together on the capital survey, but there was still tension between the two men. They were in the midst of a minor confrontation in the aspect of surveying most important to many in the profession at the time: map sales. Each had advertised a street map of Washington; Ellicott's was published; Freeman's probably didn't receive enough subscribers to warrant publication. Ellicott was well-known and quite brilliant— and so his map of the nation's capital vanquished the one from the man who had actually finished the job of putting the city on the ground. The fact that life can be unfair probably didn't surprise Freeman by that point in his career, but he still clung to the belief that he belonged in the first tier of American surveyors. On that ambition, he wrote to George Washington in immaculate handwriting, requesting the opportunity of "ascertaining & adjusting the

---

* An old Irish proverb meaning, roughly: "If you don't have someone appealing with whom to spend time, be glad for someone tawdry."

Western limits, and bounds of the United States as contemplated in the late Treaties."

Freeman's superiors, the commissioners of the capital project, supported him with a recommendation, telling President Washington that they "found him steady, sober and attentive to business." Although Washington refused to be pressured—despite the best efforts of the many people Freeman egged on for references—he did finally make the appointment in May 1796.

Five months later, Freeman was on a boat sailing west on the Ohio River with Ellicott and a growing party that included Ellicott's nineteen-year-old son, Andy, as well as thirty woodmen to help the survey team fight through the brush. A rather offended Mississippian later pointed out that there really wasn't any need to import *woodmen*; at least one or two of the locals undoubtedly knew how to use an ax. Ellicott probably suspected that, but he wanted his own posse. He also brought a washerwoman on the barge, although the Lower Mississippi region could presumably have provided one of those, too. Arriving in Natchez in February 1797, the American surveying party waited expectantly for the preliminary step—the Spanish surrender of their forts east of the Mississippi River. It had been two years since the Treaty of San Lorenzo had taken effect, after all. Ellicott and Freeman couldn't start work with guns symbolically trained on them. Yet nothing seemed to budge Lieutenant Governor Gayoso or his soldiers.

Some residents of Natchez and its vicinity had been in "a continual apprehension of a war with the United States" over the forts and they actually looked forward to the arrival of the American members of the surveying party to precipitate the withdrawal of the Spanish troops, once and for all. Neither Freeman nor the Ellicotts were likely to intimidate the commandants, though. They arrived, Gayoso remained, and the citizens of Natchez continued to wait for the future to begin. Months went by.

And then a year went by and the Spanish were still in their forts.

Three

THIS PARADISE OR PANDEMONIUM

Early in 1798, Freeman started his second year of doing nothing in Natchez. He accepted his salary of $125 per month while waiting for Spain's troops to withdraw from the eastern banks of the river, but he wasn't happy about it. Andrew Ellicott wasn't complaining about the delay, though. Freeman had previously known his colleague as one of the profession's more famous men, respected by Washington and Jefferson and the recipient of an honorary diploma from the College of William and Mary. But by the beginning of 1798, the two were getting to know one another much too well.

According to Ellicott, he was working hard, engaged behind the scenes in "worrying the Spaniards out."

According to Freeman, Ellicott was causing the delays in order to "make a job out of his office."

Either could have been right. Motivations on every side remained as entangled as ever on the eastern bank of the Mississippi. Governor Carondelet, undaunted by the treaty, was working every last possibility to find support for an insurrection there against the Americans. As he waited for something to gel, he parried with Ellicott, who was making scattershot threats on behalf of the United States and simultaneously antagonizing local residents by accusing them of secret complicity with the Spanish. Among all of the many controversies reshuffling Natchez locals onto different sides with each passing day, only one line permanently divided the populace: the one between the pro-Ellicott and anti-Ellicott partisans. (It would still exist a hundred years later in western Mississippi.)

Ellicott was no doubt right to accuse *some locals* of being complicit with the Spanish *some of the time*. The future of the eastern Mississippi River bank had been nebulous for so long that a policy of tentative flexibility was only prudent for residents. Spain, France, or Britain could still easily seize the region from the wispy grip of the United States.

No person in Natchez mastered the art of benign internationalism with more suavity than William Dunbar, the younger son of a Scottish baronet. During six years as a resident of Natchez, Dunbar had served as a magistrate in the Spanish government; founded the local aristocracy with British expatriots, and traded constantly with Americans wherever he found them. Dunbar's oft-stated attitude was that he didn't care about politics. He didn't have to. Cotton production was skyrocketing, while slaveholders had recently been given a free hand in the region. And William Dunbar was a zealous slaveholder. He and his wife lived on a five-thousand-acre cotton plantation called the Forest, located nine miles south of Natchez and about four from the Mississippi River. The house, with tall columns in the front, was large enough to accommodate the seven Dunbar children. Five acres behind the house were devoted solely to Mrs. Dunbar's formal gardens. Ranked with the richest men in the region, Dunbar was unique in his scientific discipline and curiosity. In attitude, though, he was just another of the single-minded adventurers who had descended on the region over the course of a generation.

Dunbar was born in Scotland in 1749. His father, Sir Archibald Dunbar, headed a prosperous family with a history going back to 1025 in County Moray. Sir Archibald's large landholdings provided an independent income and a way of life that included two large homes, one in the country and a small castle in the county seat.

Sir Archibald was more interested in outdoor sports than in books, as were the first three of his four sons. When the youngest, William, displayed a natural aptitude for studies, especially in math and astronomy, the emergence of a scholar was something new in the Dunbar family. Eventually, William was sent to King's College in Aberdeen. After he graduated in 1763, though, his financial future was uncertain. According to the laws of Great Britain in the eighteenth century, and more important, the customs of the Dunbars, a younger son could not expect to inherit property. Dunbar did, however, inherit the bearing of his upper-class family. He was reserved, yet exuded unshakable self-confidence.

Dunbar ultimately set aside astronomy for another area of research: the English products that Native Americans in the Great Lakes region coveted most. As a young man, his plan was to enter the fur trade—that jagged line that connected the backwoods of North America with the fashion capitals of Europe. European manufactured goods were typically used to pay for pelts. The business had been booming for more than a century but had long been dominated by the French in the Great Lakes region. At the end of the French and Indian War in 1763, Great Britain took possession of the territory, and almost immediately its more rapacious subjects rushed west to take over the fur trade.

Along with the manufactured goods used to pay for pelts, the second mark of Europe brought by the fur trade, then refined under the English, was credit. All along the line, from Indian trappers to transporters known as "voyageurs" to traders such as Dunbar, to jobbers in Philadelphia or Albany, and finally to market makers in London, survival depended on credit. Then, as now, simple loans were rare—and they were hard enough for many people to fully understand. In the 1760s, the use of credit and its derivatives opened easy opportunities to take advantage of Indians, who were not born and raised with such concepts. The fur trade became controversial in the colonies, as the English sometimes introduced terms that made vassals of Indian trappers. And abrupt reversals in the trade could ruin anyone along the line who lacked ample capital.

Dunbar arrived in Philadelphia at the age of twenty-two with one valuable asset: entrée with a fellow Scot there named John Ross. An established wholesaler, Ross suggested that Dunbar take his manufactured goods to Fort Pitt, three hundred miles west of the city near the fork at the headwaters of the Ohio River. It wasn't yet Pittsburgh and, in fact, it wasn't yet in Pennsylvania: the frontier was so ragged that Virginia insisted that it owned Fort Pitt.

Working out of a base near Fort Pitt, Dunbar persevered in the fur trade, thanks to his association with John Ross. He didn't get rich, though. By the time he had arrived in America, the easy years were over for the British trading furs in the eastern Great Lakes. Fur traders were compelled—and pushed by companies—to go ever farther into the backwoods for ever less of a chance at a fortune. Dunbar was in the position, again, of looking for another option. He decided to leave Pennsylvania in 1773—the year of the Boston Tea Party, when the threat of rebellion, as well as the discussion of rights, dominated the American colonies. Under the circumstances, the fur trade was liable to be interrupted by any sort of break between the colonies and Britain. And Dunbar felt no loyalty to Pennsylvania or the American cause. He had a lot of loyalty to himself, however, and so he formed a new partnership with Ross and started for the British territory of West Florida. Yet another boom was in the works there, offering a new path to wealth. The Floridas had been reluctantly ceded to Great Britain by Spain ten years before.

Dunbar obviously preferred the farther outposts of the British Empire, where the culture of entrepreneurship prevailed over all else. Near Baton Rouge, then called Richmond, he picked out a parcel of land for a plantation. He then went on to New Orleans and sailed for Jamaica, where he bought twenty-two African people from a slave trader, transporting them in chains to Baton Rouge.

Within a few years, Dunbar's Baton Rouge plantation was not really a plantation at all. It was a factory operation, specializing in making staves (the wooden slats in barrels, which were in high demand for the rum trade in the Caribbean). Dunbar was only moderately successful; sugar plantations farther to the south were enjoying explosive growth, while he was steadily turning out staves. For years, his journal mentioned little in the way of a social life and nothing of the science he'd loved as a student. He wrote about his slaves continuously, but only rarely with individual interest. One of those instances was in his description of a weeklong stave-making contest he sponsored among Pollux, Jamie, and Isaac, the prize being a green jacket. Jamie got the jacket.

Overall, the journal was probably an accurate reflection of life on the plantation; Dunbar watched the slaves, counted them often, and listed them over and over again, along with their jobs or output. Beneath the minute records, he was continually trying to detect any sign that they might rise up or run away, the two great fears with which he lived day in and day out. He had cause to be nervous. In fact, there were frequent runaways, some successful, and a major rebellion that set his operation back drastically.

As a slave owner, Dunbar continually emphasized how humane and kindly he was. The record doesn't show it. At the time, Dunbar counted about twenty-eight slaves, using others on a contract basis. Those accused of so much as discussing escape were executed. Dunbar meted out punishment and oversaw the hangings. For other infractions, anyone deemed guilty was confined to a sweatbox of Dunbar's own design. The entries from Dunbar's journal show a man disposed to one thing where the slaves were concerned. He explained it in a letter to his partner, Ross, who had expressed concern for them. With rare passion, Dunbar answered:

> Men who do not own slaves, and who have not studied their character, are not qualified to make laws for their government. Slavery can only be defended perhaps on the principle of expediency, yet where it exists, and where they so largely outnumber the whites, you must concede almost absolute power to the master. If this principle be not admitted the alternatives are, insurrection, with all its horrors, or emancipation with all its evils!

Dunbar sidestepped the Revolutionary War entirely, never returning east to the States. It was America that came to him, to the West and to the unconcerned pursuit of wealth that seemed to go along with it in Dunbar's day. After the Spanish once again took charge of West Florida in 1783, though, policies on slave importation and rights were far stricter than those in the territory under the British. Dunbar was ready to move on.

During the early 1790s, when Spain was fighting to retain Trans-Appalachia, it made land near Natchez available at no cost to those willing to undertake an oath of allegiance. As a further inducement, laws regarding the treatment of slaves were reduced or suspended in the region. So it was that in 1792, Dunbar and his wife of six years moved to Natchez, obtaining a grant of one thousand acres. They called their new estate "the Forest," and Dunbar immediately became active in the promotion of cotton as a new crop there. Finally, he had edged himself into a boomtown during its golden era—or more accurately, an expedient era for the Dunbars.

William Dunbar became rich during his first half-dozen years

in Natchez and then increased his fortune through the wise investment of his plantation profits, in cooperation with Ross. He used his
newfound wealth to indulge his fascination with scientific equipment, ordered from instrument makers in London and Edinburgh.
Constructing his own observatory at the Forest, he equipped it with
a ten-inch telescope, one of the largest on the entire continent at the
time. Dunbar was not the only member of the Natchez planter class
to engage in scientific research, but he was by far the most sophisticated.

In late March of 1798, the Spanish in New Orleans finally capitulated. Carondelet having moved on, the new governor-general
was Manuel Gayoso, formerly of Natchez. Following the very letter
of the Treaty of San Lorenzo, he ordered the withdrawal of Spanish soldiers from the forts on the east side of the Mississippi. The
Ellicott-Freeman party could finally set forth on the 31st parallel—
not only as a surveying project, but also as an early and closely
watched trial of federally sponsored exploration.

The only chore remaining for Gayoso was to appoint the two
Spanish commissioners who were to work with the Americans on
the survey of the border. His first choice was obvious: William
Dunbar. The second was Stephen Minor, an American by birth
who had long served in the Spanish military. While Minor was an
educated man, he was not in the same intellectual league as Ellicott
or Freeman—and neither of them was the equal of Dunbar. Minor
would fade into the background of the mission, his talents eclipsed
by the other three. The feeling was that the 31st parallel, wherever it
existed, could never elude Ellicott, Freeman, and Dunbar, all working together.

The 31st parallel coincided with the Mississippi River about forty
miles south of Natchez. Dunbar arrived there to start the survey
with a veritable jewel box of precision equipment, setting up his own
portable observatory near the more rudimentary one Ellicott and
Freeman were using. The following months may well have consti-

tuted the best summer of his life, as he reveled in the chance to use his instruments as they were meant—"to subject the phenomena of nature to the laws of mathematics," as Isaac Newton once wrote. At the same time, Dunbar was equally taken with all that was immeasurable in the beauty of the plants and animals of the wilderness.

Freeman and Ellicott had a somewhat less lofty summer. After living separately in or near Natchez, the two American representatives formed a camp south of the town, approximately where the 31st parallel would intersect with the Mississippi River. "My colleague [Ellicott] seems very much disposed to be on good terms with me," Freeman wrote to the American military attaché in Natchez, Major Isaac Guion. If that were true, then Ellicott should have saved his charm for someone else. In August, Freeman wrote from the outpost:

> Ellicott landed here on the 10th and camped with his gang. They have done nothing since but eat salt pork and guzzle whiskey. . . . His inconsistencies, duplicity, absurdities and immoralities are disgusting.

Ellicott, reconsidering his own attitude as time went by, wrote to his wife that "Mr. Freeman . . . has turned out an idle, lying, troublesome, discontented, mischief-making man." Even as Ellicott boasted to her that their son, Andy, was "enterprising, industrious, and one of the most valuable persons concerned in the business," Freeman was discovering that Betsey, the washerwoman who accompanied the Ellicotts from Philadelphia, was actually their prostitute, attending to both father and son, simultaneously.

Freeman later described the situation:

> So far as their conduct came within my observation afterwards, they continued to pay mutual friendly and familiar attentions to her. It was said, and generally believed, that that extraordinary trio, father, son, and washwoman, slept in the

same bed, at the same time—I did not see it, but believed it. I was even pressed myself by the old sinner, Ellicott, to take part of his bed with his washerwoman and himself, for the night . . . It was my opinion, and I understood it to be the opinion of every gentleman of both parties, American and Spanish, that the Ellicotts, both father and son, held and continued a beastly, criminal and disgraceful intercourse with the said harlot, Betsy.

Along the frontier, many new arrivals flung aside the mores of Beacon Hill in Boston, Walnut Street in Philadelphia, or Bond Street in New York City. That was nothing new in human behavior. Freeman knew that. He also knew that he had everything to gain by keeping his outrage to himself, completing the work, and walking away with plump savings for the first time in his life; he might even expect a good recommendation from the famous Ellicott. Freeman, however, couldn't overlook conduct he considered immoral. That made him unique, at least at a camp just south of Natchez. He wrote letters to officials, especially in the military arm of the new territorial government, complaining about Ellicott's behavior. Before long, he was warned by his friend Major Guion to stop; the newly appointed American governor in Natchez was threatening to have him arrested for it.

The 1798 Sedition Act, a hallmark of the Adams presidency, gave the government the power to jail anyone for "writing, printing, uttering or publishing any false, scandalous and malicious writing or writings against the government." The opinion of Ellicott's friends was that Freeman was guilty of nothing less in making accusations against the American commissioner. In Philadelphia, Vice President Jefferson was leading an enraged opposition to the Sedition Act, but the law was in effect as of mid-July, and it frightened Freeman's associates on his behalf.

The other surveyors were well aware of the problem. Stephen Minor was pulled into the mire, despite his best efforts. Even while Ellicott accused Freeman of "abuse of the spanish commissioner my friend Major Minor," Minor was writing to a mutual acquaintance, saying of Ellicott, "He is not the man we took him for, nor has he a friendship for any man in this world. No regard for the social proprieties. Some day you shall know it all."

The fourth surveyor, William Dunbar, did what he always did when people cared enough to step up, fight the good fight, and let their voices be heard to make a better world. He left. But he did it with logic and style, suggesting that he could work on a different, shorter part of the line. He took part of the crew and moved on.

Dunbar completed his fieldwork, and later in the year he returned to the Forest to organize the details for his portion of the official report on the 31st parallel. While he was engaged in that process, he received an unexpected letter from the vice president of the United States, who was also the new president of the APS. No sooner had Thomas Jefferson heard from a friend in New Orleans of "a son of science" living along the Mississippi than he initiated a correspondence, capturing Dunbar as though he were a bird formerly believed extinct. He wrote his first letter in an engagingly respectful tone, inviting Mr. Dunbar to report on any natural or scientific subjects related to the Mississippi River region. "A lover of science," Jefferson wrote of himself, apologizing for a letter that was chock full of requests, "cannot want the zeal requisite to engage his aid in it's promotion."

In Philadelphia, Jefferson had embraced the presidency of the APS to occupy his spare time—a commodity he had in abundance as vice president. Whether he contacted Dunbar in Natchez as a lover of science or an inveterate politician, he certainly didn't want for zeal, believing that the secrets of America's past and future were both locked in the West. What he did lack at that point were people in the region capable of acquiring knowledge useful to his ends. Seeking out others who could provide him with an eye on western lands, Jefferson also made contact with General Wilkinson's former assistant Philip Nolan, who was then living in New Orleans.

Nolan was another type of rarity useful to Jefferson: an authority on the regions farther to the west of the Mississippi River. The Irishman, who had been associated with Wilkinson in Louisville, later moved to New Orleans as his agent in trade, and in matters of espionage, as well. In the Wilkinson mold, Nolan was personable, rakish, and certainly energetic. Carondelet, a notoriously tough critic of non-Spanish men, called him "a charming young man whom I regard very highly." Nolan soon embarked on a very different type of business, one that Carondelet's successors ultimately would not approve and in which Wilkinson's influence remained withal. He was going to Texas to capture wild horses.

NOLAN WAS THE earliest of America's storied westerners, personifying the tradition of folk-hero cowboys who thrived on the open range, riding herd by day with a posse and making the most of an open campfire every night. That was Nolan's way of life on his trips into Texas, but he was also the first westerner—of many—to confide that the rugged life as he'd experienced it was "less pleasing in practice than in speculation." A sardonic sense of humor was part of his unpredictable nature. Dunbar grew to know him and often entertained him at the Forest. "Altho' his excentricities were many," he wrote, "yet he was not destitute of romantic principles of honor united to the highest personal courage with energy of mind."

During his early days in New Orleans, Nolan heard that in the Texas region of New Spain, magnificent horses ran wild. A fine horse was a valuable commodity, and it did not take Nolan long to recognize that he could make as much money in one expedition collecting mustangs in Texas as he could make in twenty years as a bookkeeper. There was a reason, however, why all of the little bookkeepers in New Orleans didn't hurry into Texas with a lasso and a handful of horse treats. The Spanish were loath to allow any encroachment into Texas from the east. Even though they also possessed the area between the Mississippi River and Texas proper—modern-day Louisiana (or "Lower Louisiana")—they saw the two regions very differently. Lower Louisiana was to be developed. Texas, on the other hand, which was practically unpopulated except for a string of missions and a scattering of Indian nations, was to be left as a buffer zone. It existed, hot, wide, and barren, to keep Americans out of Mexico. To the north was another barrier: a muddy, messy moat called the Red River. And keeping Americans out of Texas from the east were dedicated contingents of Spanish soldiers.

A no-man's-land seventy miles wide separated Texas and Lower Louisiana. The sister towns of Natchitoches (in the western part of what it now the state of Louisiana) and Nacogdoches (in the eastern section of Texas) served to define the borderlands and offer checkpoints. The two towns and the goodly distance between them proved that no border at all made for even more security than a specific line of demarcation—a philosophy in which the Spanish placed great faith, but which they backed with a force of a thousand soldiers posted at Nacogdoches.

Promising to bring back horses for Lower Louisiana's Spanish ranchers, Nolan charmed his way into the necessary credentials for a trip into Texas. He started from Natchitoches and then, as necessary, talked and lied his way past the various Spanish authorities and dubious Indians he met along the way to his first roundup. Once in the hinterlands of Texas, Nolan and his men encountered the legendary herds of wild horses, a symbol ever since of the American West, and he was the first Euro-American ever to see them.

A half-dozen years later, Jefferson heard about Nolan from

Senator John Brown of Kentucky and became interested in learning more about his observations of the frontier. On behalf of the American Philosophical Society, Jefferson wrote to the horse wrangler in 1798, the same year he contacted Dunbar, to inquire about Texas and its mustangs:

> I have understood that there are large herds of horses in a wild state in the country West of the Mississippi and have been desirous of obtaining details of their history in that state. . . . The circumstances of the old-world have, beyond the records of history, been such as admitted not that animal to exist in a state of nature. The condition of America is rapidly advancing to the same, the present then is probably the only moment in the age of the world and the herds above mentioned the only subjects, of which we can avail ourselves to obtain what has never yet been recorded and never can be again in all probability. I will add that your information is the sole reliance, as far as I can at present see, for obtaining this desideratum. You will render to natural history a very acceptable service therefore, if you will enable our Philosophical-society to add so interesting a chapter to the history of the animal.

Jefferson went on to request periodic updates on the West, in general, writing, "If, after giving in a first letter all the facts you at present possess, you could be so good, on subsequent occasions, as to furnish such others in addition as you may acquire from time to time, your communication will always be thankfully received." Jefferson's open-ended inquiry might have struck some people, especially those from Spain, as espionage or reconnaissance, but Jefferson would have protested that the only intelligence he sought pertained to science. Unfortunately, by the time his letter to Nolan arrived in New Orleans, the entrepreneur was already on another trip to Texas.

Daniel Clark Jr., to whom Nolan had entrusted his correspondence, replied to Jefferson instead. Clark, an Eton-educated Irishman, worked for the Spanish civil authority and in private business, both with enormous profit. A partner of General Wilkinson's, he was on his way to becoming the richest man in New Orleans. At the time that Clark received Jefferson's letter, he was entertaining Ellicott as a houseguest in New Orleans—which may indicate why work on the 31st parallel tended to drag.

In a long, slightly obsequious letter to Jefferson, Clark was full of praise for Nolan, "that extraordinary and enterprising man" with whom, he wrote, he was "connected in the strictest of friendship." He also offered what information he could about the wild horses of Texas.

Eventually, Jefferson managed to locate Nolan himself and the two corresponded. The episode on its face reflects nothing more than men discussing a fascinating breed, new to Americans. Through the interest in horses, though, Jefferson sought a firsthand picture of far-off Texas from a reliable observer, knowledge that was invaluable to his strategy for American security. William Dunbar, Jefferson's other new correspondent, answered the same need on the eastern side of the Mississippi.

With Dunbar's separation from the rancorous 31st parallel surveying party, the animosity between Ellicott and Freeman only increased. In continuing to charge Ellicott with immorality, Freeman was risking his career and even his freedom, but his disgust couldn't be contained. Finally, the military leader for the territory had to be summoned. The newly named commander was none other than General Wilkinson, the handsome, capable, duplicitous officer who had previously lived in Kentucky. At the time of his visit to the campsite along the 31st parallel, he was secretly on the payroll of the Spanish as well.

Wilkinson met with the two American surveyors and "discovered at once, from Mr. Ellicott, that the character and interests of the service, required their separation." Speaking of Freeman, Ellicott happily wrote to his wife, "At the desire of General Wilkinson . . . I expeld him from the camp." He considered it a victory and regarded Wilkinson as an ally. After Freeman left, though, Wilkinson immediately hired him to work as a surveyor at the newly acquired Spanish forts along the Mississippi, an act that enraged Ellicott. From his point of view, it was essential that Freeman be discredited.

Ellicott nervously wrote his wife a few months later, enclosing a miniature portrait of himself: "When you look at the picture you will see the face of a person whose life has been devoted to the service of his country who has ever since he left Philadelphia been up by brake of day and thro the encampment except when sick, and then he was lifted into a chair at the usual time of his rising." It was so heartrending a portrait of dedication, so admirable and pathetic at the same time, that she must have known at a glance he was guilty of something. With Wilkinson, Ellicott was just as unsettled. His fury over the general's rescue of Freeman had shrunk into a small, sharp blade of suspicion. He was darkly aware that Wilkinson, a master of the art of manipulation, might well be holding Freeman as a trump card against any future trouble from him.

By astounding coincidence, within just one week of Wilkinson's employment of Freeman, Ellicott came into possession of secret evidence of Wilkinson's Spanish salary. (He may have come by that information through Daniel Clark, the spider at the center of New Orleans's web of intrigues.) Ellicott evidently felt that it was time for him to play his own trump card. He wrote in code to the State Department, describing the monetary relationship between Wilkinson and Spain. Ellicott's shocking communiqué failed to do more than elicit a few questions, though. Wilkinson evaded the charge, explaining to his superiors that while he had indeed ingratiated himself with the Spanish, his only loyalty was to America.

For a man who did have so many of his own secrets, Wilkinson took a risk by alienating Ellicott, yet it was his intercession that probably saved Ellicott from public scandal at the hands of a scorned Freeman. The survey of the 31st parallel fascinated the general populace, in part because it represented an American triumph and a Spanish concession. The project was closely followed in newspapers, and so Ellicott might easily have been ruined, had the scandal been made public. Certainly, Wilkinson rescued the career of Freeman, who continued to build a reputation as a "steady, sober and attentive" frontier surveyor. For his part, Dunbar completed his own report on the survey near the end of the summer, after returning to the Forest. Ellicott, alert to a good opportunity, turned his diary of the survey into a published book—in which there was no mention at all of Thomas Freeman. In the end, all but one member of the famed 31st parallel survey emerged from the project stronger than before.

Despite the feuding, the final result of the survey was masterful. Some of the stones placed by the party can still be seen, marking a line that has never required correction. As a precursor to government-sponsored exploration in the United States, however, the 31st parallel survey was a wholly depressing episode. The lesson that it offered for the future was that whether the leaders of an expedition had lofty morals or slipshod ones, they couldn't coexist without having largely *the same* morals. Once they left behind the ties to American civilization, no other understanding would remain.

In traveling home to Philadelphia in April 1800, the Ellicotts booked passage on a schooner for the last leg up the Atlantic coast. A young man from Natchez who was on the same boat wrote a letter home after he arrived, describing the sad fate of Betsey and his frustrations with Ellicott:

> Mr. Ellicott and the rest of us had a very disagreeable voyage
> from Savannah to this city. The woman Mr. Ellicott brought

to Natchez with him and had with him on the survey, became deranged on the passage, and but for Mr. Collins, M.
Anderson and myself, would have killed herself. She is now
frantic, and chained in a mad-house.

The return from the wildness of the West was, as usual, impossible for some. While aboard the boat, Ellicott made no reference to
Betsey, but he did compose a letter, dated April 1, 1800, congratulat-
ing Dunbar on his recent election to the American Philosophical
Society. "If you do justice to your own abilities, and observations,"
Ellicott wrote, "you will do credit to the Society by your communications." Dunbar had every intention of trying.

Just two weeks before, a blazing phenomenon said to be the size
of a house had hurtled over Baton Rouge, streaking across the sky.
Dunbar couldn't resist making inquiries and writing up a *philosophic*
description of it for his new friend, Vice President Jefferson. The object was apparently a meteor, an object little understood at the time.

As Dunbar prepared his first substantive package of research for
Jefferson, he included his "Description of a Singular Phenomenon"
with a copy of his weather records for a one-year span and a small
vocabulary of Indian languages, along with two other short manu-
scripts. He sent the packet in mid-July of 1800. If he was in a hurry
to spread the news of the flying phenomenon, though, he made one
mistake: sending anything of a timely nature to a man running for
president. Jefferson, then at the end of his term as vice president, was
pitted against the incumbent John Adams and he had few spare moments to respond in the late summer of 1800, when Dunbar's letter
arrived and was pushed off to the side of the desk.

The election of 1800 started as a bitter fight, but a legitimate one,
over federal powers and the role of the president. Jefferson thought
that Adams had overstepped his bounds and was guilty of "a *monarchie masqué*," a masked monarchy. It was a matter for sober constitutional debate, but the campaigning soon devolved into personal

attacks, with Adams's followers winning the early rounds. It was intimated in many quarters that there was something sinister about a man with *philosophical* pursuits. Jefferson's side answered back in a style just as slithering. Meanwhile, the animosity against Jefferson soared to a strangely flattering exuberance. Federalist predictions credited Jefferson with organizational skills even he would have envied. "Murder, robbery, rape, adultery and incest will all be openly taught," predicted a Connecticut newspaper, "—and practiced."

In mid-December, as the election votes were being tabulated, Jefferson correctly anticipated that Adams and his party would go down to defeat. Satisfied in his expected victory, he at last allowed himself the luxury of catching up on his nonpolitical mail. Jefferson read through Dunbar's bundle of writings, left waiting since July. Impressed by the contents, he decided that the American Philosophical Society should publish them.

Jefferson sent an official letter to Caspar Wistar, the APS vice president, suggesting that Dunbar's "sundry communications" should be printed in the Society's *Transactions*. "So learned a correspondent," he added, "planted a thousand miles off, on the very verge of the great *terra incognita* of our western continent, is worthy of being cherished."

With even more enthusiasm, Jefferson immediately composed a second letter for Wistar, this one confidential. He wanted to make the suggestion that Dunbar be offered membership in the American Philosophical Society but waited to discuss his idea with Dunbar until he had the impressions of the society's vice president. That was just as well—because Dunbar was already a member of the society. Jefferson had uncharacteristically missed that point, but then, he was a recruiter at heart. For all the many things he collected, from vegetable seeds to fossil bones to practically any book with the word "Virginia" in the title, he was at his most alert in looking for people of promise.

Although Jefferson had been confident in an easy victory, as of late December, the presidential election was "under dilemma," as he put it. Because of a procedural anomaly, it was apparent that Jefferson and his erstwhile running mate, Aaron Burr, were going to receive the same number of votes in the Electoral College, giving them each an equal right to the presidency. The ugly campaign of 1800 squabbled on, straight into 1801, with an ominous note of chaos.

On January 12, Jefferson turned, as though for respite, again to his friend in Natchez, finally responding to the letters from July. He considered Dunbar's reports "vedette," a naval term meaning "surveillance" or "watch." "Philosophical vedette at the distance of one thousand miles," Jefferson wrote to Dunbar, "and on the verge of the *terra incognito* of our continent, is precious to us here." He couldn't resist repeating from his December letter the image he had of Dunbar living on the very edge of known America. The West fired his imagination and so did the thought that a meticulous reporter similar to himself could be situated so close to it. If Jefferson couldn't escape to Monticello and what he called "the attractive nature of country employments," he could at least write a long letter to a kindred spirit. He addressed each of Dunbar's essays, some in depth.

"I have never been a very punctual correspondent," he closed, "and it is possible that new duties may make me less so. I hope I shall not on that account lose the benefit of your communications." With that, Jefferson returned as though from a long way away to the presidential election of 1801.

In February, with a tug of war over practically every vote, the election dragged through more than twenty-five rounds in the House of Representatives. Despite all of the issues of real import, the election was easily compared to a viper pit. The fact that Jefferson ultimately won didn't make him the best of statesmen. For the moment, all that he was, was the reigning master of politics at its worst. As he often bemoaned, a large part of him only wanted to be at Monticello, dedicated to his projects or drawing vigor from his land. That life was exactly the kind that William Dunbar was leading. As Jefferson wrote of him, "He is easy in his fortune, master of his own time, and employs it in science." The description reflected an ideal that Jefferson found elusive, in all three respects.

Four

A WALL OF BRASS

By 1801, Barón de Carondelet was no longer the governor-general of Louisiana, but his opinion of Americans as lawless and messy, temporal and gun-happy, remained the prevailing attitude among the Spanish. "A young, thriving, nation" was Jefferson's description of the United States, "loving peace and the pursuit of wealth . . . enterprising and energetic as any nation on earth." The intrinsic clash represented the closest that the United States ever came to a cultural war with Europe.

In Louisiana Territory and the Floridas, Spain inculcated a quiet, traditional rhythm of life—low on violence, high on permanence—with a covenant that demanded absolute respect for authority. It was not unlike the model that was working in Spanish holdings further west, such as the provinces of California and New Mexico, although there, the Spanish built communities around churches or missions and placed a priority on converting Indians to Roman Catholicism. That was never the case in Louisiana, where pressure regarding religion was suspended in respect to the Native nations, the policy being liberalized owing to economic priorities. Despite the despotism and genocide of Spanish rule in Central and South America, especially in the sixteenth and seventeenth centuries, the reputation of Spanish Louisiana was that it was similar in spirit to an easygoing backwater section of Southern Europe. The same could not be said for any community where Americans held sway. They were different, as the Spanish officials could see.

Many Americans, especially those living in Trans-Appalachia, were driven by competitive obsession, while others took the concept of liberty to be an inherently antigovernment initiative. Pioneers circa 1800 were inspired by the founding generation, but not necessarily by a patriotic attachment to the United States. With the opening lines of the Declaration of Independence as a template, many were open to planning their own republics, finding without much effort "abuses and usurpations" in whatever power was governing them at the time. Carondelet and his successors had something very real to fear from the influx of Americans; something geopolitical, as the strategists looked at it, but also personal, regarding the disruption of the culture that Spanish Louisianans had been trying to build, one they loved.

In 1798, the French foreign minister, Charles-Maurice de Talleyrand, had played on the fears of the Spanish in North America, writing a blunt message intended only for the royal court at Madrid: "There are no other means of putting an end to the ambition of the Americans than that of shutting them up within the limits which nature seems to have traced for them; but Spain is not in a condition to do this work alone. . . ."

He then went on to suggest that the best solution was for France to hold Spanish lands in the American West:

> Let the court of Madrid cede these districts (the Floridas and Louisiana) to France, and from that moment the power of America is bounded by the limits which may suit the interests and tranquility of France and Spain to assign her. The French republic, mistress of these two provinces, will be a wall of brass forever impenetrable to the combined efforts of England and America. The Court of Madrid has nothing to fear from France.

Talleyrand's requests fell on deaf ears in Spain, but at home, they hardened into a policy for French expansion into North America. The idea of that conquest, as indeed nearly any conquest, was attractive to Napoleon Bonaparte, who soared to power in post-Revolutionary France. In 1799, he became First Consul, effectively a dictator.

Spain's relationship to France was complicated by twisting exigencies, but at the core of them all was the simple fact that Spain had sunk to the level of vassal by 1800, the royal family and its government existing at the pleasure of Napoleon. On that basis, the Spanish unenthusiastically agreed to the Talleyrand plan: to give its Louisiana territories to France during a process of negotiation that started in the fall of 1800. It continued in strict secrecy through the winter of 1801.

As the winter waned across the Atlantic in the United States, the election of Jefferson was finally official on February 17 and in the wake of the news, he wrote to Meriwether Lewis, his old family friend. He led off with a declarative statement reflecting his victory. "The appointment to the Presidency of the U.S.," he began, "has rendered it necessary for me to have a personal secretary. . . ."

Jefferson's insistence on an economical federal government started with his own staff. Aside from a handful of clerks, the personal secretary would be the president's only employee in his offices at the newly constructed White House. Primarily, the new president needed an alert conversationalist and an attractive surrogate to receive visitors and gather information around Washington. It was a ripe opportunity, and Jefferson already had a long list of applicants for the job by the time he offered it to Lewis, who was then stationed with the army in Pittsburgh. In terms of patronage politics, Lewis had done nothing at all to bring in blocs of votes or even one congressman to either of the Jefferson elections. But the new president nonetheless allotted one of his few available appointments to Lewis, baffling disappointed job seekers. Jefferson, however, had definite reasons, far beyond mere fondness for a friend of the family from Albemarle County—though Lewis was that. The appointment was a shrewd political gesture for a president so narrowly elected.

Lewis's mother, Lucy Meriwether Lewis Marks, owned a property called Locust Hill, just to the west of Charlottesville and less than ten miles away from Jefferson's home at Monticello. She prepared the smoked hams that were served at Monticello. Over the course of decades, the Jeffersons and the busy Lewis/Meriwether family remained close. The Lewises at Locust Hill were, as Jefferson put it, "of my neighborhood."

The elder Lewises in the mid-eighteenth century were labeled "Barons of the Potamac" by Virginia historian Moncure Conway. By the end of the century, the clan's various branches still measured land by the thousands of acres, but they were not among the area's richest families. Many of the sons became army officers, leaving their tracts to others for long stretches. More privately, the family was haunted by medical problems that Jefferson described as "hypochondriac affections." He added that in Meriwether's case, the strain "was a constitutional disposition in all the nearer branches of the family of his name and more immediately inherited by him from his father." Jefferson identified the basis of the Lewis affliction specifically as depression, manifested in anxiety-ridden pessimism.

Active and always enterprising, Lucy was keenly interested in natural medicines—possibly because she had married into a family of ailments, real and imagined. Eventually, many of her neighbors also came to rely on her for "simples," or the basic ingredients for medical remedies. At home in the wilds, looking for minerals and herbs, Lucy was said to have inspired her oldest son, Meriwether, who came to love the outdoors.

When Meriwether was seven, his father died of a very real case of pneumonia. He had fallen off his horse while trying to cross the cold waters of the Rivanna River when it was swelled by late-winter floods. The following winter, young Meriwether went out, in a sense, after him. Jefferson wrote: "When only 8. Years of age, he habitually went out in the dead of night alone with his dogs, into the forest to hunt the raccoon & opossum, which, seeking their food at night, can then only be taken. In this exercise no season or circumstance could obstruct his purpose, plunging thro' the winter's snows and frozen streams in pursuit of his object."

For the image of little Meriwether tromping through the dark, Jefferson apparently relied on an unsigned sketch supplied to him late in life, when he was gathering information for a short biographical memo about his protégé. The writer of the sketch included several details that Jefferson didn't use, writing that Meriwether "was early remarkable for intrepidity, liberality & hardihood ... He might be tracked through the snow to his traps by the blood which trickled from his bare feet." By either version, Lewis was an unusual personality, being hardy to a degree that proved something about what he was and who he wasn't, even when he was a child.

Mrs. Lewis remarried and the family moved to Georgia, but Meriwether returned to Charlottesville alone when he was in his early teens. The family reunited there a few years later. The Lewises' Locust Hill property encompassed nineteen hundred acres, which Meriwether tried to help farm as a young man, but agriculture didn't interest him. The house and the town in which he'd grown up didn't offer the comfort that others might have described

as home, perhaps because his tendency toward depression seemed
to be held at bay by new sights and surroundings. In 1794, Lewis
followed his father's footsteps into the army, leaving Charlottesville
to join the Virginia militia. Jefferson mentored his military career,
ultimately helping him to receive a commission in the regular army.

Lewis was diligent, and by early 1801 he was a lieutenant serving as a paymaster at Pittsburgh's Fort Fayette, the more modern
replacement for heroic old Fort Pitt. It was a busy place, but very
dull for anyone interested in action. Keeping track of the soldiers'
money there may not have constituted the rugged life, but with
most of the activities of the army focused on the Old Northwest,
Fort Fayette was at least a conspicuous posting. Part of the job involved travels to Ohio and Michigan, which probably helped to al-
leviate Lewis's moodiness. And as paymaster, he reported to General
James Wilkinson.

Wilkinson's military career had only burgeoned since the 1790s,
when he first perfected the posture then in vogue: tugging behind
his back on the future of Kentucky. By 1801, he was commander of
the entire U.S. Army. When inviting Lewis to accept the position
of personal secretary, Jefferson wrote simultaneously to Wilkinson,
courteously seeking permission to hire one of his subordinates. As
he entered the presidency, many in the military or associated with it
distrusted him to the point of hatred. They were loyal to his opponents, the Federalists, in large part because Jefferson was known to
favor a smaller army and a downright emaciated navy. Furthermore,
officers presumed that since Jefferson had never been in uniform
himself, he would curtail the moneymaking ventures that often
blended into the service.

By the time Jefferson's letter to Wilkinson arrived at Fort Fayette in early March, the general was already en route to Washington for the inauguration. In a clear display of the military's attitude
toward Jefferson, not one of his ranking officers chose to accompany

Wilkinson and attend the ceremony. In fact, soon after Wilkinson left, Fort Fayette erupted into dissent over the new president. Soldiers who despised Jefferson had no idea how to celebrate his inauguration on March 4, much less how to serve under him for four years after that. Many officers made drastic plans to resign and some actually did. In anticipation of Inauguration Day—then a colorful holiday across the country—Fort Fayette was filled with people noisily making plans to ignore it. Only through the most potent coercion on the part of Fort Fayette's commandant (and the promise of fireworks from Mrs. Wilkinson) did the core of Jefferson's army give up a day to honor his inauguration. No mere orders, however, could restore enthusiasm up and down the ranks after the day was over.

Jefferson was keenly aware of the antipathy of most army officers. In selecting Lewis as secretary, he chose one of the small number whose personal loyalty was certain. At the same time, Jefferson paid a public compliment to the army, giving it, in effect, another seat in his administration. To that end, he was careful to specify that Lewis would maintain his rank, as well as his seniority for advancement, during his tenure as secretary. As Jefferson had written to Wilkinson:

> In selecting a private secretary, I have thought it would be advantageous to take one who possessing a knoledge of the Western country, of the army and it's situation, might sometimes aid us with informations of interest, which we may not otherwise possess. A personal acquaintance with him . . . has induced me to select him, if his presence can be dispensed with, without injury to the service.

Jefferson made the same mention of the western country in his letter to Lewis, referring specifically to the Old Northwest. Even

Jefferson, a man who could be bafflingly omniscient regarding affairs across his own nation, couldn't have known how glad he would soon be to have identified and collected so many people, including Dunbar, Nolan, and Lewis, who were familiar with the West.

In late March of 1801, Rufus King, the American ambassador to the Court of St. James's in London, was hearing whispers—whispers about a seismic change in North American geopolitics. King, a New Yorker, may have been a holdover from the Adams administration, but he was an excellent representative, loyal to any U.S. president. He immediately notified Jefferson, via his bulletin's six-week transatlantic crossing, that Spain's King Carlos IV was preparing to cede vast territory in North America to Napoleon's France. By the time the message arrived in Philadelphia, the treaty covering the cessation was merely awaiting Spanish signatures before the entire Louisiana Territory changed hands.

The Spanish found comfort in the idea that France would preside over Louisiana. The nation that kept the rest of continental Europe from the Spanish homeland would henceforth keep America away from Mexico. High-minded French culture with its knack for organization would blend into existing settlements, reinforcing the European atmosphere of Louisiana Territory. In any guise, though, France would bring money and soldiers in abundance, more than enough to contain the Americans.

In late May, Jefferson received King's communiqué. "There is considerable reason to apprehend that Spain cedes Louisiana and the Floridas to France," the president wrote to James Madison, his secretary of state. "It is a policy very unwise in both, and very ominous to us." Jefferson couldn't say much more than that, because he didn't know much more. In the diplomatic corps, King was soon joined by two Jefferson appointees, Charles Pinckney in Madrid and Robert Livingston in Paris. None of them could learn the detail that concerned Jefferson most: whether the Floridas were included in the cessation. In fact, the secrecy with which the treaty was handled was remarkable for Europe in 1801. The intended date of the transfer was also murky, but that was a secret mostly by virtue of being unknown even to those involved.

The Spanish royal family had placed all of its faith in Talleyrand's touching sentiment about His Catholic Majesty's court having nothing to fear from France. During the summer, when a panic of remorse suddenly gripped the court at Madrid, Napoleon sent a remarkably sensitive and caring message through one of his emissaries. "His Catholic Majesty has been forthcoming in expressing the wish that France should not sell or relinquish, in any manner, the property or possession of Louisiana," the note acknowledged. "I am authorized to declare to you, in the name of the First Consul [Napoleon], that France will never relinquish it." With Napoleon's assurance that France would *never relinquish* Louisiana, Carlos IV rested easy.

In August, while impatiently awaiting more information about Spain's maneuverings, Jefferson heard again from William Dunbar, who had waited to write back out of fear of intruding on the new president's time. Dunbar had always been apolitical, but with his permanent home established in Natchez, Mississippi Territory, U.S.A., and having a personal friendship with the American president, he became a vociferous Jeffersonian—an American, at last. Most persuasive to a committed slaveholder like Dunbar, though, the American government had permanently lifted Spanish laws giving Africans and African Americans (whether enslaved or not) reliable rights.

Dunbar dutifully fulfilled his role as Jefferson's eyes and ears in the West, filling him in on regional news of interest, along with descriptions of the Mississippi River and a short report on fossils reported to have been found west of the river. He then brought Jefferson up to date on a mutual correspondent, Irish American horse wrangler Philip Nolan. "Mr. Nolan," he said, "has formerly given me some intimation of fossil bones of great magnitude being found in various parts of new Mexico [the Texas region], but we have lately been cut off from our usual communication with that Country by the imprudence of Mr. Nolan."

Philip Nolan was important to Jefferson in much the same way as Meriwether Lewis; the latter knew something of the Old Northwest from his days traveling for the army, the former was the president's expert on the Old Southwest (the western part of Lower Louisiana, the Red River, and especially, the wilds of Texas). News of Nolan would've been of keen interest to Jefferson.

In 1799, Nolan had married into an established family from Natchez, subsequently using his horse-trading profits to settle in the border town of Natchitoches. Spanish officials there regarded him as an American. All was well for the dashing Irishman, yet he felt compelled to leave his sedentary life behind later that year for yet another expedition to Texas. "Mr. Nolan," as Dunbar told Jefferson, "persisted in hunting wild horses without a regular permission."

A half-dozen years before, Spanish officials in Louisiana Territory thought Nolan amusing. But by the time he was preparing his 1800 expedition, at least two officials expressed concern to the governor-general of Texas province, Juan Bautista de Elguézabal, that the Irish American seemed to be laying plans to take over the whole of Texas. Of course, Nolan could never take over a huge and unwieldy territory with twenty miscellaneous horse wranglers, but the intimation was that Nolan was involved in an initial phase of a plot pertaining to his old boss Wilkinson. It likely wasn't true, but such rumors persisted among the Spanish—and were in fact then being stoked by Daniel Clark, the New Orleans man who had boasted to Jefferson that he was Nolan's friend.

If Nolan was on any mission for Wilkinson, his orders may well have pertained to the Red River, which he crossed on his approach to Texas. Mostly flowing from the northwest direction, the Red divides the present-day states of Texas and Oklahoma before moving downriver on a sharper southeasterly diagonal across Louisiana. Little was known to Europeans or Americans about the river above the town of Natchitoches, but the geography of the Red River would have been valuable to American leaders, including Wilkinson, who took a particular interest in Texas. As a double agent working for both governments, it behooved him to know a little more about that borderland than the leaders in either of the capitals that paid him.

Perhaps the best evidence that Nolan was innocent of a plot to become "the king of Texas" came from someone with no reason to defend him. Andrew Ellicott, the confirmed enemy of Nolan's friend Wilkinson—and the friend of Nolan's betrayer, Daniel Clark—was asked a few years later for a statement vindicating Wilkinson over alleged acts of sedition. Ellicott declined the opportunity to say anything good about Wilkinson, but he did volunteer that he did "not recollect to have ever received a hint that . . . Mr. P. Nolan was concerned in any plans or intrigues injurious to the United States. On the contrary, in all our private and confidential conversations, he appeared strongly attached to the interests and welfare of our country."

With or without other motives, Nolan set off to find mustangs with about twenty men. To avoid both of the portal towns, Natchitoches and Nacogdoches, he made a circle to the north and over the Ouachita River. Nolan puckishly sent his regrets to the commander of the Spanish militia post along the river: "I have not provided myself with a passport," he wrote, "and knowing that you cannot with propriety permit me to go through your settlement, I have determined to Pass to the North." He then met the Red River for a short span before turning across open land to the southwest to begin the work of capturing wild horses. Incensed by the simple fact of an American in Texas, Governor Elguézabal ordered the military commander at Nacogdoches to locate Nolan and capture him for interrogation. A detachment of one hundred and fifty Spanish soldiers under the command of Manuel Múzquiz tracked Nolan. "They surrounded our camp at about one o'clock in the morning, on the 22nd of March, 1801," wrote Ellis Peter Bean, a young Tennessean accompanying Nolan. At the very moment that the Spanish court was preparing to cede Louisiana to France—and thus cede the problem of unwelcome Americans in the West—Spain's soldiers circled Nolan in the darkness. "We were all alarmed by the tramping of their horses," Bean continued, "and, as day broke, without speaking a word, they commenced their fire. After about ten minutes, our gallant leader Nolan was slain by a musket-ball which hit him in the head." Nolan was the only man killed.

Múzquiz cut off Nolan's ears and took them to Governor Elguézabal as a trophy. Because Nolan was a celebrated American with powerful friends, Elguézabal knew that his execution wouldn't go unnoticed. In fact, he wanted the news to spread throughout the Louisiana Territory, a warning that would keep Americans in the future from drifting across the border on any pretext. Reports of Nolan's death did sweep Lower Louisiana and while there couldn't be any retaliation as he had indeed been trespassing, it left blood on the border and a widespread belief that war with Spain was near.

Nolan's captured men were taken to Mexico, where they were variously shot or sentenced to "eternal slavery" in prison. The fact that some of them were remanded to prison in Acapulco, that they typically didn't have to remain in their jail cells, and that Bean, for one, had a lengthy affair with a rich Mexican woman, didn't mitigate the horror. To keep the prisoners in fear, the Mexicans every so often put one before a firing squad.

The wrath of the Spanish in the face of American incursion had been raised to a lethal level. Nolan and his death were much discussed, becoming the stuff of lore along the borderland. Later explorers couldn't ignore the fact that their lives, like his, were nothing more than symbolic to distant powers attempting to make a statement about sovereignty.

LATE IN 1801, the terms of the Spanish-French treaty were at last known in the United States, though the details were incomplete. Madrid may or may not have retained the Floridas, but the Louisiana Territory was definitely to be French. By early 1802, with the transfer yet to take place, Jefferson was maneuvering. As he turned away from France, he was suddenly full of condescending praise for the Spanish authority in Louisiana. "Her pacific dispositions, her feeble state," he wrote fondly, "would induce her to increase our facilities there so that her possession of the place would be hardly felt by us." It may have been a bit premature for nostalgia, though, because Spain continued to administer the territory, not always to Jefferson's liking.

Jefferson's concern was not with the greater part of Louisiana Territory. The president of 1802 was still the secretary of state of 1792, and he carried forward his greatest concern from his earlier job: that the Mississippi River and New Orleans absolutely had to be open to American commerce. "There is," he told Livingston in a memorable line, "on [the] globe one single spot, [the] possessor of which is our natural and habitual enemy. It is New Orleans, through which the produce of three-eighths of our territory must pass to market."

Anticipating trouble over navigation on the river, Jefferson instituted a dramatic change in policy. He was ready to fight with France. Personally, he loved French culture, while other Americans were mixed; New Englanders, in particular, regarded France with antipathy, for all of its help in the Revolution a generation before. All such opinions were academic, though, since France across the ocean was far different from France on the Mississippi River. Jefferson directed his diplomats to make known a startling new national intention: at the very moment France took possession of New

Orleans, "we must marry ourselves to the British fleet and nation." The balance he'd once celebrated between Spain and Britain was to be replaced on the same fulcrum by *France* and Britain. The only difference was that in confronting Napoleon's France instead of an anemic Spain, Jefferson was staring down a nation that was far from "pacific" and anything but "feeble."

Jefferson was putting aside his prejudices against Great Britain in favor of American security. Britain and France happened to be in the midst of a negotiated two-year truce (the Treaty of Amiens), but another war between the two was anticipated, if not scheduled. In Jefferson's view, America's strength depended on its patience to await that war.

By the beginning of 1802, Napoleon had finally made his move, though Americans weren't certain what to make of it. The French emperor had equipped ten thousand troops and ordered them to New Orleans. He couldn't resist committing them to a quick stop on the way to help an even larger force subdue an uprising in Saint-Domingue (later renamed Haiti). The troops were expected in New Orleans by summer. Knowing that the French forces were on the way, residents of the Mississippi Valley were worn out from worry. "Every eye in the U. S. is now fixed on this affair of Louisiana," Jefferson wrote in April, as his young nation awaited a confrontation with the most powerful empire on earth. Even at that late date, though, the French troops had yet to leave the Caribbean island.

In late July, Dunbar wrote to a trading company in New York City with which he did business, sharing his thoughts on the situation:

> You will be surprised when I inform you that we still remain in the dark respecting the future fate of our neighbouring province of Louisianna. . . . It is impossible to predict what embarrassments may be placed upon the navigation and commerce of this river by the aspiring ruler of the French

nation; but we must be willfully blind not to see that the
position of the U.S. in this quarter must be . . . unfavorably
altered by the expected change.

As of October, there was no change; the French had yet to arrive in New Orleans. Napoleon's regiments were still engaged in the
Haitian campaign, their troop strength withering due to the guerilla
tactics of the defenders and the even more lethal efficiency of the
mosquitoes spreading yellow fever. While Americans were waiting
to see what the French would do in Louisiana, a Spanish official still
wielding power in New Orleans effectively closed the port to U.S.
shipments. When the Americans complained—and they did—the
Spanish administrator said that only one person could restore full
rights to the Americans on the river: the king of Spain. The Americans regarded that as a cynical evasion. "The surplus produce of the
West," reported Mississippi's territorial governor, W. C. C. Claiborne, "will be lost to our Country."

Jefferson's worst nightmare had come to pass, but it was precipitated by the wrong country. He had assumed that France would be
the enemy in control of New Orleans and his solution was an alliance with Britain. As of early November, when he heard the news
of the retraction of rights, he found himself facing "docile" Spain,
which seemed to be in the throes of some last, desperate attempt to
nullify the treaty of cessation. If the retraction was supposed to be
disruptive, it succeeded. While members of Congress and residents
of Kentucky and Tennessee expressed their outrage, the president—
more incensed than any—considered his options. The most obvious
and tempting was the type of action that the British ambassador,
Edward Thornton, termed "a measure of vigour."

For the United States, the most tempting "measure of vigour"—
military action—was not viable, since France was expected to enter
the theater of concern imminently. With that, the nascent United
States would be in its first world war, and it was unprepared for a

conflict of that scale. The possibility, however, remained. A diplomatic response was almost impossible to implement, because Jefferson had already outlined his potential alliance with Britain on the basis of French advances. Adding a coda with yet another set of alliances, in case Spain turned out to be the enemy, was not only impractical, but mealy. There was no good option, and so while Jefferson would not speak publicly of war with Spain, he pressed hard in private for his government to prepare for it.

Secretary of War Dearborn immediately launched efforts to rebuild the army's ranks through mandatory reenlistment orders and recruitment drives. The largest force was to be moved into position at Fort Adams, just north of Natchez, with other concentrations at posts along the Mississippi and the southern border with the Floridas. Forts along the Great Lakes were bolstered, especially at Detroit and Niagara. Jefferson gamely prepared for three potential theaters of war: against either the Spanish or the French across the Mississippi River, against one of the same in the Floridas, and most surprisingly, against Britain—America's contingency ally—in the north.

Heavy settlement would also be a part of the strategy. While the War Department was gathering troops for the east side of the Mississippi River, Jefferson initiated a program to bring American civilians into the region. He revised his land policy to make it easier to sell government land in smaller allotments in the Trans-Appalachia region.

Even as Jefferson rushed to ready the country for war, he presented a cool-headed and serene facade. He needed to make a statement of action, not words. During the hectic month of November 1802, with cabinet meetings on the rush to war almost every day, he had no time for his own interests, least of all natural history and the search for indigenous mammals, birds, trees, or fronds. Jefferson, whose administration was based on a frugality bordering on parsimony, wouldn't request an expenditure simply to satisfy his

personal interests—and the Congress of 1802, with its own reputation for stinginess, would never have taken up such a matter. At
least one member of Jefferson's cabinet, however, was agitating for
further information on military aspects of the Upper Missouri, in
the event that Britain attempted an invasion from the region west
of the Great Lakes.

Preparations were intense, but Jefferson needed something more
immediate to show the three European powers that the United
States was firmly engaged in the future of the Mississippi Valley and
the West. At the same time, he was under pressure to obtain strategic information regarding those regions. Making an impression on
the Europeans and simultaneously gathering intelligence—the two
goals were mutually exclusive, except as they merged in *philosophic*
interests. And in exploration. It was in mid-November 1802, amid
unceasing talk of war in Washington, that President Jefferson made
the decision to sponsor an expedition along the Missouri River and
on to the Pacific.

Five

"THEY PRETEND IT IS ONLY TO PROMOTE KNOLEDGE"

Jefferson expressed an interest in the sciences—especially the natural sciences—throughout his life, but it was never more than an avocation in relation to his true calling. In the 1780s, when a British scientific expedition announced its intention to cross western America to the Pacific, Jefferson wasn't enthusiastic. In fact, he scoffed at the whole thing. The explorers were well-educated specialists with academic goals, but that didn't fool him. "They pretend it is only to promote knoledge," Jefferson wrote. "I am afraid they have plans of colonizing into that quarter." The British trek never materialized, but Jefferson's response said much more about his view of scientific expeditions than perhaps he intended. According to his own 1802 plan for a Missouri River expedition, Americans would be taking steps in the West and they truly would pretend it was only to promote knowledge.

Jefferson needed to pull a plausible expedition together quickly.

In that, he was at a distinct disadvantage to the late Spanish king Carlos III, whose interest in scientific discovery was comparable to that of Jefferson. The king actively committed his reign to "the methodical examination and identification of the products of nature of my American dominions." Carlos III truly wanted scientific results. Before sending out even one expedition, though, he founded academic institutions where field scientists would be trained in botany, zoology, geology, and other natural sciences. Fine artists were recruited as well. The Spanish patiently prepared their explorers, and when the corps were fully manned by experts, they fanned out across South America, the Philippines, Mexico, the Caribbean, and the Pacific coast in North America. At the end of the eighteenth century and during the first years of the nineteenth, Spain's scientists collected thousands of specimens and also brought home an unmatched pictorial record of Native life and the natural world, thanks to the fine artists who accompanied the men of science. As an initial repository for their New World collections, the Spanish had previously created a botanical institute in Mexico City, organizing plants under Linnean classification, a demanding and complex system—the very latest thinking of the time.

The American exploratory effort was launched somewhat differently. It started in the office at the White House where Jefferson looked across his desk and hired his first explorer, a highly intelligent if unsophisticated man anxious to undertake a two-year-long expedition on soldier's pay. For Jefferson's purposes, a military man was mandatory, and yet he had to make a selection without distracting from the military buildup that Dearborn was organizing. No one was as easily available as Lieutenant Lewis.

Jefferson later intimated that before choosing Meriwether Lewis, he had looked for someone more qualified. As though apologizing to his scientific friends for choosing the novice, Jefferson maintained: "It was impossible to find a character who to a compleat science in botany, natural history, mineralogy & astronomy, joined the firmness of constitution & character, prudence, habits adapted to the woods, & a familiarity with the Indian manners & character." What Lewis did have, in addition to his army uniform, was a unique character, matched to the furthest possibilities. Jefferson, in his later biographical sketch of Lewis, was extravagant in his praise for Lewis's courage, knowledge of nature, and leadership abilities, but the characteristic that best suited the young officer for the expedition under discussion in November was one of the first that Jefferson mentioned: "a firmness & perseverance of purpose." Like Evans and very few others, Lewis had the quality of single-mindedness. Levi Lincoln, the attorney general, even worried about it, observing, "From my ideas of Capt. Lewis he will be much more likely, in case of difficulty, to push too far, than to recde [recede] too soon." Neither Evans nor Lewis, as first-time explorers, was tied by family or romance. They were both oblivious to profit. And to see a faint reflection of Lewis in Evans's life, they were both at the same stage in their twenties when they were blanks by themselves. Each was transformed under the name of a hero—a Madoc or a Jefferson made them invincible.

Jefferson had noted Lewis's depression during his two-year tenure at the White House. Such pessimistic tendencies might easily have hurt the young man's chances of being chosen for a wrenching trip, since the Missouri River had so far crumpled the hopes of all who had challenged it from the European settlements to the east. And while the extent of the Rockies hadn't even been measured yet by European Americans, it was known that the terrain there could be counted on to pulverize more than hopes. The sheer duress of such a trip had to have been considered, as Lewis "renewed his sollictations to have the direction of the party," Jefferson wrote. Lewis didn't just want to go on the expedition—he wanted to lead it. Jefferson recognized that his young friend was a unique case, requiring "more dazzling pursuits," not safer ones. Before long, Lewis was appointed as the leader, being a man who was better off with danger, exertion, and no time to think about himself.

While Lewis began researching the requirements and expenses of a journey west, Jefferson turned to an area of his own expertise: the use of information. As soon as possible—long before he told Congress about the proposed expedition—he very purposefully planted the idea of it with the European powers. Not only was time of the essence, diplomatically, but in the event that Congress denied the funding, he'd have already made his point with the trio of over-armed Euro-giants leaning in on the United States as 1802 turned to 1803.

Jefferson needed to inform a short list of foreign ambassadors about America's ambitious plan for exploration of the West. First, he requested an interview with the Spanish ambassador to the United States, Carlos Martínez de Yrujo. Though Jefferson presumed that by the time Lewis arrived in Louisiana, the territory would belong to France, his priority lay in showing Spain the strength of American ambitions west. Spain, after all, was the nation that was testing America by holding back free use of the Mississippi. Jefferson wanted to throw down his own gauntlet. Yrujo arrived at the White House from his base near Philadelphia for a talk in late November. A Spanish grandee in every sense, Yrujo enjoyed finery as much as Jefferson did, dressing extravagantly and denying himself little in the way of fashion or fine living. That was part of the reason he chose to live and work in the tony Philadelphia suburb of Germantown, rather than the hollow spaces of Washington. Another factor was that Yrujo was married to an American, the daughter of Pennsylvania's governor, in fact.

During their conversation, Jefferson grew animated as he told Yrujo of the intention to send a group of Americans to "explore the course of the Missouri River." Yrujo listened politely. What he was thinking all the while, as he later reported to his home office, was that according to Jefferson's enthusiastic description, the explorers:

> would nominally have the objective of investigating every-
> thing which might contribute to the progress of commerce;
> but that in reality it would have no other view than the ad-
> vancement of geography.

Yrujo was tacitly repeating Jefferson's sentiment about the Brit-ish explorers long before: they were going on a mission of expan-sion, not a purely intellectual one. Apologizing to the president for being blunt, he said that such a trip "couldn't fail to give umbrage" to the Spanish government. That was no setback for Jefferson; it showed that the threat of expedition carried a certain sting. Yrujo then swept the notion of an American mission off the table, treating Jefferson to a fastidiously one-sided talk about the history of explo-ration along the Missouri River and beyond. What he didn't high-light in his talk was the long-held Spanish assumption that whoever was the first to spot a body of water laid claim to all it touched, and thus the country that explored the Missouri to its source would be, as he averred, "the dominant nation there afterward."

Yrujo concluded his report of his November conversation with Jefferson by noting:

> The President has been all his life a man of letters, very spec-
> ulative and a lover of glory, and it would be possible he might
> attempt to perpetrate the fame of his administration not only
> by the measures of frugality and economy which characterize
> him, but also by discovering or attempting at least to dis-
> cover the way by which the Americans may someday extend
> their population and their influence up to the coasts of the
> South Sea.

As Yrujo left Jefferson's office, he believed that the idea for an expedition was dead, thanks to his smooth talking. Having quashed the president's dreams, he did what any grandee would do: he sent Jefferson two hundred bottles of champagne. Jefferson followed suit by doing what any man evading a gift would do and immediately made arrangements to pay for it out of his personal funds.

His talks with Spain concluded, Jefferson turned to the British and the French for passports, official permission to enter foreign territory. The French cooperated, having no reason to antagonize their future neighbors. The need for credentials from the British was largely gratuitous, although the last part of the journey did promise to take Lewis through disputed lands along the Pacific. Additionally, the British were still floating plans to gobble up the whole of the Louisiana Territory and the Floridas before spitting out New Orleans and the lower part of Louisiana for the Americans. Still, Jefferson wanted no chance of a future British move to the south; he wanted the Foreign Office to know that Americans were headed due west.

Although Britain's claims to any lands on the expedition's route were tenuous, Ambassador Thornton duly furnished a passport for Lewis. "A very great change has gradually taken place," he reported to the foreign secretary in London, "in the opinions of all ranks in this government in favour of Great Britain." It wasn't quite that simple, of course. In 1803, America's attitude toward Britain went only as far as proving that catchy old Napoleonic-era axiom that "the enemy of my enemy's enemy is probably—but not definitely—not my enemy this week." By the end of December, in any case, all three foreign powers knew of Lewis's trip. It had been barely more than a month since Jefferson received word of the crisis over American shipping rights on the Mississippi.

As the weeks went by, talk in Washington grew louder over the tension in the West, which an incensed Congress blamed variously on either Spain or France. Opinion was mixed about which of the two was actually the culprit, but after the strife of the 1800 election, the country was remarkably united early in 1803—solid in anger. "There is," Secretary of State Madison wrote, "but one sentiment throughout the Union with respect to the duty of maintaining our rights of navigation and boundary." That same adamancy put more political pressure on Jefferson than anything ever had; he needed to win back full use of the river. In early January, Congress overwhelmingly passed a resolution vowing to maintain U.S. rights throughout the Mississippi. Jefferson timed his next move to follow. With Lewis's help, he prepared a secret message to Congress, pressing the case for the funding of an expedition. It wasn't hard to sell. He was talking about sending men to the West, and with that alone he had Congress's attention. After describing the journey, Jefferson predicted that Spain, "regarding this as a literary pursuit . . . would not be disposed to view it with jealousy."

As Jefferson knew firsthand from his dealings with the volatile—if well-dressed—Ambassador Yrujo, Spain certainly did not regard the proposed trip as a literary pursuit. His Catholic Majesty's government was angry, resentful, and most of all surprised to hear that Lewis was going ahead with the expedition, even without a Spanish passport. As Jefferson was aware, the last person who tried that died where he fell in Texas, surrounded by Mexican guns and wild horses.

Congress during the 1802–03 term was notoriously tight with money, but in the atmosphere of the confrontation with Spain, it favored any "measure of vigour" and appropriated twenty-five hundred dollars for Lewis's journey. With an official congressional blessing, Lewis devoted the rest of the winter of 1803 and all spring to preparations for the trip. Jefferson wanted to equip Lewis with a means of coded communication to send back messages regarding sensitive information or, as Jefferson perceived it, "whatever might do injury if betrayed." The need for his education on that point betrayed the trip's priorities.

To custom-design a code, the president turned to the brilliant Philadelphia mathematician Robert Patterson. A native of Ireland, Patterson had grown up without the privilege of a formal education. He learned advanced mathematics on his own, entirely from books. Emigrating to America, he was a schoolteacher and farmer at first, but his intellectual reputation grew. Despite the fact that he had never been to college himself, he was named the professor of mathematics of the University of Pennsylvania in 1779. One of his grandsons recalled that in personality, Patterson was "cheerful, and even animated." For example, when giving out his address on Chestnut Street in Philadelphia, he'd often say only that "the second digit is the cube of the first and the third is the mean of the first two."* In general, he was at his most comfortable with higher math and, as a natural-born teacher, was certain that everyone else was fascinated by it, too—or, at least, that they could be. He set to work on creating a system of encryption for the western expedition.

During February and March, Jefferson kept details about the expedition largely quiet. There was a false story about Lewis heading only as far west as the Mississippi River, in order to discover its source. Many newspaper editors spotted that tale for a fake but wrongly guessed at Lewis's real mission. "The Private Secretary of the President, Mr. Lewis, is to proceed in a few weeks on political business in the Mississippi country" ran a note in the Boston *Columbian Centinel*. It was generally surmised that Lewis was rushing toward the areas affected by the suspension of shipping rights—notably Kentucky, Tennessee, and the northern part of Mississippi Territory—as an agent of President Jefferson in order to squelch talk of its secession from the United States. Lewis wasn't involved in any such mission, although it was true that a growing number of Americans along the river were preparing for their own attack on New

---

* He lived at number 285. It is the only three-digit number that answers his description.

Orleans—envisioning a Mississippi nation, independent from the United States. As February came to a close in 1803, farmers along the Mississippi were downright desperate; the growing season was about to start, and their produce would be stuck until New Orleans opened to American trade. All over the country, the suspension of full rights on the river was responsible for "extraordinary agitation produced in the public mind," in Jefferson's words. In response, Congress rose up and fairly shouted out resolutions in mid-February inciting the president to take New Orleans by force. By all appearances, the administration was planning for it. Ambassador Yrujo, for one, was convinced by the preparations. He sent communiqués to the court of Madrid advising that Spain had two choices: restore full rights to Americans on the Mississippi or go to war over them. Privately, Jefferson had set April 1 as a deadline, by which date he expected the rights to be returned to Americans on the river.

In an effort to spread his confidence to the West, Jefferson wrote to William Dunbar on March 3 of that year, taking up current events for the first time in their friendship. Dunbar was stunned to be addressed on Jefferson's official business, but as a resident of Natchez, he lived on its front line. Jefferson argued against the talk of war, which was overcharged in Natchez, and made the case for "what we believe a more certain, & more speedy means. . . ." The new development was that only the day before, Jefferson had sent word to his diplomats that the United States would be willing to buy from France greater New Orleans and the Floridas (operating, as he was, on the misinformation that France had acquired the Floridas from Spain).

While awaiting a response from the diplomats, Jefferson faced an early problem with Lewis's planned trip. Whatever the purpose of the expedition—reconnaissance, commerce, science, geopolitics, sociology—the preparation of a map would be at its core. A seminal motive of the trip was, as Secretary of the Treasury Albert Gallatin put it, "a perfect knowledge of the posts, establishments & force kept by Spain in upper Louisiana, and also of the most proper station to occupy, for the purpose of preventing effectually the occupying of any part of the Missouri country by G.B.[Great Britain]." It would not help very much to know that there were posts and soldiers in the West if Lewis couldn't identify their exact location. With navigation as a top priority, Lewis studied the subject on his own over the winter in Washington.

Lewis was still hoping to leave for the West by the beginning of summer, but Jefferson recognized how ill prepared the younger man was, especially in navigation. He wrote to members of the APS in and around Philadelphia for assistance. One of the two men who agreed to further Lewis's training was Ellicott, then stranded in the civil service in Lancaster, Pennsylvania. Years before, Ellicott had studied the subject of celestial navigation with Professor Patterson, the second man asked by Jefferson to help prepare Lewis for the trip.

Ellicott and Patterson hovered over Lewis as though they were two Pygmalions who had been challenged with turning Lewis into a working physicist in ten days or less. They were. Under their tutelage, Lewis made great progress in his study of spherical trigonometry, which was critical to celestial navigation. Accurate maps would write America's name on the West in too many respects to allow for the chance of failure; Lewis had to think like an expert once he was in the field.

The members of the expedition were expected to make continuous notes on the basis of dead reckoning—charting a direction using a compass and then measuring, or more often estimating, the distance between turns. Nearly anyone could make an effort at dead reckoning, but celestial navigation, based on longitude and latitude, was by far the more reliable means of positioning. According to the well-proven theory, any location on the earth can be pinpointed by its relation to one or more heavenly bodies. The relation is expressed using the framework of geometry or its more sophisticated variation, spherical trigonometry. After someone understands the basic theory, as Lewis soon did, the next step requires mastering the instruments. Sextants and octants are the most common ones used to measure the relationships of selected planets, stars, or moons with whatever rock pile one is, at that moment, standing on.

The third step is the mathematical calculation of the longitude or latitude, based on the findings. Calculation of longitude requires about ten steps of its own over the course of a day. It could take even more, since a plethora of different formula sets all led ultimately to the right answer. A surveyor chooses which one to use on the basis of which readings could be made accurately that day, according to factors such as the terrain, the weather, or the availability of particular instruments. If a surveyor were missing a particular reading for use in one formula, he could use others to calculate the outstanding figure. Out of seemingly arcane measurements, an expert can interpolate a number that can interpolate another number, and so on, eventually arriving at the one needed to figure the longitude.

Ellicott was proficient with the calculations required for celestial reckoning on that level. Dunbar was comfortable with them, too, as an armchair exercise. Patterson, however, was the best in America.

In March, Professor Patterson sent Jefferson a letter outlining the twenty-seven-step formula that he liked to use to calculate the longitude using lunar readings. The letter, looking from a distance like delicate wallpaper, was apparently impenetrable to Jefferson. The master of all trades was not even a jack when it came to spherical trig. He later apologized to Patterson for "having never been a practical astronomer, and a life far otherwise spent having even rendered me unfamiliar with the detailed theory of the lunar observations." That being the case, Jefferson must have wondered about his ill-trained mind on reading in Patterson's accompanying note that the twenty-seven-step formula was, in the professor's opinion, "extremely easy even to boys or common sailors of but moderate capabilities." After seeing the extent of the twenty-seven steps, Jefferson explicitly forbade Lewis from making any but the most necessary calculations during the course of the journey. With all the uncharted land that was awaiting the expedition, he didn't want it to bog down on the math.

Ellicott seemed to have more of a sense of the urgent need to streamline the material and make it accessible. Lewis found two good masters in Ellicott and Patterson and he gamely tried to serve them both. During his stay in greater Philadelphia, he was also tutored by specialists in other sciences, even as he spent some of his time placing orders for equipment to be used on the expedition. Jefferson was in constant communication with suggestions for Lewis. He also peppered him with personal errands, indicating a lingering condescension toward his secretary—asking that Lewis buy him some of his favorite fleecy socks, among other requests, even in the midst of final preparations for the expedition of a lifetime.

ON THE FRONT lines of the effort to absorb the West, Thomas Freeman was crashing around the brush of Indiana Territory early in 1803, hearing little from the east or the south, except that Jefferson was anxious to speed up the process of freeing lands for American settlers. It was another part of his mandate to show strength to the West. William Henry Harrison, the territorial governor of Indiana, was instructed by Jefferson to purchase Indian lands or otherwise move tribes, including those of the Lenape (Delaware), the Miami, the Ojibwe (Chippewa), and the Potawatomie. Harrison started with 1.6 million acres surrounding his capital city, Vincennes, and Freeman was engaged to survey it.

Since being chased off the 31st parallel survey, Freeman's reputation had stabilized. In the aftermath, he was accorded respect for having been hired for the prestigious job, but no one ever mentioned that he'd subsequently been fired from it by Ellicott. Wilkinson's intercession helped Freeman move eventually to the job in Indiana, where his work on the Vincennes Tract was as important as any in the country at that time; Freeman led a party of at least ten assistants into raw terrain, the forefront of a process critical to Jefferson's plans. A later Indiana surveyor described Freeman as he would have looked:

> with his Jacob staff in his right hand, his compass swinging on his left shoulder and on his right hip, his buckskin pouch swinging from a shoulder strap containing his instructions, papers, field notes and ink horn, opened at the smaller end containing homemade ink brewed from the forest bark; another horn opened at the larger end containing dry sand to be used as a blotter; a dozen or more wild goose feathers from which to make quill pens.

A hundred and seventy years later, grains of sand were still caught in the fading pages of Freeman's notebooks on the Vincennes Tract. Experienced surveyors who examined them through the years marveled at the meticulous detail Freeman included. They also admired his flowing penmanship, as easy to read as type in a book, a feat made even more impressive by the fact that Freeman typically made the notes crouched near a fire at a campsite. The paths that Freeman chose evolved into roads and automobile highways over the years. After months of living in the wild, he ultimately succeeded in determining the location of the northeast corner of the Vincennes Tract, a spot known to Indiana history as Freeman's Corner. Surveyors have been astounded ever since at the expertise required to mark that corner, which served as an anchor for Indiana Territory; from it, expansive land tracts were laid out over the following ten years to the north, east, and west. When those lying to the east were later surveyed, they fit neatly against established lands, requiring no adjustment.

Once Freeman's survey was ready in spring of 1803, Governor

William Henry Harrison's job was to convince the Native nations in the region to abandon their lands. For a couple of hundred years, Indians in the Trans-Appalachian region had coexisted with Europeans and Americans amid tumbling borders and policies. Land sales were largely private, conducted between companies and tribes. The interaction was violent at the edges, but the process had a quality of osmosis, proceeding slowly enough that Indians felt a measure of control. Jefferson changed that. As America's first expansionist or even imperial president, he set drastic precedents for policy on new lands.

Jefferson could have allowed the system of slow encroachment and predominantly private land sales to continue, but he was in a hurry for reasons of defense against the Spanish or French in the West. It was a hurry with which he was comfortable. As in the case of Lewis's expedition—and hundreds of government projects since—the looming threat of war gave the president a free hand in a season of action.

Indian culture wasn't based in land ownership, while Jeffersonian culture wasn't based in anything else. In his own way, though, he was as spiritual as many Indian nations in regard to land, but his closely held feelings were antithetical to theirs. The owner of Monticello had grown up believing that whoever owned the ground created the world upon it. His understanding of land had nothing to do with sharing, but was individualism at its most intensive. The person glorified the earth, not the other way around, and so it was that the little mountain at Monticello wasn't finished until Jefferson had left his mark on the land; exactly the man to do it.

Because individual people in the tribes east of the Mississippi didn't similarly attach themselves to specific holdings, Jefferson assumed that it didn't matter to an Indian where he or she lived. It was a fallacy he repeated often. Jefferson proclaimed it a kindness to support their transformation into farmers rather than hunters. It was callous in concept and set a far-reaching precedent in practice. With a war in the Mississippi Valley growing more probable in the spring of 1803, Jefferson ordered wholesale, widespread, and unequivocal displacement of Indians in the Trans-Appalachian regions, especially Indiana. He wrote to Harrison in late February, explaining the urgency to "bend our whole views to the purchase and settlement of the country on the Mississippi, from its mouth to its northern regions, that we may be able to present as strong a front on our western as on our eastern border, and plant on the Mississippi itself the means of its own defence."

"The crisis is pressing," Jefferson emphasized, after discussing the many ways, aboveboard or below, that Harrison could take Indian lands. One of the chiefs forced to surrender land at a preposterously low price was Buckongahelas, a respected chief of the Lenape nation in Indiana. He was then in his eighties or nineties—he had known Washington in the 1750s and fought against George Rogers Clark in the 1770s. Buckongahelas won fame in the Old Northwest for his gentlemanly bearing, becoming an influential humanitarian in his time. He was pained to see that his way of life would be erased by Jefferson's agenda, but there was no other choice. "Should any tribe be foolhardy enough to take up the hatchet at any time," Jefferson advised Harrison, "the seizing the whole country of that tribe, and driving them across the Mississippi, as the only condition of peace, would be an example to others and a furtherance of our final consolidation."

By 1803, one of Buckongahelas's closest friends was his former adversary in war: George Rogers Clark. They had different problems but were in the same predicament, on the losing end of a legal process. In the aftermath of Harrison's land grab, many of the affected Indian chiefs made detours to the village of Clarksville, near the Ohio River, just to visit Clark. It no longer mattered which army they'd fought for a generation before; they'd ended up on the same losing side.

In 1802 and 1803, when the Indiana town of Vincennes counted less than twenty households, a large number of them were in the business of suing, defending, or judging George Clark. Late in 1802, Clark had been at the end of yet another chapter in his descent, leaving Kentucky and escaping creditors to a small parcel of land he owned close to Clarksville.

Most of the prosperous members of his family lived across the Ohio River in and around Louisville. By 1803, Clark had been a problem to them long enough. Increasingly, he was also forgotten by the general public, even in the Old Northwest and Kentucky territories where he had once been revered. He seemed to take refuge in the very obscurity of Clarksville. His estate there didn't amount to very much beyond a two-room log house and a gristmill. But it was the location on a point looking up and down the Ohio River that gave it meaning for Clark, as it put him between all the places he was from and all the ones he thought awaited him.

Clark couldn't run the mill himself, because he suffered from enfeebling health problems, including rheumatism. He could and did entertain old friends, many of them Indians he'd known or fought in the old days. Buckongahelas was one of the frequent visitors, calling Clark "Long Knife"—his name from the days of war. Many others also visited Clarksville to "drink and boast," in the disparaging words of one of Clark's relatives. Yet Clark and the various chiefs had a kinship, with an understanding of what it was like to be pushed off land that had once been wrapped tightly around their lives.

The responsibility for George Rogers Clark's care still fell to his youngest brother, William. He had left the army in 1796, after four years of service, coming into the largest part of his late father's estate in 1799. With that, he could have finally separated himself from his brother's troubles and become in due course a very rich young planter. Over the next few years, though, William dedicated much of his own inheritance (including the family plantation) to satisfying his brother's creditors. It was a magnificent gesture, but unfortunately, the proceeds were equivalent to a drop in the ocean. William then began again with George in Clarksville: not a dapper member of Louisville society, but an occupant of obscurity.

It was, according to all reports, not easy to be George Rogers Clark's keeper. And yet there was a reason why the people who understood him stayed by. His generosity led him to hand those he loved—whether a brother or a nation—all that he had. The previous December, George Clark had written to President Jefferson, in response to a question about the location of forts in the West. At the end of his letter, he added a personal note:

> I have long since laid aside all Idea of Public affairs, by bad fortune, and ill health. I have become incapable of persuing those enterpriseing & active persuits which I have been fond of from my youth—but I will with the greatest pleasure give my bro. William every information in my power on this, or any other point which may be of Service to your Administration. He is well quallified almost for any business. If it should be in your power to confur on him any post of Honor and profit, in this Counterey in which we live, it will exceedingly gratify me. I seem to [have?] a right to expect such a gratification when asked for—but what will greatly highten it is, that I am sure it gives you pleasure to have it in your power to do me a Service.

The dissipated soldier still held his vanity high, certain that it would give the president pleasure to do him a favor. Indeed, it would, but the letter was more than an example of commonplace nepotism; on the contrary, George had something very real to lose if William were to go. His remarkably capable little brother had turned out to be the best hope he'd had since the war: someone who just might be able to straighten out his life, at long last. Yet George not only gave his blessing on a route out of Clarksville, he gave William what was left of the hero. He told Jefferson that whatever good he remembered in George Rogers Clark, he would find henceforth in William Clark.

Six

"THE OBJECT OF YOUR MISSION IS SINGLE"

The city of Washington celebrated a surprise announcement on April 17: Spain was reinstating full shipping rights in New Orleans to Americans. Those inclined to cheer soon found that it was something of a moot point. In the same communication, Spain's foreign minister stiffly informed Washington that Spain no longer owned Louisiana. While political observers in Washington tried to decipher the reasons for Spain's sudden change, the Mississippi River sprang to life with loaded boats headed for New Orleans. Spain, at long last, accepted the fact that Louisiana belonged to France. But that, too, was soon moot. Less than two weeks later, Jefferson's representatives in Paris signed a treaty buying the whole territory for the United States.

The Louisiana Purchase came about quickly—instigated by France not for diplomatic reasons, but for military ones. The Treaty of Amiens was on the verge of dissolving and war with Great Britain was imminent. Napoleon opted against trying to service a theater of war in North America. It would have involved the defense of more than 820,000 square miles of Louisiana against invasion from the British in Canada; in addition, France's attempt to subdue Saint-Domingue had already cost more than twenty thousand troops, including many of those intended for New Orleans, wearying Napoleon of transatlantic ventures. Another factor may well have been the highly charged movement in Congress for the use of military force to seize New Orleans from France. Against the inevitability of losing the Louisiana Territory, one way or another, Napoleon decided to take American dollars while he could. Possession of the entire scope of Louisiana hadn't even been a topic of discussion within the Jefferson administration. Jefferson's ambassador in France, Robert Livingston, freely admitted that the idea of obtaining it never once occurred to him until the moment it was offered.

On the day the Purchase was signed in Paris, Jefferson was writing to a friend in Massachusetts, boasting of his overall success in foreign relations and outlining his plan for obtaining New Orleans. He presumed that his friend had heard the news about shipping rights in New Orleans and bragged "that, by a reasonable and peaceable process, we have obtained in 4. months what would have cost us 7. years of war, 100,000 human lives, 100 millions of additional debt." Then Jefferson looked at the future, admitting that while he wasn't optimistic about buying New Orleans, he was

> confident in the policy of putting off the day of contention
> for it, till we are stronger in ourselves, & stronger in allies,
> but especially till we shall have planted such a population
> on the Mississippi as will be able to do their own business,
> without the necessity of marching men from the shores of
> the Atlantic.

Six weeks later, in the same vein, Meriwether Lewis wrote to William Clark, whom he'd known when they served in the army together. With Jefferson's permission, Lewis asked Clark to accompany his expedition, offering him an equal share in the leadership. At the end of the letter, dated June 19, he added:

> You must know in the first place that very sanguine expectations are at this time formed by the Government[;] and the whole of that immense country watered by the Mississippi and it's tributary streams, Missourie inclusive, will be the property of the U. States in less than 12 months from this date; but here let me again impress you with the necessity of keeping this matter a perfect secret.

When Lewis confided that secret to Clark, news of the purchase had yet to reach America, at least not publicly. A Boston newspaper was the first to break the story ten days later, on June 28. A private letter sent from Le Havre had delivered the news to Boston just about as quickly as the logistics of the day allowed. Lewis had presumably been repeating what the president had told him, based on the earliest official bulletin from Paris, and Lewis chose to betray the secret to Clark, in order to assure him of the importance of their mission.

On July 3, the president confirmed the preliminary agreement for the Purchase. His first reaction to the newly acquired land was relief and delight that it rendered New Orleans secure for U.S. commerce. On the mere suggestion of trading the Louisiana Territory away for the Floridas, he wrote not long afterward, "I would not give one inch of the waters of the Mississippi to any nation." Remarkably, in the weeks that followed, the number of papers with stories about the Purchase was only about equal to those still printing articles discussing the reinstatement of shipping rights in New Orleans.

The acquisition of Louisiana was a vision of the future, but Spain's affront in New Orleans had yet to stop stinging Americans—including Jefferson.

While Jefferson was making the public announcement, Lewis was focusing on his last preparations before leaving for the West. Jefferson had given him a detailed set of instructions in late June. On July 2, Lewis wrote to his mother in Virginia and told her not to worry. He assured her that he'd be just as safe in the wilderness as he was at home, which in Lewis's case might have been true. He'd grown bored with his lot in Washington and his mind didn't fare well with boredom. Before leaving, Lewis carefully inventoried the items he'd purchased, from medical supplies and dried soup to colorful presents for the Indians and navigational instruments.

Still awaiting word from Clark, Lewis left the White House on July 5, with the president and a few members of the staff assembled outside to see him off. He probably looked like any other nervous American departing for new places, incessantly checking and yet still forgetting to bring the guidebooks or the passport. However, in Lewis's case, it was his wallet—Jefferson had to send it by express after him.

After eight months of talk and preparation, Lewis rode a horse in the general direction of the west in mid-July, enjoying the open road across Pennsylvania. He wasn't even discouraged to hear that the teamster hired to deliver his supplies to Pittsburgh had refused to pick up the second part of the load, which was still waiting in Harpers Ferry. The driver drove on, complaining that his wagon was already groaning under the mountain of items Lewis shipped from Philadelphia. The next teamster Lewis engaged took one look at the load and did the same thing, only without even stopping.

Lewis didn't have many days to spare. On July 20 he was due in Pittsburgh to take delivery of the keelboat he'd commissioned. It was crucial to leave for the West as soon as possible. According to the schedule, he and the rest of the expedition would cross the Mississippi River, make some headway—perhaps two hundred miles—on the Missouri River before winter, and then send back a message to Washington describing what they'd found up to that point. That would answer the political need to feed the public's hunger for news of the expedition.

Even though Lewis had lost a day or two, he pressed hard and, after straightening out his problems with the shippers, arrived at Pittsburgh on July 15. Within an hour, he sent the very first report of the expedition, writing to Jefferson: "I . . . can with pleasure announce, so far and *all is well.*" But that was only the first hour of the expedition.

Lewis had yet to take his first walk around the city. With two thousand people, Pittsburgh was not so much a village as a very tiny metropolis, racing with itself to become the first big American city west of the mountains. Industries were starting, but Pittsburgh's hopes were pinned on the Mississippi Valley. Adventurers who arrived ignorant and empty handed could leave as fully prepared pioneers. They only needed money. So many impatient people left for the West from Pittsburgh that the town offered everything from maps, supplies, and tools to a fully rigged boat, large or small. Potential crew members tended to collect there, too, in the form of single men anxious to trade deck work for a ride downriver.

Pittsburgh had a problem that hobbled its many ambitions, though—liquor there was, in effect, free. "Most of the inhabitants," wrote a visitor in 1802, "distill from rye, or corn, a strong liquor, which they call whisky. It is not uncommon to see men so debilitated, as not to preserve their faculties at an age when they ought to enjoy them in their most perfect vigour." The result made for a unique situation—starting an industrial empire in Pittsburgh was easy. Getting workers to come back the second day was the hard part. Lewis would soon find that out for himself.

The first time that Lewis made his way to the shipyards to see his newly built keelboat, all finished and ready for launch, he would have first passed the biggest ship yet built in the city: a three-hundred-ton schooner under construction at the Tarascon Brothers, James Berthoud shipyard. Amid all of the excitement and headlines of the summer of 1803, the great ship was named the *Louisiana*.

But Lewis's humble keelboat wasn't being built at Tarascon Brothers, James Berthoud. The shipyard that Lewis had hired was far away, at least in spirit. When he arrived and looked for his boat, he didn't spot it at first. Then he looked closer. His keelboat consisted of a keel. And nothing else: in the discussions that followed, the builder promised that the boat would *without fail* be finished on August 5. Lewis believed him.

In Washington, Jefferson was awaiting the political response to the news of the Louisiana Purchase. Although he did worry about the constitutionality of the expenditure, he was braced for trouble of the more usual kind, as he saw it, felt it, and even smelled it in his mind:

> [with] what bloody teeth & fangs the federalists will attack any sentiment or principle known to come from me & what blackguardisms & personalities they make it the occasion of vomiting forth.

The *Washington Federalist*, an untiring source of anti-Jefferson slander, was among the first to print an editorial about the Purchase, on July 8. Jefferson must have been shocked anew as he read:

> It appears by the latest intelligence that Louisiana is ceded to the United States. Americans of all political parties cannot be otherwise than highly gratified with a cession, so important to the present, so immensely important to the future prosperity of the United States.

Jefferson's opponents apparently needed extra time to think of what it was they hated about his Louisiana Purchase.

AMBASSADOR YRUJO, SPAIN'S representative in the United
States, was also pleasantly disposed. He carefully considered the
Purchase and wrote to his superior, the Spanish minister of state,
Pedro Cevallos y Guerra, on August 3. "I do not look upon the
alienation of Louisiana as a loss to Spain," he started. "That colony
cost us heavily and produced little for us." Yrujo continued on that
theme and then went on to argue that there wasn't anything good
about Louisiana, anyway. Its most attractive characteristic, Yrujo
believed, was that it would inevitably ignite into a civil war that
would tear apart the United States. The message stretched so long
that Yrujo proudly gave it a title: "Important Reflections on the Cession of Louisiana."

It was a letter he later wished he hadn't mailed.

Even though Yrujo, the socialite ambassador, was a full-blooded
Spaniard, he was described by one historian as "half-American."
The attitude of his "Important Reflections" was an American one
where Spain was concerned, saying tacitly: just let Louisiana go.
Writing simultaneously to Yrujo, Minister Cevallos had a rather different opinion. The court at Madrid was then solidifying plans to
get Louisiana back or to get something for it, something more valuable than cheerful dreams of an American civil war.

Somewhere in the middle of the Atlantic, Cevallos's letter crossed
paths with Yrujo's, eventually landing on the diplomat's desk. With
that, the lights must have stayed lit long into the night in Germantown. Yrujo had misread the situation in Spain and he was stuck
with that sickly sense of regret, but once he reversed his opinion he
was more staunch than anyone in leading the defense of Louisiana.
To prove it, he immediately fired off an indignant letter to Madison,
informing him that "the sale of Louisiana which was lately made by
France is a manifest violation. . . . France has no authority to alien-
ate said province without the approval of Spain." Of course, he sent

a copy of his dramatic letter to Madrid, so that Minister Cevallos could see the new Yrujo for himself.

At Monticello, Jefferson perused a sheaf of papers related to the Spanish reaction and read into their rising strategy. "I think it possible," he told Madison, "that Spain, recollecting our former eagerness for the island of N. Orleans, may imagine she can, by a free delivery of that, redeem the residue of Louisiana: and that she may withhold the peaceable cession if it."

"In that case," Jefferson added, "no doubt force must be used." Yrujo was thinking the exact same thing. Ownership of Louisiana would be settled by war. His superior, Minister Cevallos, was an experienced lawyer and wouldn't stir trouble without basis. Cevallos's position was diplomatically sound, or might have been, had his country sported a bigger army and more money. With that in mind, Cevallos took his case to the French, who could be counted on for both.

But Jefferson was a lawyer, too. He delved into his own research on Louisiana. In fact, Jefferson's domestic enemies had found something to complain about in how little was actually known about Louisiana—only that it was big. And that was not necessarily an attribute. A nonpartisan newspaper in New York explained in September that:

> Mr. Livingston . . . describes it to be an *insalubrious marshy*
> *country, in a burning climate.* This description is supposed,
> however, to have a particular reference to the *Southern* parts . . .

The same paper concluded that the new territory was likely to be

> worse than useless to the United States, . . . *Louisiana* is a
> foreign country: it lies beyond the vast body of water [the
> Mississippi River] which till very recently has been consid-
> ered as the ultimate limit of the United States.
>
> Why overlap this boundary? Why transgress the or-

dination of nature, which has seemingly said, "Hitherto shall ye come, and no further?"

Americans in the East couldn't answer that question. They didn't have any connection with the land beyond the banks of the Mississippi. Jefferson needed to change that for his plans to work. The people in France or in Spain had thought Louisiana just as obscure when their countries owned it. In fact, in histories of France written for French readers, Louisiana is barely mentioned, if at all. Jefferson had to make it mean more than that to Americans, especially to those along the seaboard.

New Englanders were smitten with the Purchase for only one reason: the agreement also called for France to repay debts to American merchants, many of whom were based in the northeast. It was up to Jefferson to provide a broader basis for excitement. He began delving into the books he had or could acquire, in order to learn something about Louisiana.

Overall, the president needed to convince Congress and the nation at large that he knew what he'd purchased. Just as pressing, he needed to show Spain that he had proof of the rightful boundaries of the Louisiana Purchase. For the moment, he didn't have any idea where they should be and neither did anyone else. It hadn't mattered during the years when Spain owned all of the West south of Canada. Geography books commonly listed the borders of Louisiana as "indeterminate." Livingston and Monroe did, of course, ask about boundaries during the negotiations for the Purchase, suggesting that they wanted to know more precisely what the United States was buying. That was one quagmire Napoleon was smart enough to sidestep. With penetrating intelligence and a reluctance to give Spain and the United States anything tangible to fight about, he declared that "if an obscurity did not already exist, it would perhaps be good policy to put one there."

Jefferson feared that the Spanish would establish the Louisiana-

Texas border as far east as possible (and likewise, the West Florida–Louisiana border as far west as possible). Within ten days of hearing about the Purchase, he appointed two "Special Commissioners on the Spanish Border," residents of the region with an understanding of law. He also sent a list of seventeen questions about the Mississippi Valley to several people, including Daniel Clark—who could hardly wait to cooperate. Clark, like many others at the time, made no secret of his personal ambitions for public office in American Louisiana. In late July, Jefferson sent the same questions to Dunbar. In fact, one of the things that Jefferson undoubtedly found refreshing about Dunbar was that there could actually be a person in the region who didn't want to be governor.

During the first days of August, Captain Lewis was still in Pittsburgh, awaiting the new delivery date for the keelboat, which had been firmly set for August 5. Even though the delay had been a catastrophe in terms of the schedule for the year's travel, it was still the best thing that could have happened to Meriwether Lewis.

Lewis's June 19 letter of invitation to William Clark took longer than expected to reach Clarksville. One day after it was received, Clark wrote an enthusiastic acceptance. He was so excited at the prospect of going west that he had to start over a few times, before the letter was just right. He still managed to mail it within one day of receipt, on July 18. By then, though, his response was sorely late. Lewis already had someone else in mind, a soldier at Fort Fayette.

Had the keelboat been ready, as ordered, and had Lewis left on July 20, as planned, he wouldn't have received Clark's response and would have engaged the replacement. With Lewis's indomitability, a switch to someone else from Clark wouldn't have distressed him as much as any further delay. A little later, William Ewing Patterson— the son of his kindly mathematics teacher in Philadelphia— expressed a fervent interest in joining the crew of the expedition, but when he missed an appointment in Pittsburgh, he was dropped by Lewis forthwith. Until the expedition came to an end, Lewis's idea of leeway was that there was none.

Not in the nick of time, but actually two weeks beyond it, Clark's reply finally arrived in Pittsburgh. It was probably August 2. On reading the first lines, Lewis's thoughts about a replacement vanished, of course.

Clark was effusive and almost flowery; Lewis, writing back, was mostly officious, but as they made plans to meet in Clarksville along the Ohio River, they slipped into the style that suited both as a partnership. Friendly in a plain way, they handled the business at hand as efficiently as words would permit.

Lewis remained in his own kind of agony in Pittsburgh through the whole month of August, the promise of the boat on the fifth having dissolved. He described his life there, writing to Jefferson in frustration that he had yet again placed his faith in the boat builder, but

> according to his usual custom he got drunk, quarreled with his workmen, and several of them left him, nor could they be prevailed on to return: I threatened him with the penalty of his contract, and exacted a promise of greater sobriety in future which, he took care to perform with as little good faith as he had his previous promises with regard to the boat, continuing to be constantly either drunk or sick. I spent most of my time with the workmen, alternately presuading and threatening, but neither threats, presuasion or any other means which I could devise were sufficient to procure the completion of the work sooner than the 31st of August; by which time the water was so low that those who pretended to be acquainted with the navigation of the river declared it impracticable to descend it [the river]; however in conformity to my previous determination I set out.

Lewis took care not to send word of the delay to Jefferson until he could report that he had left Pittsburgh, lest anyone in Washington suggest that with the late start of the trip, it should be postponed for a year. That was unthinkable, as was anything else that threatened success, in which cause Lewis threw his efforts to the point that they themselves threatened success.

In the great Jeffersonian tradition, Captain Lewis had left almost nothing unpurchased in the Commonwealth of Pennsylvania. Before leaving, he had to divide his supplies between his overloaded keelboat and an extra boat called a pirogue—also packed beyond its capacity.

In the frontier's inexact nomenclature, further broadened by Lewis's expediency, a pirogue could be almost any small craft, built for sturdiness and payload rather than speed, elegance, or maneuverability. The mule of western rivers, a pirogue was sometimes a log dugout (or a series of them lashed together); sometimes, it was constructed of planks. Pirogues carried one to six people, typically confined to seats and exposed to the weather. In Pittsburgh, Lewis paid extra on his pirogue for a sail and oarlocks used with oars, as opposed to the paddles seen more commonly on such craft.

Bystanders warned Lewis to lighten the boats, in view of late summer's shallow water levels, but he found it impossible. With that, he pressed on with a temporary crew of about a dozen and all of the speed that two heavy boats could manage in a river that was at least as low as the most pessimistic authority had predicted. Sometimes, when the water was only ankle deep, the keelboat had to be unloaded, while horses or oxen dragged it. "I find them the best sailors in the present state of the navigation of this river," Lewis wrote wryly to Jefferson.

In early October, as Lewis was making slow progress out of Pittsburgh, Jefferson was at last prepared to make a public statement on Spain's effort to block the Louisiana Purchase. Jefferson was never known as an orator, and the mere fact that he delivered a speech when it wasn't required drew attention to his message. Appearing before a joint session of Congress, he explained his determination to prevail in the latest confrontation with Spain. The speech was satisfactory—but not nearly as effective as a single paragraph that ran soon afterward in the papers. It was immediately the most talked-about story in the nation, an excerpted letter sent from New Orleans, which read:

> A schooner is just arrived here from Havana with orders to the Governor not to give up the possession of Louisiana to either France or the United States.

If Jefferson didn't write it, he should have. The outcry among Americans soon whipped itself into outrage. People who barely knew or cared where Louisiana was vowed that Spain wasn't going to keep the United States from buying it, or anything else. Congress immediately voted to extend powers to the president for military action in anticipation of war. Jefferson called a cabinet meeting that amounted to a war council.

Jefferson's plan, discussed at the special cabinet meeting on October 29, called for the march of five hundred soldiers from Fort Adams, near Natchez, on New Orleans; the muster of seven thousand militiamen would augment them and assist in surprise attacks on Spanish-held towns, including St. Louis. The government was in agreement, and details of the military plan were leaked with impressive efficiency the next day. Secretary of State Madison's specified position was that if Spain continued to stand in the way, the United States would move, and "if things came to this extreme they [the Americans] would also attack the Floridas."

Amid the tension with Spain over the Purchase, Jefferson thought it imperative to effect a new phase, in the form of an old idea that had never really left him. He wanted to send more expeditions to explore the Louisiana Territory, timing them as a means to assert America's possession "by a reasonable and peaceable process." The idea of the Lewis and Clark expedition had been well received, in a related vein, but it wasn't necessarily the only mission accorded funding by Congress in February. The president wanted to use that expenditure to send at least three others, mostly to the south where the new friction lay.

Lewis was thinking along the same lines. Jefferson received a letter from him dated October 3 from Cincinnati. Knowing that the original schedule had been laid waste due to the boatbuilding delays, Lewis felt "in the most anxious manner a wish to keep [Congress] in a good humour on the subject of the expedicion." Still eleven days from his rendezvous with William Clark at Clarksville, Lewis more or less informed Jefferson that he planned to use the upcoming winter—when travel up the Missouri River would be impossible—to ride a horse by himself from St. Louis to the Southwest in the vicinity of Santa Fe.

During the first part of November, when Jefferson opened Lewis's letter, he had every reason to believe that the Spanish would welcome a stray officer from the U.S. Army with a firing squad, especially an officer who was alone, ill prepared, and patently not collecting specimens in a scientific pursuit. The president's reply was unambiguous: he told Lewis to concentrate only on the trip to the Pacific, via the Missouri. "The object of your mission is single," he admonished. Jefferson then added that it would be the job of other expeditions to explore the Lower Louisiana region: "It seems generally to be assented to, that Congress shall appropriate 10 or 20,000 D. for exploring the principal waters [tributaries] of the Missisipi & Missouri."

The new expeditions would be shorter than the Lewis and Clark journey and were expected to be completed long before it was. The result, in Jefferson's strategy, was that citizens in the East, no less than diplomats in Europe, would receive a steady stream of reports on Louisiana in the eyes of Americans.

Seven

CAPTAIN MERRY

As the probability of military action rose in November of 1803, the mail brought yet another stroke of bad news for Spanish ambassador Yrujo. At his most dramatic, he had chartered a special boat to Spain to carry crucial information regarding the situation in Washington. War was coming and every day counted. But then Yrujo opened another envelope from Madrid. A ship going in the other direction had brought a proclamation announcing that King Carlos IV was ready to formally surrender Louisiana to France. The rest of the purchase could go through. The threat of war receded.

It didn't matter that Yrujo had chartered the boat unnecessarily and wasted some of the court's money—a lot of it, actually. But it did matter very much that the Spanish position changed so often that Yrujo, an able ambassador, could have predicted it just as effectively by flipping a coin. For Jefferson the situation was more disturbing. He didn't have the luxury of falling out of step with the darting inclinations of Spain or other European powers. Jefferson was closely engaged with absorbing Louisiana and averting war using every means at his disposal, mainly by showing Spain the shadow of an army at the ready. Expeditions were another facet, smaller than an army, but with an even longer shadow.

On November 30, France formally assumed control of Louisiana as Spain made the cessation. "It is painful to acknowledge it and to experience it," wrote Casa Calvo from New Orleans, "but it will be much more painful not to use all our forces, while there is still time to remedy it." From the vantage of Casa Calvo and other Spanish officials in North America, the coin was still up in the air—they were not yet ready to forfeit such a large part of the continent they still championed.

While Spain's intentions were inconsistent, largely to be cunning, Jefferson made America's policy regarding Louisiana crystal clear. His compilation for Congress about the territory had not only grown longer over the summer, it had risen from a mere report into a full book, prominently featuring the president's opinion on the extent of the Louisiana Territory. If Napoleon was a man to put "obscurities" into a border, Jefferson was a man to take them out. His interpretation of the facts might have been questionable and biased in favor of American expansion, but he certainly succeeded in laying out an argument for all to see. Arranging to have his book published in Philadelphia, he gave it the title *An Account of Louisiana, being an abstract of documents, in the offices of the Departments of State, and of the Treasury.*

An Account of Louisiana, compiled specifically for members of Congress, began with Jefferson's certainty that however murky the rest of the territory, Louisiana included West Florida. That information was on page one. In later pages, he elaborated on the boundaries, grandly enveloping Texas and Oregon Territory, as well as East Florida, into Louisiana. At about the same time in Madrid, a special committee under the aegis of Cevallos likewise did research in old papers, on the topic of Louisiana's borders.

Only two men were doing more than talking about the ragged border. Captains Lewis and Clark had arrived on the eastern banks of the Mississippi on November 14. The date was an awkward one, being early enough to tempt them to start west, yet late enough to preclude truly worthwhile progress before winter. Neither Lewis nor Clark had left a record of their reunion at Clarksville exactly one month before, but on that day, the renewal of their friendship would have received its very first test, a severe one. Clark, who had been promised a commission as captain to match Lewis's, was only accorded the rank of second lieutenant by the army. It was a slight with its origins in Jefferson's original emphasis on a smaller, less top-heavy military; the openings for officers were limited, and they were filled by that very class of senior officers who resented the president, if they didn't despise him outright. Lewis assured Clark that he would do everything in his power to raise his rank, as soon as possible, but that didn't change the serious disadvantage in pay, in the meantime.

For William Clark, the sting must have been especially painful, since he'd dwelled so long amid the unfair treatment of his older brother by the government. At some point, the Clark family had every right to give up forever on government service, but Lewis's arrival in Clarksville was not that moment. Boarding the keelboat, Clark somehow adjusted to his status as a second lieutenant. Lewis never did, insisting on sharing an equal rank for the duration of the expedition, long after hope was lost for Clark's official captaincy.

Having welcomed the expedition's coleader, Lewis was concerned with signing dependable crewmen along the Ohio River. The Ohio was a boulevard of all kinds of people in a rush to the West, but, as others had learned before Lewis, not many could be described as dependable. The expedition did benefit from another addition at Clarksville: York, the enslaved servant who had grown up with Clark and attended him through most of his life. The two were companions and in some ways friends, but Clark didn't think of York as free, in any sense. An impressively strong man, York was expected to share the burdens of the corps, but he would be answerable only to Clark.

Starting from the confluence of the Ohio River with the Mississippi, the expedition made an objective of the town of Kaskaskia, ninety-three miles up the Mississippi. Kaskaskia was located on a curve in the Mississippi River so sharp it was almost like a peninsula jutting into the water. While the ultimate mission was the unexplored headwaters of the Missouri River, the northern reaches of the Mississippi were just as obscure at the time that the expedition was rowing northward on it. Heading to Kaskaskia, the men were forced to pull against the current for the first time, rowing hard just to average a mile an hour; as a result, it took almost a week for the party to arrive at the town, despite the crew rowing twelve hours every day.

A hard week on the water had inspired Lewis's resolve to double the size of the expedition roster in Kaskaskia, where the army manned a fort of the same name. Rather than balance the crew in advance, Lewis had set out from the East alone and filled in his roster along the way. That didn't prove easy to do in parts of the country where daily life was enough of an adventure—and where energetic men counted on making large amounts of money for two years' worth of trouble. Some of those who were then serving under Lewis and Clark were from the army; others were qualified civilians inducted into the army solely for the purpose of the expedition. The new recruits sometimes had training useful for the expedition, such as hunting or carpentry. None had an expertise in science, and the captains weren't even looking for help in that regard. They wouldn't have found it at Fort Kaskaskia.

Located on a bluff, the sturdy wooden fort offered extra scope down each arm of water from four parapets. Secretary of War Dear-

born gave Lewis permission to recruit anyone he needed at Kaskaskia, America's farthest outpost west and northwest. For Lewis,
it was the last wholesale opportunity to add to the "Corps of Discovery," as he slickly named his company. He scoured the fort for
soldier volunteers, conferring all the while with the commanders
of the infantry and artillery regiments there. His last-ditch efforts
were a far cry from the meticulous recruitment process employed
on Carlos III's expeditions, yet they resulted in a dozen additional
crewmen.

At the fort, Lewis met often with a twenty-four-year-old officer
who exhibited the requisite hunger for adventure—a refined and
deceptively delicate lieutenant, Zebulon Pike. Lewis couldn't hope
to add an officer to his roster, but Pike would no doubt have wanted
to go. At the time, he specialized in logistics and record keeping.

Born in New Jersey, the son of an army officer, Pike had joined
his father's regiment at the age of fifteen. As a young man, he was
described as "a boy of slender form, very fair in complexion, gentle
and retiring spirit, but of resolute spirit." Pike's gentle and retiring
side was seen less as he chiseled himself into a leader of men. He
remained slim, but a fellow officer emphasized that he was sturdier
than he looked, noting Pike's height at about five foot eight. Joining the army in 1794, Pike was moved around among postings in
Pennsylvania and Ohio. Through no fault of his own, the most conspicuous opportunity that he had for displaying bravery during the
early part of his career was in his choice of a wife. On his way west,
he infuriated the elder members of two families, one being his own,
by eloping with a young woman named Clarissa Brown. She was the
daughter of a ranking army officer as well. While all four parents
predicted the doom of Pike's military career, Pike found a home for
Clarissa in St. Louis and then reported for duty at a fort across the
river. He admitted to his father afterward that he might "possibly be
a little too independent," but then, it was hard to fully apologize for
his strongest attribute.

Coming of age before the establishment of West Point, Pike was a self-taught student in the art of war, collecting French books on the subject—and then learning the language, just so he could read them. He took the peacetime army seriously as a career, an attitude rare enough to draw notice from the territorial commander, General Wilkinson, who became his mentor. While Lewis and Clark were camped near Kaskaskia, Pike probably handled the payroll for the corps.

Naturally restless, Lewis was impatient to know where his boats would be headed when they left Kaskaskia—up the Missouri River or to winter quarters along the American side of the Mississippi. The decision didn't belong to him, though. It was to come from the Spanish lieutenant governor of Upper Louisiana, Charles de Lassus, who was still in control of the territory from his capital in St. Louis. No one there had yet learned that Spain had ceded Louisiana to France in late November. With most of December left, Lewis decided to meet personally with de Lassus and request permission to enter Louisiana with the expedition. "I determined to loose no time in making this application," he wrote.

Lewis took advantage of the fact that the expedition was, as Jefferson put it, "double-manned." While Clark continued north by water toward Cahokia, an American town across the river from St. Louis, Lewis took the quicker route by land on December 5. He had another reason for hurrying. In early November, Lewis and Clark had heard something about the availability of a Missouri River map, said to be in the possession of a "Mr. Hay of Cahokia," who apparently coveted it for himself. Lewis, fixated on finding something as valuable as a map of the unknown, rushed ahead to Cahokia, where he first paid a visit to the postmaster. He was met with a surprise after introducing himself there, though. The postmaster was John Hay.

Hay was also a merchant and a fur trader, in addition to being the nation's first Lewis and Clark fanatic. He had indeed been prickly to others about the map, but only so that he could give it to Lewis or Clark on their way west. His map, itself a copy, was based on the explorations of the late John Evans, as drawn under the auspices of his commander, John MacKay.

Hay enthusiastically accompanied Lewis across the Mississippi River to St. Louis. He even brought along another local man to provide translations from either Spanish or French, as needed. The trio arrived in St. Louis, probably on December 7, and made their way to Government House.

Lieutenant Governor de Lassus, the Spanish commandant, was a bright man with a certain busy charm, and he was glad to greet the American explorer about whom he had heard so much. De Lassus described the meeting to his superiors in New Orleans, writing that Lewis brought papers showing that

> his intention was to continue his trip penetrating the Missouri in order to fulfill his mission of discoveries and observations. . . . [I] observed to him that he surprised me for not having provided himself with a passport from our Spanish Minister in Philadelphia [Yrujo]; that if he had had a passport in the name of the King my master, he could have removed all difficulty. He answered me that when he left Philadelphia that it was already at the beginning of July, that he thought he would find here [in St. Louis] the French, that for that reason, he had not believed it necessary to carry a passport from *Señor* Marqués de Yrujo; that he thought that then it would be useless.

Lewis may have neglected to mention that Yrujo had indeed been asked—and had almost spit on the White House floor at the mention of a passport for an American explorer. However, while Yrujo had been frank, trying to disabuse Jefferson of the idea of an expedition, de Lassus took a different position with Lewis. When the moment came for him to rule on the application, he gave Lewis advice, good wishes for success, the kindness of concern regarding the dangers of the trip—and dinner. He pointedly did not give Lewis and Clark permission to enter Louisiana.

De Lassus's underlying orders were to stall Americans at every turn, and he did so. Lewis's underlying orders were to avoid confrontations and he did so too. "Thus defeated in my application," as Lewis wrote, he returned to the eastern side of the Mississippi River, his new home for the winter. With Clark, Lewis set up a comfortable camp along the river Dubois about twenty-two miles to the north. Translating that name from French into English, they called their encampment "Fort Wood."

The bad break dealt by de Lassus was actually a boon for the expedition, giving the captains, especially Clark, time to train and temper the corps. It also gave them a chance to reconsider the personnel selections and improve the permanent roster as it expanded over the winter to the final number of twenty-nine, in addition to the two leaders.

Lewis spent long spans of time in St. Louis, promoting the expedition, looking for information about the West, and socializing. Amid the cold-war conditions that existed between the United States and Spain, he had strong reason to suspect that de Lassus, who had offered him free access to the city, was in fact spying on him and threatening those who lent material assistance. Even in the face of the veiled danger, Lewis and Clark remained desperate for clues about the journey ahead of them. If de Lassus was playing a spy's game, they proved themselves willing to join in, whatever the stakes.

James MacKay, the person that the captains most wanted to meet and a man who might shed some more light on the map in Hay's possession, lived near the village of Femme Osage in Upper Louisiana, about thirty miles away from Camp Wood via the Missouri River. Still traveling the frontier occasionally, ten years after his attempt to trace the Missouri with Evans, MacKay earned a living as a civic official and businessman. The captains felt that he'd be a source of advice on the Evans map and might even have an original copy of it. Unfortunately, de Lassus had made clear that entering any part of Spanish territory except St. Louis was specifically forbidden for a member of the expedition—or for any American military man.

As the new year of 1804 began, Clark was feeling sick, having let his feet get so wet in the cold that his shoes and socks had frozen to his skin. With a break in the weather, though, he sent a private in the corps, Joseph Field, across the river to find MacKay. The orders were to ask the veteran explorer to pay a visit to Camp Wood. By any description, that was espionage. If Private Field was caught, the Spanish would very probably end his life. If that specter didn't give the captains pause by itself, the history of their expedition would surely have been changed—or ended on the spot—by the capture of a corpsman under orders on enemy territory. Moreover, the history of two nations might have been changed, the capture or death of an American private being just the spark to ignite two powder kegs leaning across a band of water against each other.

Field succeeded without complications, arriving at Camp Wood by canoe with MacKay. The details of the meeting are lacking, but he apparently helped with geography and may even have left an updated map. Perhaps it was worth the gamble, but the risk itself measures the anxiety that Clark and Lewis felt to know as much as possible in advance.

The Louisiana Territory was formally transferred to the United States on December 20, 1803, in a ceremony in New Orleans that included all of the usual baubles: flags, bands, cannon, General Wilkinson. The moment was dramatic, the spectacle memorable, but the Americans were no more ready to fully assume control of the complicated city, that "shapeless composition of all countries," than the Spanish were ready to fully vacate it. Afterward, Casa Calvo wrote to Minister Cevallos, arguing that Spain must keep control of Louisiana. His wording was significant; Spain no longer had control of Louisiana—at least, not legally.

Back east, Yrujo went a little further in his own agitation over the transfer of Louisiana. As the year ended, he was steering the preparations for a war that would be waged from the Spanish strongholds of Cuba and Mexico in order to seize the Louisiana Territory back from the United States. Then in January, an envelope from Madrid arrived and, as ever for Yrujo, that was a bad omen. The court had written its usual letter, telling him to stop what he was doing—the policy had changed. He was ordered to drop his plans for all-out war and to concentrate on the border debate.

Jefferson was privately calling Spain "ridiculous," while Minister Cevallos was describing the United States as "a nation of calculators." Neither was entirely wrong. Two very different nations were on the brink of war—or taking advantage of the chance to bluff on that point while inching toward better ground. Casa Calvo, on hearing the new Spanish policy, interpreted it in his unique way: he used his influence to launch military expeditions with orders to stop Lewis and Clark.

Jefferson's friends in Congress were just as stealthy, but they had their own methods, choosing late February to bring to a vote a very specifically designed revenue bill. It was dullish legislation, except for one component, a hidden salvo buried in section 11 that asserted America's possession of West Florida by virtue of connected tributaries. The bill passed on February 28. Two days later, Yrujo stormed into Madison's office, "with the gazette [containing the act] in his hand and entered upon a very angry comment on the eleventh section." Madison gave the usual explanations, and Yrujo responded with "a rudeness which no government can tolerate," as Madison described it. Madison refused to ever again see Yrujo or communicate with him; the French ambassador would thereafter serve as intermediary.

But the common hatred of Spain was no longer enough to unite public opinion in the States. Opposition to Jefferson rose up as people quietly sided with Yrujo in exasperation at what they saw as an uncoupled, unconstitutional land grab in West Florida. After the signing of the bill, the *Washington Federalist* threw away its truce and labeled Jefferson the "Emperor of Louisiana." Jefferson's doctrine stated that if any portion of a river was in U.S. territory, then America owned the whole of that river, including the surrounding territory—which gave the United States at least one of the Floridas, as well as Texas. The logic of a waterway offering contiguous land rights smacked of the Spanish assertion that if they claimed Panama's ocean coast, then they owned all of the land in Alaska, too. And Tierra del Fuego.

EVEN AS JEFFERSON'S doctrine expanded on the Louisiana Purchase, he was aware that maintaining those territories depended on demarcation of the rivers. To that end, he put his allies in the government to work. While Congress was passing the Revenue Act, it was discussing a recommendation from Representative Samuel Latham Mitchell of New York City on the exploration of Louisiana. Mitchell was one of the most erudite members of Congress, a lawyer, a doctor, and a pioneering magazine publisher in addition to his political activities. Mitchell edited the *Medical Repository*, described as America's first medical journal, though it was in truth a reflection of Mitchell's boundless interests, one of which was exploration and another of which was Thomas Jefferson. (Hence it was the *Medical Repository* that printed the only known review of Jefferson's *Account of Louisiana*.)

Mitchell's congressional report, ostensibly from the Committee on Commerce and Manufactures, was a marriage of Jefferson's predilections and Mitchell's grasp of facts. "By a series of memorable events," it started, "the United States have lately acquired a large addition of soil and jurisdiction." No one could deny that, but the report described those lands as including everything from the Mississippi River to the Rocky Mountains and beyond, including the Northwest above California. It was an expansive view, especially when adjoined to the explicit claim already made for West Florida and the implicit one for Texas. Jefferson was pushing the borders to the stretching point in every direction. If he kept working at it, the Louisiana Purchase would have included Japan.

Mitchell's report made specific recommendations on expeditions, including two tracing the Red and the Arkansas Rivers. Expanding on the purpose, it argued:

> An expedition of discovery up those prodigious streams and their branches might redound as much to the honor, and more to the interest of our government, than the voyages by sea round the terraqueous globe have done for the polished nations of Europe, who authorized them. Such liberal enterprises will befit the present season of prosperity, and may be expected to succeed best during the reign of peace.

With that, the report pinpointed Jefferson's concept of the geopolitical use of exploration. Other nations of his era used war for conquest; America would use exploration instead, just as European sea powers had done three hundred years before. In spring of 1804, even as Congress considered the Mitchell report, Jefferson was already initiating his program of expeditions—changing the way that the United States defined itself. He wrote a long letter to Dunbar describing his plans and inviting—or conscripting—the brilliant Dunbar to be one of his key leaders.

Dunbar's grasp of scientific method was beyond reproach. Moreover, he was celebrated as a colleague by the local Spanish officials, who could never paint him as an enemy interloper. Dunbar was as safe a representative as Jefferson was to find, and as respected a scientist. After reminding him of the details of the Lewis and Clark expedition, the president wrote to Dunbar:

> Congress will probably authorise me to explore the greater waters on the Western side of the Missisipi & Missouri, to their sources. In this case I should propose to send one party up the Panis river[*] to it's source, thence along the highlands to the source of the Padoucas river,[†] and down it to it's mouth. Another party up the Arcansa to it's source, thence along the highlands to the source of the Red river, & down that to it's mouth, giving the whole course of both parties corrected by astronomical observations. These several surveys will enable us to prepare a map of Louisiana, which in it's contour and main waters will be perfectly correct, & will give us a skeleton to be filled up with details hereafter. For what lies North of the Missouri we suppose British industry will furnish that. As you live so near to the point of departure of the lowest expedition, and possess and can acquire so much better the information which may direct that to the best advantage, I have thought if congress should authorise the enterprise to propose to you the unprofitable trouble of directing it. . . . Still this is a matter of speculation only, as Congress are hurrying over their business for adjournment, and may leave this article of it unfinished. In that case what I have said will be as if I had not said it.

At the time, Dunbar didn't respond to the invitation. Living at the edge of disputed territory, he was acutely aware that the Spanish

---

* This is now known as Ponca Creek in northern Nebraska.
† He was referring to the Kansas River and/or the confluent Smoky Hill River in southern Nebraska.

were prepared to turn back interlopers—or shoot them and bring back their ears. Since Jefferson had mentioned that Congress first needed to fund the trips, Dunbar delayed his decision about directing the program of expeditions in the Southwest. Not long after his note from Jefferson, though, Dunbar started to receive rather strange letters from Secretary of War Henry Dearborn, the second of which began, "Sir: Directions have been given Doctr. Huntur to procure about six hundred dollars worth of trinkets and other light articles proper for presents to the Indians." It closed: "I presume you will not think it improper to advance the gentlemen you shall employ, more than four months pay."

Dunbar had no idea why he should be concerned with trinkets and doctors named Hunter; and he wasn't about to employ anybody for four months or five minutes. Dearborn had been given the impression that Dunbar was definitely managing Jefferson's second western expedition. That didn't put Dunbar in a good mood.

Even as Jefferson tried to enlist Dunbar in the Southwest expeditions, the president devoted time in late March to the recruitment of other potential leaders. George Hunter of Philadelphia had been one of the first to consent. He'd probably been suggested to Jefferson by a mutual friend, Dr. Samuel Brown, in Louisville. Hunter had taken a second journey to the West only two years before, and Dr. Brown had seen him pushing through backwoods, oblivious to obstacles, but never for a moment forgetting his goal. On the second trip, Hunter was no longer dreaming about land, though; he was looking for any substance that could be mined for a profit. That was fitting; he earned his living as a chemical wholesaler in Philadelphia—thanks to his occupation, Hunter looked at a mountain and knew the value of every dram within it. Since Dr. Brown was similarly interested in finding something worth mining, their conversations were narrowly focused on getting rich, a characteristic that Jefferson would forever attach to Hunter.

On March 9, 1804, three weeks after Mitchell's report was read in Congress, both Lewis and Clark were in St. Louis to witness a pair of rituals in the plaza of the small city. In the first, the Spanish yellow-and-gold flag was lowered, folded and taken away. The French tricolor was then raised. In the next day's ceremony, the tricolor was duly lowered to make way for the American Stars and Stripes. As an exercise, it was of interest to no one more than Meriwether Lewis and William Clark. At the moment that the American flag touched the top of the staff, the captains knew that they finally had legal access to Louisiana.

Casa Calvo, thinking the expedition had already started and was on its way to the Pacific, wrote from New Orleans to Minister Cevallos in Madrid, asking "that the most efficacious steps be taken to arrest" Lewis, whom he called by the much more memorable name "Captain Merry." Casa Calvo argued that until the borders were set, the explorers were bound to trespass on Spanish property at Louisiana's western edge—wherever it was. Jefferson would have responded that borders could not be set until the raw territory was explored. With a measure of logic on both sides, all that was left was the contest. Governors in Spain's western provinces, notably California and New Mexico (neither of which had a defined northern border), were given strict orders in the aftermath of the Louisiana transfer against "the introduction of foreigners." The Spanish governors didn't yet know that Lewis and Clark were only the first of the American explorers heading into the blurred borders. In the last days of March, Congress acted on Mitchell's recommendation, voting an appropriation for the new expeditions, as Jefferson hoped, although the amount was only one-fifth of the ten thousand dollars he had anticipated.

On April 15, 1804, Jefferson wrote a long letter to Dunbar, although he hadn't yet received a reply to his March 13 invitation to direct at least one of the expeditions. Sitting at his desk at Monticello, Jefferson decided that "presuming" Dunbar's consent would suffice. In fact, Jefferson was uncharacteristically anxious about the expeditions, and his short letter to Dunbar was paced by phrases of impatience. Dunbar couldn't have missed the point.

In his letter, Jefferson related his decision that the second expedition, after Lewis and Clark, would trace the Red and Arkansas Rivers, which run in roughly the same southeasterly direction in the region north of Texas. It was his area of first concern in the "obscurity" of the Louisiana border. Having already chosen Hunter as the chief scientist on the trip, Jefferson entrusted Dunbar with the selection of "the person who is to direct the mission."

While Jefferson was writing to Dunbar, the Mississippian was responding to Secretary of War Dearborn in an unusually blunt manner to complain that not only wasn't he qualified to choose the leader of an expedition, but that the government should have selected "characters properly qualified from the Seats of Science or under their own Eye." He was right about that. In fact, Dunbar laughed at the idea of finding anyone well qualified in his region, since the few scientists who lived there rendered serious study "subservient to this all devouring passion of gain." Dunbar, of course, knew something about that. Long before, he'd dedicated himself to wealth above science, but he'd since reverted to his first passion. His letter brusquely advised Dearborn to find an army officer to lead the expedition, along with soldiers to staff it. He thought men of science had no place amid the dangers of the West.

A day after Dunbar did his best to sidestep the role of director for the second Jeffersonian expedition, the first one was at last departing from Fort Wood, pushing into territory new to Americans. It departed at four p.m. on May 14. Clark was in charge of the expedition fleet: the keelboat and two pirogues. As he noted in his journal, the big boat had twenty-two oars and the pirogues had six and seven oars each. But ironically, the Lewis and Clark expedition left without Lewis. On the day that Lewis had been awaiting for so long, he was in St. Louis, arranging the journey of a group of Grand Osage chiefs to Washington, where they were to meet the president. The

Osages were going under the aegis of Pierre Chouteau, the powerful businessman in St. Louis who had been helpful to both Lewis and Clark over the winter. Lewis made himself useful in the last preparations for the Grand Osage trip. Even as Jefferson was destroying Indian homelands in Trans-Appalachia, he had insisted that Lewis court western tribes and cordially arrange for as many chiefs as possible to visit Washington. Lewis started with the Grand Osages. Or at least Chouteau did, demonstrating how naïve Lewis and his boss were, in relation to the Indians of the West.

The Grand Osage nation, the largest in the vicinity of present-day Missouri, was led by a chief named White Hair (Gra to Moh se). The nation was in the midst of a fierce internal struggle, with a segment of the people having left for the southern part of their territory (in modern-day Oklahoma), under the leadership of a chief named Big Track (Cashesegra). Included in this group was a young man named GraMoie, more commonly called by the European-ized "Clermont," who held a hereditary right to the chiefdom of the united nation. The reason for the split was that White Hair's new position as chief had been granted mainly through the intercession of the Chouteau family, which was seeking to maintain its influence in the fur trade on Osage lands. Lewis dutifully packed the Grand Osage chiefs off to see the president, believing that the trip was integral to peace efforts, though it was more likely to have the opposite effect. As the Clermont bands would see it, the trip to Washington was in fact meant to solidify the position of White Hair and therefore that of the Chouteaus.

While Lewis remained in St. Louis, Clark set out with the boats from Fort Wood, traveling for only about three or four miles across the Mississippi and up the Missouri. Then he purposely stopped—a technique used by experienced boatmen, who typically spent the first night on a journey within easy reach of the home port so that missing items could be retrieved while it was still easy to do. Starting again the next day, Clark made unhurried progress up the first twenty-one miles of the Missouri, tying up in the town of St. Charles, where he and the rest of the corps awaited Lewis. In St. Charles, the men bid farewell to all that they would miss about European culture by partaking in it all night.

Just as they were going to sleep, Lewis was setting out from St. Louis on horseback, escorted by a posse of fashionable friends. Meeting wave after wave of thunderstorms, they were forced to stall their journey and take shelter, but Lewis couldn't bear it. Having let the better part of a week go by in St. Louis, he was newly reminded of the value of a day. "As I had determined to reach St. Charles this evening," he wrote, "and knowing that there was now no time to be lost I set forward in the rain." He had pressed through eighteen months of chatter and planning, drunken shipbuilders, points of legal procedure, octant lessons, opinions, lists, passports, people's good wishes, rumors—and blank waiting. The prospect of one more day of it was apparently scarier to him than instant electrocution from one of the storm's lightning bolts. Ignoring the raging weather around him, he arrived in St. Charles in time for dinner, exactly according to plan.

On May 21, Lewis, Clark, and their corpsmen set out into the water, an expedition at last. As the people and problems of the East dropped away behind them, one phrase out of all of it remained and bound them forward; in the words of Jefferson, "the object of your mission is single." When their boats lapped into the Missouri current and drifted west in the wind, they were just that much closer to the Pacific.

Every river has its own character, and Clark and his boatmen were soon acquainting themselves with that of the Missouri. It was a capricious and dangerously playful river, marked by sharp turns and variance in depth, new courses, and even occasional changes in direction. The careless river made quick decisions, transforming itself in a moment or a day and rolling over new land as easily as it did the plans of the people in the region. While Indian nations, Americans, Spanish,

French, and English struggled with one another for control, it was the Missouri that really presided over a massive section of the West.

Because Lewis and Clark were going upriver, they soon discovered that the Missouri offered an ever-changing pattern of currents. The slowest rate of flow allowed them to make the most progress (with the least effort), but the Missouri didn't betray its many simultaneous moods. A boatman had to react almost constantly to the river. It also hid an array of underwater hazards. The captains and the sergeants who were charged with spotting the waters ahead had to be alert, whether the keelboat was propelled by sail, oar, towrope, or pole. Whenever it was moving, making its average of ten miles per day on the Lower Missouri, the expedition's sergeants (Charles Floyd, John Ordway, and Nathaniel Pryor) were typically posted in their three stations: bow, center, and helm. The first was the most important, as Lewis wrote: "It shall be the duty of the *sergt. at the bow*, to keep a good lookout for all danger which may approach, either of the enemy, or obstructions." The fact that the keelboat was overloaded made it even more unwieldy when dangers did approach. On May 23, Clark wrote an unfortunately typical entry: "Set out early run on a log: under water and Detained one hour."

The following day, he described a treacherous near-disaster, as their fully loaded keelboat spun out of control:

> we wer verry near loseing our Boat in Toeing She Struck the Sands (which is continerly roaling) & turned the Violence of the Current was so great that the Toe roap Broke, the boat turned Broadside, as the Current Washed the Sand from under her She wheeled & lodged on the bank below as often as three times, before we got her in Deep water.

Clark was keeping the only official journal from 1804 that is extant, though the crewmen were also asked to write diaries of the trip and a few of them did.

As the expedition settled into a routine, the two leaders easily defined their own roles. Clark was always available to handle the operation of the boats, and he seemed particularly intrigued—if aggravated—by the Missouri's waters. He was also taken with its expansive views. Lewis was more likely to walk alongside the river, looking at the plants and the rocks. If there was an easy differentiation to be made, Lewis bent over to get close to the land; Clark stood as high as he could to observe "the most butifull prospects imagionable."

After two and a half months, Clark wrote of a single day but also summed up the whole first segment of the journey: "every thing in prime order men in high Spirits. . . . Great no. misquitors."

Eight

A SECOND EXPEDITION

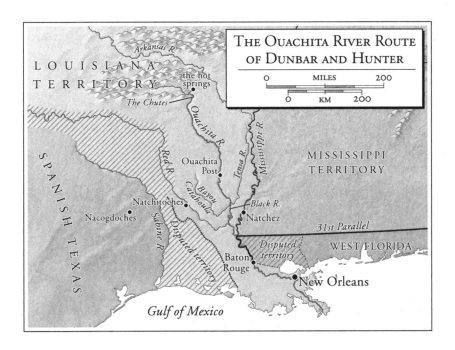

George Hunter was a busy man in Philadelphia in 1804 when the president asked him to drop everything and tour an alligator-infested, lumber-clogged river in the parched Southwest. He could

have said no. Hunter was the head of a respectable, close-knit household and a business that was successful enough to provide a comfortable living for his family, and also for any unemployed relatives
who turned up in Philadelphia in need of work. George and his
wife, Phoebe, had five children of their own, ranging in age from
just one year to sixteen.

With at least four other expeditions to fill, Jefferson had also
been sending inquiries to others, but without success. Some men
couldn't meet his schedule; the president was in a hurry for results
and wanted people to leave for the West within three or four months.
Jefferson's priorities were political—international and domestic—
and in both, he was being chased by circumstances. In his opinion,
the people along the eastern seaboard needed to know that America
had arrived in the West. And, moreover, the Spanish had to know it.

Some of the men who were best qualified to lead an expedition
had issues with character: a violent temper in one case, a habit of
abandoning wives in another. Most who were contacted made their
own excuses, though, and declined the opportunity to devote time
and energy and perhaps their lives to the unknown. Citing age, illness, work schedules, or family obligations as reasons, the main point
was that the vast majority of those invited just wanted to stay home.

As to the chance to become a national hero—that precedent had
yet to be set. In the spring of 1804, Lewis and Clark didn't present
much of an inspiration—quite the opposite, in fact. At the same
time Hunter was expected to leave his comfortable town house, the
unconfirmed story about Lewis and Clark was that they "and their
companions, had been fallen upon by Osage Indians and put to
death, only two men escaping." The rumor may have grown from
Lewis's efforts in May to send the Grand Osage chiefs to the East,
under the aegis of Chouteau, but none of that was known in Philadelphia when Mrs. Hunter was trying to get used to the idea of her
husband following Lewis and Clark into Louisiana Territory. The
common knowledge was that they were dead.

The Hunters would never hear the news that would have changed their mind about risking everything for the sake of Jefferson's West. In February and March of 1804, General Wilkinson was in New Orleans, preparing a report for Spain on American encroachment in the West with his advice on the best means to eradicate it. His long outline, charging that the United States "with their boundless designs" wouldn't stop short of overthrowing Mexico and Peru, might have been an example of the provocation and intimidation techniques of a deft double agent, except that he brought Jefferson's explorers to Spain's attention, sometimes by name. "An express ought to be sent to the governor of Santa Fe," Wilkinson advised, in order that the Spanish "may detach a sufficient body of chasseurs to intercept Captain Lewis and his party, who are on the Missouri River, and force them to retire or take them prisoners."

Wilkinson also made a direct reference to the work of Dunbar, exaggerating it by referring to Jefferson's "astronomer, who is at this very moment in the province of Louisiana, with the duty of determining by all practical investigations the relative positions of the mouth of the Rio Bravo or Rio Grande." He garbled Dunbar's assignment, pressing it closer to sensitive turf with the mere mention of the Rio Grande (known in Mexico as the Río Bravo). Enlarging upon the explorations did play into Jefferson's strategy—and anyway, officials in Madrid had already been goaded by Ambassador Yrujo with many of the same intimations regarding Lewis and Clark—yet Wilkinson's report crossed a significant threshold. The commander of the American army had placed Jefferson's explorers on the field of battle that existed between the two nations—until soldiers started to march, Wilkinson made them the only standing symbols of supremacy in the West. That might not have disturbed Jefferson so very much, in principle, but dangling Lewis, Clark, and Dunbar before the Spanish was still drastic and dangerous.

In looking to recruit other leaders, Jefferson continually tried to make a virtue of the self-sacrifice of Louisiana exploration, but for the time being, the men he approached sidestepped that opportunity. They would be trailblazers in both a literal and figurative sense, leaving new paths on the ground and doing so in a way that made exploration on behalf of the United States a privilege. That was a tradition that had yet to be established. For the time being, it was not a prospect drenched in glory. The work itself was at best uncomfortable and at worst deadly—and for most, a waste of time in any case. To Hunter's contemporaries in 1804, the western reaches of the Red River were as remote as outer space and about as important to their lives.

Yet when the president of the United States asked, Hunter didn't pause over the myriad reasons that he had for staying home. Newspapers of the era often made reference to the "Spirit of '76"; it was a potent phrase, especially in Philadelphia, and was used specifically to jolt the reader back to the idealism present in the American Revolution. George Hunter had had the Spirit in '76.

Hunter was from Scotland, though with very different origins than those of William Dunbar. Dunbar was raised in luxury in the rugged north; Hunter was from the city of Edinburgh in the southern part of Scotland. His father had been a cooper, but he died young. George, the oldest of two sons, was undoubtedly a bright young man, training with "an eminent druggist," before the Hunter boys, their mother, and her second husband (who was barely older than her sons) moved to America in 1774, settling in Philadelphia. The timing was unfortunate, unless they believed in a republican form of government enough to live through a war over it. Within a year, the shooting began and the two Hunter brothers and their stepfather, a coachbuilder by trade, stepped up.

"In the winter of 1776," Hunter wrote, "we all three entered as Volunteers with the Philada. Militia, were present at the Engagements of Trenton & Princeton, which gave a turn to the scale of American affairs."

Before those two battles, General Washington had been on the run from a series of defeats toward New York City for his amateurish army. Near Philadelphia, he made a fairly desperate attempt to regroup. Marching out toward Trenton on Christmas Eve, the Philadelphia Militia added about 500 recruits to the 2,400-man army. The best that could be said for Washington's men on the new offensive is that they were, on average, even fresher and less well-trained than before: row after row of druggists and coachbuilders. Nonetheless, they followed orders and made their way with Washington across the Delaware River, the faces in the background of the famous painting. Having routed Trenton, the Continental Army marched on Princeton nine days later and drove out a strong British force there. That was the "turn in American affairs" of which Hunter wrote—and was a part.

In 1778, George Hunter transferred to the Hospital Department of the Army, building on his knowledge as a druggist. After three years, he qualified as a doctor and sailed as ship's surgeon on a navy vessel called the *Hetty Bound*, amassing a small fortune. Whether he did that by trading goods at distant ports or in the time-honored method of cheating at cards with newly arrived sailors, his original stash increased sixty-fold. Judging by the investments he later made with the money, he probably shipped out with the equivalent of roughly $200 and came home with about $12,000. Hunter had managed to find a branch of service in which he could do his job and simultaneously realize a steep return on investment. On returning home, he started a chemical factory, which burned down, and then started over with a drugstore.

When the family's carriage-building business took a fall, though, George was the only one who could save it from ruin. The business happened to be almost directly across High Street from the house that Jefferson rented when serving as secretary of state in Philadelphia. George, on hiatus from the drug business, didn't have the expertise to help manufacture carriages, but he could sell them, continually advertising carts, wagons, and coaches that were "completely repaired" or "as good as new," in his sunny phrasing. When Jefferson first arrived on High Street, he would be more likely to order a new set of spokes from George Hunter than engage him in philosophic investigation or to speak to him about their common fascination with the West.

Even while Hunter applied himself to reorganizing the carriage business, chemistry remained his passion, and in 1794 he was at last able to return to his own profession. He described his new business in a Philadelphia newspaper ad:

GEORGE HUNTER, CHEMIST

At his Laboratory, 114, South Second Street

Informs his former customers and the public that he has begun the DRUG business again on an extensive plan.

He has for sale a general assortment of FRESH DRUGS, CHEMICAL PREPARATIONS, and PATENT MEDICINES.

Likewise—painters' colours, dry and ground in oil, paint brushes, window and coach glass, dyestuffs, linseed oil, oil of turpentine, copae oil varnish and japan, warranted good.

Allum, copperas, madder, ground redwood by the hogshead or smaller quantity.

As he imports the simples from the best markets, and makes the compositions and preparations himself, he is enabled to vouch for and warrant every article sold out of his Laboratory, and likewise to dispose of them at the most reasonable rates.

Hunter wasn't a theoretical experimenter and didn't seem to correspond with those who were. In looking for a man to lead an expedition, Jefferson might have been more comfortable with someone more esoteric who fit his grand vision for a man of science, but Hunter had a characteristic others lacked. He was a simple patriot, a Scottish-born American who said yes to George Washington and then yes to Thomas Jefferson when others did not.

NO SOONER HAD Hunter agreed to go to the Red River in April than Secretary of War Dearborn sent him an inventory of required supplies, "the selecting and purchase of which," Hunter wrote, "together with the necessary arrangement & preparation for such a journey, having occupied the chief of my time for the present month." He made that note on May 27, the day he left Philadelphia for Natchez, which was to be the staging area for the expedition. Because of Jefferson's rush to launch the trip, Dunbar had finally agreed to serve as coleader—but only for the first section of the Red River. The corps could start out from Natchez and make some headway before another leader, yet to be found, took over in Natchitoches.

While Lewis had been accorded about six months in which to ready himself for the Missouri River expedition—and even that wasn't enough—Hunter was pressed to start his expedition after only six weeks. In all of his preparations, "dispatch was necessary," as he put it. Before he left Philadelphia, he received permission to bring along his son, George Heriot Hunter, who was then just shy of his fifteenth birthday. Young George may have been Hunter's version of an unpaid batman. As a father, Hunter would no doubt enjoy having one of his children around on the expedition, pounding tent stakes, carrying barrels, chopping brush and cutting trees, stacking trunks, pulling boats through mud. It would be educational.

The father and son set out for Pittsburgh, having previously forwarded by wagon "all the Indian presents, medicine chest, Tools, mathematical instruments &cc destined for the use of the expedition to explore Louisiana." Arriving in Pittsburgh on June 4, Hunter found that the busy city had no existing boats for sale of the right size and no room on any westbound vessels for him, his son, and their wagonload of supplies. Unlike Lewis, he hadn't commissioned a boat in advance. As it was, space wasn't expected to become available for at least five weeks. "Dispatch" being necessary, Hunter decided to have a boat custom-built in Pittsburgh.

Hunter designed the boat himself, in the "Chinese stile" of a junk. It had a large rectangular sail and an oversized rudder to steady the course in place of any sort of keel. "She is 50 feet long 6½ feet Beam very strong," Hunter wrote to Dearborn. "Can accomadate 25 men under cover who being properly speaking in close quarters cannot be easily stormed by any number of Indians & carry a considerable burthen." Hunter remained at the shipyard full time to oversee construction. It was finished in less than ten days, indicating that his years in business had given him skills in industrial management that Lewis might have envied.

With six men in the crew, Hunter scheduled the launch for June 15, the day after the boat was finished. All was ready as the men arrived at the dock, the adventure to begin. Then they saw Hunter's adaptation of the Chinese stile. "Three of our hands left us being afraid to go in our Boat," Hunter wrote. The three unbelievers bought a vessel of their own and left at the same time as Hunter, who was insulted enough to turn the early part of the trip into a race. "They soon had reason to repent their imprudence," he declared, "for much stormy & rainy weather soon came on with thunder & lightning which forced them to lay by at nights, whilst we continued floating on." Eventually, he stopped tracking the other boat.

"I pay nothing for hands," Hunter boasted, speaking of the labor of the three men who were left guiding the boat downriver. Of the crewmen, one was described by Hunter as "An Old Spanish Fencing Master," one was a German, and one a shoemaker from Switzerland, all working for their passage. Hunter was an inveterate bargain seeker; on his first trip down the Ohio, on the *Illinois* in 1792, he had struck the same deal with his crewmen. But then, they jumped ship.

Hunter's version of a Chinese boat survived the Ohio River, to the surprise of everyone except Hunter, who confidently left it in the charge of George Heriot for a few days in mid-June. The boat continued downriver while Hunter took a detour on horseback across northern Kentucky. His main stop was Lexington, where he seemed to know more people than ever, meeting Dr. Brown and many others.

It was a busy summer in Lexington. Only about two weeks earlier, the Grand Osage Indian chiefs had passed through with Chouteau, moving steadily east toward Washington. According to a description reprinted in newspapers across the country, the Osage chiefs appeared "almost naked." Depending on the weather, the Grand Osage used buffalo robes or put on buckskin leggings. The typical Grand Osage man shaved his head, leaving a circle about one-half inch wide of long hair around the crown. The hair was used to secure hanging ornaments; their ears were pierced for the same purpose. The local paper in Lexington described the chiefs as "gigantic" and noted, "They are represented as a ferocious people who wish to be at war with all the other tribes of Indians." The Caddo, who lived to the south of Osage lands, would have been quick to agree. The Osages did prey on their neighbors, especially the Caddo and the Witchitas, but their nation was among the oldest of all Indian cultures and was unusually stable in many ways—they had occupied the same territory in what is now southern Missouri and Arkansas for over a thousand years.

The Osage chiefs who visited Lexington were anything but ferocious, the people of central Kentucky finding them to be mild in temperament. By the time Hunter arrived, heading in the opposite direction, talk about the chiefs was fading. He supplanted the Indians on the city's center stage, formally beginning his career there as a figure of national importance. For the first time in his life, he was newsworthy, as an article in the *Kentucky Gazette* began:

> Dr. Hunter of Philadelphia arrived in this town on Sunday last [June 24], on his way to Natchez, where he is to be joined by Dr. Dunbar of the *Mississippi* Territory; both of whom are commissioned by the President to ascend Red river to its source.

Whether Dunbar had changed his mind about the Red River and was actually planning to "ascend it to its source," Hunter would have to learn in Natchez. In fact, Dunbar was so ambivalent about the project that he was thinking at the time that if he and Jefferson failed to find another leader, Hunter could head the expedition by himself, "should we in the end be obliged to accept a person of moderate talents," as he wrote to Jefferson. If Dunbar's intrinsic haughtiness wasn't the source of this low opinion of Hunter, then the only explanation is that Jefferson remembered Hunter from Philadelphia as selling used coaches—the furthest pursuit possible from that of serious exploration—and that he retained an opinion he may have communicated to Dunbar. As summer drew near, though, the president needed the expedition to start as soon as possible and both Hunter and Dunbar were keenly aware of it.

By the time Hunter arrived on the banks of the Ohio River to meet his boat again, it had been waiting for him for four or five days. That and the less than inspiring command of a fourteen-year-old interim captain had made for changes on board.

"At Louisville we lost our Spaniard & German," Hunter wrote, "whom we did not regret as they were grown saucy & Lazy." That left a crew of one—the Swiss shoemaker on his way to Natchez.

The boat had a trying trip downriver, a large, unwieldy vessel with a shorthanded crew that was, in Hunter's words, "much fatigued with rowing, want of rest & want of regular and good meals,

& above all continually pestered by Mosquetoes." With stagnant water, the Mississippi in July could be more of a long, narrow pond than a river. Hunter learned that firsthand, as he and his crew were forced to row as strenuously going downriver as they would have going up.

While Hunter was battling just to reach Natchez as soon as possible, Dunbar was actively engaged in research for the expeditions. His interest had finally risen to the level of the president's unwavering imperative, in part because he'd gotten his way in the matter of personnel, receiving permission from Dearborn to contact U.S. Army posts in search of leaders and crewmen. At the same time, Dunbar learned what he could about the Red River, enticing Jefferson with the prediction that "many important objects will present themselves to the curious inquirer: Plants useful for food in medicine, dying [of cloth] & other arts are said to be in profusion along the known parts of the red river." With that, he lamented that the congressional appropriation didn't allow for a trained botanist. In terms of geography, Dunbar made it clear that he had no enthusiasm for the Arkansas River, which seemed to him to be a pale twin of the Red River, but he did let Jefferson know that

> the Washita [Ouachita] river is supposed to offer many Curious objects, it diverges considerably from the red river, of which it is a branch . . . [about] 200 miles from the red river, here is a Curiosity which I am apprehensive will be too far out of the tract of our party, otherwise would merit to have its position ascertained; it is called the boiling Spring or fountain.

Dunbar planned to explore the Ouachita on his own after the Red River expedition left—or after he left the Red River expedition. He knew that, from Jefferson's point of view, an extra report on a river in the Louisiana Territory would be an asset in Washington.

JEFFERSON HAD HIS first chance to personify the new territory in early July, when the Grand Osage chiefs arrived in Washington. Among them was White Hair, who had recently won the power struggle to become the main chief. The Osages were the city's very first sensation, as Jefferson showed them around—and showed them off. Even while he was anxiously arranging expeditions and awaiting reports, the Louisiana Territory had come to his door.

Amid the festivities, Jefferson had the chance to directly address western Indians for the first time. Most of his official messages to the Osages pertained to something of great interest to him, but of little attraction to them: American exploration of their lands and those adjoining. He didn't say anything at all about the Osage right to keep their tribal homelands (which, indeed, he would pressure them to cede during his second administration), but he did include a long passage about the explorer who launched their trip toward Washington, "a beloved man, Capt. Lewis, one of my household." He further invited them to explore the eastern seaboard and acquire the same knowledge "on this side the Missipi, which we are endeavoring to acquire of that on the other side, by sending trusty persons to explore them." He listed at least five rivers to be visited, including a specific reference to the Red River expedition. Such was the theme of Jefferson's remarks to the Osages: the Americans were coming.

While courting favor with Jefferson, White Hair was also trying to sully the reputation of Big Track, Clermont and their associates. So it was that when he heard that the American Red River expedition was due to begin within two months, he took care to deliver a sobering description of what the Clermont bands would do to Hunter, Dunbar, and the crewmen. Jefferson was impatient for exploration of the Red to begin, but he listened carefully to White Hair and decided that Big Track and his breakaway group posed too great a danger. In truth, the Clermont bands were not bloodthirsty people and probably wouldn't have had any problem with the explorers—at least not until Lewis blundered by entertaining White Hair without also approaching the Clermont contingent of Osages. Convinced by White Hair's warning, Jefferson sent an urgent warning to Dunbar the next day, July 17, and even specified that if necessary, the letter should be forwarded—without delay.

As of July 17, Dunbar was at the Forest in Natchez. Hunter was still on the Mississippi, about 250 miles away, and the prospect of being attacked by angry Osages would have seemed appealing if it meant he could stop rowing. The temperature was rarely below ninety degrees Fahrenheit, and the number of men working on board his boat had been reduced to two—Hunter and his son. The Swiss shoemaker had fallen ill. Hunter administered to the patient, taking time away from the navigation of the boat. By July 21, he wasn't sure where they were, but could only hope that they were nearing Vicksburg (known then as Walnut Hills). That afternoon, he needed yet again to look through the maps at the back of the boat. At about two thirty, Hunter watched the shoemaker's condition worsen. Turning his attention to the maps momentarily, he heard a splash and then saw that the patient was gone, his hat floating at the surface of the river. Hunter wrote:

> Reflecting on this awful event, I commonly think that either he went over in the delirium of the fever, or not being perfectly awake from his sleep or perhaps from design, & he once mentioned since the commencement of his sickness, that he never would see Natchez. We continued in a melacholly manner to look over the side & all round the boat for a considerable time & and at length concluded it was in vain, as no person could live so long under water.

Even though the drowned man was not a member of the expedition that had yet to start, his final weeks were intertwined with it:

an understaffed crew to save money, an awkward boat because of the need to save time. If there was anyone back in Switzerland to wonder what happened to him, the answer never came. He was one of the many who went into the West, sooner or later to be enveloped by it. After the fatality, the Hunters kept moving around the clock, and miraculously they arrived in Natchez before the end of July. In the span of three months, Hunter had, with a certain desperation, readied himself for the Red River.

Nine

A SPECIAL KIND OF WAR

On July 25, Dunbar welcomed his fellow Scot with the crisp, clean hospitality of the Forest. The region's heat wave had seized Natchez for more than a month, but a local judge, Thomas Rodney, wrote home to his relatives in Delaware that week that "it has now much abated and the nights have become pleasantly Cool and refreshing."

When Hunter arrived at Dunbar's plantation, about eight miles from Natchez, he regarded it as "an elegant Situation & finely improved," adding that he was "politely and kindly received." The next day, Dunbar met the Hunters at the riverside to see the boat. He was ill impressed. If Hunter happened to use the name "Chinese junk" to describe it, Dunbar would have agreed, heartily. Unfortunately, he didn't know of any other available boats in Natchez, or he surely would have replaced it.

Dunbar politely suggested that Hunter take the boat to New

Orleans, where he could also pick up provisions from the army garrison. Hunter was to show his boat to the commander, who might be induced by the sight of the oddity to find a replacement. Of the detour, Hunter wrote to Dearborn on July 31, "This will delay our final departure from this place to explore the Rivers at least 5. Or six weeks, which I much regret." Dunbar may not have approved of the Chinese boat, but as a cotton man, he couldn't bear the sight of any vessel above the size of a canoe leaving for New Orleans with room on deck and so he sent twenty-seven bales of his cotton with Hunter's boat. Since that alone delayed the work of the expedition by at least two days, it was exactly the kind of opportunism that Jefferson—and Dunbar—feared in their explorers.

While Hunter was delivering cotton—in the wrong direction—Lewis and Clark were on course, navigating the Missouri River to the northwest, through present-day Iowa and Nebraska. If they had one thing in common with Hunter on the Mississippi, it was mosquitoes. "Abutifull Breeze from the N W. this evening," Clark noted on July 27, "which would have been verry agreeable, had the Misquiters been tolerably Pacifick, but thy were rageing all night, Some about the Sise of house flais." The insects were debilitating. Clark wrote that he "found the Misquitors So thik & troublesom that it was disagreeable and painfull to Continue a moment Still." Moreover, mosquitoes carried two of the most deadly communicable diseases: malaria and yellow fever.

Along the Missouri River, the progress made by the expedition's flotilla was steady, despite the nearly daily problem of finding consistently deep water. If there was any disappointment for Lewis, in particular, it lay in the fact that they had been nearly alone on the river for the first two months of the journey. All of the Indian villages that they passed were deserted. The Iowa had moved on; the Missouria (Niúachi) were decimated by war, and every tribe in the region had suffered from a slow, stubborn smallpox outbreak in 1800–1802. Plains Indians, living in uncrowded conditions and often in villages that were temporary, developed even less immunity to newly introduced diseases than other American Indians. The Native populations on the Northern Plains were dramatically reduced over the dozen years between Evans's trip and that of Lewis and Clark. On July 28, when the expedition was in what is now northeastern Nebraska, it finally intersected with another person: a hunter from the Missouria tribe.

A bright man, the Missouria explained that he was on an elk-hunting trip with a group of twenty Otoe (Jiwere) families, camping about four miles away, but that the "great gangue" of Otoes were on a more distant hunt for buffalo. The captains were anxious to contact the nearby group of Otoes to start the mission of meeting Native people and communicating to them what Jefferson had described in his instructions as their "wish to be neighborly, friendly & useful to them." The next day, Lewis sent a French Canadian crewman known as La Liberté with the Missouria hunter to invite the chiefs and warriors to a meeting on neutral ground. By the end of the day, La Liberté hadn't returned. Although Lewis and Clark suspected that he had been killed, they continued with the plan to receive the Indians. The expedition settled into a camp on high ground, eagerly awaiting the Natives. Days passed without any sign of La Liberté or the visitors.

While the captains were waiting, the men tried to make the most of their time. Sergeant Floyd used the break to rest, having been ill with what he called a cold. Another of the men captured a young beaver that he tamed as a pet, making it one of the luckier animals to find itself in the path of the expedition.

Between the hunting that was done for food or oil and the collection for study, the expedition's campsites were typically very busy abattoirs. On July 30, as the men continued to wait, one of those assigned to hunt for meat brought in a badger, the first that anyone on the expedition had ever seen. Lewis knew what it was and took a great interest in having it stuffed. "This is a singular anamal not common to any part of the United States," he wrote in one of his rare journal entries that year. "It's weight is sixteen pounds.—it is a carnivorous anamal. on both sides of the upper jaw is fexed one long and sharp canine tooth.—it's eye are small black and piercing."

Clark also took an interest in the badger, but he couldn't stop thinking about the deer that had also been brought to camp from the same hunting trip: "One inch fat on the ribs," he noted. He wasn't being zoological. The next day, he turned thirty-four. "This being my birth day," he wrote, "I order'd a Saddle of fat Vennison, an Elk fleece & a Bevertail to be cooked and a Desert of Cheries, Plumbs, Raspberries Currents and grapes of a Supr. quallity." Clark relaxed into his indulgence, the greasy hunks of venison and the wild fruit salad. The fruit that astounded Clark was also important to the nutrition of the entire crew. "The Praries," he wrote, "Contain Cheres, Apple, Grapes, Currents, Rasp burry, Gooseberris Hastlenuts and a great Variety of Plants & flours not Common to the U S." While wild fruits and berries stayed ripe for only a short time, they often had intense flavor and tenderness. Along the Lower Missouri in summer, the members of the expedition had as balanced a diet as they would have during their entire trip.

During the same day, the captains prepared the peace pipe that they had brought along, and the next day the expected group of Otoe and Missouria chiefs finally arrived, with a similar number of warriors. Clark noted most of their names and included translations of several. Shon-go-ton go (Big Horse) was the grand chief. Others in the party were We-ar-ruge-nor (Little Thief); Sho-Guss-Con (White Horse); We-tha-a (Hospitality); Wau-pe-ur; Au-ho-ningga; Ba-Za-con-ja, and Au-ho-ne-ga. Sergeant Floyd described the way that the two bands of well-armed strangers, Indian and American, approached one another on the plains. Surprise was the greatest danger. Referring first to the Indians, he recorded that "thay fired meney Guns when thay Came in Site of us and we ansered them withe the Cannon thay Came in about 2 hundred yardes of us Capt Lewis and Clark met them at Shakeing Handes we fired another Cannon."

Lewis and Clark were wary but welcomed the Otoes and Missourias, as well as a French trader who accompanied them with his family. The Indians in the group were stout, light-skinned people, with open expressions; one of the corpsmen, Private Joseph Whitehouse, noted that "they all use paint in order to compleat their dress." A ceremony known as a council was scheduled for the next morning, and the Indians set up a camp a short distance away. The captains, who were still uncertain about the fate of La Liberté, took the precaution of putting their men on high alert for an attack.

The next morning, Lewis, Clark, and the men in the expedition camp woke up—to their surprise—and the council went on as planned. It began on the American side with the creation of the proper setting. A sail was stretched over a frame onshore to create an awning for the leaders. Next came a parade of men in arms. Medals were presented, according to the rank of the various chiefs, and Clark made a long speech, informing his guests that the United States was the new power in the region and advising them on the best way to interact with the Americans. Two of the Indian chiefs made speeches in return. Clark, a star of the show, described it all in detail, including his satisfaction that he didn't waste valuable presents on the rather insignificant chiefs. Sergeant Floyd also liked to note fine points of the meeting, but he had an even greater inclination to get on with the business of exploration. He summed up the morning in his own way: "the Council was held and all partes was agreed the Captens Give them meney presents thes is the ottoe and the Missouries The Missouries is a verry Small nathion the ottoes is a very Large nathion So thay Live in one village on the Plate River after the Council was over we took ouer Leave of them and embarked at 3 oclock P. m."

The Otoe delegation returned to their own encampment in the afternoon, but that didn't mean that they were finished with the

Lewis and Clark expedition. During the talks surrounding the council, Lewis or Clark almost certainly asked about La Liberté and learned his fate at last. He had gone to the Otoes, as ordered, but had decided to stay among them; since he was a civilian rather than a military man, he was nominally within his rights to quit. Nonetheless, his departure marked a turning point for the expedition. While the Indians had often seen Europeans making the trip upriver, the members of the Lewis and Clark corps were for the first time confronted by Northern Plains culture. An army private named Moses Reed found the inherent temptation overwhelming. The night after the visit of the Otoe and Missouri chiefs, he stole a gun and some ammunition, hid it with his clothes, and then told the captains that he had forgotten his knife at the previous night's camp.

Lewis and Clark gave Reed permission to retrieve the knife. With that, the private fetched his hidden stash and made a beeline for the Otoe village. The chiefs, in the afterglow of the council, made him welcome. They were fond of Reed. That and the experience of previous explorers suggest that he was offered what companionship he wanted. As Reed knew, the expedition was on its way upriver, farther and farther away, which must have made him feel safer by the minute.

The next important stop for Lewis and Clark was the Big Village of the Omaha. A dozen years earlier, a boat could not have expected to pass the Lower Missouri without paying homage to the Omaha tribes and the nation's bustling Big Village. Under Blackbird, the Omahas could handle Europeans, toy with them, and very often fleece them. Unfortunately, their contact with foreigners also brought a disease they couldn't fight, and in 1801 the nation suffered massively from the outbreak of smallpox. In the epidemic, Blackbird died—at least according to the usual understanding of that term. The Omahas believed that he continued to preside over his river, retaining his former powers and guiding the fortunes of his people.

Accompanied by about ten members of the expedition, Lewis

and Clark climbed a three-hundred-foot bluff to reach the grave of Blackbird. It overlooked the river for sixty miles and took in the plains to the horizon, with animal life abounding upon it. Because Omahas visited the grave regularly, as did many other Indians, the captains brought a memorial banner. With that, they went back down the bluff to the river of Blackbird: treacherous, rich, and for so long a time, indomitable.

Reed was starting his second week at the Otoe village, when he was surprised by a search party composed of five crewmates from the expedition. They came with orders to kill him if he resisted, but Reed buckled immediately. The group made their way to the north by land, also escorting Big Horse and two other chiefs, to whom the captains had extended a second invitation, having further diplomatic goals in mind. With Private Reed in firm custody, the search party arrived at the expedition's latest campsite on August 18. Lewis and Clark needed to discipline Reed, who was not only a core member of the crew, but an enlisted man in the army. They couldn't abide a stampede to "Venus' country" at every accommodating village that the expedition might pass. After a formal court-martial, Reed was officially dismissed as a member of the expedition; he was to travel with it, though, until return passage could be arranged at the Mandan villages. In addition, he "ran the gauntlet" four times, the other members of the corps beating him with a switch as he passed.

Sergeant Floyd's journal didn't mention Reed's punishment. His entry for the day was rushed and terse, even by Floyd's blunt standards. He was feeling ill again. The next day, he was so uncomfortable he couldn't stand up. Whitehouse called the ailment "a bilious cholic"; modern medical opinion surmises that it may have been appendicitis. With the expedition stopped for the day, Sergeant Floyd was tended by York and others. Clark was concerned with the soldier's condition, but he had other problems. The captains had summoned Big Horse and members of his band so that they might travel

together to visit other nations. The Americans wanted to negotiate
a lasting peace for the Otoes and Missourias with other tribes, such
as the Omahas and Sioux. It was a masterful plan, except for two
points. Lewis and Clark couldn't find the Omahas. And Big Horse
turned out to be a rather trying guest.

After Lewis and Clark made those realizations, their options
were limited and so they called another council. The formality of
the ceremony offered just the right note of finality and farewell,
allowing the two parties to separate with diplomatic gravitas. The
crewmen erected the awning again, paraded in arms again, and prepared for a second time to sit through the speeches. Lewis made
much the same talk as had Clark—but then Big Horse went off
script. There comes a time in diplomatic relations to abandon sub-
tlety, and Big Horse seemed to have reached it after traveling with
the thick-headed Americans for days on end.

> I went to the hunt Buffalow I heard your word and I re-
> turned, I and all my men with me will attend to your
> words—you want to make peace with all, I want to make
> peace also, the young me[n] when they want to go to war
> where is the goods you give me to Keep them at home, if you
> give me Some Whisky to give a Drop to my men at home.
>
> I came here naked and must return home naked. if I
> have Something to give the young men I can prevent their
> going to war. You want to make peace with all, It is good
> we want Something to give my men at home. I am a pore
> man, and cant quiet without means, a Spoon ful of your
> milk will quit [quiet] all.

The Indian's slang use of the word "milk" came through clearly,
even in translation. Big Horse wanted whiskey, in addition to certificates and better medals than before. Clark and Lewis scrambled
to exchange the presents already given for finer ones—which Big
Horse and his companions didn't regard as any improvement, send-

ing the captains back to the storage lockers yet again. "Those people became extremely troublesom to us begging Whisky & little articles," Clark wrote.

Big Horse had explained clearly why his chiefs couldn't guarantee peace without presents, but Lewis and Clark "finally blew up and rebuked them verry roughly for haveing in object goods and not peace with their neighbours." The chiefs took offense at these verbal blows. Fortunately for Lewis, who had been ordered by Jefferson to treat Indians "in the most friendly & conciliatory manner," the chiefs relented before a minor Indian war erupted. They even apologized, just before beginning to ask for presents again.

Lewis and Clark had thought that the expedition's first encounter with the same Indians—that first council on August 4—had been a well-orchestrated success, putting them in control. Only two weeks later, they could see what a failure that exercise had really been. American diplomacy looked like a honeypot to Big Horse and felt like one to Lewis and Clark, trying to extricate themselves from the sticky need to give the Otoes and Missourias presents, almost continually.

Finally, all agreed that the Indians would leave in the morning. At dawn, Big Horse was ready to go home, along with his companions and an array of presents, a fine medal, provisions, supplies, and a brand-new certificate. Just before he broke camp, Big Horse must have thought of one more reason to stay, though. At the last minute, according to the official journal, Clark pressed a container of whiskey on him. Big Horse left.

In mid-August, Dunbar was at the Forest in Natchez, awaiting Hunter; the decision had been made to upgrade and improve the Chinese junk in New Orleans. Even while the boat was still under reconstruction, Dunbar disdained it—and he was right: it was too heavy and unwieldy for use anywhere, let alone on shallow rivers. He was also complaining about gaps in the staffing of the expedition, especially in the need for a trained botanist. Moreover, he wanted a guide—someone like the late Philip Nolan, who had been to the country past Natchitoches and not only knew what to expect on the slovenly Red River, but how to get over, around, or by it. Dunbar thought the expedition needed a skilled linguist or translator, a geographer, and an experienced hunter, too. In lieu of any of the above, he had a wholesale chemist from Philadelphia, who was at that time spending his nights ripping apart everything that the boat builders in New Orleans did to his boat during the day. "Having but very indifferent workman, tools & materials," Hunter wrote, "I am obliged to attend personally & frequently to tear to pieces what they have done." Even worse, George Heriot was seriously ill, having come down with a condition that Hunter blamed on severe exhaustion after the arduous journey down the Mississippi. Nursing his son and arguing with boatbuilders must have weighed on Hunter, but he did have one pleasant evening of celebrity, dining with the territorial governor, W. C. C. Claiborne, in mid-August.

Claiborne was Jefferson's sentry on the Spanish officials who were still in Louisiana. While no one could seem to get rid of them, he closely monitored their activities. In August, the nebulous borderland between Natchitoches (Louisiana) and Nacogdoches (Texas) was riled with hostilities on both sides, effectively closing travel past Natchitoches to Americans without special passports. The obvious conclusion was that an expedition along the Red River would be regarded as an encroachment and stopped. That was the basis of the rumor that reached New Orleans and Natchez in August, to the effect that the Spanish would immediately arrest any Americans exploring the Red River.

In Natchez, the mail in mid-August brought a letter from Jefferson for Dunbar; it was the one written a month earlier, during the visit of the Grand Osage chiefs. Believing White Hair's warnings about the dangers of the Clermont bands under Big Track, Jefferson suggested that they "conclude to suspend this expedition till this spring."

Dunbar couldn't have been disappointed when he read that line. Like all residents of Natchez, he had heard the reports about the

Spanish intention to arrest explorers on the Red River. Jefferson, who was no doubt deeply unhappy with the delay, responded with his usual reflex, however: a new plan, one that would ensure that someone would explore something immediately.

Optimizing the postponement, Jefferson suggested that Dunbar should immediately "go to what distance, and in what direction you please, return when you pleas, but in time to report to us the result of your researches, which report will probably induce Congress to enlarge the appropriation, and in the spring the party may start under better prospects. This delay gives us an opportunity too of appoint[ing] a person fully qualified to head the expedition." Jefferson was persistent, starting with what he wanted: a report on the new territory, any part or region, it didn't matter. He concluded his letter by telling Dunbar again to go somewhere with an expedition and get back to Natchez in order to "report their progress in time for the consideration of Congress."

Dunbar made an immediate decision to explore the Ouachita River and the hot springs located in the modern-day state of Arkansas. The two features weren't connected, but the river, starting in the central part of what is now the state of Louisiana, passed only about nine miles overland from the springs. Altogether, the Ouachita wound its way with frequent curls and turns more than six hundred miles, as far as the mountains of Arkansas. Dunbar didn't propose a trip that far, in search of the source, but wanted to study the river only up to the point near the hot springs: a trip of about four hundred miles, though he couldn't be sure of that beforehand.

Dunbar calculated that the Ouachita would be at its most navigable at that time of year (late summer or early fall), and moreover that the hot springs would make for newsworthy subject matter in a report, titillating Congress and inspiring more expeditions. With the lingering image of himself waiting out the rest of his life in a Mexican jail, he was also aware that the Ouachita River was in territory less disputed than that of the Red River and that an American detachment had already taken charge of the former Spanish outpost on the southern end of the river (the fort that Nolan had jauntily by-passed). Dunbar promised Jefferson "a mass of information, which I have no doubt will induce Congress to make a more liberal provision for the more important Expedition of the ensuring season."

Although dogged in their efforts to prevent American exploration, the Spanish regime in Louisiana Territory was almost out of money; in fact, as of September, officials such as Morales and de Lassus were voluntarily accepting half pay. Casa Calvo, who had been replaced as governor-general by a dour career bureaucrat, Juan Manuel de Salcedo, remained in New Orleans in a semiofficial capacity. He and the other veterans of Spain's Louisiana administration continued to believe in the cause of retaining most of the Louisiana Purchase for Spain, living day by day for the small victory that would coax the necessary money from Madrid or Mexico.

Salcedo wrote to Cevallos in an August 20 letter:

> Although it is almost eight months since the United States of America took possession of this province, they are maintaining themselves in the greatest inaction and are guarding a most profound silence concerning the time when they are to begin the marking of the boundaries. Meanwhile with great activity and care they are sending expeditions to the Upper Missouri, Missouri, Arkansas and Red Rivers in order to reconnoiter their sources and courses, examine the lands, and attract and conciliate the Indian nations to them, which with study and cautious skill they will separate from our friendship with their extended trade and presents.
>
> In hand we have a very recent proof of what we have just assured. On the twenty-sixth of last July Dr. Hunter arrived at Natchez with all the necessary apparatus to explore the west bank of the Mississippi. He is a botanist and mineralogist. He is to accompany the expedition which

is to ascend to reconnoiter the Red River as far as its origin, descending afterwards with the same motive from the source of the San Francisco de Arkansas river to its mouth—in the Mississippi.

The immediate goal was one and the same for the Americans and the Spanish: do something along the rivers to generate excitement in their respective capitals regarding the last push for the Louisiana Territory. Salcedo was wrong about one thing, though, in addition to Hunter's not being a botanist. The Americans were not in the midst of "inaction" on the question of the border. Like the Spanish, they were energetically engaged in drawing those lines in their favor.

The tension over the Louisiana Purchase was a special kind of war, and in August 1804 the parameters of aggression became clear on both sides. Two nations were trying to hold forth possession of a vast tract, but neither side had the requisite population, army, money, or strategic location for a real war, such as it looked to the world in the early nineteenth century. Instead, it was a war of insinuation, rather than conquest, with only a few people on each side aware of the stakes. If occupation without means was the goal for each of two vying nations, exploration was accepted as the weapon of the war.

Ten

TOWARD THE OUACHITA

Jefferson was at Monticello in August 1804, conspicuously aloof for a man in the midst of a presidential election. Down the hill and under the clouds, the rest of the nation was gasping through a summer of national scandal; at the root was a story of unending shock value, with the sitting vice president, Aaron Burr, shooting Alexander Hamilton, the former secretary of the treasury, in a duel to the death. Jefferson was probably the only person in the country who had nothing to say about it. He didn't comment on the shooting at all in his official capacity. He hardly mentioned it in private, either, according to available records, and yet he knew both of the men involved so well that the Aaron Burr–Alexander Hamilton duel was like a three-way collision at an intersection, in which two vehicles are mangled and one keeps going, untouched.

Looking forward, not back, Jefferson focused his attention on his upcoming summer vacation at Monticello. He was still tinkering with crop rotation, trying to simplify it for a professional farmer to whom he had leased one of his plantations. Since leaving for public office seven years before, Jefferson hadn't been able to manage his productive lands any more minutely than that. "There is never a moment, scarcely, that something of public importance is not waiting for me," he wrote to Philip Mazzei, a friend in Italy, on July 18, 1804, the eve of his trip to Monticello.

Even when Jefferson "scarcely" had an extra moment in Washington, he took his daily ride on horseback for an hour or two after lunch. Hacking along the Little Falls branch of the Potomac River in Georgetown, he especially liked to stop at the nursery owned by Thomas Main, who would talk about horticulture for as long as a customer liked. A rugged but amiable Scotsman, Main succeeded in solving one of Jefferson's long-standing conundrums: the live fence. As he was happy to tell the president, he had refused to give up when others scoffed, and he doggedly searched the Mid-Atlantic for a wild pricker bush to cultivate as a hedge. The only hiker in history who actually hoped that his sleeve would get torn, Main finally found the thornbush he wanted near Wilmington, Delaware. He put his discovery out for sale in Georgetown: "this cheap, easy and elegant manner of fencing," as he termed it. Jefferson studied Main's display of American thorns in the ground, aged one to five years. In just that amount of time, a farmer could have miles of fences that never needed painting. The president ordered four thousand.

Returning to Monticello during the summer of 1804, Jefferson's time was taken by presidential matters to an even greater extent than on previous vacations. As the election approached, the Twelfth Amendment was added to the Constitution, removing any chance that a presidential election could ever again end in a tie between members of the same party. Jefferson asked New York's retiring governor, Henry Clinton, to run for the vice presidency on his ticket, while the Federalists nominated the impressive South Carolinian Charles Cotesworth Pinckney for president. Their vice presidential candidate was New York's Rufus King, who had been useful to Jefferson as ambassador to the Court of St. James's until 1803. In fact, King had been the first to bring Jefferson news of the European maneuverings for Louisiana.

Even without opinion polls, political observers were confident that Jefferson was unbeatable. He had not, as his enemies predicted in 1800, taught courses in violent crime. Even more to his credit, the federal government was relatively quiet for the first time in its history. If the 1804 election was a referendum on Jeffersonian democracy, it generated little debate.

Surprisingly, it wasn't the Jefferson Republicans who trumpeted the Louisiana Purchase during the campaign. In fact, they barely mentioned it, if at all. A year after the announcement, the Purchase was a Federalist issue with the potential to reveal a serious vulnerability for Jefferson. "Fifteen millions of debt have been imposed upon us for the purchase of Louisiana," railed a critic in Frederick-Town, Maryland. "Except for Salt Mountains, horned frogs and naval backed hogs, we yet see no advantage from the purchase." That couldn't be denied, but another Federalist argued the same point with a bit more bite by complaining that "while so much of the public money is expended in the purchase of Louisiana, exploring that country, taking the latitude and longitude of particular points, &c., government leaves our sea-coasts and dangerous banks and shoals unsurveyed." The theme repeated by Federalists across the country was that when it came to Louisiana, Jefferson had paid too much and bought too much.

"We wanted free navigation of the Mississippi, which we held by treaty," wrote a New Yorker, "and everything more was injurious. . . . Any addition was wrong, could we have obtained it for *fifteen cents*, instead of *fifteen millions of dollars*." Another Jefferson critic, writing for a Philadelphia paper, complained that the vast tract was in actuality no more American than it had ever been:

Mr. Jefferson and his friends appear to have done puffing the purchase of Louisiana—its extent, soil, climate, good qualities, and innumerable advantages to the union. Perhaps they are waiting for major Lewis' report of exploration, some part of which will no doubt be received about the time of the next meeting of congress, and commented on. It is hoped that the administration will at the same time give us the real boundaries of the territories over which they are to exercise at least a temporary jurisdiction, and the *protest* of Spain to the transfer.

Federalists were not merely frustrated by the slow progress in absorbing the Purchase, but by Jefferson's ability to direct and, in their view, misdirect the nation's perception of the new territory. "A perfect Eden," spat one, who was more than fed up. Most Americans, however, were willing to give Jefferson time to work out Louisiana's place in the Union, horned frogs and latitudes included.

The Spanish court, meanwhile, was convinced that the United States was embarking on conquest of all the Americas. The latest rumor was that Americans were colonizing the islands off of Chile, in order to launch attacks on Spanish commerce in the Pacific. That wasn't true, but it reflected the fact that diplomatic channels were cluttered with every kind of bad feeling. Madison still flatly refused to be in the same room with Yrujo, the Spanish ambassador, after their shouting match. Yrujo didn't regard his banishment as a hardship. He called Madison's messages regarding Louisiana "as full of subterfuges, evasions, and subtleties, as they are destitute of logic, solid reasoning, and devoid of . . . good faith." Yrujo was agitating for war as the only remedy, and his compatriots in New Orleans were organizing the local citizenry in continuing loyalty to His Catholic Majesty. Casa Calvo remained prominent alongside Governor Juan Manuel de Salcedo, who was such an ineffective and self-promoting presence that it reflected on Madrid's interest in the local situation in New Orleans, where Spanish loyalists were clamoring for a strong leader. He was not, however, the only figure of significance amid the friction. Nor was he the only one named Salcedo.

The commandant of the Spanish Internal Provinces, which included most of the regions on either side of the Rio Grande, was General Nemesio de Salcedo. Having been spurred by Casa Calvo, General Salcedo pressured the governor of Spanish New Mexico, Fernando Chacón, to take immediate measures to stop Lewis and Clark. Both General Salcedo and Chacón thought that in terms of geographical knowledge, the best candidate to find Lewis and Clark was Pedro Vial, a Frenchman who had been traveling Mexico's northern frontier on behalf of the Spanish for more than twenty years. He spoke an array of Indian languages and was friendly with most of the nations in the region known as the Comancheria: the eastern area of what is now the state of New Mexico, and the western parts of Texas, Oklahoma, and Kansas. With the benefit of intelligence gathered from Indians along the way, Vial could find the American expedition, even in the vast spaces of the West. He arrived in Santa Fe in the summer and met with Governor Chacón about the new mission.

Vial liked to travel light, typically with only one companion. Two men weren't likely to intimidate twenty-nine Americans, though, and so he organized a party of twenty, comprised of Spanish civilians and Taos Indians. Vial left Santa Fe on August 1, heading north through the Comancheria. He was aware that Lewis and Clark were still somewhere on the Lower Missouri River. Maintaining a far faster pace than the Americans, Vial was at the Arkansas River in what is now eastern Colorado after only two weeks. Lewis and Clark, unaware that a Spanish detachment was on its way to intercept them, continued up the Missouri. They were in no particular rush, since they had plenty of time in which to reach their winter quarters at the Mandan villages. The plan was to send a boat back with specimens representing the region, "some part of which will no doubt be received about the time of the next meeting of congress," in the words of not Lewis or Clark, but the editorialist in Philadelphia.

In Madrid, Ambassador Charles Pinckney (cousin to the Federalist presidential candidate) was negotiating directly with the minister of state, Pedro Cevallos. They were supposed to be discussing the border issue, in the hopes of reducing the chance of the cold war giving way to shooting. As far as Cevallos was concerned, young Pinckney—good-looking, energetic, ambitious, egocentric—represented America all too perfectly. Likewise, Pinckney felt that no matter how much the bland Cevallos talked, he personified Spain's "fixed & determined plan to do nothing." They worked together in an atmosphere just about as cordial as that of Madison and Yrujo. At a meeting in early July, though, not long after Pinckney took it upon himself to threaten war (his stated reason being Spanish treatment of Americans in their ports), Cevallos suddenly erupted. He apparently wasn't as bland as he seemed. Pinckney was taken aback, reporting to Madison that Cevallos insisted that

> the Americans had no right to expect much kindness from his Majesty—that in the Case of Louisiana, they had paid no attention to his repeated remonstrances against the injustice and nullity of that transaction, whereas if they had had the least friendship they would have done it.

Cevallos wasn't finished, letting Pinckney know that Americans "were well known to be entirely a Nation of Calculators, entirely bent on making money and nothing else." It was familiar invective on both sides, but it had reached new levels. Cevallos advised the French government that hostilities were drawing near over the border question and, using the language of the duel, foresaw "the necessity of exacting satisfaction for an insult which is as good as inflicted." With France inserting itself into an American-Spanish relationship that was abrasive at every level and in every locale, a bad situation was in descent even as Jefferson took his summer vacation at Monticello.

On August 25, word of Dunbar's decision to substitute the Ouachita River for the Red reached Hunter in New Orleans, where he was still overseeing improvements to his Chinese boat. Hunter wasn't disappointed but wrote that he was "pleased with Mr. Dunbar's arrangement of the small excursion." Without missing a beat, Hunter then paid a visit to a Dutchman named Baron de Bastrop, who was in debt to Hunter's firm. Bastrop wasn't actually a baron and wasn't really named "Bastrop," but few people, if any, minded that. He was disarmingly, even dangerously, attractive. No sooner did Bastrop hear that Hunter was headed to the Ouachita than he offered him land along the river at a half dollar per acre. Bastrop owed Hunter $822, making for a debt that could be traded for 1,644 acres. Hunter was tempted.

Ten years before, the Spanish had granted Bastrop more than thirty-one square miles in the northernmost part of what is now the state of Louisiana—with the stipulation that he bring five hundred families to the region. But not even the magnetic Bastrop could draw that many people. He tried for eight years, without success. By the time Hunter visited Bastrop, the original grant had been nullified, mortgaged, and confiscated, and for good measure, the land itself was flooded into a state of ruin, but Bastrop was willing to sell some of it to Hunter anyway. In fact, he suggested that in exchange for all of his many debts, Hunter could have 50,000 acres.

A Louisiana resident who was very fond of Bastrop memorialized him succinctly: "He ruined all who became interested in his projects." Hunter wasn't ruined, because he didn't strike a deal for Bastrop's land, or lack of it. At the end of the month, he left New

Orleans with his boat, his son, and a detachment of U.S. Army soldiers assigned to the expedition, traveling north on the Mississippi
toward Natchez, where he planned to meet Dunbar.

The going was slow, although Hunter and his son no longer had
to resort to rowing, as on the way down. They had soldiers for that.
More often, though, the soldiers walked along the riverbank, six at
a time, pulling the boat with a towrope. Considering that most of
Hunter's other journal notes recorded the lengths of the alligators
they saw in the water and on the shore, the soldiers demonstrated
that even with the chance of losing a leg or two, towing the heavy
boat was easier than rowing it. En route, Hunter also noted in his
journal that they met an interesting man: "Major Ellis from a tour
up the Ouachita to the boiling springs where he had been for his
health."

Between the stragglers who lived on the Ouachita and the people
with ailments who made their way to the hot springs for relief, the
Dunbar-Hunter expedition wouldn't be breaking into terra incognita. With humans roaming for so many reasons through hundreds
of centuries, there wasn't much untrodden land anywhere in the
world by 1804. Someone who knew Ellis was even working on a report based on his own trip, for the hawkeyed editor Samuel Latham
Mitchell. Dunbar and Hunter would be, however, the first to explore the Ouachita as a national initiative. The very fact that they
were Jefferson's men made their trip different from any other.

The Ouachita expedition remained a crucial step for Jefferson
and significant for American science. That river, that boulevard, was
in recently foreign territory, making any official expedition there an
incident of serious intent. According to some reports, the territory
there was already in peril. As Dunbar expressed it, "The rumor prevails that the Indians on [the west] side begin to threaten & they are
set on by the Spanish Gov. at Nacadosh." Such rumors abounded
in the region, but in a wider sense, the Ouachita expedition would
be the first government-sponsored scientific project in United States

history to present results. Planned as a four-month journey, it would finish before any of Jefferson's other explorations. The Federalists had correctly pointed out that Jefferson needed proof for Congress of the U.S. government's progress in the new territory. He wanted proof for Madrid, too. The Ouachita expedition promised it, but the downward risk was even steeper than all upward potential. Failure would inevitably reflect on subsequent scientific projects.

Hunter, on his return from New Orleans, reported to the Forest, where Dunbar was as hospitable as ever, though he was feeling ill and staying in bed. While Dunbar recovered, Hunter purchased a "large Canoe to enable us to cross barrs and shallows." After storing it on the boat, he rechecked the supplies, including presents for the Indians and food for the expedition: flour, bacon, and whiskey, along with 10 gallons of molasses, 100 pounds of brown sugar, 40 pounds of coffee and 4 pounds of tea. He also stocked what he called "Hospital Stores," in case anyone became sick. Soon after all of that had been delivered and secured in the boat, Dunbar called Hunter into his room and calmly handed him a shopping list of extra food solely for the officers:

> 240 pounds of brown sugar
> 40 pounds chocolate
> 50 pounds of coffee
> 6 pounds of tea of the Hyson variety
> 60 pounds of lump sugar
> 30 gallons of molasses
> 17 gallons of brandy
> 12 bottles of Madeira
> 2 bottles of cucumbers
> Pepper, mustard, cloves, nutmeg
> 12 bottles of smoked anchovies
> 3 boxes of smoked herring

1 case of gin

1 box of split peas

The part of the boat holding the officers' food was apparently going to sit low in the water. And there were only three officers: Dunbar, Hunter, and an army lieutenant named Wilson.

As September began, Vial and his expedition were closing in on Lewis and Clark. A tribe of Pawnees some distance from the Missouri River gave Vial an accurate estimate of the location of the Americans, who were by then moving up the river only about one hundred miles away in what is now Nebraska. Vial decided not to give chase, despite the fact that he could have expected to catch up before winter. The weather may have been a factor anyway. Vial was familiar with the peoples and terrain in the Lower Midwest and the Comancheria, but he may not have been as confident continuing into the Northern Plains, populated by a very different set of Indian nations. A further factor, underscoring the others, was that Lewis and Clark would be available at a later date; they were on a long, long trip. By the end of September, Vial headed home to Santa Fe; Lewis and Clark, still unaware that anyone had been ordered to "force them to retire or take them prisoners," were safe from the Spanish for the time being.

As September drew to a close, Dunbar had yet to regain his strength and close his business at the Forest. With nowhere to bivouac the soldiers in the interim, Hunter prepared to find camping grounds near Natchez—someplace not unlike Fort Wood, the staging area on the Mississippi River used by Lewis and Clark. First, though, Dunbar unexpectedly invited the army officer Lieutenant Wilson to dine at the Forest. Over the course of the meal, he told Wilson to return to New Orleans, that he wouldn't be needed on the short journey. Hunter was probably away scouting camps, but it's likely that he knew what Dunbar had in mind. There is no reason to think Wilson was dismissed because he wasn't a good officer, although he had been in trouble in a previous posting at West Point over a duel. The difference probably lay with Dunbar. He took his role as master seriously and was certain he could handle the peacetime soldiers on his own, without the help of a military man. He also may have worried about wasting the services of an officer in treacherous times. Whatever the reason, Dunbar dispatched Wilson, leaving just himself and Hunter to lead the soldiers.

Sailing a few miles south, Hunter found an amicable spot called St. Catherine's Landing, full of fish, game, and sunshine, at which to await Dunbar. Nearby, white bluffs reached two hundred feet over the river. Hunter was nominally in charge of thirteen army men and his son, George Heriot. About two weeks later, on October 16, Dunbar arrived in grand style, feeling strong and sweeping onto the Chinese boat with two slaves, a personal servant, his luggage, and a collection of wooden cases. The luggage was loaded on the boat, followed much more carefully by the cases containing his scientific instruments. He probably couldn't help noticing that the boat, fully loaded, sank into the water with a draft of two feet. His gaze would then have shifted to the bow, and all of the tons of water in front of it that had to be moved so that it could go forward. It was, in effect, a snowplow rather than a sled.

Several of the boxes remained on the riverbank, including one containing Dunbar's exquisite circle of reflection, made in London. Dunbar needed to start the trip by taking readings, although he was only a matter of a few miles from the marker that he and Ellicott had set seven years before. He knew without looking that they were within range of the nationally famous 31st parallel.

To take his initial readings, Dunbar carefully set up a stand for the circle, something that impressed Hunter all by itself. "Mr. Dunbar's excellent Circle of Reflection," he wrote, "being supported by a pedestal of brass with three feet, rests solid on the ground, & nicely contrived by a variety of joints & screws, so as to be capable of every kind of motion however minute, & so well balanced as to rest there; by which the Observer is enabled to be very exact & minute & have as great confidence in his operations as any instrument can give." Dunbar did not want for confidence; he was the man who had recently detected a running error in the standard reference book, published in London, listing the sun's diameter on each date of the year. And so he used his equipment to make his own corrected measurement and then calculated the latitude, choosing to use a more sophisticated equation instead of the standard one.

In the field of celestial navigation, Dunbar's mind could be simultaneously occupied by three versions of the same idea: the almost infinite one of the geometric relationship of the heavenly bodies and the Earth; the mechanical one depicted in the gauges and needles of his instruments; and the abstract one, captured by the equations at his disposal. Dunbar was at home in all three. Watching him take his readings and puzzle them through to a latitude and longitude made others on his trips watch with awe and feel like fumblers.

Within two hours, with the expedition ready to leave at last, Dunbar dutifully made note of his readings: latitude 31°26'30" North. Carrying through the data collected for the longitude, he wrote: "6h 5' 56"—west of Greenwich." To reach the Ouachita, which was to the north, the expedition first had to go south on the Mississippi River and turn northwest onto the Red River. After another turn, on the Black River, a short stretch almost due north would then lead to a fork, one prong of which was the Ouachita. Overall, the route would be shaped something like a fishhook.

Hunter provided a succinct description of the expedition, as it must have looked from the banks of the river:

> Our Boat was made somewhat in the form of a ferry flat, with a mast fixed to strike occasionally, & were provided with a

large sail, manned with 12 men and a Sargeant, rowed twelve
oars, was 50 feet long & about 8 feet beam on deck at the
mast which was her extreme breadth, tapering to the stern.

With eighteen men aboard, it would have been a crowded deck
even if had it been completely empty otherwise. But it was also laden
with provisions for three months, scientific equipment, and luggage.
Most of the supplies were stored on the ship in what was called the
"pavilion," an awning equipped with tarpaulins that could be lowered in rough weather. Some of the deck space was also taken by a
cabin at the back for the use of the officers. Without room to walk
a straight line, the boat was a machine for transport but nothing
more.

At about three in the afternoon, the Chinese boat pushed away
from the bank with all hands on deck. The exploration of the southern part of the Louisiana Territory had begun. The sail was hoisted,
oversized and very white, snapping full of wind to carry the boat
easily into the channel and downriver.

Eleven

———

RIVER OF DIRT

Within an hour, the wind from the north that had so cheerfully escorted the Chinese boat out of St. Catherine's shifted. The soldiers reluctantly pulled down the sail and took seats at the oars, fighting against newly southern winds. With the Mississippi offering little in the way of a current, it was as discouraging as ever to have to row downstream—and row hard, at that, to make headway.

There was a choice, of course. If one didn't have to make real progress, one didn't have to row hard—and the soldiers didn't. Dunbar looked at them, and his watch, and the apparatus that he'd brought to measure the distance covered by the boat. Dunbar's regard for time was more emphatic than that of most others—more modern, in fact. In an era when being busy was not yet a bragging point, Dunbar dismissed leisure and expected a steep return from his days. Constantly looking at time in terms of success or failure, he wanted to get to the hot springs and back as soon as possible. Two days into the trip, though, as the boat turned from a southern course on the Mississippi to a brief westward push on the lower Red River, he dutifully noted the vines and willows on the riverbanks, the ducks and geese eating "greedily" there, and then he settled down to business and calculated that the boat was averaging 1¼ miles per hour.

"Very slow," Dunbar wrote, as though he were trapped. "Soldiers do not exert themselves at the oar," he complained, "came to, for the night having made nearly 13 miles." Dunbar made his point, but used a rounded-off distance, which was uncharacteristic for him: the geographer's equivalent of a slow oar. Later in his journal entry, he fastidiously corrected his own notation, revising it to "$12\,^{55}/_{60}$ miles."

On the same day, October 18, traveling upriver against a lively current, the Lewis and Clark expedition beat the progress of the Dunbar-Hunter boat by a half mile—or $^{35}/_{60}$ of one. They made 13½ miles that day, and that was in the choppy water of the Missouri River—where they could count themselves grateful that there was enough water to be choppy. Over the previous weeks, the going had been rugged for the men assigned to keep the boats moving. In increasingly shallow water, the river bottom caught the hull of the main boat so often that on some days, the expedition made as little as 4 miles. With the air turning cold, the crew was forced to wade around in water that was even colder, extricating the boat with brute force or reloading crates so that it might actually float on its own. Two of the men, John Newman and the former deserter Moses Reed, groused openly about the task in front of them. Newman went so far as to blame the captains for the struggles that dogged the expedition's progress. Normally, at least some muffled remarks might be expected from people doing heavy labor in frigid water, especially after weeks of much the same thing. But Newman and Reed were in the army and more than that, they were in a tightly operated unit. The captains charged them with insubordination.

After a review, Reed was exonerated (he was already set to be banished at the Mandan villages), but Newman was taken into custody and confined to one part of the boat. Sensitive to any blush of disloyalty, the captains charged him with

> having uttered repeated expressions of a highly criminal and mutinous nature; the same having a tendency not only to distroy every principle of military discipline, but also to alienate the affections of the individuals composing this Detachment to their officers, and disaffect them to the service for which they have been so sacredly and solemnly engaged.

A court-martial was convened on October 13. Two hours later, the majority in a jury of Newman's peers among the men found him guilty. Private Newman was "discarded from the perminent party engaged for North Western discovery," meaning that he would be returned to St. Louis after the expedition reached the Mandan villages. Furthermore, he was reassigned from his usual work to "drudgeries . . . to the general relief of the detachment," and, more immediately, he was to receive a flogging on his bare back. As far as Lewis and Clark knew, the most lashes allowed in the U.S. military was a hundred (the number was officially reduced to fifty while the expedition was under way). On the morning of October 14, Newman took seventy-five whip strikes on his bare back.

The punishment was witnessed by a chief from the Arikara tribe, who was deeply upset, crying openly at the sight of the beating. Clark carefully explained to him that the lashing was intended in part as a deterrent to others. The chief agreed in theory, but not with the method. He "observed that examples were necessary," Clark wrote. "He himself had made them by Death, but his nation never whiped."

Dunbar decided to address his own problem with discipline in the ranks on the third morning out of St. Catherine's landing. Only a few days—long days—from the Ouachita River and the main push of the expedition, he called the men together, in his role as titular head of the expedition. "Having given the Soldiers this morning a few words of advice and encouragement," he later reported, "they improved considerably in activity and cheerfulness." Under normal circumstances, those doing the rowing don't tend to be cheered by advice, especially not from a man traveling with three servants, but Dunbar had his say. He delighted in the response.

All Jefferson's expeditions were faced with the same concern—maintaining discipline in isolation from the rest of society. That challenge is commonly associated with ships at sea. The detachments in the Louisiana Territory were no different, as self-sufficient bodies of men, far from the evidence of order. Out in the wilderness, people weren't held in place by the proximity of judges and jails, payrolls and bills, major generals, older sisters, newspaper columns, and all the other ominous reminders of the fragility of an unbothered life. The dangers of disobedience were still lacking in the Louisiana Territory, yet so were the dangers of a truly life-threatening environment that hang over ships at sea to motivate discipline in the ranks. Neither the Missouri nor the Ouachita had yet presented enough risk to frighten the men into cooperation. Without society at large and without danger, the leaders had to establish their own hold over the men. Dunbar gave advice in a pep talk. Lewis and Clark, by contrast, were at the ready with a whip.

The difference showed was a very basic contrast between a man who made his living as a slaveholder and two who were military officers. Dunbar, who believed so firmly in the dominance of the white master, was nonetheless constantly intimidated by the slaves working his plantations. He related to them in extremes: bribes for productive behavior and killing or torture for any sign of revolt. He wasn't any different from any other slaveholder whose prosperity was balanced on a needle of fear.

Lewis and Clark, both of whom did own slaves, were trained in command by something else—their army experience. It was a key reason they were chosen to lead the longest of Jefferson's western expeditions; they knew exactly why they were in charge. In a military outfit, the officer's role as "master" is secure, granted by common advantage and mutual subscription to the hierarchy—two factors not known at the Forest or any similar plantation. Lewis and Clark, may have been harsh, but they brought the entire army with them, losing no chance to remind the men of it. Whatever relationship prevailed at Fort Fayette existed every moment of the day on the Missouri.

Perhaps if Dunbar really knew why he was master of the workforce at the Forest, he might have been able to hold himself forth as master of the soldiers on the Chinese boat. Instead, he relied on advice and encouragement, with his first talk resulting in a record for the week of about $11\frac{1}{2}$ miles per day—less than the previous one of $12^{55}/_{60}$.

Dunbar and Hunter typically started the boat moving early, at about six a.m., stopping for a one-hour breakfast at eight. The men wedged themselves into position and pulled on oars for hours at a time, but when they stopped, it was almost a necessity that they get off the boat and stretch. At nine, they would start again, continuing until eleven thirty, when they stopped for a two-hour break, which offered the men another chance to rest while the leaders took measurements. Like Captain Clark, Dunbar relied on dead reckoning to note every turn in the course, taking readings for longitude and latitude only during the longer stops and when conditions allowed.

Of all of the rivers that the expedition navigated on the route to the hot springs, the Red offered the fewest choices for making stops. Though its waters were slow moving in October, it flooded every spring, leaving its low banks covered with a tangle of plants that could survive a few weeks or months underwater.

The October depth of the Red River, about six feet, was fortunately more than adequate for the boat, which had a draft of about two and a half feet. The water itself was opaque and heavily clouded with sediment—reddish, of course. That only made it mysterious, shrouding anything it chose to hide under the surface, and that obscurity was sure to make the boat travelers nervous, knowing that just beneath them lurked deadly alligators. Growing huge and yet invisible in their own murky world, Red River alligators calmly waited for prey to come within a snap of their jaws. They were the true lords of the Red, even when a long, narrow blur slipped by above.

With the threat of the alligators only increasing near the bank, Dunbar and Hunter had to choose their landings carefully, but they were taken aback one day when they spotted a canoe onshore. Looking carefully, they saw an African or African American man nearby, dressed shabbily in plain trousers and a shirt. At a time when clothes were sewn to order for nearly everyone, mass-produced (and usually ill-fitting) garments were easy to spot and immediately indicated that the wearer was a prisoner, a slave, or a common sailor. The man disappeared into the brush when the Chinese boat approached.

Eager to learn more, Hunter and Dunbar set a trap for him, landing near his abandoned canoe and encouraging the soldiers to enjoy their lunch. They departed as noisily as possible an hour later, but only after two of the soldiers had hidden themselves in the bushes. As the boat glided into the water, it made slower progress than ever, the oars hardly making a sound as they hit the water. Everyone was listening for some sort of commotion that might indicate their fellow crewmen had found the African. Before long, shouts could be heard. The boat turned around as quickly as an overloaded Chinese boat could.

Hunter and Dunbar's plan had worked. Shortly after he thought the party had left, the stranger had been drawn to the temporary encampment, probably looking for discarded food, and was easily captured by the soldiers. "They had got a black man," Hunter wrote, "a stout fellow who called himself Harry."

Harry claimed that he was free, but his clothes indicated otherwise. Dunbar described him as a "runaway negro," but Hunter wasn't quite as sure. "We took him into the Boat," Hunter continued. "He was half-famished, we gave him plenty of ham & biscuit to eat, which he devoured with a voracious appetite." Harry wouldn't say much about himself, but with a canoe on the Black River, he was well on his way to freedom in Nacogdoches, a few days away by water. Hungry and perhaps disoriented, he gladly accepted the invitation to accompany the expedition north. As he found a place helping the crew, he was treated as a free man, with no firm evidence to the contrary. There didn't have to be. Within a few days, a man stopped the boat, claiming to be Harry's master, and took him away. In a year when Americans were acutely aware that Spanish Texas was undermining their economy in the lower Mississippi Valley by offering a haven to Africans and African Americans, the prevailing attitude toward runaways was harsher than ever. Some owners would execute a runaway, especially a male; some would level other punishment, but there was almost no doubt that in Lower Louisiana in 1804, Harry's fate would be showcased to meet and match the image common among slaves of the life of freedom that awaited in Nacogdoches. The meeting in the wilderness with the Dunbar-Hunter expedition had seemed like a chance for Harry. It had been his undoing.

The expedition carried on. The Black River, which took the boat northward from the Red, was clear all the way to the bottom, its waters presenting a strong contrast to those of the Red. According to Hunter, the Black River also had fewer alligators than the Red and smaller ones, at that.

The banks of the Black River were also different. They were more "stable," to use Dunbar's word, than those of the Red—"more elevated," Hunter wrote, "dry and healthy." Dunbar took samples of the soil as the mud on the banks turned to marl and then to sandy granules and finally, along the Black, into a fine-grained, rich dark soil. With good land and clean water, the Black River offered an attractive place to live, except that even the higher points along the banks flooded in spring, during the rising waters that were known as "the great freshes." With accurate hydrology and a bit of poetry, the name reflected the fact that the top layer of soil was scoured out and replaced every spring. By the time the expedition reached the four-way intersection where the Black River became the Ouachita River, the men on the boat described seeing a house every so often—although "house" may have been a generous word. Dunbar described one of them as a "covered frame of rough poles without walls."

At first glance, the flimsy homesteads on the lower Ouachita River conjured up the disdain of Barón de Carondelet. Ten years later, Dunbar expressed a different opinion. His journal abruptly rang out with pride in the American settlers of the West, who put down roots, even when they had no walls. "How happy the contrast, when we compare the fortune of the new settler in the U.S. with the misery of the half starving, oppressed and degraded Peasant of Europe!!" he wrote—expending two of the only three exclamation points in his whole journal. The difference between the impoverished American settler and the impoverished European peasant was in fact the same as that between Carondelet's American squatters and Dunbar's Ouachita farmers: land ownership. Because of the Louisiana Purchase, Americans were entitled to buy their own holdings, and the earliest and most determined of them were already doing so along the lower Ouachita at absurd prices—as low as ten cents per acre.

At that first glance, the messy homes that the settlers built didn't look much different from those of the squatters who preceded them ten years before; the tip-off that a new era had begun could be detected in the use of the land. Squatters, if they cultivated anything at all, threw seeds into any fairly level, fairly clear patch. The first settlers, on the other hand, laid out fields intended to be perma-

nent. The fields were as regular as possible, because they weren't
to be abandoned after the first harvest, but plowed again the following year. The farmers situated themselves near a reliable source
of drinking water, though that wasn't hard to find along the river.
At the same time, however, they didn't want too much water and
needed the protection of either altitude or a natural levy during the
great freshes. Squatters had no such concerns, showing up in April
after the water receded and leaving before winter.

From the deck of the boat, Dunbar and Hunter witnessed the actual beginnings of Ouachita settlement. Schemers like Bastrop had
tried to settle the rich sections of Ouachita before, in league with
the Spanish, but promises of enduring hospitality from His Catholic
Majesty had a hollow ring. And the plans of the hustlers were far too
grand, as they unfurled maps showing bird's-eye views of bustling
cities surrounded by plantations. What Dunbar and Hunter saw—
people making homes of nothing more than a roof and the sound
of flapping tarpaulins—that was the beginning of U.S. civilization
in the West and the absorption fifty acres at a time of the Louisiana
Purchase.

One of the earliest European settlers in the vicinity, a Monsieur
Cadet, arriving from southeastern France eighteen years before, had
been given his choice of locales. He selected well in terms of the geography, at a site near the four-way intersection of rivers: the Cata-
houla River's entry into the Black, and the Tensas River's entry into
the Ouachita. Touring his property, Dunbar and Hunter agreed
that it presented an inevitable locale for a large city. Five thousand
years before, an Indian tribe had felt the same way, literally lifting
the landscape into a geometric pattern. Monsieur Cadet had built
his home on an ancient mound that kept it well above the highest
waters in spring. Hunter marveled at the size of the mound, "100
feet broad & 300 feet long" and two stories high. The Frenchman,
he noted, "took the pains to go round with Mr. Dunbar my son
& me to shew us the curiosities of the place." Of course, they were

then standing on one of the curiosities. Moreover, they were in the shadow of the most astounding man-made sight in the whole region, an earthen tower growing out of the mound and reaching eighty feet in height. Hunter reasoned that it and the mounds in general had been even bigger when they were new. The discovery was the kind Jefferson sought, proving that American civilizations were far from primitive.

"If one may judge from the immense labor necessary to erect those Indian monuments to be seen here," Hunter wrote, "this place must have once been very populous." The visit to the enormous mounds was enthralling for both Hunter and Dunbar, offering a glimpse at a world unlike anything they'd seen before on the trip—or even in their lives. As they gathered the men and resumed the journey, however, the problems of managing the expedition remained. Dunbar watched over the crew for another day, as they made only nine miles in easy waters. It just wasn't a good trip for a man carrying a watch, especially one as obsessed with efficiency as he was. Dunbar wrote that evening:

> Made slow advancement as usual with our oars; found the shore favorable for tracking or towing, which mode we continued nearly all day making at the rate of five perches pr. ½ minute, which is about half a perch more than by rowing

The "perch" is a unit of measure that was obsolete even in 1804, having been rejected in part because it was so local in definition. For a Briton, a perch could reflect any distance from 10 to 24 feet, depending on the consensus of the neighborhood; Dunbar assumed 16½ feet. Even the modern man of science reverted to the way his father had taught him to put numbers to land back in the hills of Moray. His fellow Scotsman, Dr. Hunter, joined in the use of the perch, at least in his notes. On the basis of a 16½-foot perch, Dunbar's evidence was that the boat was moving at 1.87 miles per hour when pulled by men walking onshore, a slight improvement over the 1.69 miles per hour it made when rowed. Either way, the boat couldn't even have kept up with the average duck, which paddles along at 2 miles per hour. With abundant time to consider the matter, Dunbar concluded that it was unlikely they would ever speed up. "Our Soldiers seem at certain times to be without vigour," he observed, "& now and then throw out hints that they can work only as they are paid."

The crew had apparently discovered, despite Dunbar's pep talks, that there was no officer on board. With every mile that the expedition slipped farther away from Natchez and New Orleans, Washington, and London, the twelve soldiers became nothing more than twelve men, who seemed more and more convinced that the "service for which they have been so sacredly and solemnly engaged" was ferrying a couple of rich businessmen to the springs. The only thing sacred about that was the chance to extract extra pay from the one with three servants and a jar of smoked anchovies. If the men were staging an unspoken slowdown strike on the trip, the weather was on their side, with temperatures that ranged between sixty-eight and seventy-five degrees Fahrenheit. Days went by and didn't seem to matter.

The fact that progress was disappointing presented problems to Dunbar in particular. He was more sensitive than Hunter to the fact that the president had authorized the Ouachita trip largely to commission a fresh stream of news regarding the Louisiana Territory. To that end, Dunbar and Hunter were diligent in collecting scientific data on the environment of the river. Moreover, they took measurements for the calculation of the latitude and longitude several times per day if the sky was clear. Unlike the captains to the north, each took his own readings, and with two separate sets of instruments, to boot. Hunter—a chemist by training—fumbled with the sextant he'd brought from Philadelphia, which was intended for use on ships. Mostly, it was giving an accurate reflection of the shakiness of his hands. Like a struggling student in the next row, he couldn't help noticing how confidently Dunbar came up with the right answers.

To indicate the horizon, Hunter's sextant featured an artificial mercurial horizon, which was a narrow box partially filled with mercury. It sprung a leak the day after the expedition left the Indian mounds. Hunter was left a thousand miles from Philadelphia without an artificial horizon. There was no way for him to continue the readings. If he looked around, he would've felt a thousand *years* from Philadelphia, finding himself in a part of the river that Dunbar described as a veritable tunnel primeval:

> The twining vines entangle the branches of the trees & expand themselves along the margin of the river, in the richest and most luxuriant festoons, and often present for a great extent a species of impenetrable Curtain variegated and spangled with all possible gradations of Color from the splendid orange to the enlivening green down to the purple & blue and interwoven with bright red and russet brown.

Like Lewis and Clark, both Hunter and Dunbar—well-traveled men, all—were often stunned by the overabundance of color in the American West. Late in October, the vegetation was still in full bloom along the river, a shock to the eyes even of Dunbar, who lived only about twenty miles away. "The ground here," Hunter marveled, "is inexhaustibly fertile."

On a stretch that had been called "rapids" by Monsieur Cadet, the French settler, Hunter and Dunbar met their comeuppance for the deep, easy course they'd described day after day as "gentle with little current." Instead, they were met by the opposite combination: rushing water, barely knee deep. "The rapids or rather shallows," Dunbar called them. Already suspicious that the Chinese boat was too heavy, he was no longer counting miles per hour. The whole affair was beginning to depress him. After the boat became little more than a sledge, the best he could hope for was a mile a day. "Sent people into the water to search the best channel," he wrote on October 25, "and after being frequently aground and dragging the boat, we got up into a situation about a mile higher, where we were in a manner embayed, being shut in by a gravel bar upon which there was scarsely in the deepest part a foot of water."

Hunter, for his part, was anything but discouraged, referring to the shallows as "but a trifling obstruction." Nonetheless, the expedition was in trouble, attempting to move a massive boat, suited to the South China Sea, up a trickling brook. Hunter and Dunbar thought it best to give the crew the rest of the afternoon off. Embracing the challenge of finding a channel, Hunter waded into the current to see if the water, in any direction, happened to be deeper than it looked. Quite the opposite, in examining the gravel bar, he found that the water above it was only six inches deep in some places. What they needed for the boat was a set of wheels.

Instead, Hunter staked out the course for a channel, 108 feet long. It would have to be dug out by the men, to a depth of at least 2½ feet. He laid it out so that whatever current existed would flush the loose gravel away. The men understood the idea. Perhaps it was ominous that they didn't use the word "channel." They called it a "canal."

Work was to start the next morning, but there was plenty to do in preparation. Hunter was using his extra time during that part of the journey to resuscitate the sextant—just another "trifling obstruction," as far as he was concerned. He started with the construction of a pedestal, which he fashioned out of a combination of wood and buffalo horn, picked up somewhere in his travels. As a chemist, he was able to devise a way of "balancing the weight of the Sextant with lead cast in sand for the purpose." Having made the sextant immobile, he then had to find a way of making it, conversely, adjustable. "Instead of screws," he explained, he "used wedges, to

tighten or slacken the several joints, thereby acquiring full command of every motion." The pedestal, created on a backriver, was
ingenious. He was still left with the problem of his artificial horizon,
which differed from the natural one in that his dripped mercury.

The next morning, the temperature was unfortunately low, at
about forty degrees Fahrenheit. Dunbar and Hunter decided to
allow the men to have breakfast before tackling the channel. That
was a change from the routine, in which the men worked for a couple of hours before getting any food, and it indicated the inclination of the leaders to ameliorate a difficult situation—the soldiers,
already lacking motivation, were being asked to work harder than
ever. After they had eaten, the digging of the channel began.

The morning was clear, and while travel was stalled as the men
kept digging, Dunbar took advantage of the break. "The day being
fine," he wrote, "made some observations for the regulation of the
watch & for the magnetic variation." Regulating a watch by the
position of the sun is an advanced procedure; by the time Dunbar
was finished, his watch was as accurate as any in or out of the Royal
Observatory in Greenwich.

The separate and even more difficult challenge of accounting for
the magnetic variation required a long page of calculations. Dunbar
busied himself with that and then took a reading. "At noon," he
reported, "had a fine observation, from which the Latitude of this
remarkable place was ascertained to be 31°.48' .57".5." It was good
that Dunbar thought that part of the river remarkable.

After a morning of working on the channel, the soldiers quit.
The uprising couldn't be called a mutiny, it being hard to mutiny
when the boat won't budge. Setting the captain adrift in a dinghy
was out of the question. They were surrounded by gravel. But the
soldiers did calmly and resolutely refuse to continue digging, even
though the channel was not yet at the specified depth. "When midday came the channel was but half done," Hunter wrote. "The men
seemed jaded or unwilling to work at it any more."

As a compromise, Hunter and Dunbar agreed that they would try to move the boat through the channel despite its unfinished state. The men consented to work from the boat and use leverage to nudge it along with poles called pikes. "It was concluded," Hunter acknowledged, "to try to force the boat thro it with hand pikes. This we attempted & got thro only a few feet when we were obliged to stop for want of force." They were gondoliers in dirt.

Dunbar's report was terse: "After dinner [the midday meal], the boat was moved into the channel, where she stuck fast."

Twelve

LOUISIANA FRESHES

Even with the boat resting on dirt, thereby blocking the only channel, Hunter remained optimistic and resourceful, examining the alternatives. Dunbar was gentlemanly, if nothing else. Had it not been for his respect for Jefferson, one can assume that he would have called his servants, packed his gourmet food, and walked home to the Forest. As it was, the head of a nation was awaiting their observations and so they all waited, if not for the great freshes five months hence, then for someone to think of a new way to move the boat. With Dunbar's watch working perfectly, he could listen to it tick, whether he wanted to or not.

ON THE MISSOURI River, the northern expedition was in what is now South Dakota in the third week of October, seeing cold rain, sleet, or snow every day. The corps was anxious to reach the Mandan villages, in order to set up winter quarters; with each passing day, they were vulnerable to early winter storms. They knew, however, that they had to pass other Indian homelands first.

South of the Mandan villages along the river lay the Arikara (sometimes known among themselves as the Sahnish), a nation of affiliated villages near the confluence of the Grand River. The Arikara had lived along the Missouri for about a thousand years, longer than any of their neighbors. To the south of them was the larger Teton (or Lakota) nation; they had been in the region for about a hundred and fifty years. Effective hunters and fierce warriors, they terrified most of the Europeans who had tried to navigate the Missouri River. Only the previous month, the Tetons had put Lewis and Clark into a nervous state of defense, the first since the expedition began.

While Clark was onshore with three of his men, a band of Teton warriors nearby seized the towrope of the keelboat, as though to take charge of it. Immediately, they drew their bows. In response, Clark raised his sword. As soon as Lewis, standing on the boat, saw that arms had been brandished, he ordered the men on deck to draw their guns, even training the swivel gun at the bow on the warriors. The Tetons backed down.

The tribe was even more frightening the next night at a banquet intended to make amends. Amid the speeches by the chiefs and dancing by the women, the Tetons conspicuously displayed the evidence of a raid on an Omaha village thirteen days before: sixty-five scalps and more than two dozen prisoners, all of them women and children—sending what they hoped was a very clear message to their American guests. It was the Teton policy to be aggressive; they had that reputation and benefited from it. Lewis and Clark were supposed to recognize that the Tetons needed to be feared.

But Clark, in particular, refused to notice their efforts. When they served roasted dog as the main course, he disdained it. He also gave gifts to the prisoners to cheer them up. And when women were offered for companionship, he and Lewis flatly refused them, on behalf of the entire corps. All three actions bordered on diplomatic insults, yet there was a message to be returned to the Lakota regarding America's own aggressiveness. The fact that the Lakota chose not to take offense betrayed their respect for the captains.

Clark, a voracious carnivore, reduced the population of practically every North American species as he traveled on the expedition yet could not bring himself to look on dogs as food. Oddly enough, Lewis, who was entirely attached to Seaman, a companion dog he'd purchased in Pittsburgh, had no such misgivings, to the detriment of hundreds of dogs en route.

After leaving the Teton country, Lewis and Clark were understandably on edge, and in mid-October, when they arrived at the Grand River, they were tentative in approaching the Arikara. The Arikara were used to visitors' hesitations after more than a hundred years of living next to the belligerent Tetons. They knew how to greet travelers who had skirted their warlike neighbors on the way north, and how to make them feel once again at ease. The Arikara were planters and because of their dependence on farming, Arikara villages were permanent, unlike those of the Tetons, and they were well fortified. Typically, they consisted of earthen lodges, surrounded by a deep ditch, as well as a stockade of pointed poles. At Grand River, Lewis and Clark encountered two Arikara villages in close proximity on the west side of the river (or the "left side," as Clark described it). A third was located at that time on an island four miles to the south.

The Arikara were part of a loose confederation that stretched across what is now South Dakota, northern Nebraska, and eastern Montana, with bands living quite independently. They didn't even speak the same dialect, as Clark noted: "Their language is So corrupted that many lodges of the Same village with dificuelty under Stand all that each other Say."

The Arikara were united most significantly by their religious be-
liefs, which revolved around the "sacred bundle" of artifacts and
icons that each village treasured and used during rituals. The Arikara were one of the only peoples encountered by Lewis and Clark
to dedicate a building in each village to religion (though the same
structure could also be used by the village doctor, medicine being
another Arikara priority). They believed in a number of deities, but
depended on one as a matter of everyday life, called Mother Corn.
She remained a constant presence in the tribe, reportedly the most
reliable friend that human beings had. Mother Corn was also said
to have given the Arikara the main staple of their diet and whole
way of life.

The captains handed out presents as usual, but the Arikara were
unique in giving the expedition equally important gifts: corn in
various forms, cooked, baked, or on the cob, each with the hope
that it would influence a tie between the visitors and Mother Corn,
their entity of goodness. In exchange, Lewis and Clark were giving
the Arikara flags, medals, and certificates in order to induce them to
bond with the Great Father—Thomas Jefferson.

The Arikara weren't always quite so benevolent, having recently
killed two Mandan chiefs and subsequently finding themselves in
a state of war. They seemed to regret the murders and made the
suggestion to send one of their chiefs north with Lewis and Clark
to work out a peace agreement. The captains were delighted to accept, since fostering peace among the tribes was one of the directives
they'd received from the president. The chief chosen for the trip was
named Ar-ketarna-Shar. As the expedition left the Arikara settlements in mid-October, one of the other chiefs bade them a memorable farewell, saying, "We Shall look at the river with impatience
for your return."

Some of the other tribal members didn't say good-bye, though.
They followed the expedition. "The Ricaras," Clark explained, referring to the Arikara, "have a custom Similar to the Sioux in maney

instances, they think they cannot Show a Sufficient acknowledge-
ment without [sending?] to their guest handsom Squars [squaws]
and think they are despised if they are not recved[.] The Sioux followed us with women two days we put them off. The Ricarries we
put off dureing the time we were near their village—2 were Sent by
a man to follow us, and overtook us this evening, we Still procisted
[persisted] in a refusial—"

The refusal seems to have dissolved soon thereafter. Within
two days, Sergeant Gass was referring to one or both of the women
as "our squaw," and at another Arikara settlement along the river,
Clark reported with no further concern that "their womin verry
fond of carressing our men." The Arikara were a highly spiritual
people, who placed an emphasis on the intangibles to be gained
from the other person in a sexual encounter: strength, knowledge,
or power. But at the same time, women in the society were accorded
little power over their own lives. The desire of the Arikara women
for the Corps of Discovery emanated from cultural dimensions that
the members of the expedition didn't pause to understand. Whether
it reflected part of the Arikara's spiritual discipline or a complex system of relationship, the Americans indulged without any such basis.
In that, there was a risk.

Soldiers by nature are expected to suspend and then readopt basic
mores, in combat and then back on the home front. The transition
back and forth can be more hellish than the battlefield, because during the transition, however long it takes, there is no norm. For the
members of the Lewis and Clark expedition, the suspension of their
own mores when they came in contact with the Indian nations was
quite the opposite of battle, bringing not horrors, but the guiltless
pleasure of a liaison unlike any in the United States—unlike any,
because it didn't have to be arranged, induced, concealed, limited,
remunerated, or sanctified. Taking one part of the Indian culture,
without all of the rest of it, though, the Americans were, by definition, going a little wild. Consuming the dog meat was another

example of a line not crossed back in the United States. For most members of the expedition, suspending their own society's rules for the duration wouldn't matter at all. The same kind of actions put others, though, in a state of transition that wouldn't lead them back easily when the trip was over.

On October 25, Lewis and Clark were on board the keelboat, making only fair progress at a rate of about eleven miles per day, but with no particular effort, thanks to gentle winds on the sail. The Missouri River, which leans to the northwest as it passes through the present-day state of North Dakota, widens into bodies of water that look like lakes in mid-autumn, when the waters are not pushed from upriver. As Lewis and Clark made their way north so late in the season, the waters were, like those of the Ouachita, dangerously shallow for a large boat. Looking at the map John Evans had made while searching for Welsh Indians, the captains were aware that the Mandan villages were drawing near, though. If the map didn't tell them, then the increase in traffic along the river would have made it obvious. The five Mandan villages served as the commercial capital of an extensive region, stretching across the plains from the northern Great Lakes to the Rocky Mountains.

The sky was cloudy, and the temperature barely above freezing, but the brisk day brought the wind that the crewmen loved best: a gentle one from the southeast. It filled the sail of the keelboat and guided it up the river, past rounded hills mostly barren of grass. The trip was pleasantly monotonous until the crewmen were sure they heard something. As the boat drew a little farther up the river, "a great many of the natives," as Patrick Gass wrote, "some on horseback and some on foot appreared on the hills on the north side, hallooing and singing."

The members of the expedition were looking at the Indians gathering on the "up land," as Clark called the rises overlooking the river. The Indians were looking back. Yet the Americans couldn't pay a visit, the boat being stopped in the only navigable water, which was on the opposite side of the river. Even though it was still afloat, the captains were fearful that the increasing number of sandbars ahead would stop it completely and stall any further progress.

With the plan to send at least one barge full of materials and notes from the Mandan villages the following spring, Lewis wanted to complete the first leg without any last-minute problem. It was true that the Mandans and their allies could be aggressive on territorial matters, but their priority was trade. Placing a premium on commerce that was downright Hanseatic, they took great interest in new arrivals, and so it was that the Mandans made their way down the riverbank in droves the following day to see the boats of the expedition, piled high with goods.

As evening fell, Lewis grew edgy and decided to walk on to the first village. Clark preferred to watch over the boat, probably never straying too far from the swivel gun. His rheumatism was flaring up again as the temperatures sank toward freezing during October. Lewis was perfectly willing to go by himself, a lifelong predilection. He was accompanied by several Indians and an interpreter, but it was an intrepid gesture, nonetheless. It was also abrupt. But Lewis felt he had no time to waste; he had promised Jefferson to reach the Mandan villages before winter and so it was that on October 26, he set off on his own, determined to make it a reality.

DURING THE DIMMING days of late October, Jefferson was at the presidential mansion in Washington, a couple of weeks away from the election. His campaigning seemed to consist mainly of telling people in and around town that the current race would be his last and that he could hardly wait to return to private life at his farm after his term. While others handled the sharp politicking, Jefferson could afford to protest his passion for leaving office, four years before the fact. He knew perfectly well that he would be reelected.

Aaron Burr knew perfectly well that he wouldn't be. He spent the heart of the campaign season in a rented house on St. Simons Island off the Georgia coast. Burr's nearest neighbor lived a half mile away. Except for a staff of servants, he was alone in the house, and by every expectation of human emotion he should have been despondent. He knew that he was ruined politically, even telling people to stop bothering to call him "vice-president." He was ruined financially. And he couldn't go back to his former home, as he was facing charges in New York for arranging a duel and was in the process of being indicted, in absentia, in New Jersey for the deadly outcome. "The subject in dispute," he joked, "is which shall have the honour of hanging the vice-president."

If Burr wondered how things could get any worse, he didn't have to wait long. Right on cue, as in the last act of a melodrama, nature unleashed a terrifying and ultimately deadly hurricane on the Georgia coast.

Burr thought the thrashing storm was "distressing," but nothing would convince him that he was in any last act. For those who watched him closely, that was exactly the problem. He was the monster of optimism. Burr still wanted to be a leader for anyone seeking their lost liberties, but he needed somewhere to put them, and himself. While he was in the South, he made a concerted effort to visit Florida. He never divulged the reason for his trip, but Florida was foreign soil, belonging to the Spanish. The only thing that Burr found there, circa 1804, was women smoking cigars.

Burr was, in fact, on course to return to Washington, which was for the moment the perfect theater for him. Bright as ever, he had a merry time wherever he was welcomed en route to the capital. Without coincidence, General Wilkinson, the commander of the army, was also on his way to Washington in late October. Wilkinson intended to be named the governor of the Territory of Louisiana, and he wasn't at all discouraged by the fact that it didn't yet exist. As of October 1, the original Purchase was divided into two sections, known colloquially as Lower and Upper Louisiana. The Lower section, which was by far the more glamorous of the two, embraced much of present-day Louisiana (including, of course, New Orleans) and some of southern Arkansas. Upper Louisiana encompassed everything to the north. They might as well have been called Moneymaking Louisiana and Money-Losing Louisiana. The former, Lower Louisiana, was officially called Orleans Territory and a swarm of people campaigned privately to be named governor there. After Jefferson's own choice, the Marquis de LaFayette, turned it down, the appointment was won by W. C. C. Claiborne, a Jefferson loyalist who had formerly been the governor of Mississippi Territory. In truth, it wasn't an enviable posting.

There may well have been as many political factions as there were people in Orleans. One group of wealthy citizens marked the birth of the new territory by writing to Jefferson to express their utter lack of faith in the United States. To make their point, they wrote the document in French. Casa Calvo was still holding court, and only a bit more officially, so was Governor Salcedo—in fact, it was hard for most Orleanians to tell which was the shadow government, his or Claiborne's.

Upper Louisiana needed government, too, and would soon receive its own territorial designation. Once that was made, a governor would be appointed by President Jefferson and approved by the Senate. And so James Wilkinson headed for Washington. His interest in the governorship of the presumptive territory made him unique—but not just because he expected to hold both military and civilian power simultaneously. Wilkinson's new ambition distinguished him as one of the very few people with any interest at all in money-losing Upper Louisiana.

Working on his Annual Message to Congress, to be delivered November 8, Jefferson summed up the political situation in the Louisiana Purchase in terms so vague that they credited nothing to the present tense. Acknowledging that a "form of government thus provided having been considered but as temporary," he professed himself "open to such improvements as further information of the circumstances of our brethren there might suggest." He went on to discuss Upper Louisiana with few details and the assurance that at some point, "it will also be in its due state of organization."

Jefferson's interest in the practical administration of the new (or fairly new) Purchase was surprisingly offhand, a fact gratefully noted by everyone with a plan for tilting the future of the West—including the conniving Wilkinson. Those connected in any way to that future were looking at the region carefully in late October, perceiving it in one of two ways. They saw it either as an entity of land to be gained or as an entity of people—also to be gained. The two were not the same. As the people of Orleans sought strong leadership, Jefferson remained one of those who was then more interested in the land itself, as a thing of flags and borders.

In terms of both the West and the Deep South (the Floridas), Jefferson's mind was a map. Acquisition was his goal. Had he been to either Orleans Territory or Upper Louisiana, he might have been more aware of the imperative of the people there. Instead, awaiting his own version of the West, he anticipated the reports from Lewis and Clark, who were then on the verge of the Mandan villages, and from Dunbar and Hunter, who at that same moment were along the Ouachita River, hanging pulleys on the trees in an effort to keep their expedition moving forward.

Thirteen

MANDAN, AMATARI, AND MINITARÍ

The pulleys were Hunter's idea. His logic was that if the gravel of the shoal was strong enough to hold the boat tight, then what was needed was something even stronger. As he looked around the frontier, only one possibility presented itself. "I then got a runner & tackle fixed to a tree on the opposite bank," Hunter wrote. According to the plan, the battle would no longer match the gravel against the boat. It would be the gravel against the tree trunks, with the boat in between. It was an ingenious solution, except that it had the problem of so many brilliant ideas through the centuries—not enough rope.

When all of the spare lines on board wouldn't reach, the crew took down the mast and raided it for extra footage. With every scrap tied in, the span was finally met. "We then divided our force," Hunter wrote, "set six of our strongest men to use the hand pikes upon the boat in the water & the rest to the tackle ashore."

As the men pushed on pikes and tugged on ropes, the trees held hard, locking in every incremental gain. It was the gravel that gave way. The boat moved forward slowly, yet at the end of the day, it was still resting on gravel. The next morning, as Dunbar wrote, "the people were directed to get their breakfasts and prepare to use their exertions in getting the boat over the shoal." After another half day of digging, cursing, pulling, pressing, and prying, the boat made a final slide and "got entirely over into floating water," as Dunbar put it, "on the opposite shore." The only sensation more exhilarating for a boatman than that of being floated is that of being refloated. "The men," Dunbar wrote in the moment of euphoria, "upon this occasion exerted themselves to my entire satisfaction."

Hunter was likewise overjoyed. "We then dined & set forward & soon got thro the rest of the rapids; where we found the river as before a smooth, & peaceful stream with scarce any currents."

Both men were deluded. In Hunter's case, it wasn't long before he realized that they were not nearly through the rest of the rapids—or that "rapids" was a cruelly inaccurate word for that part of the Ouachita at the end of October. Two days later, the boat was stuck again. "Got on a shoal," Hunter wrote on October 31, "& were for some time embarrassed by the shallows." Dunbar didn't shrug off the situation as delicately:

> From the experience we have had of this river and the information obtained, it appears that the present is the least favorable season for ascending this river with a boat of so considerable a draught of water as ours; the spring of the year is the most advantageous, the Mississippi then flows up into the beds of the inferior rivers, raising their waters sometimes within a few feet of the top of the banks; the small current is then often in favor of the ascending boat . . . in our actual situation our dayly progress seldom equals 14 or 15 miles, which is a sad drawback upon the accomplishment of the objects of an exploring expedition.

Since the expedition had entered the so-called rapids, the mark for daily progress wasn't "14 or 15 miles" a day, as Dunbar had written. It wasn't even 4 or 5. On some days, they couldn't manage to move the boat a half mile. And yet they had to keep going: for Jefferson.

Analyzing the trip two weeks out, Dunbar tried to categorize the nature of the disaster in which he was enmeshed. It wasn't a spectacular, epochal disaster, like a shipwreck or a hurricane. It was an incremental disaster. In considering the situation, however, Dunbar hit on a problem at the core of Jefferson's western expeditions, both those in progress and those still in the planning stage.

Dunbar had been understandably frustrated to learn from locals that if he and Hunter had timed the expedition more cleverly, they could have taken their trip *downstream* to the north and then *downstream* again to the south, all on the same river. And yet, collecting such intelligence, or any facts at all, about a new place is the very purpose of exploration. On their expedition, Dunbar and Hunter—a pair of sophisticated scientists—were not engaged in "observation and research," as Dunbar had wistfully written, but in a test of brute strength, augmented with desperate field engineering. Leaving at the wrong time of year, they exemplified the fact that in exploration, somebody has to go on guesses, so that all others can follow more efficiently with informed decisions afterward. Lewis and Clark had yet to meet with such frustrations, in large part because they had yet to do any real exploring. The first part of their trip was based on Evans's map of the Missouri River, along with advice from people who had seen the region.

So it was on the Ouachita that instead of researching or observing, William Dunbar—the outstanding scientist of the South—was gathering evidence, day after day, on how much better boats work when there is water underneath.

Late on the evening of October 26, Lewis returned to the expedition's camp on the Missouri River after a brief walk to the first of the Mandan villages, Mitutanka. As early as possible the next morning, he and Clark formally approached the village on behalf of the United States and President Thomas Jefferson. They were politely received, and within days Lewis was standing before a council of chiefs, delivering "a long Speach Similar to what had been Said to the nations below," as Clark described it. If Lewis had given the same assurances and promises to Natives before, the chiefs had heard them all before, too, in one European language or another. One of the chiefs, an elderly Minitarí, grew "restless before the Speech was half ended" and slipped out early. His village, he had just remembered, was unprotected. He had quite possibly been more attentive when the French, British, and Spanish had expressed much the same sentiments over the previous fifty years.

The area known as the Mandan villages consisted, north to south, of two settlements occupied by the Mandans, one by the Amatari, and two by the Minitarí. The Minitarí lived on the Snake River, a relatively quiet tributary of the Missouri. In fact, the Minitarí had many names, including the Hidatsa, the Willows, the Hewaktoktu, and, most memorably, the Big Bellies. The last grew out of an error in translation that confused the Minitarí with another tribe actually known by that name (which derived from a tendency to beg). Despite the unfortunate mix-up, the Minitarí/Big Bellies were to be taken very seriously; they were relentless warriors when roused, making Lewis and Clark constantly wary of them during their stay near the Mandan villages.* The third tribe in the enclave, the Amatari, occupied the middle village of the five. More closely related to the Minitarí than the Mandans, they had a small population, about one-tenth the size of that of either of their neighboring nations.

———

* To further the confusion, Lewis and Clark later referred to the original Big Bellies, who lived farther west, as the Minitarí. The western Big Bellies referred to themselves as the Atsina.

DURING THE FIRST one hundred sixty days of the expedition, time had been loosely filled for Lewis and Clark, as well as the other members of the corps. Over the first three days at Mitutanka, though, everyone was in a rush. In addition to the excitement of arrival, the changing weather provided a strong imperative to settle in as soon as possible. The captains were scanning the lay of the land, looking for a site for the expedition's winter quarters; it would be made of wood.

The Mandans and their neighbors were more practical, living in earthen lodges called *amati* that had rounded roofs, guiding the winds of the plains up and over the building. The wood fortress that Lewis and Clark planned, on the other hand, would try to block it. Two or three families lived in each *amati*, bustling around a central fire pit, along with their horses and dogs. Whatever else the animals added to the atmosphere, they raised its temperature—as both species give off a lot of heat. The *amati* included bedsteads that were completely encased by hide curtains, the people sleeping three or four at a time on or under animal skins. Even during the coldest winters, the lodges were said to be comfortable and the tented beds warm.

Amid the cosmopolitan atmosphere of the Mandan villages, Lewis was pulled in every direction, continually meeting chiefs, as well as European traders who were on the scene doing business or using the villages as a base. Most of them were attached to the North West Company, which had a regional headquarters in undisputed British territory to the north, at a river called the Assiniboine. Lewis's dual diplomacy—establishing a benign sovereignty over the Indian nations while indicating a more prickly attitude toward the foreigners—was at the core of Jefferson's directives for the expedition. Lewis circulated almost continuously among the villages, presenting a New World concept of nonaggressive strength to each side. In company with Clark, he met the traders and held forth U.S. sovereignty over the territory, without touching on anything more controversial, such as impending changes in the rules for commerce. To the contrary, during the expedition's first week at the villages, Lewis wrote a formal letter to Charles Chaboillez, the Canadian fur trader serving as the North West Company agent at Assiniboine, promising American protection. "This we are disposed to do," he wrote, "as well from the pleasure we feel in becoming serviceable to good men, as from a conviction that it is consonant with the liberal policy of our government."

Lewis left murky the identity of those from whom the North West traders would be protected. It might have been marauding Indians, the troublesome Russians along the Pacific, or the Spanish— and every other Caucasian west of the Mississippi River. The people from whom the British in the Northern Plains truly needed protection, however, were the Americans. Perhaps not Lewis, perhaps not Clark, but the next wave and the one after that.

As a means of mutually agreeing to bide their time, Lewis and Chaboillez wrote correct, even sunny, letters back and forth across the plains. Even while Chaboillez was ingratiating himself with the Americans, he was hastily launching his own party to navigate the Upper Missouri and stake a claim to trade with the Indians there. The fact that the British expedition didn't transpire wasn't as significant as Chaboillez's response: competition for knowledge of the Missouri.

Another point of business that demanded Lewis's time was the need for accord between the Mandans and the Arikara, who were still feuding over the murder of two Mandan chiefs. Ar-ketarna-shar, the Arikara chief, pressed Lewis to proceed with the peace talks, a diplomatic challenge in view of the American reliance on the Mandans for accommodation during the winter. Lewis couldn't go too far in his seeking an accord on the criminal case if it meant risking the success of his expedition.

In the midst of the busy days of arrival at the Mandan villages, Lewis overlooked one of his duties. "The Chronometer ran down today," he wrote on October 29. "I was so much engaged with the Indians, that I omited winding her up.—"

The chronometer was a specialized pocket watch that had cost Lewis $250 in Philadelphia. He'd been guided in the purchase of it by Professor Patterson. At the cost of a small house, the chronometer was not, actually, supposed to keep perfect time. That's not only unrealistic for any watch, even up to the present time, but it's also unnecessary for an instrument used in celestial reckoning. The prime advantage of a chronometer—over a personal watch—is that it will gain or lose time at a predictable rate. In other words, accuracy isn't as important as consistency. But Lewis's chronometer offered neither. It ran slow at all different rates. And then it stopped, because Lewis didn't wind it.

Even in the open, Lewis and Clark had long since learned to set the chronometer using their artificial horizon and the sextant. The technique, known as equal altitudes, consists of noting the time on the chronometer during four readings of the sun's altitude in the morning and then again during the afternoon, with the sun at the corresponding altitudes. Averaging all of the times together results in a preliminary indication of the chronometer's relative accuracy to noon. Another calculation is needed to account for the declination of the sun, but the use of equal altitudes is fundamental in celestial navigation. In addition to its use in setting a chronometer, it was the main part of the most common and accessible means of deriving the longitude.

Lewis did not use equal altitudes, however, to derive longitude. Under the tutelage of Professor Patterson, he used a little-known method that worked even when visibility was less than perfect. Known as the Problem 4th, it was a great enthusiasm for Patterson, a man who, it should be remembered, had an unusual mind—one that reaped satisfaction from the endless expanses that open up in the abstract through complication. Most people prefer simplicity. Most explorers require it, being surrounded by an overabundance of endless expanses in the real world. Lewis, however, continually opted to take his measurements in keeping with the Problem 4th.

From the vantage of the route west, the stars and the moon were indeed obscured at times by clouds and at other times by mountains or trees. Perhaps for that reason, Lewis stayed with the Problem 4th, taking arcane readings for its revelation of the longitude. That is not to be regretted; he was the student of two expert mathematical astronomers, Patterson and Ellicott. Unfortunately, he was uncertain in the best of times and in possession of a dubious chronometer all of the time. What is to be regretted is that when he and Clark reset the chronometer, which was probably often, they didn't make notes on the equal altitudes. The contents of their scratch pad would have been more useful than the readings they took in such earnest for the Problem 4th.

Lewis needed the presence of Dunbar, who was working that day on his latitude on the Ouachita, along with several readings of ancillary interest. But had he been at the Mandan villages with Lewis, he would have started by making the watch jibe, whatever its idiosyncrasies. Or he could have swept the whole thing aside and told Lewis to stick to the equal altitudes, as any beginner should. At the same time, ironically, Dunbar needed Lewis just as much down on the Ouachita, to keep the boat moving.

Having spent some of October 29 "in the rearrangement of our benches and oars," Dunbar wrote, "we advanced with a little better speed; about 6 perches pr. ½ minute." Just in case that sounded like something akin to joy, he added, "which however does not exceed 2¼ miles pr. hour in water without any sensible opposition from the Current." With Lewis around, there would have been a court-martial for anyone who wasn't pulling hard enough. That was one way to increase the speed. As a coleader, though, Hunter was himself a remarkable asset—the personification of the saying that where there is a will, there is a way. He didn't know despair, even when he probably should have. Since the root of their current troubles—

the design of the Chinese boat—was his responsibility, though, he could never be the hero of the means he found to extricate it from disaster.

As partners in the expedition, Dunbar and Hunter were cordial, but formal. While their colleagues to the north referred to one another by last names in a jocular way, "Doctor Hunter" and "Mr. Dunbar" were always that on the boat. They hadn't known each other before, as had Lewis and Clark, and it is a testament to good manners that they got along at all on a trip so aggravating. Dunbar, of course, was remembered as the man who retained his composure during the raucous survey of the 31st parallel with Ellicott (and party) and Freeman; the slow progress on the Ouachita was a different kind of challenge for the sort of gentleman to whom "bland" was a compliment.

Dunbar did have his survival techniques, though, one of which was detachment. As the attitude of the crew deteriorated to a new low, he had less and less to do with them. He focused on the verdure. Hunter stepped up without compunction to command them, but even he found it wearing, as he confided to his journal:

> The men, or rather some of them often grumbling & uttering execrations against me in particular for urging them on, in which they had the example of the sergeant who on many occasions of trifling difficulties frequently gave me very rude answers, & in several instances both now and formerly seemed to forget that it was his duty in such cases to urge on the men under his command to surmount them rather than to show a spirit of contradiction & backwardness.—In the same spirit this day when at the helm he steered inshore too much although I cautioned him to keep out.

As Hunter watched, the sergeant defiantly kept to the course near the riverbank. Dunbar was looking past them both, intently keeping his eye on the foliage. "The Willow tree pendant over the water," he noted, "presents a fine deep yellow along the outline of the plant. . . ." Dunbar's yellowish-green tree may have been the exact "pendant willow" that the sergeant failed to see as the bow of the boat slipped underneath it. But he couldn't miss it when it lopped off the mast of the boat.

Seeing his boat decapitated, Hunter was infuriated. Fortunately, the next day, the expedition rowed into a small but important settlement, the Ouachita Post. The men from the derelict boat fairly fell upon it.

The Ouachita Post was near the site of Spain's Fort Miro, from which a detachment of young soldiers had chased Philip Nolan's party three years before. The Spanish fort having been torn down, a rudimentary American one was constructed early in 1804. The newly named commanding officer of the fort was Lieutenant Joseph Bowmar, a steady, personable Kentuckian who welcomed Hunter and Dunbar, while effortlessly providing a dose of army discipline to the soldiers in their party.

Dunbar saw his chance at the post to make major changes, but first he took advantage of the opportunity to mail a report to the president. Dunbar wanted to tell Jefferson honestly how the expedition was faring, and why. It's unlikely that he showed the letter to anyone else before sealing it. He then expressed an immediate interest in finding a guide for the rest of the route to the hot springs. Hunter agreed, describing the need for "a man acquainted with the river & the adjacent country, as a Pilot, as well as a hunter to explain & point out the proper manner of passing the shoals, where to get game in plenty, where we might look for salt springs, minerals &cc. And in short every remarkable object in our voyage which without his assistance might be overlooked." They wanted a predecessor, in the Evans tradition, to free them from trial and error.

While looking for the right person, Dunbar and Hunter were met with the discouraging news that the hardest part of the journey wasn't even behind them. In the words of those who knew, as Hunter noted, "There were many places between this & the warm springs where there was but little water, many falls & rocks."

The leaders couldn't help pondering the image of a river that presented—simultaneously—very little water and lots of rocks. The most daunting of the waterfalls was called the Chutes, "which," Dunbar noted, "it was supposed at the Post that we would never be able to pass with so large a boat." A canoe was recommended instead, since it could be portaged around the Chutes.

At the Ouachita Post, Dunbar and Hunter also came to realize that the time of year was inopportune not only for navigating the river, but also for finding a guide. Many of the likely ones were already engaged in hunting in mid-November, but Dunbar and Hunter managed to hire a local farmer named Samuel Blazier to accompany the expedition. He had been to the hot springs the previous year; it cured his dropsy, so he said.

Dunbar had disdained the Chinese boat for months, but at the post he finally reached the brink of reason. "Mr. Dunbar," Hunter wrote, "concluded to hire another boat." Finding a boat rental in a fledgling community wasn't easy, but finally, for the steep price of $1.25 a day, Dunbar contracted for a barge that was somewhat smaller than the Chinese boat, at fifty-five feet long by nine feet wide, with a cabin for the use of the officers. It featured a short pole where the mast would normally be—but not because it had been lopped off by a low-hanging willow branch. That pole was a standard feature of Ouachita boats, used for towropes to be tugged by men wading ahead. Because it was a lightweight barge, Dunbar enthusiastically predicted that it would draw half as much water as the old boat. Even that had a downside, though, as a barge built of light lumber would gash all the more easily on the rocks. Unfortunately for Dunbar and Hunter, there was no cargo boat on earth entirely suited to a trip up a wild river.

On November 10, the crew loaded the barge as sparingly as possible and it proved to be a marvel, drawing only one foot of water. Hunter and Dunbar looked forward to setting forth again for the hot springs on the following day. But just before going to bed, Hunter couldn't resist walking out to the barge, to check it one last time, by moonlight. It was sinking. "Found our new boat half full of water," Hunter wrote. As fast as he could, he woke up the soldiers.

Hunter was too pragmatic a man to waste time on despair. Had he been in Philadelphia, he might have raged at the owner of the boat, but he was in the Ouachita Post, with a slippery hold on the only available vessel that could carry Jefferson's orders forward. Hunter gathered the soldiers and directed them to bail the barge out, while he made arrangements for repairs the following day, a Sunday. Far from looking upon the foundering barge as a disaster, Hunter optimistically concentrated on the fortune of finding the leak before all of the expedition's supplies were ruined.

Late on Sunday afternoon, November 11, the seams in the hull having been recaulked, the barge was loaded and launched once more. The expedition had traveled a little over three hundred miles in twenty-six days; they had about two hundred and fifty to go before reaching the hot springs.

The barge veritably shot forward at three miles per hour, a new record for the expedition, as Dunbar was pleased to note. The men were still difficult, exerting the least possible effort in response to orders, but the improvement in the boat gave the illusion of new energy. On Monday, the corps made more than sixteen miles—"16 miles and 32 perches," as Hunter recorded it. The following Sunday, they traveled eighteen, using such easy days to make notes on the plant and animal life. "We thought we had lost sight entirely of the Alligators since two days journey beyond the Post," Hunter wrote. "Were surprised to see a small one basking in the sun on the bank. Saw this morning for the first time a solitary tho stately Swan in the river which or [our] guide said had probably lost its mate by the Hunters." The temperatures had dropped to about forty degrees Fahrenheit, although the water temperature was about fifteen degrees above that. In the evening, the expedition camped on the riverbank as usual. "Our canoe came up with us," Hunter wrote, "having been behind us this afternoon." He went to see if the hunters had caught anything, and they "brought the Swan that we saw this forenoon." Hunter saved the skin, intending to have it made into a muff.

Several days later, the expedition was abruptly met by a tragedy awful enough to rock Jefferson's dream of exploration. The animosity remained between the leaders and the soldiers, while Hunter came to the conclusion that Mr. Blazier, the newly recruited guide, was an ignorant liar. A nicer way of putting it was that he was a teller of tall tales; when the scientists leading the expedition asked him a direct question about the river, he made up what he didn't know. On the morning of November 22, the barge was moving along the river quietly, the water being noticeably calmer than the lingering tensions on board. During that otherwise usual morning, the quiet of the barge was suddenly shattered by a gunshot from the cabin. Inside, Hunter had shot himself almost point-blank in the face. "Doctor Hunter was employed in the Cabin of the boat loading one of his pistols," Dunbar reported. "He held it between his legs upon a bench with his head almost over the muzzle: while in the act of ramming down the ball, the pommel [the handle of the gun] slipt from the bench & the cock of the lock came with force against it, which giving way discharged the pistol."

Hunter had violated an important tenet of gun safety, well-known in the early nineteenth century. The rule, as Charles James's 1802 *Military Dictionary* put it, is that "in loading the pistol, the barrel is to be kept to the front." The fact that Hunter had his "head almost over the muzzle," as Dunbar wrote, indicates his lack of experience with guns. He later described how close the bullet came to ending his life, as it traveled so near his skin that it burned his face:

> by the motion of the boat or otherwise [the pistol] sliped & immediately went off in my face. The whole charge with ball and ramrod went thro between my right thumb & two principal fingers, which were thereby lacerated considerably, & then passed along my face, burning my eye lashes & eye brows entirely off & the skin round my eyes & nose. the charge bruised my forehead & caused two black eyes, & then passed thro my hat within an inch of my right temple & finally thro the roof of the boat.

The force of the explosion even burst a powder horn lying on a table nearby. Dunbar made sure that Hunter was not seriously hurt and then turned his attention to something more interesting to him: the gunpowder on the table went the wrong way. He couldn't help considering the dynamics of the "concussion of the air"—how transferred energy opened the horn and scattered the powder in a reverse direction from what might be expected. Hunter was musing on the same phenomenon, but from a different perspective, behind burnt eyebrows. Even in the aftermath of "an accident that had nearly cost me my Life," he recognized that if the spilled gunpowder "had taken fire (& it was a miracle it did not) the cabin & all the people in it would have been destroyed."

To recover from the incident, Hunter lay in bed a full day. The next morning, sporting two black eyes, he slowly reclaimed his duties, circulating on the deck with his ghoulish face a reminder of the cataclysm that had visited the barge and nearly incinerated it.

Within two days, the expedition was tested in a more familiar way, as the Ouachita River once again fell apart, flopping its way through shoals and rocks. The barge floated easily over some of the obstacles that would have ensnared the Chinese boat, but the advantage was limited. Through the last leg of the journey to the hot springs, the Ouachita may have looked slovenly, but it was cunning nonetheless, raising the difficulty of its hazards, until it presented its ultimate expedition killer: the Chutes.

From November 27 until December 6, the barge was in trouble every day, as it had to be extricated from gravel, wrestled into abruptly rushing currents, or eased between jagged rocks—or all three at once. Dunbar's record of the daily mileage indicates the growing resolve of the Ouachita River:

> November 27—13 miles, 39 perches
> November 28—12 miles, 255 perches
> November 29—8 miles, 2 perches
> November 30—7 miles, 28 perches
> December 1—7 miles, 148 perches
> December 2—6 miles, 118 perches
> December 3—7 miles, 218 perches
> December 4—4 miles, 164 perches
> December 5—3 miles, 128 perches
> December 6—2 miles, 32 perches

Thomas Jefferson (1743–1826) sat for Robert Field in Philadelphia around 1796. The sketch was not finished.

A Mandan Indian dressed in a buffalo robe on a bluff overlooking the Missouri River.

BELOW: A Native American with his dugout canoe on the Columbia River in the vicinity of the Dalles.

NO. 147. NATIVE WITH DUGOUT CANOE.-CELILO.-COLUMBIA RIVER, 1897.

In *Ball-Play of the Women, Prairie du Chien*, George Catlin painted a lively Dakota outing along the Mississippi River; women played the sport, while men were the spectators.

George Rogers Clark, his glory days as a Revolutionary War officer behind him, as drawn by an anonymous artist. In middle age, he was supported by his youngest brother, William.

Marquis Carlos Maria Martínez de Yrujo y Tacón (1763–1824), a vibrant and volatile man, was the ambassador to the United States from Spain. He married the daughter of Pennsylvania's governor, and the couple lived in Germantown, near Philadelphia, where he sat for this painting by Gilbert Stuart circa 1799.

William Dunbar (1750–1810) helped Jefferson direct western expeditions and was coleader of the party that explored the Ouachita River for him.

Dunbar's journal, compass, and other personal items from his exploration of the Ouachita River with George Hunter. As the first of Jefferson's expeditions into Louisiana Territory to return, their mission was critically important to the president.

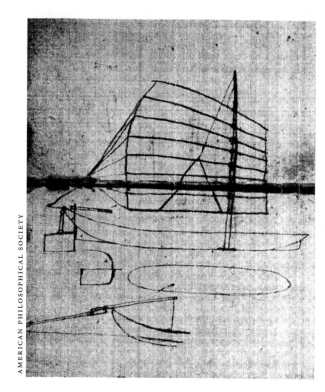

George Hunter (1755–1823), a Scottish-born chemist in Philadelphia, fulfilled Jefferson's need for an explorer with a background in hard science. He made his own sketch for a boat to use on the rivers.

William Clark (1770–1838) was painted in 1807 by Charles Willson Peale.

Meriwether Lewis (1774–1809), recently returned from the West and laden with souvenirs, posed for Charles de Saint-Mémin in his expedition clothing. His mantle, composed of ermine pelts, was a gift from Cameahwait, the Shoshone chief who was also Sacajawea's brother.

BELOW: The Lower Missouri River, which changed route frequently, took a serpentine course northwest from the hill on which Sergeant Charles Floyd was buried. Floyd, who served with Lewis and Clark, was one of two Jeffersonian explorers to die en route. George Catlin painted the view in 1835.

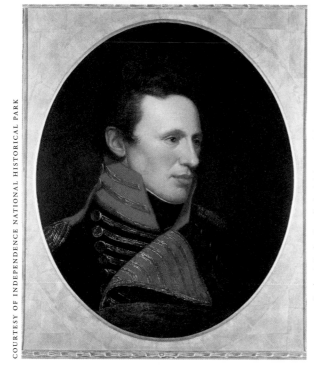

Lieutenant Zebulon Pike (1779–1813) enjoyed national celebrity after his return from two western expeditions. This portrait, painted by Charles Willson Peale, was reproduced widely. It was displayed in many American homes and schools.

Saint Anthony Falls presided over the Mississippi River at the site of present-day Minneapolis. It was photographed in 1852 before it effectively disappeared, its waters diverted and tapped for waterpower. The falls were profoundly important to both the Ojibwe and Mdewakanton nations. Lieutenant Pike explored the region in 1805–06.

Thomas Freeman (ca. 1760–1821) was invited to dine at the White House with Jefferson on November 10, 1805, and he accepted in meticulous script, which was not much less precise than the field notes he made on the frontier. Freeman's trip up the Red River was the most significant of all Jeffersonian expeditions in its time.

For hundreds or even thousands of years, the Red River had been clogged with logjams (known as "rafts") like the one above, photographed in the 1870s. The Great Raft, which confronted Freeman's expedition in 1806, stretched to over one hundred miles.

Pike's Peak, much as Pike would have seen it: in the winter snow and rising tantalizingly in the west. No matter how far he marched each day, however, the mountain remained out of reach.

The view from Thomas Jefferson's home at Monticello, looking west.

Fourteen

NEW YEAR'S

Hunter could barely write, having only recently shot the skin off of his hand, but he did note ominously in his brief entry for November 27: "The river continues to run with gradual increase of swiftness." Rapids and shoals alternated in the Ouachita, demanding brute force in return from the men. The shallows and shoals looked friendly, though, compared with the far more dangerous stretches of white water that began to meet them. Worst of all were the ledges, like steps carved of rock on the riverbed—or, like practice waterfalls in anticipation of the Chutes farther upriver. The ledges weren't clean—they were arrayed with sharp boulders. The soldiers had to find ways to hoist the barge through the gaps and over the ledges often with no room to maneuver on either side, rushing water constantly pushing the boat back, downriver, down off the ledge, and down from the hope of dominating the Ouachita. Each day offered a new and grueling reason for the members of the crew to pipe up and say whatever seditious and disloyal thing that had gotten Private Newman seventy-five lashes on the Missouri six weeks before.

On the Dunbar and Hunter trip, though, it didn't matter what anyone said. The soldiers had already complained about the leadership, just as acerbically as Newman ever could have and much more often. They had cursed the expedition and one another. They insulted Hunter to his face. Not a man to take guff from anyone, he no doubt scrapped right back at them. Dunbar was not a man to take guff, either, but he wouldn't stoop to debate his inferiors; no longer offering his signature pep talks, he seemed to have disengaged from the crew. The morale on the barge was bad, and it kept getting worse until the day that Hunter almost shot his head off—an event that became an unexpected turning point in the expedition.

Perhaps it is easy to wish someone were dead, until they almost are. The sight of Hunter lurching around with his black eyes and burnt hair may have humbled the men, or solicited their pity. Even if the accident was entirely Hunter's fault, it was a reminder that the man hadn't handled a military weapon since George Washington crossed the Delaware. Maybe Hunter wasn't perfect, but he didn't stay where it was safe and neither did they, being soldiers. They could see in his burnt face some of themselves—their hardscrabble spirit and dogged pursuit of impossible goals, ones that, as a practical matter, they had no business pursuing.

The shift in morale could also be attributed to changes in the river as much as with poor, disfigured George Hunter. The worse the conditions that the river threw at the men, the more they rose to meet it, shoulder to shoulder. After a span of time, living without those many laws, superior officers, and courts-martial that clamp people together within the confines of society—whether they like it or not—a more innate unity took hold on the Ouachita.

However the transformation occurred, Dunbar responded to it, as though he'd merely been away and had decided to come back.

"The Soldiers," he noted with pleasure in his journal, "seem desirous that we should accomplish the end of our voyage." It is true that they could have had that inclination on October 16, when the expedition left St. Catherine's. But they didn't. It did finally come to them in late November and that was good enough.

The Chutes consisted of an uneven waterfall, one to two feet high, reaching the full breadth of the river, an expansive two hundred yards wide. Selecting a likely passage for a "frail bark like ours," as Dunbar put it, meant choosing space with enough rushing water to provide insulation from the rocks, but not so much as to emphasize the double danger of a wall of angry water above a sheet of indolent stone. No matter what happened, it was a mismatched game. At the critical span in the Chutes, the boat was placed in line with a likely passage between two boulders, but it was only inches wider than the boat.

Adding materially to the difficulty was the noise from two hundred yards' worth of tumbling water. In an era in which there weren't many extended loud noises except in battle, the assault on the ears was comparable to only one thing, at least in Dunbar's experience: the sound of the "horrid din of a hurricane in New Orleans in the year 1779." Not only did the unending noise make speaking almost impossible, it was just plain uncomfortable for people raised in the prevailing quiet of the eighteenth century.

With ropes and brute strength, soldiers pulled the bow of the barge up and partially over the ledge, despite the rushing water. That left the rest of the vessel hanging off the edge. Overall, it was jammed so tightly into the gap between the rocks that it couldn't be maneuvered. There was no room to play it side to side and walk it fully over the ledge. The expedition was almost completely stuck. Dunbar explained what happened:

> The water tho' extremely rapid was not deep & we got four of
> our boldest men into the water at her bows, as far as possible

from the suction of the fall, who by feeling for rocks on which she rested, & raising her sides with all their might, enabled us to advance a step or two farther, beyond which it seemed impossible to move: it was now night, the stars were visible, the water was cold, and altho' the weather was not freezing, it was far from being mild, the thermr. being at 45°; we now repented that we had made the attempt to pass so late in the evening.

The boat went from being *almost* completely stuck to being stuck solid—or so it seemed. All but four of the men were ordered to the river's edge to pull on the towrope. The other four would push on the pikes in hopes of prying the barge loose.

In the dimming light and the unending din, the men suddenly started running through the water from the shore back to the barge. They reported that the rope was fraying from all of the weight on it and seemed likely to snap at any minute. One strand was already broken. If the rope was of standard construction, it only had two strands remaining. And if they were weakening, as the men reported, then there was little time left before the rope gave out entirely. When that happened, the boat would become miraculously unstuck—blasting back down the river and onto the rocks below, as though shot from a cannon. "No force onboard could have prevented us from being dashed to pieces," Dunbar exclaimed.

Every man on board stood by the rail with a pole or any other tool, bracing the barge against the sudden snap of the rope. One man—a quick one—was chosen to take another rope and fasten it to a tree upriver; no one breathed easily until he returned. Once the boat was tied again, nine soldiers took their places in the water, tried to stay strong in its forty-five-degree (Fahrenheit) grip, and then pulled with all the vigor they had left. The boat slid forward in a line straight enough to avoid the rocks that embraced it. The men kept pulling, hand over hand, until the barge was onshore and with that, they were, one and all, "greatly rejoicing," as Dunbar described it.

The Chutes, however, were only the beginning of three and a half more days of white water. According to both leaders, with each passing day, the effort became only more baffling, exhausting, and dangerous. On December 6, the barge had to nose against a strong current and uphill over a four-hundred-yard stretch across which the river rose by four and a half feet, including one ledge of about fifteen inches. All along the way, the going was "rocky and intricate," in Hunter's description. Some men pulled on the rope, meeting the river in a tug-of-war extraordinaire. Some poked the bottom with poles in order to finesse the hull around the rocks. "Great exertions were necessary," Dunbar wrote. "She however passed without touching any other obstacle but the impetuous torrent and in a few seconds was drawn into moderate water to the infinite joy of the whole party."

The journey upriver was finally over.

After safely mooring the barge, the expedition was only a short distance overland from the hot springs. An advance party consisting of the guide and several of the soldiers was immediately dispatched to verify the trail, which stretched about nine miles.

OF ALL THE millions of people who have visited the hot springs through the centuries, few have been more deserving of a respite by the waters than the members of the Dunbar and Hunter expedition. None, it is safe to say, ever had a harder time getting there, since no one else had need of such a large boat before the river was dredged and channeled, and none except Dunbar and Hunter had to rush for the sake of presidential business.

"Our people returned from the hot springs," Dunbar wrote in his journal the following day, "each giving his own account of the

wonderful things he had seen." Hunter and Dunbar followed, organizing the soldiers into parties for the job of transporting the baggage from the barge across a nine-mile trail. They intended to stay
for about one month.

Over the years, Indians and others had built cabins or more rudimentary shelters in the vicinity of the springs. December being
the off-season, the members of the expedition had the place to
themselves. There were ample rooms for everyone. At a temperature
of 145 degrees Fahrenheit, the springs were dangerous to touch (the
hottest bathwater is about 110 degrees). A usual practice, handed
down from the Indians, was to lie on a stretcher of sticks just above
the surface. Many of the party took advantage of the restorative
properties of the steam, but neither Dunbar nor Hunter expressed
the same delight as their men had in the springs themselves. Instead,
the leaders filled their days with experiments on the composition
of the water, the resulting steam, and the surrounding soil, as well
as minute observations on the geology and botany of the vicinity.

Jefferson was in Washington when he finally received Dunbar's
letter from the Ouachita Post. Probably arriving in late December,
it was the first message he'd received from any of his explorers in the
field, although he'd had seen secondhand reports in early November originating with traders on the Missouri regarding the progress
of Lewis and Clark. Unfortunately, Dunbar had written his letter
from the low point of the expedition and for him, it was a tirade,
as he described it "a voyage of trouble and retardment." He devoted
most of the first paragraph of the letter to a description of the boats
and then began the second paragraph with the even more dismal
news that "hitherto we have nor Seen any thing interesting which is
worthy of being particularly communicated to you at this moment."

The news that the expedition was foundering and the river dull
was of no use to Jefferson in his immediate plan to elicit more funds
for exploration of the Purchase. He was still in a good position,

though, to promote his interests even without an exciting report from the field. By December 29, the presidential election result was official, if not certified, as Jefferson and Clinton won all but three states: Connecticut, Maryland, and Delaware. Jefferson had the luxury of grousing a bit about Delaware, but altogether it was a stunning victory, even at that young stage of post–George Washington presidential politics.

As Jefferson's new vice president prepared to move to Washington, his disgraced old one was still employed, presiding over the Senate. Many in Congress wished that Burr would forgo his last session as the president of the Senate. Among other business, he was scheduled to oversee the first impeachment proceedings in Senate history, against a Supreme Court justice—for an infraction far less serious than murder, as many in Congress noted. "Mr Burr," so went the common grumbling, ventures "to take his seat among men, the natural color of whose hands is unchanged." It was hard to forget, even for those few who tried, that Burr had Hamilton's blood on his hands. And yet the facile vice president would do his best to make his colleagues do just that. The president was reportedly more receptive to Burr after the election than he ever was before it.

Not only was Burr to be safely vanquished, effective March 3, but he was handling his final duties as president of the Senate assiduously—and as luck would have it, they were very difficult and critically important during that session, with the impeachment looming. Initiated through a congressman friendly to the White House, it was a hotly anticipated trial. The defendant was Supreme Court Justice Samuel Chase, and the impeachment was arranged by Jefferson to quash the rising profile of the Supreme Court. The House had voted in favor of impeachment over the fall, leaving the Senate to pass the final judgment. With the coming trial in mind, Jefferson was very likely currying favor with his Burr, as he listened to his suggestions for several key posts in the new territories of the

West, including the two primary positions in Upper Louisiana, as it headed for territorial status.

Burr's choice for the lesser one, territorial secretary, demanded the most of Jefferson. Burr suggested his own brother-in-law, Dr. Joseph Browne, who was one of the few people in New York City who had publicly spoken in Burr's favor after the duel. Jefferson agreed to name Browne to that position. The appointment was seen by many as Jefferson's tacit absolution of Burr for the shooting of Hamilton. For the main job, the governorship, Burr touted James Wilkinson, the commander of the army, who was also in Washington at the time.

Wilkinson had known Jefferson well since the first years of the republic, when both were working for President Washington in Philadelphia. The fact that Wilkinson wanted to be governor of Louisiana was well-known in the capital. He not only made sure to be there all through the fall and winter, doing his own lobbying for the job, but he moved around within the city in a glittering procession. As described by a biographer, it was led by Wilkinson arrayed in "his magnificent uniform—of his own design—his stirrups and spurs of polished gold, his saddle-cloth of leopard's hide with dangling claws. Behind him rode his son and aide, James Biddle [Wilkinson], arrayed in almost equal splendor. Smart orderlies brought up the rear, alert to receive the General's bridle reins when he dismounted."

With that specter blinding the streets, it was easy to see that very few people could earn as much money as General Wilkinson spent. The common assumption was that the money-hungry general craved any job with a plump stipend—and the governorship was going to pay two thousand dollars a year. One newspaper editorialized Wilkinson's pursuit of the post with nothing more than a little poem, in Wilkinson's voice and with reference to John Adams and Thomas Jefferson:

This is a truth, I will maintain
Unto my dying day, Sir
That whether John or Thomas reign
I'll be in CONSTANT PAY, Sir

The relationship of Jefferson and Wilkinson is shrouded, neither having left a written appraisal of the other. It was, however, left in deeds. Even in an era of slow mails and prohibitive travel, Jefferson kept abreast of the leanings, however minute, of individuals all over the country. He wasn't often fooled or caught by surprise. Wilkinson's seditious activities in Kentucky ten years before had not diminished Jefferson's faith in him, and neither had the evidence of his continuing relations with Spain. Jefferson depended on Wilkinson as the head of the army, just as both Washington and Adams had counted him in the highest ranks of the military during their administrations. Some have theorized that Wilkinson had a blackmailer's hold over each president. For his part, he insisted that in acting so much like a traitor, he was only brilliantly pretending—an agent provocateur—and that everything he did served the interests of the United States, shrouded as his true motivations may have been. A more substantive explanation for his special status is that each of the three received what they wanted from the army when he was in charge.

In the same manner as Jefferson, Wilkinson was sensitive to the posturing of others all over the country. Mainly, though, he was aware of the needs of the president, any president. Jefferson's eye turned naturally to the West, and Wilkinson's experience there went back as far as America had a West—first in trans-Allegheny Pennsylvania, then in Ohio, Kentucky, Illinois, and, as of 1803, across the Mississippi, in both Upper and Lower Louisiana. Serving Jefferson, he not only became the administration's foremost expert on the frontier military, he was Jefferson's legs on the land. During

1802 and 1803, Wilkinson traveled fifteen thousand miles. By comparison, Jefferson traveled about five hundred miles a year, and at that, he was far above the average for his time. Wilkinson was the only ranking administration official to make the trip from the East Coast to the Mississippi Valley—and he made it regularly, usually twice a year.

If Jefferson was the inside man where the West was concerned, Wilkinson was the outside man, circulating among the frontier's rougher elements. He thrived there, among all those adventurers who need, by definition, to start anew more than once. There was a reason why Wilkinson could fit in with such people.

In Washington over the winter of 1804 to 1805, Wilkinson admitted to renewing a lively friendship with Burr, who had by that point already contacted the British about cooperating with him on a plan to seize New Orleans from America. Wilkinson, however, later denied that, in their talks in Washington that year, the two were anything more than a couple of old campaigners, fellow officers in the Revolutionary War, feeling "how strongly the sympathy, produced by hardships and dangers, binds men together."

In that spirit (perhaps), Burr did what he could to help Wilkinson gain the governorship, speaking up for him at the White House. Wilkinson helped his own cause, too, when he visited Jefferson at the White House, discussing the military outlook for Orleans and Louisiana across a desk in the East Room. Until the newly drawn territory had a congressional directive to establish a government, though, Jefferson couldn't officially select a governor. A bill on the subject was expected during the winter. For the time being, Jefferson's most publicized representatives above New Orleans were not moving much in any particular direction. Whether on the Ouachita or the Missouri River, his explorers were snowbound and poking at fires as 1805 started.

Having spent almost a month at the hot springs, Dunbar and Hunter felt that they had all of the descriptive information of the

environs that they could expect to glean at that time of year. The
expedition had been scheduled to return to Natchez and the Mississippi River by mid-December, but the rough trip upriver had extended it by well over a month. Camping at the edge of the Ouachita
River, Dunbar was impatient to go home, having done his job.
Every added day away from the Forest was a waste, as far as he was
concerned. The soldiers were just as anxious, but mainly because
they were running out of food. Many of their rations, including the
flour and bacon, were all used up. The leaders, who were still well
supplied with enticing foods, gave some of their flour to the men.

On New Year's Day, Dunbar and Hunter were in a tent at the
riverside, waiting out a blizzard. Although they were new to the
area, they still regarded it as unusual weather for the vicinity—and
complained accordingly. The storm was too harsh to allow for the
return voyage, and the level of the river was also discouraging, con-
juring up memories of November. The water was a little deeper than
it had been then, but not by enough to accommodate the draft of the
barge. Dunbar decided to wait out the storm, and when it passed,
he would watch the river a few more days, anticipating that the level
would rise. In the meantime, everyone was stranded in tents.

Dunbar was at his happiest when he was measuring something
and he began to look more closely at the snow. It had accumulated
outside his tent, knee deep and all too tempting. Designing a means
of determining the amount of water that the flakes contained, he
found that 9.346 inches of lightly fallen snow melted at thirty-three
degrees Fahrenheit turned into 1.07 inches of water. Even though he
didn't admit it in his journal, his interest in the hydrology of snow
was probably motivated by his interest in predicting exactly how
much the Ouachita River would rise once the snow melted. Tossing
1.07 inches of water out of the tent, he immediately looked around
for something else to measure and found it, on a slide under his
microscope. The mosses that he collected from the hot springs were
home to tiny organisms, which fascinated him as they went about

their lives on the slide. He described them as bivalve testaceous animals, and not surprisingly, he decided to measure them. A large one measured one-fiftieth of an inch in diameter.

At the Mandan villages, Lewis also stayed close to his quarters on New Year's Day, but he celebrated the holiday in a more conventional way, doling out a portion of liquor for each man in the corps. They heralded the start of 1805 with a couple of blasts from the swivel gun, the shots probably scaring distant Indians, who couldn't immediately discern the difference between exuberant holiday cannon fire and the kind that left craters in crowds of people.

The Indians in the vicinity well understood the need for midwinter diversion, though, some of the Mandans having apparently invited the corpsmen to perk up the gloom by demonstrating their own style of dancing. With Clark doling out another portion of liquor, it isn't entirely clear whether the explorers were actually asked to show off their dancing at the village or just arrived to do it anyway, with a violin, a tambourine, and a horn in hand. The dance detachment, sixteen in number, stood in the middle of the village and gathered a crowd by alternately firing their guns and playing music. A number of Mandans were happy to come out to watch, enjoying the sight of the dancing so much that it continued all afternoon inside the lodges.

For all of the fun of New Year's Day, with Lewis passing out yet another glass of liquor for each man, the winter camp returned that night to its disciplined routine. "Fort Mandan," as it was called, reflected the two immediate concerns of the captains, both of which fell under the priority of security: protecting the men and then the supplies, including the guns. The triangular fortress included barracks, secure storerooms, and a defensive facade surrounding a bare yard. The swivel gun from the keelboat was mounted at the front vertex of the fortress. From the start, Fort Mandan was operated crisply as a military post, Lewis and Clark trusting the members of the corps and absolutely no one else. Sentries were on watch, night and day, even when sharp winds brought temperatures in the single digits.

Within a week, the Mandan were ready to turn the seasons in their own way. On January 5, the elders instigated an all-day ceremony that called the buffalo back to the river. It also honored the spiritual strength of the tribe's storied hunters who had grown feeble with age. There was a sexual element to the dance, in which young husbands asked—and in fact, begged—the doddering old hunters to have such relations with their equally young wives. Clark described it in some detail. The fact that the assignation wasn't always a success made the couples turn in desperation to visitors, leading to Clark's boastful report that "one of our men, much more hearty and potent, due to his youth, this night preserved the honor of four husbands."

Clark's description of the Buffalo Calling ceremony was so vivid that early editions of the expedition journals printed it in Latin. And yet, Clark's description is also significant, reflecting nothing of the dance, but only of the American lens through which he looked at such Indian scenes. The Buffalo Dance in its entirety affirms and rejuvenates a complete connection between animals and humans— more broadly, between nature and humans. Those who attained that connection strongly were venerated in a host of ways during the wide-ranging ceremony.

The members of the Lewis and Clark expedition had long since known that Indian cultures had attitudes toward connubial and sexual relations that were diametrically different from American ideas—confronting that reality was part of the fabric of their daily existence. A relationship of that kind was considered a way to receive something of the spiritual strengths of another person. Having failed to develop the perspective particular to the Natives, though, Clark left a description of the buffalo dance that would have been unrecognizable to any of the Mandans who were there.

On the day of the Buffalo Dance in the Mandan village, Dunbar and Hunter were standing next to the Ouachita River, gauging its depth. The amount of water in the river had become their obsession, and it was also their main occupation. Just before New Year's, the river had been about three feet deep at the landing, but that figure didn't bode well for the levels farther downstream; five feet would be more encouraging. Dunbar and Hunter had a plan, though. When the snowfall of 18 inches melted, it would become, as Dunbar could easily figure, 2.060774662957415 inches of water. Accumulating as runoff, the snowmelt would bulge into five or even ten times that much by the time it found its way to the river. On that basis, Dunbar looked forward to the transformation of the Ouachita from a slightly damp stone quarry into a veritable cradle of water two yards deep all the way to the Forest, or at least to its junction with the Black and the Red Rivers. Day by day, Hunter's journal noted the fast-moving changes in the level of water:

> Decr. 30th, 1804, Sunday. . . . we found the river about 1½ foot higher than when we came up [upriver], yet Mr. Dunbar judged it safer to wait for a further rise . . .

> Decr. 31st. . . . We are now waiting for a thaw to raise the water in the river . . .

> January 1st. . . . The river continues to fall 1 foot every twenty four hours, or more.

> 2nd. The river still continues to fall.

> 3rd. The River now falls but slowly.

> Jany. 4th, 1805 . . . Clear & pleasant. The river continues to fall a little; although the snow gadually [sic] melts a little in the day, yet it is not felt in the river.

> 1805 Jany. 5th . . . We are still detained by the want of water of the river . . .

The only evidence of snowmelt was inside the leaders' tent. Wild rivers break quickly, though, and after a week the river suddenly tripled in depth, adding "3 or 4 feet," as Hunter wrote, during just one day.

Much to Dunbar's delight, they struck the tents on January 8, loaded the boats, and left. With the water luxuriantly deep and the current strong, the boat glided along with real speed. For the first time on the trip, the going was easy. The challenges weren't always obvious, though. Because the boat was moving quickly, a collision with a submerged rock would do irreparable damage, and loaded as it was, almost any pinhole would sink the boat. Back when it was being towed upstream by the hands of men, such collisions were common, but harmless. Thanks to some good advice from the guide, Dunbar and Hunter chose to nose the boat into the bank frequently and then scout the river ahead on foot. It was worth the trouble. Meeting the rapids over which they had all but portaged the boat on November 16, they "passed along with the rapidity of an arrow in perfect security," according to Dunbar. The dreaded Chutes went by in a blink, safely separated from the hull by four feet of water.

Farther on, the riverbed of the Ouachita was smoother, and the expedition set new records for itself: nineteen miles in a day, or as much as two and a half times the progress upriver. At that rate, the hospitality of the Ouachita Post was only a few days away. For the first time since leaving, the struggle was over. Anticipation was spent; Dunbar and Hunter had accomplished all that they set out to do, except returning the soldiers safely to their post. There was, at last, time to think about something other than the trip. And that is exactly when an expedition is over.

Fifteen

THE ARCANSA AND
RED RIVER EXPEDITION

Returning to civilization at the Ouachita Post on January 16, the soldiers found less available food than they'd hoped for—and a lot more work. Hunter described their arrival. "We delivered up the boat Mr. Dunbar hired," he wrote, "& took possession of our own again [the Chinese boat] which looked more weatherbeaten than if we had used her all the time." In Hunter's reckoning, the Chinese boat needed a complete cleaning, six new oars, a new mast, restored rigging, work on the sail, and a careful reloading in hopes of keeping the deck above water.

It was then that Dunbar announced that he would forgo the rest of the journey. He, his servant, and one of the soldiers would leave the next morning and go ahead in a canoe. With that, he would leave behind the Chinese boat, the unending baggage, the corps of moody soldiers—and Dr. Hunter. Where the road from Natchez met the river, Dunbar intended to buy a couple of horses.

Bypassing the one-hundred-fifty-mile journey by water, he and his servant could continue overland to the Forest, a distance of only thirty miles.

For his part, Hunter didn't resent Dunbar's escape, since it wouldn't materially affect the job at hand—the return of the soldiers and the boat. At the Ouachita Post, Hunter described Dunbar's departure as "a shortcut home to his family whom he had received letters from at his Arrival here." Hunter understood; he was homesick, too.

Dunbar couldn't be called a quitter in any sense; he had proved himself a brilliant investigative scientist. But his only connection was to the work, not to the men with whom he had been working for three months. He and Hunter had been polite and certainly productive throughout the trip, yet the futility of their relationship was betrayed in a single word that Dunbar used in his journal toward the end of the exploration of the hot springs—on Christmas Day, in fact:

> We amused ourselves with farther experiments on the hot waters; the conduct of the analysis being left to Doctor Hunter as a professed Chemist, the results will be hereafter given.

It was the gratuitous word "professed" that separated the two men. The word itself wasn't an insult; Hunter was self-professed, not having been affiliated with any institution of study. But it was a classification, the nearly invisible weapon of the British aristocracy.

On January 26, Dunbar arrived home, finding that his family was well and his house the same social hub he'd left in October, with a wife of many hobbies, children on the verge of adulthood, and friends with time on their hands continually coming and going. Even in a formal home such as Dunbar's, southern hospitality was real and so were the many guests dropping in to spend an hour or receive an invitation to dine. Dunbar resumed his place in the commotion and devoted the free time that he had to organizing his notes from the expedition. He especially focused on calculating the longitudes and verifying the latitudes from the data he had collected.

Only five days later, Hunter arrived at St. Catherine's, thereon traveling with his son to the Forest. "We arrived at Mr Dunbar's about dinner time," Hunter wrote, "but as usual here there was so much company that I could not enter upon business until the next day." They each had weeks of work left organizing the supplies and the expense accounts.

The Dunbar-Hunter trip was the first of Jefferson's expeditions to be completed, a victory in the effort to take possession of the far side of the Mississippi. In the battle of perceptions, a corps of a dozen and a half had made history—or started history. With the return of Hunter and Dunbar, tugging stacks of journals stuffed with observations on the ecology of the Ouachita watershed, the United States had proof that it had started west in the new territory. More than just a smattering of settlers, the government itself had taken the initiative and arrived with a claim of interest on the Ouachita.

To an even greater extent than Lewis and Clark, the leaders of the Ouachita expedition set a standard for reporting in an academic context. Not long after returning, Dunbar wrote to the president, summarizing the research and concluding that the hot springs

> are indeed a great natural Curiosity; the temperature of their
> waters is from 130 to 150 of Farheneit's thermometer; the heat
> is Supposed to be greater in Summer, particularly in dry
> weather. In water of 130 which was comparatively in a state
> of repose to one side of the Spring run, I found by the aid of
> an excellent microscope, both Vegetable and animal life; the
> first a species of moss, the latter a testaceous bivalve of the

Size of the minutest grain of Sand; I do not despair of being able to reanimate these as soon as I can procure a little leisure. the meanders of the rivers have been carefully taken as high as we went; the latitude was ascertained every favorable day & the Longitude was not neglected at convenient or important points. . . . I shall only now mention that from our analysis of the water of the hot Springs, it appears to contain lime with a minute portion of iron disolved by a small excess of Carbonic acid: this is indeed visible upon the first view of the Springs; an immense body of Calcareous matter is accumulated upon the Side of the hill, by the perpetual depositions from the hot waters, & the bed of the run is coloured by red oxid of iron or rather Carbonated iron.

Hunter also had extensive reports to prepare, when time permitted. Wrapping up both government and personal business, he and his son paid a visit to New Orleans, where they officially relinquished the troubled Chinese boat to the army. Hunter was soon writing to Dunbar with the news that the boat had, without the slightest delay, been selected for another trip all the way to Natchitoches—the commandant himself had chosen it, a fact that Hunter made sure to mention to Dunbar. That was a point of personal pride, but he was also pleased to tell Dunbar that the commandant had overseen the return of the soldiers, all of them in good health. In the city, Hunter and his son had dinner one night with the Orleans governor, W. C. C. Claiborne, who treated them with "civility & politeness." While Hunter dined with one governor in the old Louisiana Purchase, Jefferson was still deciding on the appointment of the other, and it was an even more pressing decision—the most sensitive of his administration at the beginning of 1805.

On February 23, the Hunters boarded a brig bound for New York City, set their luggage down on deck, and for the first time in seven months let someone else worry about how to keep moving forward on the water.

As Jefferson's second term came into view, he was almost insouciant, describing America as "a nation of one party"—meaning his. In fact, during the winter of 1804 to 1805, he faced no crises and few pressing problems, an airy time of transition that was reflected in the fact that he actually looked forward to delivering his second inaugural address.

At the very outset of the Jefferson presidency, uniting the country meant the reconciliation of the two warring political parties. At the beginning of the second term, it meant the alliance of the East and West. The two regions, after all, were brought together by nothing more than opportunity. History was against them, as was culture. Too perfectly, perhaps, they were personified by Jefferson and Wilkinson, sitting side by side early in 1805.

Jefferson's biggest troubles, if he had any, were entwined with the nations that he lumped together as "the belligerent powers," notably Britain, Spain, and France. He considered that his role was keeping those troubles on the other side of the ocean. "It seems very uncertain," Jefferson wrote, "which of the two powers of Spain or England, by commencing hostilities against us first will force us into the scale of the other." That statement explained the bulk of Jefferson's second-term foreign policy. It reflected the same balance that he'd described since his earliest days at the Department of State, except that in 1805, the anticipated hostilities would occur on American soil, presumably Orleans Territory.

Neither Lewis and Clark nor Hunter and Dunbar, steering through their frothy rivers, could have been as careful as Thomas Jefferson steering in his own field. Jefferson wanted to make a show of the U.S. presence in areas of friction, without inciting attack. In keeping with his thinking, the army presence along the Mississippi had become conspicuously small. It was a strategy that the president argued would discourage a buildup of Spanish troops and so fore-stall invasion from Texas or West Florida. That left some in New Orleans feeling unprotected. It left others there eyeing the oppor-tunity for insurrection, with a few of the more sinister among them wondering whether the president was purposefully inviting war by so lightly arming the new lands.

Governor Claiborne, presiding over the swirl of opulence and discontent that was Orleans, fretted constantly about the disloyalty of his fellow citizens. Baffled but resilient, he tracked major anti-American groups—a few of which were made up of Americans. An even stronger one was composed of Frenchmen; the strongest was led by the Spanish. Jefferson let New Orleans roil and even allowed Casa Calvo, Salcedo, Morales, and other Spanish officials to remain; they were not to be trusted, and yet ironically, for the moment, they did more than Claiborne could to stabilize the day-to-day operation of the city.

The president was more concerned with the Spanish who were in Texas. With them in mind, he was open to Wilkinson's pursuit of the governorship of Louisiana Territory. As an appointment, Wilkinson would cast another rather unique American shadow across the terri-tory: a general without a field army—something to notice, but not to fear. In discussions with Jefferson during early winter, Wilkinson pressed his case, supplying the president with a fresh sheaf of hand-sketched maps of north Texas and its vicinity. He left more direct campaigning on his behalf to others, including Burr.

The concentration of the two branches of power in just one person had potential benefits in Louisiana from Jefferson's point of view, but members of the House of Representatives balked at the rumored appointment of a general to be a governor. James Elliot, a lonely Jeffersonian in the congressional delegation of Federalist Vermont, broke ranks with the president over the issue. He was one of many Republicans to do so. Elliot later wrote that "the union of legislative, executive, judicial, and military powers, in an individual, was utterly irreconcilable" with "the republican principles of the constitution."

In case that didn't sting President Jefferson, he added the conjecture that had John Adams dared to put military officers in charge of civilian governments, it "would have been considered by the republicans as unquestionable evidence of a disposition to create a monarchical system of government." Everything that Adams did provided that same evidence to his detractors—but nonetheless, the problem that Jefferson faced in the winter of 1805 was that people committed to republicanism just didn't appoint generals to be governors. As he was aware then, it was a very Spanish thing to do.

Dunbar wrote another letter to Jefferson in mid-February, revealing that the pressure he'd felt during the many delays on the Ouachita was still dogging him in Natchez. "The great irregularities and delays which the mail has experienced to and from this territory," he wrote, "has rendered it impossible that any report I might have prepared could possibly reach you before the end of the Sessions of Congress, which I presume must necessarily terminate by the 4th day of March: I am much concerned at this delay, as the information we have collected respecting the neighbouring rivers would have served to awaken the Subject & induce more liberal provision by Congress for the important object of exploring rivers much more interesting that the one we have visited."

According to the plan that Jefferson had laid out for Dunbar the previous summer, the Ouachita reports would be needed as soon as possible in Washington in order to inspire support for further expeditions. It might have worked that way, except that by the time Dunbar wrote to Jefferson, Congress had already acted, allotting a little less money than the president was hoping for new expeditions: five thousand dollars. Success or failure on the Ouachita had no bearing on the funds.

Congress closed out the session with two speeches, the first, a so-called valedictory address by Aaron Burr on March 4th and then Jefferson's inaugural address the next day. Burr's poignant and patriotic farewell electrified the Senate, giving meaning to the work there. Hailed by senators from both parties, their cheers still ringing in his mind, Burr left Washington later that same day, never to return in an official capacity. His valedictory was widely considered the finest address heard up to that time in the chambers of Congress.

Jefferson made no comment on Burr's triumph, letting the waves of praise break harmlessly over the city as he delivered his second inaugural address. It was not as lofty as Burr's speech nor, more to the point, as lofty his own first inaugural address, with its assurance that the politics meant less than principle: "We are all Republicans—we are Federalists," he had insisted to great applause in 1801. By 1805, he was pretty sure that wasn't true, referring proudly in private to "the war *ad internecionem** which we have waged against federalism." In the second inaugural address, he complained openly about what he considered the obnoxious ways of his opposition. Jefferson did make reference to Louisiana, with an argument that seemed, on the face of it, to be sorely outdated:

> I know that the acquisition of Louisiana has been disapproved by some, from a candid apprehension that the enlargement of our territory would endanger its union. But who can limit the extent to which the federative principle may operate effectively? The larger our association, the less will it be shaken by local passions; and in any view, is it not better that the opposite bank of the Mississippi should be settled by our own brethren and children, than by strangers of another family?

---

* "to annihilation"

Almost two years after the Louisiana Purchase, not many newspaper editorials were still arguing its merits, yet Jefferson still felt obligated to put up a defense of the acquisition. The more timely editorials revolved around the fate of Mexico, Texas, and perhaps Louisiana in the event that the anticipated European wars spread to the New World. To read into Jefferson's point in the inaugural address, it may be that he was preparing Americans for further expansion, beyond Louisiana—and into the Floridas, Texas, or even Mexico proper. The most pointed statement, though, that he made regarding the Southwest was in an unrelated part of the speech, when he offered that "a just nation is taken on its word, when recourse is had to armaments and wars to bridle others." With that pacific and even beneficent statement, he sent the commander of the U.S. Army to serve as governor of Upper Louisiana.

A few days later, the president wrote to Dunbar for the first time in six months, dashing off a quick note—not in Dunbar's capacity as leader of the Ouachita expedition, but in his continuing capacity as director of further exploration in Orleans and the southern part of Louisiana Territory. "Your letters of the 2d & 15th of Feb. arrive just in the moment I am setting out on a short visit to Monticello," Jefferson wrote. "It will be necessary for us now to set on foot immediately the Arcansa & Red river expedition, Congress having given an additional appropriation of 5000.D. for these objects generally." With Lewis and Clark already in the West, Jefferson wanted more expeditions without delay over more of the territories. Perhaps the money from Congress was burning him forward. Perhaps the threat of trouble from the Spanish was giving him reason. Or maybe he just wanted to take possession of the land the best way he knew—to have someone "of his own brethren and children" walking around on it.

———

ARRIVING AT MONTICELLO in mid-March of 1805, Jefferson was sixty-two years old and his health was "firm" in his own estimation. That March brought one of the most exciting and propitious moments of Jefferson's life—at least his life as a farmer. The American hedge thorns arrived.

On March 22, after Jefferson was settled at Monticello and able to oversee the planting, Thomas Main was ready with four thousand seedlings, packed for shipment. Jefferson's dream of a living fence for his pastureland was at hand. Sadly, the hedge thorns didn't produce delicious peaches, as had Jefferson's previous attempt at a living fence. But on the other hand, hedge thorns didn't allow animals to walk right on through. The four thousand thorns were supposed to be planted six inches apart, according to Main, and while that seems a little close, no one could argue with Thomas Main when it came to hedge thorns. Jefferson wouldn't, and over the course of the spring vacation, the workers, quite possibly with his help, established the beginnings of a two-thousand-foot fence.

As spring arrived on the Upper Missouri, Lewis and Clark were watching the ice carefully, seeing it fracture into a river of chards. As at Camp Wood on the Mississippi the year before, the captains devoted much of their time to the selection of personnel for their corps—which was about to divide. The keelboat would return to St. Louis with a crew of about six (in addition to the two men released from the expedition for infractions). The main part of the corps would go west in a flotilla of canoes and pirogues.

The most noticeable addition to the main corps was the legendary Indian woman Sacajawea. A Lemhi Shoshone or Snake Indian (from the eastern part of what is now Idaho), she was born circa 1788 into the Agaidika tribe. When she was about eleven, she was taken as a slave in a raid and was eventually traded to the Minitarís at the Mandan villages. They in turn sold her to a French-Canadian fur trader, Toussaint Charbonneau, who had a history of interfering with underage girls, and had attempted to rape at least one. Charbonneau married Sacajawea and another young Shoshone woman, also purchased as a slave. Sacajawea was described by an Englishman who visited the area then as "a good creature of mild and gentle disposition." She had been able to learn at least four languages while she was growing up in various homes en route from the West. For that reason, Lewis and Clark wanted both her and her husband, Toussaint Charbonneau, to accompany them as interpreters. His other wife would stay home. Prolonged and aggravating negotiations ensued at the Mandan villages between the men. Finally, after Charbonneau capitulated on major points, Lewis and Clark agreed to bring the three of them—three, because by the time Charbonneau made up his mind, Sacajawea had a two-month-old baby in her arms.

The idea of a woman on an expedition was not a novelty, inasmuch as an 1802 hunting/exploration trek led by a Canadian trader and an assistant along the Upper Missouri as far as the Rockies (at the Big Horn River) included more than twenty women. That corps of forty-three consisted entirely of Indian families, aside from the two Canadians. Yet Sacajawea was unique for the Corps of Discovery as an Indian woman with an important role to play at several junctures. Moreover, she would become a signal figure to modern Americans looking back through history, as an Indian woman with a name. There were not many that were remembered. The legend, however, emanates from more than just her gender. Although the amount of information known for certain about Sacajawea could be written on a single piece of paper, the words left by others paint a consistent picture of a bright person and a kind one, amid a life of hard circumstances.

With Sacajawea and her family in tow, the various boats of the corps started in their opposite directions on April 7. Lewis, in his journal, called the moment of departure "among the most happy of my life." Jefferson wasn't aware of the particular moment, but it would eventually be one of the happier ones of his life, too, since the other boat, the keelboat headed south, was carrying four boxes and a trunk, carefully packed with specimens and notes on the journey. They were addressed to the president. Also included were live animals in cages: a prairie dog, a quartet of magpies, and a sharp-tailed grouse.

The expedition, as it started again, consisted of thirty-three people aboard two pirogues and six canoes. Lewis, for the record, wasn't in a boat. As he had throughout the journey, he preferred to hike alongside the boats, and so it was that he walked to the West out of the Mandan villages.

Lewis's mood seemed to change dramatically as of April 7. He wrote consistently in his journal, where his entries had been sporadic before; more than that, his writing was fully engaged and candid, even passionate when he was pressed to it by his experiences on the river. During the first days, his relief to be moving toward the challenging part of the journey was apparent. Perhaps in his mind, he had been only an organizer and not an explorer, until the corps left Mandan for the truly raw lands to the west. An intense personality, Lewis had a dread of failure, yet to fail as an explorer could still be heroic. To fail as an organizer would have been crushing. Leaving behind his fears, he compared his endeavor with that of a couple of others:

> This little fleet altho' not quite so rispectable as those of Columbus or Capt. Cook were still viewed by us with as much pleasure as those deservedly famed adventurers ever beheld theirs; and I dare say with quite as much anxiety for their safety and preservation. . . . The party are in excellent health and sperits, zealously attatched to the enterprise, and anxious to proceed; not a whisper of murmur or discontent to be heard among them, but all act in unison, and with the most perfect harmony.

The river met Lewis's mood, unraveling with space enough for a man breaking out of a state of anticipation that was years long. Both he and the route were unencumbered, at least temporarily. The terrain varied between low hills and plains. The water flowed smoothly, but not too strongly. While the progress was steady, ranging between about eighteen and twenty-six miles per day, none of the boats was as steady as the keelboat had been, nor did they offer the impression of security that it had. That mattered when a section of the riverbank caved in, almost filling one of the canoes with water. It mattered when the wind blew across the water, making waves too choppy for light, shallow boats. And it certainly mattered when a wild animal was chasing a human and there was no thick door to slam, no safe place for a thousand miles in any direction.

The land surrounding the river, though it soon became monotonous with its smooth landscapes of stone, offered Lewis the thrill he'd coveted of being the first Americans in a place "on which the foot of civillized man had never trodden." His definition of civilization was sadly narrow, but if he meant that Americans had never been so far west, he was certainly right. The members of the expedition were reminded of that fact by the overwhelming array of animal species they were seeing for the first time. The sharp-tailed grouse that had interested them on the Lower Missouri was not as majestic as the animals that lived on the upper part of the river. Buffalo were common, but so were mountain sheep, rattlesnakes, and otters. They also spotted tracks of a bear they presumed was the grizzly. It was the species they most wanted to see. As Lewis wrote:

> we have not as yet seen one of these anamals, tho' their tracks are so abundant and recent. the men as well as ourselves are anxious to meet with some of these bear. the Indians give a very formidable account of the strengh and ferocity of this anamal, which they never dare to attack but in parties of six eight or ten persons; and are even then frequently defeated

with the loss of one or more of their party. . . . this anamall
is said more frequently to attack a man on meeting with him,
than to flee from him.

The grizzly bear was of interest as a species new to the explorers,
but then, so were many of the other animals and plants investigated
by Clark and especially Lewis, day in and day out. Only the grizzly
became an obsession. Because its range was confined to the western
and northwestern parts of North America, few Europeans had ever
seen one—and only then, perhaps, on the Pacific coast. It is probable that no American had ever seen a grizzly at the time Lewis was
looking hopefully along the riverbank for any sign of the magnificent bear. As a species or an individual, the massive grizzly was the
dominating force in the vast territory the corps was traversing, shaping the experience of all life there. In terms of sheer power, a grizzly
bear was unmatched—except by another grizzly. Weeks went by,
and still none was seen. The grizzly, it seemed, was in control of
everything—even its own entrance—and that annoyed Lewis.

The corps watched for the bear every day. "Tho' we continue
to see many tracks of the bear," Lewis wrote on April 17, "we have
seen but very few of them, and those are at a great distance generally
runing from us." He then indulged in a bit of wishful thinking: "I
thefore presume that they are extreemly ware and shy; the Indian
account of them dose not corrispond with our experience so far."

In all of the journals of the Lewis and Clark party, there is an unending sense of awe for the sheer amount of animal life that thrived
around them on the Upper Missouri. "The game, Such as Buffalow
Elk, antelopes & Deer verry plenty," Clark wrote on April 18. "The
Game is gitting pleantyier," Sergeant Ordway echoed. It was a hunter's shooting gallery. The animals weren't yet familiar with guns, as
the various Indians in the region more typically used nonexplosive
means of killing them: arrows, spears, or the technique of driving
them over a cliff. Clark took great pride in the fact that the corps

killed only for food, not for sport (though they would sometimes kill a fifteen-hundred-pound buffalo just for the tongue). Even Seaman, Lewis's pet dog, killed an elk swimming in the river and brought it into camp. But the favorite food of the corps, while on the Upper Missouri, was beaver, which was plentiful.

At the end of April, Lewis shot and killed a small three-hundred-pound bear that he assumed was a good example of a grizzly. His description is inconsistent, but it was probably a very young grizzly bull. He was not impressed. "The Indians may well fear this animal," he wrote, "equiped as they generally are with their bows and arrows or indifferent fuzees [rifles], but in the hands of skillfull riflemen they are by no means as formidable or dangerous as they have been represented." Once again, Lewis exhibited a pronounced skepticism regarding the grizzly, an attitude that was, in large part, a means of disparaging the Indians who thought the bear indomitable.

After Clark and another man managed to kill an eight-foot-long bear that was identified as a grizzly, Lewis's attitude started to change, especially in light of the ten bullets that it took to kill the animal. As other grizzlies crossed the path of the expedition, Lewis began to see that the Indian lore about the grizzly was, if anything, understated. The bear had an unearthly power to remain alive even after it had been—by all that was understood of ballistics—killed. A hail of bullets straight into the lungs or other vital organs didn't stop a grizzly or give it any notion of giving in.

Lewis and Clark had encountered aspects of the West that were the opposite of all that they'd learned in the society of the United States. The wilderness of the north wasn't much different, though, not at its base. Animals, including humans—including the corpsmen—wanted to keep living and arranged themselves on a to-pography of fear that guided their decisions in that interest. The journals of Lewis and Clark, as they navigated the Northwest, are full to the brim with the details of life around them and, just as con-stantly, the death, along with the fears that drive individual animals to do clever things or stupid ones. Then the grizzly came along, not just as a new species, but as a new phenomenon. By the time Lewis had encountered two or three grizzlies, he knew it. The grizzly didn't possess the thing called fear and had not the least respect for death—no belief in it.

"These bears being so hard to die reather intimedates us all," Lewis admitted, before devoting extensive reflection to the bear. When Lewis and Clark arrived in the West, an estimated one hundred thousand grizzly bears lived in the region. Weighing around eight hundred pounds, they sustain that mass mostly from plants, which make up ninety percent of their diet. They are lazy hunters, usually eating carrion, baby animals, or rodents for meat. Lewis would have his own encounters with the grizzly; one stalked him on June 14 while he was hunting about three hundred yards from the Missouri riverbank. The explorer was admiring a buffalo that he had just shot when he noticed the bear. With no ammunition in his gun and no trees within scurrying distance, he tried to walk quickly, but nonchalantly, away. The bear wasn't fooled, chasing him "open mouthed and full speed."

Lewis realized that the bear was gaining on him, but he raced over barren terrain and managed to reach the river first. Plunging in and pushing as fast as he could into the deeper water, he turned around and with menace in his eyes, he held up an espantoon (a small bat like a policeman's billy stick). The bear stood on the bank, but decided against an exhausting fight in the water over one human; he may have opted for the buffalo carcass, for a greater return on much less effort.

Aware that he owed his life to the discretion of that bear, Lewis decided on a new policy; he would stay away from grizzlies as much as possible. As a man who walked alone along the river almost every day, he vowed that he wouldn't stalk or hunt them and hoped they would do the same. With love and hate, Lewis habitually referred to the bears as "gentlemen."

The terrain surrounding the river became more dramatic as the corps moved into what is now central Montana. Cliffs and vistas gave sweep to a landscape that was arrestingly beautiful, not only in its grand textures, but in colors more verdant than any since the southern part of the Missouri. With the varied terrain, however, came a rockier riverbed. For all of the glories of the sights on the land, the corpsmen probably would have opted for more of the soft-edged monotony of the river farther east. But on May 26, there was a reward.

Clark hiked ahead to the top of a hill, where he thought he saw lines in the distance. He kept walking down into a hollow and then up to an elevated plain, where, as he wrote, "From this point I beheld the Rocky Mountains for the first time with Certainty . . . those points of the rocky Mountain were Covered with Snow and the Sun Shown on it in Such a manner as to give me a most plain and Satisfactory view." He and Lewis had the same reaction to the site, as Clark described it back at the camp. The height of the peaks and the snow that gave each of the captains a thrill of happiness from a distance were going to be something less than majestic in a close-up view.

Both Lewis and Clark were looking closely at their position, within view of the mountains of the Rockies and tantalizingly close to the source of the Missouri River. They weren't the only ones seeing the West in terms of the line of that route.

Only the day before Lewis and Clark first glimpsed the Rockies, Jefferson had written to Dunbar from Monticello in a hastened effort to launch the next expedition:

> Your observations on the difficulty of transporting baggage
> from the head of the Red river to that of the Arcansa, with
> the dangers from the seceding Osages* residing on the last

---

* the Clermont bands

river have determined me to compose the ensuing mission to the ascent of the Red river to it's source, & to descend the same rive again, which will give an opportunity of better ascertaining that, which in truth, next to the Missouri, is the most interesting water of the Missisipi. You will accordingly recieve instructions to this effect from the Secretary at War. Dr. Hunter does not propose to take a part in this mission. . . . I write to Govr. Claiborne to endeavour to get a passport from the Marquis of Casa-Calvo for our party as a protection from any Spaniards who may be fallen in with on the route

The news that Hunter was declining the expedition to the Red River was not entirely unexpected, in view of the time he'd devoted to the Ouachita. Dunbar made the same decision, though he was under pressure to reverse it and lead the journey up the loutish Red River. Alligators loved the Red River, but people avoided it.

Even as Jefferson was writing his letter, vaguely and yet emphatically outlining the expedition, the commandant of the New Orleans army post was floating up the Mississippi in a boat with forty soldiers, expecting to pick up Dunbar in Natchez and take him to the source of the Red River.

Dunbar, puttering around the Forest, met the commandant, and after a short span of confusion it was soon apparent to the visitor that the expedition was not yet ready to begin. More specifically, Dunbar was not ready and the odds were good that he never would be. The communications having been botched, the commandant said that he would come back at a later date. The problem facing Jefferson and also Dunbar, as his director of future expeditions, remained that of engaging the corps: finding the right people and hoping they'd agree.

While the commandant was being rowed back to New Orleans, General James Wilkinson, the new Louisiana governor, was on his way to St. Louis. It was June of 1805 and he'd had a stunning idea for exploration in the West. He didn't have to cajole Congress into the funding, and he certainly didn't have to wait to see if his top choice for a leader would deign to accept his offer. The choice was a lieutenant in the army.

He accepted.

Sixteen

MYSTERIES OF THE MISSISSIPPI

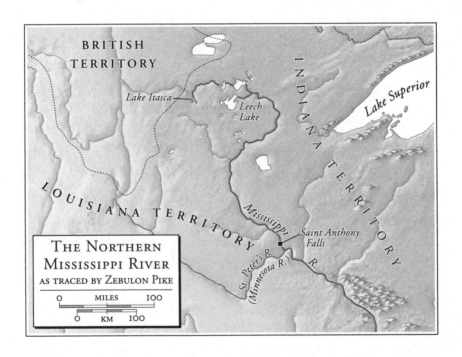

BRITISH TERRITORY

Lake Itasca

Leech Lake

INDIANA TERRITORY

Lake Superior

LOUISIANA TERRITORY

Mississippi

Saint Anthony Falls

St. Peter's R. (Minnesota R.)

R.

THE NORTHERN MISSISSIPPI RIVER
AS TRACED BY ZEBULON PIKE

0   MILES   100

0   KM   100

The residents of St. Louis already knew James Wilkinson well. As a general, he'd lived among them on and off for more than a year, and so his return on July 1, 1805, from yet another trip to Washington shouldn't have caused much excitement. Because the residents did know him well, though, Wilkinson was welcomed by a crisply mounted escort of citizens and, a little later, by a ceremonial contingent of Indians. And later still, by his soldiers, standing in formation in front of his house.

Two days later, the city of St. Louis continued the celebration of Wilkinson with a banquet at the only venue in town that could hold everyone who wanted to attend—a meadow. At a spot along the river that commanded views in every direction, the supper tables stretched out three hundred feet. To the north and south ran the Mississippi. Across the river lay southern Illinois. Just as everyone sat down for supper, a pyramid arose "as if by magic," from behind a separate table, engraved with patriotic inscriptions—a category that included, for the time being, Wilkinson's initials. But the backdrop for it all was the real star of the evening, and even Wilkinson would admit it: the Louisiana Territory to the west, where the dinner guests looked on wild animals grazing among wildflowers as far as the eye could see.

During a convivial first month, Wilkinson was faced with the challenge of maintaining the austerity of his army command, even though he was devoting far more attention to civilians than to soldiers. In one of his first major acts after returning, he issued orders for a new expedition. He wanted someone to find the source of the Mississippi River and chose Lieutenant Zebulon Pike—the dogged but delicate-looking officer from Fort Kaskaskia. Wilkinson had been mentoring him since before Lewis and Clark set out west. Secondarily, he assigned Pierre Chouteau, the St. Louis businessman, to use his contacts within the Grand Osage nation to learn more about routes to the southwest, as far as "St. Afee"—Santa Fe. Despite the fact that Wilkinson's name was clearly signed at the bottom of each set of orders, it isn't easy to trace which of his incarnations was actually responsible for them. Conventionally, as the governor, he needed to know more about his environs; as commander of the army, he was expected to know how best to defend U.S. territory. A perennial double agent, though, his life was itself a borderland, and so he needed to train his sights in terms of the European threats that closed in on all sides. And finally, as a profiteer, he couldn't make money without learning the possibilities in newly opened regions. Many reasons explain Wilkinson's rush to launch the expeditions, yet all but the governorship had existed long before the summer of 1805. One difference came from Wilkinson's long visit to Washington.

Neither Jefferson nor Wilkinson left any record of their conversations in Washington—except by their actions. In the aftermath, Wilkinson launched his own impetus on western exploration, while Jefferson tried hard to accelerate the planning for his expedition on the Red and Arkansas Rivers. Disturbed by his conviction that "the acquisition of Louisiana has been disapproved by some," and also by the creeping possibility of European aggression there, he saw it as a means to exert control of the territory. The first setback was that the trip was lacking a leader, Dunbar having withdrawn. Jefferson came by that information during Wilkinson's last month in Washington and probably mentioned it. Wilkinson knew Dunbar well—but if the president had an emergency need for a hardy mathematician with a streak of patriotic self-sacrifice or even self-promotion, Wilkinson was at the ready with a name.

Thomas Freeman, the veteran of the 31st parallel survey and its clash over morals, shortly thereafter entered into correspondence about western navigation with Jefferson. Over the previous half-dozen years, he had continued his work as a surveyor on the frontier, most recently in Tennessee, where he was employed by an old friend of Wilkinson's. Since the warring days of the 31st parallel survey, the two had remained in contact, Wilkinson occasionally finding Freeman work and Freeman managing to ignore the fact that in the realm of rumors, Wilkinson was only a little more respectable than old Andrew Ellicott.

Freeman was distantly known to Jefferson from the platting of

the new city of Washington in the early 1790s. His rise in the selection process for the Red River, though, after Jefferson had exhausted his own list of first choices in 1805, points to Wilkinson
as the one who championed the Irish-American. Freeman was still
unmarried, moving around the country—not to live in its cities, but
to map its backwoods accurately enough that cities might someday
follow as the country pushed west. Unlike many of Jefferson's previous choices to lead a Red River expedition, Freeman wouldn't have
to worry that six months in the middle of nowhere might take him
away from his regular life. That was his regular life.

According to those who worked with Freeman, he brought the
same careful, perhaps even plodding, precision to surveys a hundred
miles from the nearest town that he had to the planning of Pennsylvania Avenue in Washington. He was a meticulous worker who
refused to sacrifice accuracy for efficiency. As a civil servant stalled
in the middle range, Freeman must have regarded even a conversation with the president about such a trip as a lofty honor, and a rare
opportunity.

Wilkinson, the western eminence in Washington, had always
taken a keen interest in Jefferson's plans for exploration. Even while
he was in a position to suggest Freeman, he would have been absorbing the president's impatience regarding the West. "Our relations
to Spain & Britain on our Southern, Western & Northern *unexplored* frontiers," Wilkinson wrote to Dearborn that summer, "Suggest the expediency of attaching to us, all the Nations who drink
of the waters which fall into the Gulph of Mexico." That would be
news to Spain, since the waters of every one of its North American
provinces, except California, headed for the Gulf. So it was that in
Washington, the less obvious motivation for Wilkinson's interest
in exploration was his cultivation of Aaron Burr, with whom there
were furtive plans to take over parts of Orleans or the Spanish provinces in the Southwest.

The Wilkinson/Burr plots were never expressed on paper, but

if they were more than talk—more than the residue of two schemers circling each other—then the goal was the conquest of, at the
very least, East Texas, and, at most, Orleans and the Spanish empire in America. Burr was especially interested in South America.
Wilkinson had an open desire to invade Mexico. Whether he actually dreamed of splitting it with Aaron Burr or turning it into an
American province, Jefferson's interest in exploration would help
the cause. Wilkinson had survived by giving three presidents what
they wanted. And so, when he returned to St. Louis, he set the highest priority on putting his expeditions in motion.

Jefferson was doing the same for his Red River expedition. He
wasn't at the point of formally engaging Freeman, but the two corresponded about techniques used in celestial navigation, with Freeman taking the traditional first step: scouting the Philadelphia shops
for the president, who wanted to know what the latest instruments
could offer.

One of Jefferson's primary concerns in organizing the trip lay
with the dangers attached to territory that was disputed. As a former secretary of state, his solution was diplomatic in nature—to
obtain a passport for his explorers, in the event any Spanish officials should question them. On the president's orders, Claiborne,
the governor of Orleans Territory pressed a request for just such a
passport from Casa Calvo, his bitter adversary. Calvo, still tacitly in
charge of Spain's interests, sent an utterly gracious reply. It was an
ominous response, both in the generous cooperation it promised,
and even more, in Casa Calvo's cheerful tone. His attitude seemed
to bode well, but by then, Jefferson was resigned to postponement
of the Red River expedition until the following spring, 1806—a true
disappointment, considering that Dunbar and Hunter had been on
the very verge of exploring it in 1804.

A few days later, Casa Calvo wrote to his superiors in Spain and
Mexico with at least a partial explanation of his outrageous display
of charm. He thought he had planted a spy in Freeman's midst. As

Casa Calvo explained, he had the impression that he had convinced Dunbar to include a Spanish subject named Thomas Power on the American expedition. "Don" Thomas, as he was known, was closely associated with the Spanish in New Orleans and Casa Calvo looked forward to receiving from him "knowledge of the designs of the Americans" headed to the Red River. That was all in error, but Casa Calvo also wanted to tell Madrid about the latest news of Lewis and Clark and first of all, that there was late news. The keelboat that the captains sent back to St. Louis had arrived with the first account of the expedition in over a year.

In his letter to his home office, Casa Calvo was determinedly unimpressed. That would have made him the only one; Americans were parched for a report and newspapers devoted long columns to firsthand descriptions of the first stage of the expedition and the countryside through which it passed. Jefferson read the articles along with everyone else, quoting the points he found important in a letter to a friend: "Capt. Lewis who has been sent to explore the Missouri to it's source, & thence to pursue the nearest water com-munication to the South sea, passed the last winter among the sav-ages 1600 Miles up the Missouri. . . . Lewis finds the Indians every where friendly. He will probably get back in 1806." The cases of materials sent to Jefferson from the expedition were still in transit. He was looking at 1806 as a busier year for news from the West, but then, at that point in the second week of July 1805, he still wasn't aware of the plans for Pike to make the first trip by a European American to the Upper Mississippi River.

The orders for the exploration of the Mississippi are an oddly brief document, reflecting the president's impulse, as interpreted by Wilkinson. "You are to proceed up the Mississippi with all possible diligence," Wilkinson wrote to Pike in the first line, "taking the fol-lowing Instructions for your general government, which are to yeild to your discretion in all cases of exigency." The orders then briefly—

very briefly—covered the governor's expectations for a geographical record, interaction with Native populations, surveys of potential
sites for forts, and collection of specimens from the mineral and vegetable classes. Wilkinson wasn't nearly as thorough in composing
the orders for Pike as Jefferson had been in sending Lewis and Clark
to the Pacific. Wilkinson translated the challenge of Jeffersonian
exploration into his own terms, setting the main goal and leaving
the less interesting details to the leader, one who could respond with
"discretion in all cases of exigency."

Pike, born in New Jersey, was twenty-six years old in 1805 and
had been a first lieutenant since 1799 or 1800. "Pike," wrote the historian Elliot Coues, "had not before been distinguished from any
other meritorious and zealous subaltern, though his qualities had
already attracted favorable attention." Pike stood out amongst his
peers, possibly because there were so few meritorious and zealous
junior officers from whom to be distinguished in 1805. Jefferson's
peacetime army offered small chance of promotion, and young men
of promise typically looked elsewhere for a career. Pike was ambitious enough to ignore the odds.

Attached to the First Infantry Regiment at Fort Kaskaskia in
1803, Pike heard the news of the Louisiana Purchase and immediately compiled a description that found its way to Samuel Mitchell,
who published it in his *Medical Repository* in New York. If being
in the farthest outpost of the American army suddenly had cachet,
Pike was quick to press the advantage. Mitchell, the Jefferson loyalist, was hungry for just such reports. In the article, Pike was per-
ceptive, writing that Americans would "find it to their advantage
(after the example of the Spaniards) to divide Louisiana into two
territories, the upper and the lower. The lower province will be the
country for the cultivation of cotton, indigo and sugar. In the upper
will be raised wheat, and all kinds of small grain. . . . In this region
the curse of slavery ought not to be entailed on posterity."

Pike's article featured a description of the Missouri River, yet he didn't even mention the Mississippi—despite the fact that he was stationed at a fort overlooking it. The northern section of the river, reaching above St. Louis, was a mystery to Americans, but it was a mystery ignored. They knew it was there, with only a vague idea of its length and no idea of its features.

The eastern banks of the northern section of the Mississippi—the region now occupied by Wisconsin and north Illinois—had been acquired with the rest of the old Northwest Territory at the end of the Revolutionary War. Nothing had yet been done with it by the Americans, although in terms of Indian claims, William Henry Harrison had negotiated his biggest bargain of all, the purchase of the massive Sac lands there for a price of $1,000 per year, equal to 0.0045 cent per acre. The Sacs maintained he'd bought it from an unauthorized, minor chief named Quashquame, who was drunk during the negotiations but who came home with "fine coats and many medals." The treaty was only seven months old and still untested when Wilkinson decided to send Pike through the Sac territory. The region to the west of the northern Mississippi had, of course, come to the United States as part of the Louisiana Purchase.

Newspaper readers of 1804 and 1805, who never tired of articles about the Missouri River, found few, if any, about the northern Mississippi. The essential waterway of the first era of western settlement was the Ohio-Mississippi river system, stretching from Pittsburgh to New Orleans. As far as early Americans were concerned, the Upper Mississippi was barely a tributary of that busy waterway—and the mapmakers might just as well have given it one name, all the way from Pittsburgh to the Gulf of Mexico. The new excitement in the air, however, was that the river system of the next era of settlement was going to be the one drawn from the opposite side, by the Missouri-Mississippi. In 1805, Americans were fixated on the search for its source, believing that the Missouri-Mississippi was destined to define the West. The fact that the full length of the Mississippi would define the entire nation had yet to intrigue anyone.

Receiving orders from Wilkinson to proceed up the Mississippi, Pike was understandably reminded of Lewis and Clark, who were already famed when he met them at Fort Kaskaskia during their preparatory days. Perhaps it was their influence that made him read the orders from Wilkinson with his own emphasis on just one phrase in the fifth paragraph:

> You will proceed to ascend the main branch of the River, until you reach the source of it, or the season may forbid your further progress, without endangering your return before the waters are frozen up.

Pike read only, "Reach the source of it." He considered that he was going to discover the headwaters of the Mississippi, in the same way that Lewis and Clark were trying to find the farthest reach of the Missouri. Wilkinson looked on the fifth paragraph with a different emphasis. He believed the last phrase dominated: "return before the waters are frozen up." With Lewis and Clark not expected back until 1806, according to their own prediction, Jefferson needed reports, and he needed them in 1805. Wilkinson's overall orders may have been a bare outline of Jeffersonian exploration, expressed without the president's passionate curiosity, but his prerogative was identical. He wanted Pike back by the end of the year.

Alacrity was knitted into Pike's nature, and it was probably one of the reasons he was chosen to go. He first heard about the expedition in late June, when Wilkinson visited Fort Kaskaskia. The subsequent orders were dated July 30 and on August 9, Pike was ready to go. The corps included, in Pike's words, "one Sergt. two corporals and 17 privates in a Keel Boat 70 feet long, provisioned for four months: with orders to explore the source of the Mississippi."

While Pike couldn't be sure how far he was going, he presumed that he would be back in St. Louis in early December. On the assumption that the source was at least six hundred miles to the north, the keelboat needed to average about ten miles per day, a fair clip compared with the other expedition boats heading up the other rivers. In the boatman's tradition, he departed at four in the afternoon, to give him a chance the first night to retrieve anything forgotten.

The boat was towed or rowed upriver, being only occasionally under sail. Within only two days, Pike had left American settlement behind. As the banks of the river intermittently rose in altitude, forming high bluffs that braced the river and gave homes to the many eagles flying overhead, Pike was struck by the grand scale of the place. On August 12, he saw "on the E. shore a beautiful cedar cliff and after you pass that the river expands to nearly two miles in wedth and has four Islands whose lowest points are nearly parallel. We called them the four Brothers." The topography of the northern Midwest became only more dramatic during the first weeks of the journey.

Pike pushed on as quickly as possible, no matter how hard the river tried to hold him to its more regal pace. When the boat passed small groups of Indians, going about their business, "they'd cry 'How do you do,'" he wrote of a typical group on August 19, "wishing us to give them an invitation to come over." Pike wouldn't even reply. When he lost one of his dogs during a stop on an island, he left it behind. A few days later, he lost another dog along the riverbank, and two of his soldiers volunteered to go look for it. After a short time, he left them behind too.

PIKE'S IMPATIENCE HAD a cost. He may have been an explorer, but he wasn't an adventurer, refusing to allow the worlds that he encountered along the way to fully surround him. In fact, he dreaded just such encumbrances. While Lewis and Clark typically allowed two or three days for a visit to an Indian village, Pike tried instead to make his speech, hand out his presents, and discuss the issues of a particular village all in a single afternoon—an efficiency that confused some tribes. At a Meskwaki Sac village along the river in what is now northern Iowa, he met the infamous Quashquame. He was still a minor chief, though slightly chagrined, after sobering up the previous November and realizing that he'd just signed away his nation's homeland. The intrepid chief Ma-Ka-Tai-Me-She-Kia-Kiak, better known to Americans as Black Hawk, was then a young man living in the village. He recalled that at the time, the treaty had yet to have any impact on his people, but even so, the whole idea of the Americans replacing the Spanish in Louisiana Territory "cast a deep gloom over our people." The Indians of the Sac nation considered that the Spanish had always treated them fairly, even allowing a trade alliance with the British to flourish. Black Hawk recalled Pike's visit:

> Some time afterwards, a boat came up the river, with a young American chief. . . . He gave us good advice; said our American father would treat us well. He presented us an American flag which we hoisted. He then requested us to pull down our *British* flags,—and give him our *British medals*—promising to send others on his return to St. Louis. This we declined, as we wished to have *two Fathers!*.

Quashquame repeatedly encouraged Pike to visit Saukenuk, a nearby Sac city—or at least to allow a messenger to fetch the chiefs there. Saukenuk was home to four thousand people, about three times the population of St. Louis. At least a hundred years old, it was a walled city of wooden houses, neatly laid out in blocks, with alleys and two public squares. In order to meet its chiefs, at least, Pike would only have to extend his stay until morning. He couldn't

do it. "Not wishing to lose any time," he wrote of that day, "I embarked and made 6 M[iles] above the Village." Six miles was a fine
accomplishment so late in the day. Had he been willing to detour
about three miles, though, "he would reach the very large Sauk village of Saukenuk where the truly influential chiefs lived," as Donald
Jackson, the editor of Pike's journals, wrote. Quashquame had tried
to impart that idea, but time drove Lieutenant Pike. "When the
young chief started," Black Hawk related, "we sent runners to the
village of the Foxes, some miles distant, to direct them to treat him
well as he passed."

Pike had until the middle of October to find the trickle at the
beginning of the Mississippi, but as of mid-September, the river beneath the boat was two miles wide, by his own estimation. It was
probably more like a mile and a half; Pike wasn't a good estimator,
but the source of the river was quite apparently not around the next
bend. Pike followed the river as it veered off to the west, away from
its remarkably straight north-south axis, and along the west border
of what is now Wisconsin.

He and his men stopped in Prairie du Chien, the outpost of
British trading activity on the east bank of the river. The British,
with outsized charm, welcomed the American explorers as guests—
guests on their own territory. For the time being, that was all right
with Pike. The British operated as merchants in the region, but
Pike's priority lay with the Dakota nation, which actually controlled
the land. Continuing to the northwest on September 20, Pike and
his men encamped in a village on the prairie, established by a clan of
the influential Mdewakanton (pronounced *Em-day-wa-kahn-tahn*)
Dakotas. It was a fortunate stop, inasmuch as the local chief, Le
Petit Corbeau (Little Crow or Cetanwakumani) was also at the core
of one of the Mdewakanton's defining kinship groups.

Across what is now southern Minnesota the dominant culture
was that of the Santee Dakotas, a Sioux-language group composed

of four tribes, including the Mdewakanton, who occupied the Mississippi River exactly where Pike and his men were traveling. In their previous home farther north, the tribe had enjoyed a rather urbane diet, by modern standards, composed mainly of wild rice, freshwater oysters, and duck. In the northern wetlands, the food was abundant, but other people weren't—until the eighteenth century, when the Mdewakanton were pushed south by the Ojibwe, who remained their mortal enemies almost to the point of an obsession. The living wasn't quite as easy on prairie land, where by 1805, the Mdewakanton were gamely learning to grow corn to augment the meat they gained from hunting.

One day after leaving Le Petit Corbeau's Mdewakanton village, Pike reached the point where the Mississippi River met the Minnesota, a river he called by its European name, "St. Peter's." While he was there, he noticed a burial scaffold holding four bodies wrapped in blankets; by looking at the condition of the cloth, he reasoned that the remains had been left recently. What Pike described as the "confluence" of the two rivers, the Mdewakanton called the *bdote*, and it was the site of their most sacred ceremonies. Pike didn't make that connection. He thought the scaffold intriguing, but he had other things on his mind. He intended to buy the *bdote* as a site for an army fort.

Calling together several chiefs, including Le Petit Corbeau, Pike staged a council under an awning (made of a boat sail) on the riverbank. He started with a speech, "which though long," as he admitted, focused on the interest of the United States, first, in buying one hundred thousand acres surrounding the confluence and, second, in fostering peace between the Mdewakanton and the Ojibwe. Pike valued the land at two dollars per acre—two hundred thousand dollars—but bragged later that he managed to secure it for two hundred dollars. "You will perceive that we have obtained about 100,000 Acres for a Song," were his exact words.

Pike evinced no particular respect for the Indians that he met during the first part of his expedition. He didn't differentiate Indians from European Americans merely on the basis of cultural differences, but on human ones. Near the outset of the trip, he expressed surprise at the idea that an Indian would have personal emotions. On being told the story of a Sioux woman who chose to commit suicide rather than marry a man she didn't love, Pike called it "an impressive display of sentiment for a Savage!" *Savage*, by itself, was not a notable disparagement at the time, being roughly equivalent in use to "aboriginal" today, but his astonishment at her sense of humanity was certainly insulting to an entire race. Pike wasn't the only American of his generation to harbor that attitude, which contrasts with the fact that in the West, the French and to a great extent the Spanish were noticeably more appreciative of Indians, both as individuals and as whole tribes.

At 0.2 cent per acre, Pike's deal might have made even William Henry Harrison squirm with guilt. But two factors mitigated the basic math, as well as Pike's self-congratulation—the terms of his treaty left the actual purchase price to be determined by Congress at a later time. (In fact, Wilkinson was less than pleased that Pike left that question open.) The second point is that the Mdewakanton didn't need money—according to the way that they looked at the world, what they needed was protection from the Ojibwe. On that score, historian Gary C. Anderson wrote, they "probably thought they were getting a bargain. . . . Mdewakanton leaders obviously viewed Pike and the Americans as future allies and kinsmen." The sense of security was an important part of the purchase price, whether or not Pike and subsequent Americans fully understood it.

After finalizing the treaty, Pike was feeling lighthearted and celebratory, yet his mood turned dangerous the very next day. "In the morning," he wrote, "I discovered my Flag to be gone off from my Boat—uncertain whether it had been stolen by the Indians, or fell overboard and floated away." Either way, he was enraged at the

guard who had been on duty, dealing him an "instantaneous punishment" of one hundred lashes. That was more than was allowed
by army regulations, but Pike was beside himself. The flag, just a
piece of cloth, was not the backbone of an army unit and not its
mind, either; the flag was its very throat, according to Pike's training, and if the enemy had hold of that piece of cloth, then all was
lost. American lives remained secure on the boat, yet in their battle
for respect, the capture of the flag carried the same message as in the
carnage of true war: defeat was at hand. Pike suspected the Indians
downriver.

The day wasn't developing as a happy one there, either.

A rather vain Mdewakanton chief named Outard Blanche
(White Bustard) had suffered a cut lip—there was even a report
that his lip had been cut off, but that would have made it difficult
for him to talk, and he did a lot of that in the aftermath. He blamed
Le Petit Corbeau for his injury, confronting him. Outard Blanche
said, according to Le Petit Corbeau's account, "that his face was his
looking glass, that it was spoiled; and that he was determined on
revenge." Le Petit Corbeau drew his guns in response, impulsively
rushing to meet Outard Blanche's revenge and raise it to a higher
level. Yet at the exact moment when the two chiefs and their seconds faced off along the banks of the Mississippi, something new
suddenly happened, something none of them had ever seen before.

An American flag on a broken pole went bobbing by in the river.

Everyone stopped fighting. Le Petit Corbeau reasoned that the
flag must have been taken from Pike in violence and that they should
prioritize the day, setting aside the revenge at hand until they "had
revenged the cause of their eldest Brother."

Early the next morning, Pike felt someone waking him up and
opened his eyes to see Le Petit Corbeau. He had, Pike wrote,

> come up from his Village to see if we were all killed, or if
> any accident had happened to us—they had found my Flag

floating three miles below their Village: (15 miles hence)
From which they concluded some affray had taken place,
and that it had been thrown overboard.

On being awakened, Pike was unconcerned about the flag, even
though it had sent him into a half-mad frenzy the day before. He
did express a distant measure of concern about the feuding between
the chiefs. Counseling them that they needed to settle their differences peacefully, he handed over a number of presents for Le Petite
Corbeau to split with Outard Blanche. The consensus was that the
flag must have fallen off the boat by itself and floated downriver.
The point that Pike missed, though, was that the Mdewakanton
chief had raced twelve miles overnight and come to his rescue, not
to get presents, but because they were bonded as kin by the treaty.
"A wonderful exhibition of Sentiment," indeed, whether it was returned or not.

Seventeen

ACHIEVEMENTS LARGE AND SMALL

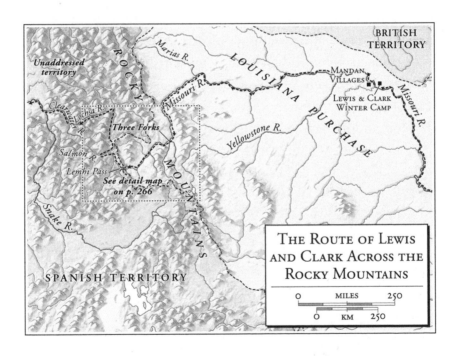

As a leader, Pike had the energy and bearing to impress. He was especially effective with his own men, leading by charismatic example. On the expedition to the Pacific, by contrast, Clark and especially

Lewis maintained a sense of reserve in relation to their corpsmen. They consistently refrained from anything that could compromise the discipline they regarded as critical to their success on such a long trip. Dunbar and Hunter gave up early on crisp discipline. In fact, they threw their hands up on the first day. They then spent three months trying to find a substitute for it in eliciting hard work, and eventually, somehow, they succeeded.

Pike's expedition developed a more natural atmosphere than either of the other two. He drove his soldiers hard, yet referred to them affectionately as "my boys." He often had fun with them. Pike didn't just go hunting, for example; he bet the crew that he could kill an elk. With that, he set off on a hunting trip that was something of a disaster, especially for all the many maimed elks who went through life with bullets in obscure parts of their bodies as a result of Pike's refusal to lose the bet. Finally, he came upon a recumbent buck that was either asleep or perhaps already dead. He shot him and headed home to tell the boys.

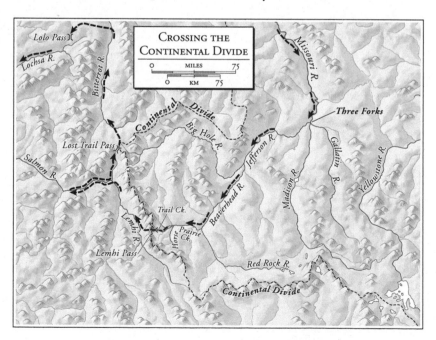

Perhaps Pike, known to be a good marksman, wasn't the best hunter of all time. In terms of his cunning with humans, Wilkinson told Dearborn, "he is a much abler Soldier than Negotiator." And modern geographers have noted that his notations on distances carried a conspicuous margin of error—plus or minus 110 percent. Pike was average or worse in many of the individual facets of exploration, but he was second to no one in determination, a half-mad sense of imperative that he deftly inspired in his men. He was similar to Lewis in his adamancy, but not even Lewis, heading west to cross the Rockies, would be tested as was Pike. An army officer with more years in the service than any of the other leaders, he had already put in time in the safety of a quiet fort. Surprisingly elegant for a frontier officer, he'd kept books, counted inventories, and logged in shipments of materiel, all the while dreaming of real action. He finally had it, and more by the day as his expedition continued north.

After negotiating the treaty with the Mdewakanton, Pike was anxious to see Saint Anthony Falls, the wide, dramatic feature that dropped the waters of the Mississippi as much as twenty-nine feet. The impression of the vertical drop ranged widely. In fact, when Pike sent three of his men to scout the falls, about two and a half miles from the confluence of St. Peter's River with the Mississippi, he was dismayed to receive three completely different descriptions of it. That was understandable. The misshapen falls jutted out in some places and caved backward in others, with islands intruding themselves on the whitewater. Saint Anthony probably didn't look the same from any two points on shore. It was always, however, said to be breathtaking.*

The only falls on the Mississippi River, Saint Anthony was a line of demarcation in the region. It refereed the Ojibwe and

---

* Saint Anthony Falls no longer exists as a natural feature.

Mdewakanton, keeping them apart, even as it gave them a place to meet in tentative talks, or at least to espy each other on their separate errands in a place held sacred by both nations. For Pike, the falls were also monumental, having the same meaning that the Mandan villages had for Lewis and Clark. They marked the last stage of the route that was known or accessible to Euro-Americans.

About two weeks remained before Pike needed to head south in order to guarantee that he would arrive in St. Louis before ice formed on the Mississippi. As a Jeffersonian explorer, he'd already made his contribution to the president's cause. The American commitment to the territory was made known to the British, as well as to three of the largest Indian nations in the region. Pike had compiled geographical information regarding the river, which could be useful, even if it didn't always happen to be accurate. He still had plenty of time to make specific findings on Saint Anthony Falls, and they would be of the same interest to easterners as were the hot springs near the Ouachita River. Pike's findings could be sent immediately to the national capital, where Jefferson would make use of them in diplomacy, foreign as well as domestic.

Continuing past Saint Anthony Falls to the source of the Mississippi, however, would give Pike his chance at matching the glory of Lewis and Clark. Jefferson's explorers shared a conspiratorial understanding that the president could no longer merely talk about the value of the American presence in newly acquired western lands—he needed to prove it. He had to bring forward in place of his words the color of the rock, the words of the chiefs, the direction of the water, and the fact that the American mind had met its frontier. The president was waiting. And he was still waiting. One of the common attributes of the expedition leaders was a nagging Jeffersonian ulcer that pressured them to provide the material that he needed *as soon as practical*. It ate Lewis up. It drove Dunbar to distraction. It was Pike's dilemma at Saint Anthony Falls.

Whether to come back before winter to feed the news cycle of the day with at least, by Pike's ambitious standards, a half-finished mission . . . or to continue in the interest of later, but bolder, headlines until the geography was known: Pike had that decision to make, even while the Mississippi River crashed down all around him at Saint Anthony Falls.

Captain Lewis had faced similar decisions in early July, weighing Jefferson's overall goals against more immediate considerations. Arduously portaging around the Great Falls in what is now western Montana, the Corps of Discovery had devoted almost two weeks to hand-carrying their belongings over rugged terrain. They built rudimentary wagons to help, but eventually ended up hand-carrying even the wagons. Most of the men were bloodied, but not by the mountain lions they'd begun to spot or the grizzlies that had become anything but a novelty. The wounds were from plants such as cactus, especially the low-growing species that bit into their moccasins, slashing their feet and ankles. Such duress had to be expected, though, in a trip across half of the continent, and, anyway, explorers aren't supposed to complain. They did, though, after twelve days of portage at the Great Falls.

By the time the men were upstream of the falls, they were on the Rocky Mountain Front, the uneven geological formation that draws the prairieland up to the mountains. Lewis had been expecting to send another contingent back to St. Louis from the eastern edge of the mountains. He and Clark had another installment of specimens and notes packed and ready to ship to Jefferson. When the portage dragged on, though, it erased the very slim chance of crossing the mountains, touching the Pacific, and then returning to the Mandan villages before winter. For that reason, Lewis was even more anxious to send the shipment with its news value to Jefferson. Other factors, though, changed his mind.

The Minitarí had warned the captains of the viciousness of their own traditional enemies, the Shoshone. As the corps drew nearer to Shoshone territory in the heart of the Rockies, Lewis and Clark began to take the warnings more and more seriously. The fact that Sacajawea was a Shoshone and had become a member of the expedition didn't mitigate Lewis's trepidation. He had to consider the fact that he'd have fewer men in his little army should he send a detachment back east. He also feared that those who were left to finish the trip might resent the division of the corps. Despite the fact that Jefferson was waiting, Lewis made the decision to forgo any shipment from the Rockies. Meanwhile, on July 15, when the expedition was finally ready to move forward on the Missouri River again, Lewis made an observation familiar to every tour group leader: the luggage was growing. "We arrose very early this morning," he wrote, "assigned the canoes their loads and had it put on board. we now found our vessels eight in number all heavily laden . . . we find it extremely difficult to keep the baggage of many of our men within reasonable bounds; they will be adding bulky articles of but little use or value to them."

The captains were among those who walked alongside the Missouri River, in order to lighten the canoes. The water had sliced canyons into the Rocky Mountains, a range that Private Whitehouse perceived was well named. "These mountains appear to be from the nearest calculation that we can make 700 feet high," he wrote, "and it appear'd to be a solid rock." As they made slow progress, the Missouri was joined from the north by a wide river, which Lewis and Clark named after Secretary of War Dearborn. Lewis was intrigued with the newly christened river and its clear waters. "It appears as if it might be navigated," he wrote, "but to what extent must be conjectural." The Dearborn River, in fact, offered a relatively smooth conduit toward a pass that sidestepped the worst of the Rockies in that region. Had Lewis been thinking in terms of an easier trip, he might have remembered that the Minitarí back at the Mandan villages had advised the captains to look for that very river. But Lewis was thinking only about his orders from Jefferson, which explicitly directed him to find the source of the Missouri. The Dearborn, as inviting as it was, meant nothing more to him.

At about the time that Lewis was walking by the confluence of the Dearborn River, Clark split off from the main expedition, ostensibly to scout for the Shoshone, but probably because the pace was so slow along the shallow river. As long as most of the members of the expedition were forced to walk, it made sense to fan out to some extent. They separated often on the way through the Rocky Mountains, sometimes for weeks at a time, as one or the other— usually Clark—would take on a side assignment and disappear. They made agreements as to where to meet, but since they didn't really know where they were going, it could be a tenuous arrangement. Sometimes, without prior coordination, they even left notes for one another, tacked to a tree or anchored to a rock. The fact that unexpected notes would be spotted indicates that by the summer of 1805, the captains had developed a second form of communication— glancing around unfamiliar terrain where the scenery itself rained colors and knowing exactly what the other would see first.

The certainty that they couldn't miss one another's notes failed on only one occasion. In early August, Lewis left a note on a tree, but a beaver cut the tree down and dragged it away.

By that time, the two leaders had been exploring together, practically every day, for almost two years. Clark and Lewis grew closer in their working relationship, which has been one part of the fascination of their expedition. Leadership wasn't an individual characteristic; it required uninterrupted loyalty from two very different men under trying circumstances. The way that their partnership developed gave the captains the benefit of solid guessing—not snatching a choice from the air, but the serious exercise of analyzing and prioritizing information, even when key parts are missing. When the Missouri River forked, for example, it was nearly impossible to tell which branch was the main river. To choose the wrong fork could have serious consequences, since a dead end might delay the expedition enough to strand the corps in the mountains when winter arrived. In serious discussions at several such forks, Lewis and Clark pooled their thoughts and proved themselves to be smart guessers, an unsung but crucial art. That record, however, undercut Jefferson's hope that neither leader would be irreplaceable.

By the time the corps reached the spot where the Missouri separated into three rivers, or forks, the right guess was just that much harder. At that juncture, the captains had already separated temporarily, and they took advantage of the opportunity to examine the terrain from different perspectives. It was also fortunate that they could rely on at least some intelligence from the Minitarí. Known as Three Forks, the spot was surrounded by just enough ridges to promise an overview, and yet so many that they blocked the sightlines for the corpsmen. With three new rivers to name, they called one the Jefferson River to honor the president, naming the other two after the members of his cabinet who had done the most to realize the Louisiana Purchase: Secretary of State James Madison and Secretary of the Treasury Albert Gallatin. Separately and together, the leaders selected the Jefferson as the best route west.

The question is why Lewis and Clark wanted to give the main fork another name at all. "Both Capt. C and myself corrisponded in opinion with rispect to the impropriety of calling either of these streams the Missouri," Lewis wrote. That being the case, they were done; they'd made their discovery. The source of the Missouri River was the Jefferson River. That sly decision—to drop the name "Missouri"—indicated that Lewis and Clark were no longer able to affirm the original intent of the mission, seeking the *true* source of the great river: that is, the most remote place from which a drop of water or a twig could find its way all the way to the Mississippi River along a single current. Faced with three viable candidates for the longest fork, they didn't have time, with winter coming, to survey each one. In effect, the captains admitted that they were abandoning the scientific search for the source of the Missouri when they renamed it, choosing what they thought (correctly) was the main branch, the Jefferson River, and following it in the direction of the more pressing goal: the Pacific Ocean.

By mid-August, Lewis and Clark were actively looking for any sign of an Indian presence in the region—more pointedly, they were seeking the Shoshone. The Shoshone were supposed to live on the eastern side of the Rocky Mountains in Montana, but Lewis and Clark hadn't seen them and, indeed, hadn't met another person since leaving the Mandan villages. At first, they'd approached Shoshone lands with trepidation at meeting members of the tribe, but that eventually changed to fear of not meeting any. With game growing scarce, the captains were hoping to trade for food. Moreover, since they had begun to strongly suspect that there was no water route to the Pacific, they wanted to obtain horses, perhaps as many as fifty, for an overland trip. Fearing and yet seeking the Shoshone, Lewis began a hike as the Jefferson River grew narrow, taking three of his men. As important, they were seeking the Lemhi Pass.

The Lemhi Pass across the Continental Divide was one of the easier sections of the Rocky Mountains to traverse; the land leading to it, more than seventy-two hundred feet above sea level, rose on a gentle incline, covered with stubble and small rocks. Having separated temporarily from Clark, Lewis came upon a river that emptied into the Jefferson, where it began. Two other small rivers also flowed into the Jefferson near its source: three forks, again. Tracing level terrain, all of the waterways were delineated by grasslands. Opting for the northernmost, the Big Hole River, Lewis followed it for a few miles, surveyed its tightly winding course and then stopped, knowing he'd chosen wrong. The Big Hole River was taking him in the wrong direction. He reverted to the middle river, the Beaverhead, which stretched out straight and strong, the most likely continuation of the Jefferson/Missouri. Clark made the same mistake on the Big Hole, following behind Lewis by a day or so with the canoes and the rest of the corps—and leg ailments that made travel excruciating. There was nothing to do but travel, however, so Clark lagged with the cargo while Lewis darted ahead once again with four of the men.

Finding some indication of recent Indian activity on the banks of the Beaverhead, in the form of foot- and hoof prints, Lewis was encouraged. His immediate goal was to find the Shoshone, but he was still intrigued with the ultimate source of the waters of the Missouri, and he presumed that the Beaverhead would serve both purposes. Then the Beaverhead forked. Lewis had another decision to make. He chose northwest over southeast, following Horse Prairie Creek. It curved up the crest not more than a quarter mile from the Continental Divide. And then *it* forked.

Letting Horse Prairie Creek continue curving to the south, Lewis's scouting party veered to the west along the little waterway they called Trail Creek.

By the time Lewis and his men hiked it to the end, they realized that they were seeing their familiar river in its infancy or, as Lewis described it:

> the most distant fountain of the waters of the mighty Missouri in surch of which we have spent so many toilsome days and wristless nights. thus far I had accomplished one of those great objects on which my mind has been unalterably fixed for many years

Clowning around, one of the men straddled the innocent little brook where it was forming a bit farther upstream, demonstrating that he was finally bigger than the great Missouri. For his part, Lewis took a drink, "pure and ice cold," from the brook. He was undoubtedly at the most distant fountain—of Trail Creek. Geologists later determined that one of the other creeks stemming from the Jefferson River was the actual source of the Missouri. That other creek spit forth from a spring in the ground: the very, very begin-ning of the Missouri River.

Lemhi Pass brought Lewis's scouting party to "the top of the di-viding ridge," as Lewis called it. It was the Continental Divide, that high-altitude wall across which water does not flow. Trotting even a short way to the west side, Lewis was affected by his new proximity to the Pacific. As he took another sip of water from a creek there, he enjoyed the fact that it connected him somehow to the Columbia River.

Farther to the west of the divide, Lewis's small party at last came across other human beings—an older Shoshone woman, with a young woman and a girl. Terrified by the sight of Lewis and his men, the three prepared to be slaughtered on the spot. The young woman ran away, while the other two sank to the ground, "hold-ing their heads as though reconciled to die," Lewis reported. It was a reflex of the Lemhi Shoshone to believe that strangers would kill them on sight.

The Lemhi Shoshone expertise lay in horsemanship and, sec-ondarily, horse stealing. Fittingly, their prime asset was their flex-ibility, avoiding stronger enemies by moving around their extensive homelands and enjoying a varied diet, so they weren't tied to any one place in particular. It was adaptation on a remarkably sophis-ticated level. Having an abundant supply of the gold standard of the West—horses—they were frequently raided by their neighbors, and, indeed, they were living on the very top of the Rockies in mid-summer because they felt protected there. The members of the tribe that Lewis and Clark eventually visited were entirely friendly, once Lewis convinced them that he was not there to hurt them, though he couldn't help noticing how many of the Shoshone horses bore Spanish brands.

One of the achievements of the Corps of Discovery was taking Sacajawea back to her own people. In one emotional scene after an-other in the Shoshone village, she was reunited with her friends and relatives, including her brother, who had become the chief. Lewis and Clark would not have gone out of their way to bring Sacajawea to her home—they were far too single-minded about reaching the Pacific—and yet they did facilitate her homecoming. Compared with finding a route to the Pacific and opening the Northwest in the minds of a young American nation, bringing back one person, snatched into slavery as a child of twelve, was in its way equal to anything else they did.

A WEEK LATER, Lewis celebrated his thirty-first birthday and reflected on the subject of accomplishments, small and large. He wondered whether it mattered what they were. The important factor was why they were attempted. Lewis had come around to a new way of judging achievement—an exercise that would have been lost on someone like Lieutenant Pike, who was born supremely, even mythologically, confident in his sense of mission. Unfortunately, the new method of self-analysis only made Lewis shudder with a brand-new way to feel that he was a failure:

> This day I completed my thirty first year, and conceived that
> I had in all human probability now existed about half the
> period which I am to remain in this Sublunary world. I re-
> flected that I had as yet done but little, very little indeed, to
> further the hapiness of the human race, or to advance the in-
> formation of the succeeding generation. I viewed with regret
> the many hours I have spent in indolence, and now soarly
> feel the want of that information which those hours would
> have given me had they been judiciously expended. but since
> they are past and cannot be recalled. I dash from the gloomy
> thought and resolved in future, to redouble my exertions and
> at least indeavor to promote those two primary objects of

human existence, by giving them the aid of that portion of
talents which nature and fortune have bestoed on me; or in
future, to live for *mankind*, as I have heretofore lived for *myself.* –

It is crass to suggest that Lewis just needed rest to cure him
of the resolve to be less selfish—but there is an impression of nervous strain left by his journal entry. Inasmuch as he was subject to
lonely bouts of doubt, it was lucky that he reunited with Clark at the
Shoshone village. They then spent several weeks there, haggling for
horses, while the corps prepared to cross the last range of the Rockies, the Bitterroot Mountains. If Lewis seriously wanted something
to regret, he would find it there.

As the expedition made its way across the Bitterroots (with
Sacajawea opting to continue with it), the Indian road tightened
into a trail, and then, around peaks and across steep drops, it shrank
to a scratch in the dirt, and then, finally, there was nothing more
substantial than the pointing of the Shoshone guide. The corps led
fully loaded horses over the rugged landscape, the worst encountered since the boats had been abandoned on the Jefferson. After a
hard snow of at least a half foot, the dismal picture was complete:
the men and horses were just about starved, they were cold and slipping around, and the risk of death abounded.

September 19 was the low point of the Bitterroot span, whatever
the altitude, as they made their way along the side of a mountain
overlooking a creek. "The road was excessively dangerous," Lewis
wrote, "being a narow rockey path generally on the side of steep
precipice, from which in many places if ether man or horse were
precipitated they would inevitably be dashed in pieces."

And then, with all the slipping, it happened. "One of our horses
fell backwards, & rolled about 100 feet down a steep solid Rock,"
Whitehouse wrote, "and dashed against a Rock, in the Creek with
his load, which was Ammunition." The men made their way down

as fast as they could, with their main objective to salvage the expedition's store of ammunition before it got wet. When they unfastened the load and pulled it away, though, the horse shocked them all. He stood up. He was fine, and twenty minutes later he was back on the trail.

"The most wonderful escape I ever witnessed," Lewis beamed in his ebullient account of the fall. He and his men were in high spirits, anyway, because in the distance they had spotted a plain. Clark wasn't hiking with them then; he was traveling a short distance ahead with a party. His health wasn't as strong as it had been a few months before, and he was suffering badly from the lack of food. In fact, he was the one who named the water below "Hungry Creek." The next day, though, Clark was the first to benefit from the end of the harrowing trek across the Bitterroots, entering what he considered beautiful country and then being welcomed into a Nimi`ipuu (Nez Perce) village. When Lewis caught up, the entire corps had enough to eat for the first time in weeks. And then, having survived the Bitterroot Mountains at their worst, they almost succumbed, or wished they could, from the Nimi`ipuu diet.

The Nimi`ipuu were respected by Lewis and Clark, along with observers ever since, for the discipline of their thinking and the quality of their lifestyle. Not, however, the quality of their food, at least for a European-American palate. Being mainly composed of smoked fish and roots, Nimi`ipuu meals sounded benign, but made many of the men violently ill, none more than Lewis. As he struggled to recover during the last week of September, Clark took the lead in commissioning boats for use on the local rivers en route to the Columbia River.

Lieutenant Pike was at Saint Anthony Falls that week. On September 26, two messengers arrived, courtesy of one of the British traders near Prairie du Chien. Characteristically, Pike had decided that he had to continue the expedition rather than return to St. Louis. The weight of the moment affected him as he drew together a packet of papers for the messengers to forward to Wilkinson. "This business," he wrote, describing his feelings as he sealed the package, "appeared like a last adieu to the civilized World." With that, Pike and his men climbed into their boats.

In Santa Fe, Vial was at the head of his second expedition to stop Lewis and Clark. The new plan was to solidify the bonds with Indian nations in the region—always a priority for Spain during its cold war with the United States—while convincing them to do the job of forcing the Americans to retire. They chose the Pawnee. It was an excellent scheme: a hundred or more warriors could descend on the expedition and either decimate it or at least scare it back home. That's exactly how it happened, too, with a nighttime attack of more than a hundred Indians on horseback until the expedition had no choice but to run. Unfortunately, the expedition attacked was Vial's. Even he could not discern the nation to which the marauders belonged, but then, he was on the run, doing his best to protect his crewmen and perhaps even more so, his horses. "Finding ourselves devoid of munitions for our defense," he wrote afterward, "we all decided to return to Santa Fe." Vial, one of the most dauntless of explorers for any flag in the late eighteenth century, had proved himself unable to move a large detachment into unfamiliar territory. His failures in late summer of 1804 and the autumn of 1805 saved Lewis and Clark from interference, but shifted even more pressure on the Jeffersonian explorers closer to the heart of Spanish North America.

At the beginning of October, Pike was strangely oblivious to the fact that he was starting north at the very onset of wintry weather. In fact, when Wilkinson received his letter, he was dismayed, accusing his lieutenant of "stretching his orders." Pike was stretching all reason, too, as he found out when the Mississippi started to turn to ice water on October 16. His own description, one of the most horrific in the annals of exploration during Jefferson's era, indicates that even he questioned his judgment:

When we arose in the morning found a snow had fell, and was still falling, which covered the ground two Inches. This was but poor encouragement for attacking the rapids, in which we were sure we must wade to our necks. But I was determined if possible, to make Le Riviere De Corbeau (the highest point ever made by the Trader's in the Bark Canoes). We Embarked, and after four hours work became perfectly useless in our limb's with cold. We put to shore on the opposite side of the River, about two thirds of the way up the rapid's. Built a large fire, and then discovered that our Boats were nearly half full of Water, both having sprung large leak's, so as to oblige me to keep three hands bailing. My Sergeant (Kenneman) one of the Stoutest men I ever knew, broke a blood vessel, and vomited nearly two quarts of blood. One of my Corporals (Bradley) also evacuated nearly one pint of blood, when he attempted to void his urine. These circumstances, with four of my men being rendered useless before; who were left on shore [farther downriver], convinced me, that, if I had no regard for my own health and constitution, I should have some for those poor fellows, who, to obey my orders were killing themselves.

Pike came to his senses, to the extent that Pike could. He immediately announced that they would build winter quarters comfortable enough for frigid weather of twenty, thirty, or even forty degrees below zero. The soldiers would stay there while he continued north largely by himself to find the source of the Mississippi River. Pike had, as he stated, no regard for his own health and constitution. To make matters worse as the temperature steadily dropped, he vowed to delay leaving until he had hunted for enough meat to sustain the men while he was gone, a promise that took Pike the better part of a month to fulfill.

Eighteen

"THE MORE DANGER THE MORE HONOR"

On November 9, a Sunday, Thomas Freeman was in Washington, the city he'd known as empty acreage fifteen years before. He pulled out a card and picked up a pen to tend to an important piece of correspondence. "Thos.," he wrote, capping the "T" with a billowing loop. "Freeman," he continued, its loop drawn to nestle inside the first one, "will do himself the honor of dining with the President of the United States on Tuesday, next agreeably to invitation." By then, Freeman was well aware that the president was ready to name a leader for the exploration of the source of the Red River, the third of his expeditions into the West, and in its day the most important.

The very first of Jefferson's expeditions was close to success on November 9—about fifteen miles from it, to be exact, after more than thirty-seven hundred miles. Rain pelted down, but Lewis and Clark were sure they'd be able to see the Pacific Ocean when the skies cleared; they had been overjoyed to spot what they thought must be the ocean the day before as a blur in the distance. Most of the time, they were stranded along the Columbia River and could see very little. The rain wouldn't let up, and the members of the corps were drenched day and night. "Not withstanding the disagreeable time of the party for Several days past they are all chearfull and full of anxiety to See further into the ocean," Clark wrote on November 9.

Actually, the men had yet to see at all "into the ocean." What they saw in the distance was only the widening of the river near its mouth, but, then, perhaps mere geography was trumped by the rule of the water. In front of their camps—and sometimes washing over them—the river was filled with seawater. When the men were wading around to bail out their canoes or haul their belongings farther up the bank, they were in a sense already in the ocean, complete with unpotable water and rugged swells.

Since leaving the Nimi`ipuu, Lewis and Clark had navigated over six hundred miles in canoes, finding ways through or around treacherous stretches of the Columbia, a younger and far more unsettled river than the Missouri. It churned through waterfalls and rapids, in addition to the Dalles, a narrows two miles in length. The Dalles dramatically squeezed a mile-wide river through a canyon only one hundred seventy-five feet wide. That middle section of the Columbia offered rich fishing, an activity of minimal interest to the meat eaters of the corps, but it was instrumental in supporting the oldest permanent human settlement in North America.

The Wasco Indians on the south side of the river and the Wishram on the north had been on the same land for more than five thousand years. They were remarkable artisans, making intricately patterned bowls and baskets, in which they stored salmon for the winter. The Wishram were the busy traders in their region, not unlike the Mandan, but they didn't make as good an impression. They struck the corps as sharpsters, continually looking for a way to get the better of visitors. They were also less hygienic by American standards, crawling as they were with lice and fleas. On the basis of just those two characteristics, more than one corpsman found the Wishram "troublesome."

Lewis and Clark were rarely out of contact with people along the Columbia as they made their way to their soggy base near the estuary. None of the Indians they passed appeared threatening, although one of the guides accompanying the expedition reported that he'd heard that a plan was in the works to massacre the corps down to the last man. Where a growing euphoria might be expected, Lewis and Clark became increasingly morose on the last leg of the journey. Perhaps a certain letdown might be expected. But the moody coastal region near the Columbia discouraged celebration. In front of their various footholds near the estuary, the waters of the river were as rough as those of the North Atlantic. After thousands of miles of travel, most of it on rivers, the corpsmen rarely went far in their canoes. Ultimately, they clung to a puddle of a camp on the north bank, watching local Indians dart around the treacherous river in their canoes as though it were a glassy pond. The Indians were far better canoeists, as Clark had to admit, watching them disappear behind high swells and then come bobbing back into view. When three of the corpsmen tried to emulate the Indians, the "waves tossed them about at will," and they fought their way back to the riverbank as soon as they could—even that took the better part of an hour.

Lewis and Clark weren't used to being the weaklings in any situation—they'd just taken Jefferson's victory tour across half a continent. With the confidence of the masters, they strode across the cultural chasm that separated Indians of the far West from Americans of the Jefferson era. Yet, just before their journey's end, the continent made them masters of nothing, reduced to standing onshore and trying to wave down "the best canoe navigators I ever saw," as Clark wrote.

On November 11, a group of Kathlamet Indians from across the river stopped at the encampment to sell fish. The members of the corps had already been fishing, but in the signature style of the expedition. They shot the fish. Eventually, they became better at spearing it. Lewis and Clark welcomed the Kathlamets and traded trinkets for salmon. As they did, they noted without surprise that most of the Indians who came by were wearing elkskin robes. The Americans hungered for elk, but were making do with fish. As they dickered for it and more Indians arrived, the captains were suddenly taken aback. One of the newly arrived Kathlamets climbed out of his canoe in a sailor's coat and trousers.

That evening, on the other coastline, Freeman arrived at the White House for dinner. The meal was typically served at three thirty in the afternoon, after Jefferson's daily ride, which lasted from one to three o'clock. Jefferson used his dinner table as a salon, in the Parisian style, bringing together people of disparate interests. Including after-dinner tea in another room, the guests might not leave until about seven. The president selected the menus and wines himself; in fact, one of the entrées that he favored most was larded salmon—which happened to be what Lewis and Clark were having for their dinner, too. Jefferson was universally recalled as an engaging host, if sometimes quiet until the plates were cleared. In only one point did he grow less generous. He had apparently seen too many people during his first term guzzle his prized vintages. He thereupon decreased the budget for wine in each year of his administration, even though the number of guests remained about the same.

Jefferson didn't dress formally, but visitors would naturally feel compelled to be well turned out in the presidential mansion. Most of his dinner guests were male—in large part because he needed to attach a woman as hostess if females were to be present. The wife of one of his cabinet members often filled in. The hostess would preside over the after-dinner tea service, which was started by the women, before the men repaired into the salon to join them. There is no record of the number who were present when Freeman had dinner with Jefferson on Tuesday evening.

If Jefferson was vetting Freeman carefully, it was because the responsibility was enormous. The previous summer, Dunbar and Jefferson had discussed the Ouachita expedition as a precursor to the *big* trip, the one on the Red River. The Lewis and Clark expedition, as expansive as it was in every way, was second to the Red River expedition, too, in its immediate importance to Jefferson. Two years after the Louisiana Purchase, he still couldn't point to the border of his nation where it met the Spanish provinces of Texas and perhaps New Mexico. The future of West Florida was a parallel issue, since Jefferson was determined to acquire it and obtain control of the Mobile River, once and for all. After negotiations over both issues twisted to a stop in Madrid in mid-1805, Jefferson quietly prepared the nation for war with Spain.

The threat had been around for decades—cold wars are typically quick to come, but very slow to go. Jefferson had never before been so closely aligned with the possibility of a shooting war as he was during the last part of 1805. It was France that unexpectedly stepped in during the autumn, diffusing the tension regarding West Florida by simply offering to sell it to the United States. France didn't happen to own West Florida, of course, but France dominated Spain and could speak for its weaker ally.

Jefferson was commander in chief of what he called "the peace establishment." Under his aegis, the garrison at West Point, New York, had become the home of the new "Peace Academy," as the president referred to it, otherwise known as the U.S. Military Academy. Not surprisingly, his name was associated with the very word "peace" in more than rhetoric—a lasting factor in his popularity. Jefferson offered a refreshing change from the standing armies that masqueraded as nations in Europe. Having a small army, the United States could afford to buy territory that it wanted, unlike the Western European countries that were in a nearly constant state of war, with the debt to prove it. The Jeffersonian alternative relied on diplomacy and gesture, including scientific exploration. Neither, however, had yet coalesced for the sake of West Florida and a border for Orleans Territory.

While Freeman was looking forward to his dinner at the White House, Jefferson was weighing Napoleon's price for West Florida. The topic would have been irresistible for Freeman or anyone else who was interested in the Red River, because France's offer included a provision concerning Texas, which Jefferson had long tried to claim as part of the Louisiana Purchase. If the United States purchased West Florida, then according to the deal, Spain would restrict its own settlement in Texas for thirty years. That wasn't a hard code to enforce, since the Spanish didn't have any teeming masses anxious to move there anyway. The northern and eastern borders, however, were left in their usual blur. The benefit that France offered was an end to Spanish aggression along the border with Orleans Territory. For the time being, the approaching deal for West Florida was a secret, but Jefferson was confident that it would come to fruition, and long before it did, he wanted Americans on the Red River.

Most western Americans expected that the Spanish would imminently send soldiers north across the Red River and east into Orleans Territory. Many of those same westerners actively hoped that the Spanish would make just such a move, so that they could start the war they longed to fight. As Aaron Burr toured the West in 1805, he contacted just such hawkish residents. Newspaper reports fueled the stories about his plans. Jefferson heard the rumors circulating on two continents and became even more adamant that the Red River expedition begin in the first part of 1806. Writing to his friend, the French philosopher, agriculturist, and world traveler Constantin-François de Chasseboeuf, Count de Volney, Jefferson explained his practical attitude:

> These expeditions are so laborious, & hazardous, that men of science, used to the temperature & inactivity of their closet,[*]

---

[*] "Closet" referred to a private study or office.

cannot be induced to undertake them. They are headed therefore by persons qualified expressly to give us the geography of the rivers with perfect accuracy, and of good common knolege and observation in the animal, vegetable & mineral departments. When the route shall be once open and known, scientific men will undertake, & verify & class it's subjects.

On that basis, in mid-November, Freeman was formally appointed to provide the geography of the Red River "with perfect accuracy." It was an honor for an ambitious man clinging to the unsung heroism of the frontier surveyor.

Freeman described to one of his friends how delighted he was to be expected in Natchez for the start, although it would necessitate traveling in the middle of winter, which he dreaded. There was no choice if he wanted his expedition to leave Natchez in early spring. Dunbar was planning to assist with the expedition even before Freeman arrived in Natchez, organizing the supplies and, more emphatically, choosing the boat. One of the chores that Jefferson and Dunbar gladly left to Freeman was finding scientific assistants. "I expect to take with me a Naturalist and an assistant astronomer," Freeman wrote, "if such persons properly qualified can be found here willing to hazard travel in the Neighborhood of *St. Afee*." His own attitude was that a

> great many difficulties, and some personal danger will attend the expedition, but, I will—"Stick or go through." The more danger the more honor.

Freeman's parting line could have been the motto for any of the explorers: "The more danger the more honor." It implied that Jefferson had warned him vividly of the troubles with Spain and how they might affect the expedition. In the name of patriotism, if nothing else, Freeman left Washington almost immediately for Philadelphia to begin the search for men who would say the same.

The year 1806 was inevitably going to be the most active to date for Jeffersonian exploration. As it began, Lewis and Clark were planning to leave as soon as possible on their return trip, hoping to reach St. Louis during the year. Pike was still on his way north along the Mississippi River. Freeman was preparing to leave for Natchez and the start of the Red River expedition. And Wilkinson had further plans—as ever—including ones pertaining to another expedition.

In Washington, Jefferson was on more dangerous ground than any of them, actively promoting a war that he knew, at least at that juncture, was not going to occur. It was as though he wanted only a certain faction of people to hear him, while others were to remain oblivious, when he said publicly on December 3 that Spain had be-haved aggressively against American interests in Orleans and that he had "found it necessary, at length, to give orders to our troops on that frontier to be in readiness to protect our citizens and to repel by arms any similar aggressions in the future." As word of Jefferson's message spread throughout America, many people were relieved, feeling that a war long overdue was finally at hand. Having all but declared war before the American people, Jefferson needed an excuse to back out of it. Like any smart president, he looked to Congress.

ON THE COLUMBIA River, the Kathlamet Indian who was dressed in the clothes of an American sailor had sparked the curios-ity of Lewis and Clark, with Clark recording that he "made Signs that he got those Clothes from the white people who lived below the point &c." The captains had been told about a person named

"Mr. Haley," their Indian informant having learned enough English from someone to describe his latest errand: he was delivering a woman "who Mr. Haley was fond of &c." Mr. Haley was a British trader working in the region.

Even while meeting Indians who were in contact with "the white people," Lewis and Clark made no effort to send a message through them, even if it could mean a ride home. Before leaving the East, the expedition had been encouraged to consider returning with a passing ship; Jefferson even provided a letter of credit for the cost it would incur. The captains undoubtedly made the decision to return by land; among other things, they had left crates of important specimens and papers at the Great Falls of the Missouri. At the very least, though, they might have arranged to send newer collections to Jefferson by sea. The interest in other Euro-Americans was perfunctory, but after thirty-seven hundred miles, the corps no longer needed them.

When the Kathlamets paddled away, Lewis and Clark continued to stay put on their toehold. They had no choice. The stoicism of the expedition was especially noteworthy in view of the fact that their soggy campsite along the Columbia River lacked tents, walls, dry blankets—anything dry—or even sufficient elevation to separate it from the river when an aggressive tide came in. After eleven days during which the longest span without rain was two hours, the expedition finally moved on, taking up residence in an abandoned Chinook village closer to the estuary. A few days later, a party of eleven men led by Clark "set out in order to go down and see the passific ocean," in the words of Ordway, who was among those in the group. Some sort of blue-grey blur had been visible in the distance, but the expedition had yet to see ocean water endless to the eye. They seem to have been worn down by the drenching of two weeks, during which time the goal was tacitly met. The more immediate concerns of food and shelter had more meaning. Nonetheless, the captains had yet to be unequivocally convinced that they had answered Jefferson's orders to establish "communication with the waters of the Pacific ocean." While Clark walked the final miles to the west, Lewis remained in the camp.

After a long hike, Clark and those with him climbed a steep hill covered with coarse grass. As they trudged over the crest, they suddenly saw it. "A handsom view of the ocean," Ordway reported. Significantly, Clark didn't describe it in terms of his own reaction. "Men appear much Satisfied with their trip beholding with estonishment the high waves dashing against the rocks & this emence ocian," Clark wrote. He didn't record his own response to the ocean, perhaps because the moment belonged to the men.

The detachment returned to their camp and settled into the search for a site for winter quarters. After crossing the Columbia River, which proved to be a scary exercise even on a relatively calm day, the corps selected an elevated field about three miles from the river and seven from the ocean. As at the Mandan villages, they constructed wooden barracks, along with a yard behind stockade fencing. Named "Fort Clatsop," after a local Indian nation, it was completed on December 30. Lewis and Clark imposed the same general orders for discipline that they had used successfully at Mandan, but it was a different atmosphere, since tribes along the coast were not warriors, but inveterate peddlers. During the warmer months, local Indians offered their wares to the ships that called near the river. Ever since the Nootka affair had opened the region to trade, traffic had been heavy enough to change the focus and even the personality of the tribes on the northwest coast. They had learned commerce in the European-American manner and plied it aggressively. Clark intimated that contact with Euro-American traders had corrupted the Indians of the coast; the brazen practice of prostitution was one obvious effect. In any case, the Indians who swarmed the ships that arrived from April to October had only one market over the winter, and it was Fort Clatsop.

Lewis was pleasantly surprised to see that the local tribe had learned to make hats in the style of men's top hats in the United States. Apparently a man of au courant tastes, he was disappointed to see that they were made in the 1801 fashion but bought one anyway, and so did many members of the expedition. Lewis—the man who had complained on the way west that the corpsmen were too acquisitive and had too much luggage—was also fitted for a bespoke coat, made of the skins of bobcats. It was finished in mid-January. Licorice was a specialty of the locals that proved popular, as were woven mats. Everyone wanted a sea otter skin, which were in short supply. A season near the Clatsops was such that even Clark took two when the Indians came by selling hats.

The winter was quietly passed, with lesser events growing to a pretense of drama. A dead whale washed up on the beach, and some members of the expedition traveled a fair distance to see it, or what was left of it. A freckle-faced, redheaded Indian visited the camp. Over the course of the whole winter, though, the most newsworthy item of all pertained to dogs.

"Two of the Clatsops who were here yesterday," Lewis wrote on January 18, "returned today for a dog they had left." The Lewis and Clark camp was by then the worst possible place in the world to lose a dog. The corps sometimes brought in dogs by the dozen to devour. The Clatsops must have rushed back to the fort, probably running to arrive before lunchtime. In fact, it could have made for a very stiff moment, but the dog was still alive.

Doing things that they wouldn't do in the United States changed the corps. They still operated crisply as an army unit; that was one identity that was carefully protected. But survival and sometimes expediency had drawn them to veer occasionally sharply in other respects. By the time they reached Fort Clatsop, they were less representatives of American society than proof of just how delicate was its hold. As in certain Indian nations along the route, dogs were looked upon as food by the corps. Lewis reflected in January that "our

party from necessaty have been obliged to subsist some length of
time on dogs have now become extreemly fond of their flesh . . . for
my own part I have become so perfectly reconciled to the dog that I
think it an agreeable food and would prefer it vastly to lean Venison
or Elk." Reversing mores for survival was one thing. Doing so as a
preference was another. So it was that the next expedition of Lewis
and Clark, crossing back across the West to find the United States
they'd left behind, promised to be an even more difficult journey for
some than finding the Pacific.

In late January, Pike was deep in the forest of what is now central Minnesota, the terrain mottled with lakes and creeks for fifty
miles in every direction. A traveler named George H. Monk, who
visited a year later, described the region: "Lakes, Rivers and swamps
are numerous in this quarter. . . . Many of the lakes, Bays & Rivers
are muddy and spontaneously produce vast quantities of wild rice,
of which the natives gather but a small part." On top of the confus-
ing mess of water, beavers built dams that changed the topography
anew. Their handiwork and the stubborn brambles that covered the
land heightened the challenge of staying in proximity of the river.

Pike brought a contingent of his soldiers with him up the Mississippi, but they inevitably constituted the rear guard. He couldn't
resist racing ahead with one or two of his men. As Pike drew within
range of the source of the Mississippi he was in the habit of scouting in front with just one soldier, John Boley. The supporting detachment followed, once a route was established. In late January,
Pike and Boley started to enter the orbit of British fur traders, who
combed through what is now northwestern Minnesota. None had
been spotted, but the Ojibwe in the area lived with apparent dependence on British trade.

On January 28, Pike was sharing a camp with his supporting
detachment, preparing to make the final push, when Boley broke
down and asked to be relieved. He "wished to decline going on"
with Pike; the physical challenge of hacking through frozen under-

brush to break the trail was a likely deterrent. Pike needed a replacement and duly gathered his men together, but no one volunteered. The boys suddenly seemed to get very busy with other things. No one knew better that Pike was relentless to a painful degree. Keeping up with him was hard, but once he started, convincing him to stop or slow down was impossible.

Just at the moment when Pike was reduced to ordering someone to join him in breaking the trail, a private named Theodore Miller stepped forward. Carrying gear, but no tents, the two of them worked to the point of exhaustion each day, cutting a trail where there wasn't one, and then sleeping outside, under the stars and in the wind. Each morning, they were chilled through just as though they'd had no blankets. In fact, Pike barely slept at all, due to the cold.

Midwinter wasn't the worst time to explore the northern Mississippi region—the brush and the insects being minimized—but it wasn't the best time to go, either. Temperatures were low, of course, and the snow was often high. Pike and Miller learned to snowshoe, because there was no other choice, except shoveling a very long trail. The area was actually far from desolate, though. Nearly every day, he and Miller came across a house or lodge occupied by Ojibwes— who could be rough with strangers. The first word, in fact, that Pike memorized in the Ojibwe language was "Chewockomen," which meant "American."

One of the largest Indian nations north of Mexico, the Ojibwe ranged through the region west of the Great Lakes. They were known to be generous and friendly with most visitors, but gruesomely, even anatomically vicious to enemies—notably the Iroquois and the Dakota (including the Mdewakanton). Ceremonial cannibalism was even practiced at one of the spiritual homes of the nation, Leech Lake. Pike was intrepid, if a little foolish, almost continually darting out ahead of the others in his party, armed as he was with little more than a word: "Chewockomen." He carried firearms, too, but a rifle and a pistol wouldn't fend off any band of Ojibwe who hadn't yet heard the news that their nation was supposed to trust the Americans.

Stopping at an Ojibwe lodge on January 30, Pike was taken aback when the residents—a married couple with five children, and an older woman—boldly went through his pockets while he was still wearing his clothes. As they roughed him up, Pike stood his ground and tried to defuse the situation, finally resorting to his word. When the family members heard that he was a Chewockomen, they immediately became more hospitable. The older woman even offered him tobacco, which he didn't use.

Her husband went a little further, offering, as Pike wrote sardonically, anything in the house, including the house, for a bottle of whiskey. (Pike demurred, though he gave him a small glass of it the next day, without charge.) Normally, Ojibwe could count on trading furs for liquor and other commodities. In fact, they no longer bothered with many of their tribal ways of life—such as gathering wild rice—in favor of trading, often at a disadvantage on credit. Sadly, even that arrangement was coming to an abrupt end in many patches of a vast territory, including Leech Lake, where beaver had become scarce, due to overhunting in the interest of trade for liquor.

The following day, Pike and Private Miller came to a fork in the river, where the mighty Mississippi was all of forty feet wide. One branch headed northwest toward, as Pike suspected, Lake Winnibigoshish. The other branch pointed west-southwest en route to Lake Leech. Pike had asked those he met along the river to advise him on its source, yet no one could help him with any real authority. The question hadn't come up before; people in the area were busy with matters they considered less trivial. It was not surprising that Pike couldn't find anyone who knew for certain where the Mississippi began or, indeed, who cared.

Someone along the way did point him toward Leech Lake, probably because it was one of the largest bodies of water in the region.

It was also a revered place in the Ojibwe perspective. Standing at the fork, Pike followed the south-southwest branch toward the lake, camping out for the night after hiking about a mile. He had been traveling with cold, wet feet so long that he was starting to suffer without respite, having apparently developed the condition known as nonfreezing cold injury, better known as trench foot. First, cold, waterlogged skin stops working properly, leading to problems with nerves and veins. Then atrophy of the muscles sets in. If trench foot isn't treated, or at least checked with rest, it leads to gangrene.

Pike was not resting. Because of that, his condition was deteriorating. He couldn't walk normally but had invented a hobble on two nearly wooden feet, past pain, and without free movement. Standing at his camp one day, all but immobile, he looked up to see a mountain lion stalking him. A mountain lion weighs about one hundred fifty pounds, the same or a little more than Pike. More important for Pike, one of the big cats could leap thirty feet with only a small start, pouncing on prey from a surprisingly long distance. At that moment, Pike made a mental note that the cat in his camp was twice the size of the panthers he'd seen farther south.

Pike instantly squatted down, giving Private Miller a direct line of fire at the mountain lion. Pike explained rather elaborately later that he crouched down in order to "entice" the animal to approach. Possibly that was his thinking, but the lion, seeing that the second man was hale, hearty, and aiming a rifle, ran away. It was all too obvious that Pike's feet were severely damaged. For him, continuing in freezing temperatures unfortunately just wasn't feasible.

And so Pike continued. Zebulon Pike was a singular man, sublimely stupid in pursuit of a goal. He limped his way to the source of the Mississippi River, because, as Freeman had expressed it two months before, "the more danger the more honor." The image of Pike wobbling before the mountain lion and then inching his way to the headwaters proves the power of the words: at least in a realm less rational.

Nineteen

HOBBLING BOLDLY

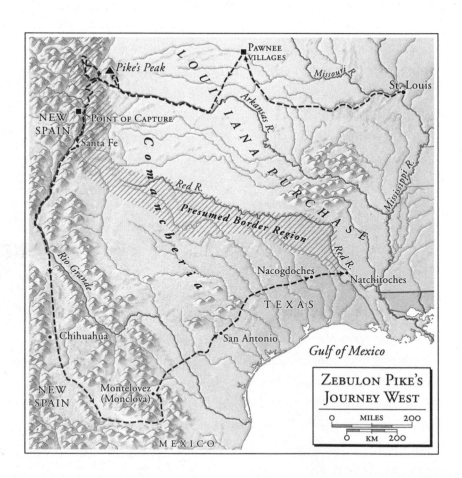

At two thirty in the afternoon, February 1, 1806, Pike and Miller took their last step up the river. There were no more steps left. At the end of the river, they stood at the shore of Leech Lake, an oval about twelve miles across. Its waters emptied into the Gulf of Mexico—after bisecting most of North America. Pike was in the moment of his triumph. "I will not attempt to describe my feelings," Pike wrote, "on the accomplishment of my voyage, this being the main source of the Mississippi."

Pike's feelings in his heart and his mind may well have been beyond words. Once the sense of awe receded, though, the only feelings that really mattered were the jagged throbs in his legs, as the flesh in his feet prepared to die off.

At some point much farther back, Pike had hobbled boldly past the point of no return, the place in some part of the forest at which he could have walked back under his own power to a base camp. Passing that point accentuated the fact that, ultimately, the finish line at the end of the river was really just a halfway point—even if it was also something magnificent. As many brambles and at least as much cold water awaited Pike on the return journey. Moreover, the mere miles were against him in his condition.

In less than an hour, Pike and Miller were ready to start moving again. They still didn't turn back, though. Instead, they started straight across the frozen surface of the lake. Pike may have been wishing all the while that the ice would break apart and put his feet out of their misery, yet his last twelve-mile trek reflects one of the anomalies of his exploration of the Upper Mississippi.

On the opposite shore of the lake was the regional headquarters of the North West Company, Britain's fur-trading goliath. Company traders, however, were oblivious to the flow of water south. They may have been *on* a source of the Mississippi, but they didn't know it, so they didn't discover it. At ten o'clock, after managing the long, last hike, Pike stumbled up to the headquarters in the silence of the dark, as only winter can make it so. By that point, he may as well have been walking on his knees. He immediately started banging on the door, but there was no response. No one was expected that evening or, indeed, that month. Pike kept pounding away, disturbing the quiet of the surrounding forest. The winter of the north had finally made him desperate. Due to the decision to cross frozen Leech Lake, his own camp was twelve miles farther away than it had been when he reached his goal at the end of the river. Plodding back across the ice to that point, only then to begin his journey back to camp, was as impossible as anything could be for Lieutenant Pike. As the rapping against the door cracked the air, anyone who was inside probably missed a heartbeat. Miller joined in, hammering on the door.

Before long, there was a stirring inside. The occupants of the building had every reason to take up their guns. But when the door opened, the local North West agent, Hugh McGillis, only looked Pike over. He then invited him inside "with distinguished politeness and Hospitality." Before long, Pike was in a warm room, having a supper of "a good dish of Coffee, a Biscuit, Butter and Cheese." It was a practically perfect *après-explore* tray.

Jefferson's other explorers tried hard, but it was Pike on that night who showed how wondrous the American West really was.

Far from empty, the West was only enormous and its exploration anything but a straight line, either on the map or through the years of history. In the West, one could discover the source of a great river and then find a hot cup of coffee in the neighborhood. Westerners of all stripes were tucked into their own spaces, without knowing or needing to know the scope of the whole. Confronted with the dizzying expanse of the West, Jefferson's explorers (and those who came later) were supposed to tell easterners what was out there. They did that, but they also told westerners *who* was out there, and gave them their first understanding of the whole.

McGillis, who was about thirty-eight years old, had started in the fur trade in the same way as Dunbar. He was likewise a Scotsman, but where Dunbar chose not to join one of the conglomerates in the trade, McGillis stayed with the North West Company and was allowed to buy a partnership in 1801. About four years later, he arrived at Leech Lake to take charge of the Fond du Lac department of his company: a small fortress in the woods. He had traced a path that might have been Dunbar's, had Dunbar remained in the north.

From Pike's perspective, the best thing about his new host was that he had wide legs, but then, most people did, compared with the lanky lieutenant. Because of the trench foot, Pike's lower legs were so swollen that his pants no longer fit and he anticipated that he would be incapacitated for weeks. While McGillis loaned him clothes, Pike made himself comfortable in the house, reading books from an impressively up-to-date library.

Finding the source of the Mississippi had been problematic. In the same manner as Lewis during the previous fall in the Bitterroot Mountains, Pike actually missed his true goal—though not by much. The source of the Mississippi is actually along the Lake Winnibigoshish branch, the one he bypassed in favor of the Leech. That route would have led to a lake later given the name *Itasca*—which is the true source of the river. From a broader perspective, neither Lewis nor Pike could have realistically expected to verify the source of a river on the basis of only a single visit. Lewis seemed to know that. The designation of headwaters is a meticulous process, requiring an array of measurements at various times of year and the examination of all of the river's tributaries.

Twelve days after arriving at McGillis's residence, Pike was finally able to move freely, going outside for the first time. He was lame, his ankles still swollen, but at least he could travel by riding in a dogsled. In that way and using McGillis's home as a base, he moved around the region, continuing the business of the expedition. On February 16, he continued his diplomatic efforts, presiding at a council of Ojibwe chiefs. Promoting peace between the Ojibwe and the Mdewakanton was one of his primary missions, according to

Wilkinson's original orders. The negotiations were hard, but there were breakthroughs, including a rudimentary peace agreement. In addition, two young Ojibwe chiefs, called Buck and Beaux by Pike, agreed to travel with the expedition all the way to St. Louis. At the end of the council, the same two chiefs pledged themselves to Pike and his young children.

Pike's attitude toward Indians had evolved after continual interactions with them during the course of the expedition. At the Ojibwe council, he proved himself to be receptive to kinship, a concept important to both the Ojibwe and the Mdewakanton. The bond was more complex than he probably understood at the time, but he was humbled by the invitation to be equals. "I was determined it should be my care never to make them regret the noble confidence placed in me," Pike wrote of the Ojibwe pledge. "I would have protected their lives with mine." That is just what Le Petite Corbeau, the Mdewakanton chief, was trying to do for Pike during the flag incident below Saint Anthony Falls. At that time, Pike was ill impressed and slightly bored. His commitment to protect Buck and Beaux started immediately. When the two young chiefs wanted to celebrate the end of the council by getting drunk, Pike refused to give either of them more than a single glass of whiskey.

While Pike had the opportunity to keep moving across the snows around Lake Leech in his sled, Lewis and Clark were stuck in the rain at Fort Clatsop, biding their time. The corps wouldn't be in any position to leave for at least a month and possibly more. Lewis industriously focused on the Clatsop Indians, providing one of the expedition's most thorough reports on Indian culture. Clark labored over his maps and oversaw the production of salt from seawater for use by the expedition.

Jeffersonian explorers were in the field, having pressed farther forward in two directions than any American had ever gone. But no one knew it yet, and the mere promise of exploration wasn't enough to satisfy those clamoring for the hard facts of the West. In the

East, Jefferson was hearing growing criticism—as usual—but in the case of Louisiana, the Federalists had come upon an argument with teeth. According to an editorial in the *Washington Federalist* on February 18, 1806, Jefferson had bought the Louisiana Territory

> and paid the 15 millions without specifying the boundaries (a thing unheard of in the annals of the world) and in order to make the transaction popular (and this has been the labored passion of Mr. Jefferson's whole public life) a forced, and false construction, was given to the treaty.

Even while siding with America's cold war enemy, Spain, the Federalists were successfully freshening old arguments about Louisiana by combining them with new developments—or, more specifically, with the numbing lack thereof. The country was dividing into two camps, neither of which matched well with Jefferson's dual public/secret policy. One faction was making plans based on a coming war. Another faction was blaming Jefferson's clumsy land grab for getting the United States into a foreign entanglement that required war. But there wasn't going to be a war, even if Jefferson couldn't announce that fact as yet. While he was waiting for France to complete the treaty regarding West Florida and Texas, he needed to provide something more than rhetoric that would refute the notion that he had administered the land he'd acquired with "neglect and ignorance," in the words of the *Federalist*. Jefferson had known that just such an exigency was coming and for that reason had impressed on his explorers the importance of sending their materials as soon as practical.

The very next day, February 19, 1806, Jefferson submitted a packet to Congress that featured documents representing his initiatives in exploration. The packet included extensive notes from Lewis and Clark from the Mandan villages and an excerpt from Dunbar's journal, describing the natural setting and attributes of the Ouachita. One can see Jefferson looking around his office for something else—something pertaining to the more incendiary Louisiana-Texas border. All that he had were a couple of letters from Dr. John Sibley, the newly named Indian agent in Natchitoches, whose descriptions were something of a pastiche, almost an inventory. Jefferson used them to fill the hole and present to Congress and the American people something of the farther reaches of the Southwest.

The letter that Jefferson sent to Congress with his reports was a masterpiece of circumspection. He nimbly failed the essayist's obligation to provide a thesis sentence, as his only point was intrinsic: his explorers were on the scene in the Louisiana Territory. In February 1806, he couldn't say anything more without risk. At the end of the letter, Jefferson did deliver the breaking news that a Red River expedition would soon be under way. For anyone who only glanced at the first and last sentences of a document, Jefferson put Captain Lewis in the first line and the Red River in the last.

Although the exploration of the Red River hadn't yet commenced, it was finally drawing closer. On the day Jefferson submitted his report to Congress, Freeman was en route to Natchez, as was a medical student named Peter Custis, who would accompany him as botanist. A native of Virginia, Custis was related to the family of the late Martha Washington's first husband. He was studying in Philadelphia when he agreed to accompany Freeman. Rounding out the party, an army officer stationed in New Orleans, Captain Richard Sparks, had been assigned to escort the Red River corps with a detachment of soldiers.

Far to the north on the day of Jefferson's message, Pike was prepared to begin the journey back to St. Louis, in company with Buck and Beaux. Jefferson had been informed of Pike's expedition by Dearborn. Although it didn't include scientific method or the collection of specimens, he had given it his approval. Even as Pike clawed his way back from the farthest reaches of the river, though, Jefferson was consulting with one of his friends on the best man to send on a "scientific" exploration of the same region. For that, he'd need funding from Congress, and so the wiser strategy for Jefferson was to remain quiet on the subject of Pike.

McGillis had not only lent Pike his breeches, he magnanimously presented him with a dogsled, including two large dogs, for the trip south to the main camp. On the day Pike and Miller left, the sleigh was packed, by Pike's eye, with "at least 750 pounds" of gear. Pike may not have been known for his powers of estimation, but his numbers were corroborated by someone with excellent acumen in that regard. One of the dogs, according to Pike, took one look at the loaded sled and ran away. "The other poor fellow was obliged to pull the whole load," Pike wrote. He soon obtained a replacement for the runaway.

The sled, if not the tender consideration that went with it, was all for naught. Within four days, the lieutenant suffered a bout of Pikean impatience and left his main party, along with his sled, to go ahead by snowshoe. Another American soldier and the two Ojibwe chiefs, Buck and Beaux, accompanied him. One day later, on February 24, he was making notes in his journal about the chiefs, and the snowshoes, which he called "rackets."

> My young Warriors was still in good heart—singing and shewing every wish to keep me so.

On that score, Buck and Beaux had an uphill fight. As Pike continued:

> My Racket String's brought the blood through my socks and Mockinson's, from which it may be imagined in what pain I marched.

Pike didn't stop. Long into each night, the red grid marks in the snow led to the south.

Apparently Pike believed that his body would adjust to whatever his brain could handle—and not the other way around. He marched by snowshoe for another ten days, reaching the stockade and the main body of his men on March 5. The homecoming, as it turned out, was even worse than the grisly trip. "How mortifying the disappointment," he wrote of his arrival.

During his absence, the men had laid waste to the stocks of food he had carefully reserved for the trip back to St. Louis. They even ate the plump venison hams that Pike was saving to present as a gift for Wilkinson. The sergeant left in charge had broken nearly every rule set by Pike and had even burglarized the lieutenant's personal trunk, looking for items to trade to the Indians. Judging by the stories that emerged, the fort seems to have been host to a three-month-long bacchanal—it was not only a breach of discipline, but a personal betrayal for Pike. He confined the sergeant until disciplinary action could be taken in St. Louis and spent most of the remaining month pointedly staying away from his "boys." By then, he was obviously tired and disenchanted, even becoming suspicious of Buck and Beaux. The greed of his men had greater consequences for the expedition than just the lost trust of its leader, though—without supplies, they all were stuck at camp for the foreseeable future. Pike, anxious to move forward at the best of times, concentrated on restoring the stock of foodstuffs so that the expedition could start south as soon as possible.

LEWIS WAS SIMILARLY concerned with laying in supplies of meat for his return trip, but that wouldn't have held him at Fort Clatsop once the weather started to improve. He was as anxious to leave as the rest of the men who made up the corps. On March 23, he even waved aside the retrieval of an elk that had been shot by one of the

men a few miles away. For Meriwether Lewis to leave an elk behind
was proof that he had only one priority: moving east. "The rain
Seased," wrote Ordway, "and it became fair about meridian [noon]
at which time we loaded our canoes & at 1 P.M. left Fort Clatsop
on our homeward bound journey. at this place we had wintered
and . . . have lived as well as we had any right to expect."

As they prepared to head back east, Lewis and Clark committed
to paper a message that they left with several different chiefs, affirm-
ing that they and all those named in the document had been to the
Pacific by way of the mountains. If the corps failed to reach home—
and they both had their doubts about the Bitterroot Mountains—
their accomplishment would still be known to the outside world,
protecting their legacy and the interests of the president. For the
moment, though, they didn't have to worry about the Bitterroots.

As soon as the corpsmen set their canoes into the Columbia on
March 23, it was apparent that the river in spring was even more
monstrous than the raucous, unmanageable waterway they'd cursed
in late fall. The corps set up a series of camps, at which they were
continually pestered by Indian peddlers and drifters, who—between
trade and larceny—rarely left empty-handed.

With the surge of the Columbia, the landscape was so different
that it was almost as if Lewis and Clark were exploring anew. Due
to a kind of optical illusion, they had missed the Willamette River
on the westward journey. That was despite its being almost 2,000
feet wide. Having heard that a major tributary existed somewhere in
the vicinity, though, Clark named it vaguely the "Supposed River."
The Willamette flows northward into the Columbia; large islands
near the mouth made it appear to the captains like a bulbous part of
the main river. On the trip east, however, they took a closer look, finally spotting the elusive river behind the islands. On April 2, Clark
decided to explore it with a party of seven corpsmen. But as they
left, Clark noticed four large canoes packed with unknown Indians
"bending," as he put it, for the corps' camp along the Columbia.

Because the camp was undermanned, he immediately thought he should return. "But on a Second reflection," Clark wrote, "and reverting to the precautions always taken by my friend Capt Lewis on those occasions banished all apprehensions."

The people in the canoes were only paying a social call, Lewis later reported. About a week later, though, he was tested in a more serious vein. At a camp further west, an Indian of an unidentified tribe searched Lewis out one night and spoke to him in the Clatsop language, which Lewis had fortunately learned over the winter. The stranger told him that three men from the nearby Watlala tribe had stolen Lewis's pet dog earlier in the day. To Lewis it was an act of aggression, and the search party that he sent to retrieve the animal had orders to shoot the Watlalas if they refused to return him. Lewis did love his dog, but the episode represented far more than personal sentiment; with an unyielding instinct for survival, day in and day out, he assiduously dispelled any impression of weakness on the part of the American corps. Isolated in the West with no such thing as a fallback position, he wouldn't allow the story of the dognapping to encourage any tribe or nation to ponder an even bigger attack. On seeing the search party, the Watlalas let the dog go, but Lewis was not mollified. Nor would he ever be.

By the time the corps reached the Dalles, where the Columbia grew even stronger, the canoes were of no use, except as firewood. Abandoning the river, Lewis and Clark set to work trading for horses, a time-consuming process due to their scarcity and the hard bargaining of tribes near the Dalles.

As Lieutenant Pike prepared to leave his camp in Ojibwe country on the Upper Mississippi, he found Buck and Beaux reluctant to follow him. They may have been willing to lay down their lives for him—in times of duress—but they weren't ready to travel through Mdewakanton lands for him. It was too naked a risk—if caught, they could face the specter of being tied alive to a tree, with their own intestines used for rope. And so, in March, Buck and Beaux

bolted and returned to their own villages, even as Pike was still trying to rebound from the betrayal of his own men.

As Pike described the two young Ojibwe, they seemed like bright
men, if perhaps callow. But they were absolutely correct in their
assessment of the effort to build peace. Their willingness to risk
slaughter on a trip to St. Louis wouldn't make any difference, not
even a little. In Pike's opinion, the process of giving the tribes a
chance to begin their relationship anew would be monumental, requiring the permanent presence of American troops. In the overall
effort to please Wilkinson, though, losing the two young chiefs was
yet another blow. No venison hams. No visiting chiefs. Pike was returning empty-handed, but he and the boys nonetheless were ready
to start back on April 7, after having been away eight months. Gliding down the smooth, fast-moving river like a leaf caught in the
current, they expected to near St. Louis in only three weeks.

On the same date, Freeman was at the other end of the Mississippi in New Orleans. He had arrived in Natchez in mid-March, a
homecoming of sorts, and a return to the years he had spent there
before and after his stint on the 31st parallel survey. "I am extremely
glad of his arrival," Dunbar wrote to Jefferson on March 17, "as no
time ought now to be lost; the waters will begin to fall with the
advancement of our Summer." The expedition was by far the most
intelligently planned of all of the Jeffersonian missions, with a roster
that included a celestial navigator (Freeman), a botanist (Custis),
an experienced military officer (Sparks), and even an astronomical
assistant (an army lieutenant named Enoch Humphrey). No sooner
had Freeman arrived at the Forest than Dunbar practically snatched
from his hands the new chronometer that he'd brought from Philadelphia. Dunbar couldn't resist a look at the latest equipment, as he
offered to test it for Freeman. There was, of course, nothing he'd
rather do, and anyway, a regulated chronometer would make the
measurement of longitude easier for Freeman and Lieutenant Humphrey.

———

PLANNING THE TRIP may have been an intriguing exercise, but Dunbar had doubts as to whether realizing it would be anything other than suicidal. Along with nearly every resident of the Lower Mississippi region, he believed that war was unquestionably imminent. As Freeman collected supplies for the voyage, the Spanish were actively gathering troops near Nacogdoches—apparently, they hadn't heard about France's plans for the future of Texas. More troubling to Jefferson, he hadn't heard much about the deal with France of late. Pressed and even coerced by him, Congress had appropriated the money that France wanted in exchange for West Florida and for the promise of peace along the Texas border. After Jefferson sent word to Napoleon that the money was available, he was still awaiting the relief that would come with the news that the deal had been struck.

Ignorant of the French arrangement, Dunbar advised Jefferson that it would be safer for Freeman's expedition to steer clear of Texas. He suggested they instead explore the Arkansas River, which runs roughly parallel to the Red River, but farther to the north—away from the Spanish and potential skirmishes that might stem from American encroachment on the disputed territory. But Jefferson insisted: it had to be the Red River. When the French deal was announced, it would seem a stroke of brilliantly strategic planning for Freeman and his expedition to be on the scene already, mapping the new border along the Red River—and also studying the plants.

The expedition was scheduled to leave from Fort Adams, although Freeman was obligated to travel to New Orleans first to accept delivery of the boats, which were under construction there. Dunbar had specified two barges for the expedition, rather than one, to ensure that neither would be overloaded. He also mentioned that two boats would make the trip "more pleasant" for the leaders, as though something in his recent experience made him think that such a separation might come as a relief.

When Freeman left for New Orleans, confident that the boats would be ready and that he would be back within a couple of days, either Meriwether Lewis or George Hunter could have told him not to rush. Freeman's boats weren't ready either, but compared with the earlier expedition leaders, he wasted far less time standing around shipyards: only three weeks. Three weeks in New Orleans was an eternity on the Red River, though. Under the best of circumstances, it was practically impassable upriver, and with each day that went by in summer, the water level only shrank.

The fact that Freeman was set to explore the Red River on behalf of the United States was not a secret, yet the intrigue surrounding it stands as a clear reflection of the loyalties of the citizens of Orleans Territory. In fact, during early 1806, the mail pouches to Nacogdoches were thick with messages from New Orleans tipping off Spanish authorities to the plans for the Freeman expedition. General Salcedo, commandant of the Internal Provinces, already knew about it, but he wanted to know the date of Freeman's departure. So did Freeman, for that matter, but he could wait. General Salcedo couldn't.

On April 4, General Salcedo acted, appointing a new officer, Don Francisco Viana, to defend the border as the commander of the Spanish forces at Nacogdoches. Viana, a native of Spain in his mid-fifties, was well trained, tough, and blunt spoken. He was at his best in a frontier setting; where others saw confusion, Viana saw only a wide gulf between right and wrong. When he heard that Freeman would be leaving soon on a trek up the Red River, he wasn't interested in whether it was a true scientific mission. The explorers were Americans and that was enough. Viana successfully sought permission from General Salcedo to use the military against the Freeman expedition.

At approximately the same time, General Salcedo ordered a lieutenant named Facundo Melgares to lead a large detachment from New Mexico to stop the Freeman expedition or any other American explorers. A veteran of battles against the Apache in what is now Arizona, Melgares mustered four hundred soldiers and marched to the western section of the Red River. In the event that Freeman managed to evade Viana's men, Lieutenant Melgares would be waiting.

While Freeman was waiting at boatyards and Dunbar was worrying about the international tensions that threatened Freeman and his expedition, Pike was enjoying a kind of reward for surviving the northward leg of his journey. Rather than plodding through snowy forests, he was floating downriver toward Prairie du Chien on smooth waters. Instead of sleeping outside in subzero temperatures, he was enjoying the sunshine. Somewhere along the way, spring had arrived on the Upper Mississippi. After four months of chronic cold, he was surprised to see colorful buds on the trees. The flocks of birds gathering along the Mississippi were so vast in flight, they made a roar like the wind.

If the land was different in April's sun, so were the people; Pike spent more time visiting tribes on the ride downriver than he had on the way up. He even pioneered sports commentary on a late-April day along the Mississippi. In 1806, Indian nations were the only ones enthusiastically playing team sports in America. Pike was invited to watch a lacrosse game near Prairie du Chien, and he left a vivid description of the action as a Sioux team took on a combination of Fox and Ho-Chunk players. Life wasn't easy then for sports reporters; the field was a half-mile long and the action continued nonstop, all day. Nor were the players' names on their uniforms. In fact, they didn't have uniforms. In fact, they didn't have clothes, as more than a hundred naked men on each side played until one of the teams scored four goals. The Sioux finally won, Pike reported, "more (as I conceived) from their superior skill in throwing the Ball, than superiority of foot . . . Fox and the Ho-Chunk were faster runners."

On the way home, the mood of the expedition was "hearty," as Pike described it, although he was less and less certain about his previous boast of leaving a lasting peace in his wake. The month before, in Mdewakanton country, he'd written that as "a subaltern with but twenty men," he had effected a harmonious attitude in the minds of the Indians. As he found, the interlocking societies of the Upper Mississippi were more complex than that, as was the range of individuals who may or may not have wanted peace.

Even more dismaying, Pike came to see over the course of his trip how thoroughly alcohol had distorted the way of life in many Indian nations—"through the instigation of the Traders." He was ultimately exasperated with the fur traders, realizing that it wasn't the minds of the Indians that needed to change—it was the minds of those who regarded liquor in the north woods as nothing more than the quickest way to obtain pelts. For a few months, early on, Pike had believed that a strong scolding from the U.S. government, in the person of a twenty-six-year-old lieutenant, could actually stop the distribution of alcohol. By the time he headed home, he looked to the establishment of a U.S. Army fort near Saint Anthony Falls as the answer.

While Freeman finished his business at the boatyards in New Orleans, Dunbar and the officers at Fort Adams became aware that Viana had arrived along the blurry border and that the Spanish army post at Nacogdoches was growing with ominous speed. They couldn't be sure what was going to happen, but they were aware that Freeman and his corps were attracting attention. The expedition would be like a gaggle of lambs sent to walk between two lines of cannon. Even if Jefferson didn't understand that the border with Texas was about to explode, someone had to make sure that Freeman and his men were safe when the war started. Before leaving Natchez, the expedition was bolstered with more soldiers, probably at Dunbar's request. The flotilla ultimately expanded to two barges and a pirogue, for three civilians and twenty-one soldiers.

"Mr. Freeman with his party left this place the 28th April for the Red River," Dunbar confirmed in a letter to Jefferson from Natchez, "very commodiously fitted out." The expedition made a stop at Fort Adams for several days so that every last detail could be tended. On the very day that Freeman set forth on the Mississippi, leaving Natchez in his fleet of custom-built boats, their hardware still tight, their planking fresh sawn, Pike approached St. Louis on the same river, six hundred miles to the north, his own barge battered by its voyage into new waters.

Eight months and twenty-one days after leaving on an expedition that grew from demanding to dangerous, the men were nearly home. On a rainy day, only about a dozen miles out of St. Louis, Pike ended the expedition just as he began it: with a runaway dog. On the way north, the unending explorer refused to be delayed. But with only one day left before reaching St. Louis, Pike looked high and low for the missing dog. He even ordered the barge back up the river, nosing the shore, searching every crag—that same explorer suddenly seeming to clutch at delay, so long as it would extend his time on an expedition.

Zebulon Pike loved his wife loyally, adored their three children, and couldn't wait to see his boss, Wilkinson. But he needed to be out in front—and that was a feeling he was about to lose. When there was at last nowhere else to look and with much of the day gone, Pike gave up and turned south again. The following day, April 30, the expedition was over.

"Arrived about 12 OClock at the Town," Pike wrote.

The next day, Custis jotted "we left Fort Adams" in his journal. As of May 1, the Freeman expedition was finally alive and running with the rivers of the Old Southwest. In Paris on the same day, Jefferson's envoy politely but firmly told Foreign Minister Talleyrand that America had satisfied all of France's demands, even refraining, as requested, from communicating with Spain about the tensions along the Texas border. And then the envoy asked when France would execute the agreement, selling West Florida to the United States (and ameliorating the tensions on the Texas border). The next day, Talleyrand submitted that inquiry to Napoleon, who produced, with not a bit of regret, a proclamation from the Spanish king refusing on any basis to surrender either of the Floridas. It was the sort of document that Napoleon would easily toss aside, or just as easily use when convenient—or for that matter, order to be written.

The deal was off. No treaty across Texas was going to secure the border or, incidentally, save Freeman. By the time that news reached America, however, he and twenty-three other Americans would be deep in the territory guarded by Spain, in the form of Salcedo, Viana, and Melgares.

Twenty

TO GO OR NOT TO GO

In the aftermath of Pike's return to St. Louis, a resident mentioned the event without any particular excitement in a letter to his father. "Lieutenant Pike returned a few days ago from reconnoitering the head waters of the Mississippi," he wrote. "All that I can understand of his tour is, that the Mississippi heads out of a large lake, and runs a considerable distance very narrow and very deep. The climate very cold." In St. Louis, there was no celebration of Pike's return, no meadows refurbished as banquet halls, no pyramids rising over dinner tables.

Aside from the lingering disinterest in the wrong end of the Mississippi River, St. Louis was in a foul mood when Pike returned. After a year of Wilkinson's governorship, a large faction of the city was outraged with the way that he expected citizens to obey laws that had long been ignored. Smaller factions lost no opportunity to attack the anti-Wilkinson residents, though not out of any attachment to the governor. As goodwill disintegrated, old rifts were cracking out into the open. "The opposition or disaffection to general Wilkinson's administration is not confined to six of *eight* disaffected inhabitants only," wrote one of his enemies in a letter that found its way into eastern newspapers, "but pervades every part of the territory, where his measures are known and felt, and is composed of the most respectable citizens (both French and American) and officers of the government.

"That Louisiana is a distracted and divided territory is melachnoly fact," the letter concluded. That much was inarguable. Wilkinson was, ironically, considered too well-ordered. A Frenchman who had known Wilkinson in New Orleans two years before called him "a flighty, rattle-headed fellow, often drunk, who has committed a hundred impertinent follies." Marvelously enough, that was just what St. Louis residents had anticipated in their new governor. Unfortunately, he didn't live up to his character reference. In St. Louis, he was serious; he was exacting. Wilkinson should have been a good politician, having juggled foreign governments for over a decade, but instead he was regarded as an impossible autocrat. The city wasn't inclined to cheer anyone closely associated with him, including Pike on his return from some "climate very cold."

Jefferson was aware of the unrest in St. Louis as he waited for news in the White House. In 1806 he came to the conclusion, finally, that he would have to buy Louisiana with action to quiet the disturbance that plagued the area. Since the Purchase, questions had threaded through rumors, which had completely encircled the future of Orleans and Louisiana. To the north, it was said that St. Louis was roiling for revolt and would turn on Wilkinson. To the east, the reports from Kentuckians pointed at odd statements from Burr about building a republic in the Southwest. To the southeast, word was that West Florida was about to be flooded by bandits and visionaries—"filibusters"—who were determined to set it free, only so they could seize it for themselves. To the south, the Gulf of

Mexico was supposedly full of British ships just over the horizon, ready to attack. To the west, the Spanish in Texas were toeing the Sabine River. Loose talk raced ahead of the Jeffersonian antidote to the swirling rumors, which was to absorb the land in spirit and then put Americans upon it.

If even one of the rumors turned out to be true, though, and crashed down on Louisiana, Jefferson would surely lose the land and the Americans there. For the first time in his presidency, he didn't leave for his spring vacation at Monticello in March. Instead, he remained in Washington, watching events and awaiting the word from Paris that would put them all into order. At the beginning of May, though, he was still at his desk in the White House waiting— and perhaps sensing that there would be no agreement from Paris.

The deal for the purchase of West Florida with an accord on the Louisiana border was already late. Jefferson must have surmised that the delay stemmed from the fact that Napoleon had won a tremendous victory at Austerlitz, Austria, since authorizing the deal. Napoleon had thereupon exacted forty million francs from the Austrian court, which might have made him less interested in American money. Jefferson remained hopeful. "We are trying to lay the foundations of a long peace with Spain," he wrote to a friend on April 27.

Jefferson believed that Spanish troops might attack Orleans Territory from Pensacola in East Florida, and from either Mobile or Baton Rouge in West Florida. After consulting with the cabinet, he informed Claiborne, the Orleans governor, that he was sending a total of nine navy gunboats to defend New Orleans (against either Spain or Britain), even while realigning the ground troops in the region. In placing the soldiers, the president took the precaution of keeping them out of the city proper, where malaria and yellow fever were at their most virulent in the rainy spring season.

Through almost two years, the president had been betting that the people of Orleans would remain safe. As of May, that was no longer probable. The timing on which Jefferson was counting had failed, and so it was that he remained in Washington in March, then April, then May to address the reality, as opposed to the plan. "According to our latest dispatches from Spain," he wrote, "that government shews such pacific dispositions, that if any hostilities take place in your quarter they will certainly not be by order of that government, but will be merely the effect of the passions & interests of her officers. Were Spain disposed, she could send no troops across the Atlantic."

General Salcedo didn't need troops from the Iberian Peninsula. One of his primary officers, Simón Herrera, was in the process of marching into U.S. territory with his own contingent of six hundred soldiers, who had taken control of an alligator haven called Bayou Pierre, a place near Natchitoches that was only strategic for what it symbolized: the first step on the way to New Orleans. Herrera's troops "advanced in considerable force & took post at the settlement of Bayou Pierre," Jefferson's wrote.

Meeting with members of the cabinet who assumed that war on the border with Texas was imminent, Jefferson made the decision to send Wilkinson to Orleans Territory, in his incarnation as commander of the army. With that, the president simultaneously pulled the unpopular governor of Louisiana Territory from St. Louis in hopes of returning the West's most stable community to its conservative ways. Dearborn drafted the orders on May 6 and sent them to Wilkinson, mincing no words about the threat at hand:

> From recent information received from New Orleans and its vicinity, the hostile views of the officers of his Catholic Majesty in that quarter have been so evident as to require the strictest precaution on the part of the United States; and the immediate exertion of the means we possess for securing

the rightful possession of the territory of the United States, and for protecting the citizens and their property from the hostile encroachments of our neighbors, the Spaniards.

Wilkinson was ordered to travel to Orleans without delay, charged with defending it against invasion from Texas or West Florida, or both. With that, the United States was at war or at least inured to being at war, a painful concession for Jefferson Republicans. Having done what he could for the moment, Jefferson left at last for Monticello. "I was able to get from Washington a few days ago," he wrote from the farm the following week, "and am here for about three weeks to unbend, as much as the current business will permit, with the aid of country recreations."

While Jefferson walked and rode the property that invariably brought his balance back, Dearborn continued to prepare, calling out militias in the region and ordering them to Orleans. The Secretary was scrounging to find as many as twelve hundred militiamen to station throughout Orleans—many of his recruits were undrilled civilians. And while he scrambled to ready Orleans for war with one of the European powers, nineteen of his most professional soldiers, ones who knew that territory well, were on a pair of flatboats, gliding up the Red River with Freeman and watching the prickly ash trees go by. In the midst of the war emergency, Dearborn didn't rush word to Natchitoches to stop the expedition and return the soldiers—quite the opposite.

On the Red River, the expedition was making smooth progress during the first week of May. Every breeze must have been exhilarating for Freeman, simply because he was in charge of a presidential mission. After years of climbing under logs and over ravines in his surveys of the backwoods of Tennessee or Indiana, motivated by a conviction that every detail mattered, he could finally rest easy. On the Red River, every detail did matter. In the national obsession with personal ambition, Thomas Freeman had climbed the mountain. He wasn't yet exploring, in the strictest sense, since the route to Natchitoches was already in regular use for trade. But that didn't mean that the lower Red had been studied as a natural setting. And it wouldn't be, at least not by Freeman.

Freeman was in a hurry as the boats made their way up the Red River, past the intersection with the clear Black River (the spot where Dunbar and Hunter had turned north). His first goal was to reach Natchitoches, about one hundred eighty miles northwest, by "the meanders of the red river," as he put it. It was not located on the Red River proper, but on a smaller, parallel waterway, the Cane River. "Owing to Mr. Freemans great anxiety to proceed to [Natchitoches] as quickly as possible," Peter Custis wrote, "I have not had so compleat an opportunity of examining the country and its productions as I could have wished." With every turn in the river, he marveled that there was another field to study. To his disappointment, however, Freeman was compelled to rush past them, owing to the rapidly falling water levels in the river.

Along the Red River, the banks rose sharply about eight feet to a level section about a quarter mile back from the river and then to a second incline, like another riverbank. The banks were heavily forested, with willows lining the route for miles on end. As the expedition moved on, Custis was excited to discover a bush he didn't recognize. As soon as the boats stopped, he looked at it according to his training:

> There is a shrub growing in great abundance every where along this River and as I have not seen the flowers am unable to ascertain what it is. It grows to the height of from ten to twenty ft. and bears a drupe [a fruit with a pit] which resembles the Olive, but is not so large. When ripe it is of a reddish-purple color. The putamen [the pit] is of a woody fibrous structure and may be easily separated by the fingers. The same peduncle [a stem with multiple buds] supports from

ten to twenty drupes. The peduncles are rameous [like wood tree branches] and subopposite [very slightly staggered].—Its leaves are elliptic.*

Freeman and Custis were well-matched colleagues. In science, their background represented the practical and the academic, respectively. Personally, the two seemed to get along well, being conscientious professionals, as were all of Jefferson's explorers. Aside from leaving late, Freeman's Red River expedition had begun on a successful note, with accurate mapmaking by Freeman and Humphrey, in addition to Custis's meticulous observations, the best botanical accounts left by any of Jefferson's explorers. Where Hunter and Dunbar had the luxury of getting on each other's nerves and Lewis and Clark had the even more welcome opportunity of taking time apart on the trail, it was crucial that Freeman and Custis work seamlessly together. They faced more violent prospects than the others, an incendiary situation that narrowed the confines of every relationship on the Red River expedition. Reaching Natchitoches on May 19, Custis noted that "the party are all in the enjoyment of health and unanimity, pleased with the prospect, & resolved on the prosecution of the expedition, let what will oppose."

The members of the expedition were well aware of the danger that lay ahead from the Spanish—"what will oppose." Freeman was concerned about it even before he arrived in Natchitoches, a town alive with the worry that he and his expedition would end up as Philip Nolan had: dead, his men arrested. Some people in Natchitoches, however, were actively working against Freeman; at least two residents immediately sent word to Spanish officials of his arrival and his schedule. Fortunately for Freeman, information

---

* The botanist R. Dale Thomas has identified the plant from Custis's description as a swamp privet. Custis was correct that it is related to the olive, though the fruit is sickening to humans, as the name "swamp privet" somehow suggests.

was also coming in from Nacogdoches—from people sympathetic to the American side. Locals in the know sorted out the intelligence. Dr. Sibley, the Indian agent who often corresponded with Jefferson about the region, greeted Freeman like an old friend but warned him that the trouble was real. The Spanish had no intention of letting him finish the voyage.

Freeman had been hearing much the same ever since his meetings with Jefferson in Washington. The news had greater immediacy in Natchitoches, because it was the last outpost of American protection. While Freeman showed no inclination to quit, he needed to manage a host of new details in view of Sibley's assurance that the expedition would be confronted, and probably attacked. The worst that could happen—outright massacre—was likely. So was a life sentence in a Mexican jail and becoming the cause of international problems for Jefferson, should Freeman botch any of the split-second decisions he would have to make in the face of Spanish opposition. It was a case of remote ambush: he learned that there would be a surprise attack, and he had no choice but to walk right into it. For a quiet-living surveyor, Freeman was at the epicenter of an intrigue of serious proportions.

Even as Freeman and Sibley had their very first talk, the level of the river was decreasing by small increments. One valuable aspect of those talks was the information Sibley imparted about the Indians Freeman might encounter on the lower part of the Red. One nation not expected to be on the list was the Clermont bands, about whom Jefferson had been warned two years before (delaying the original Red River expedition). They hadn't strayed into the region during the year, being more concerned with problems from their opposite borderlands, where the Grand Osages were making incursions. Sibley was especially interested, however, in describing the various Caddo tribes that lived along the Red River.

Caddo was actually the language used by a number of different nations, including those who farmed along the Red and Neches

Rivers. Among them were the Kadohadacho nation, the Yatasís, the Natchitoches, and the Hasinai confederacy. They were also bound to some extent culturally and under the same umbrella politically. The way of life among the Caddos was extremely stable and the pace of life gentle, when they weren't defending themselves against occasional attacks from neighboring nations, particularly the Osages. It was gentility at a price to others, though, since some of the Caddo nations became known as the arms dealers of the lower plains. Their society had a hierarchical government and developed deft diplomatic abilities that allowed them to adapt to French, Spanish, and American neighbors, in succession or, even better, all at once. In family relationships, the Caddo were far more conventional by American standards than the Indians of the Northern Plains. Sibley (a ladies' man who was reputedly not conventional in family relationships by American standards, a factor in his decision to live on the frontier) became a serious student of Caddo ways soon after arriving in Natchitoches. He made numerous trips across the Red River to tour their villages and even learned some part of the language. Along the way, he formed friendships and when President Jefferson was looking for someone to serve as Indian agent in the region, Sibley was a natural choice. His information on the tribes farther up the Red River, notably the Comanche and Pawnees, was less reliable, being based on secondhand stories.

At the time of the Louisiana Purchase, a new Kadohadacho chief named Dehahuit was rising in stature. He understood that in approaching the European-American powers, unity among the Indians was critically important. To that end, he grew his leadership one tribe at a time until he came to represent all of the Caddo and some additional nations. He was the voice of the tribes in dealings with the outside world. Dehahuit may well have been the single most important man in the Old Southwest, and he certainly controlled America's immediate future there.

EVERY DAY THAT Freeman spent in Natchitoches, the Red River was becoming more of a challenge and less of a river. Muddy in the best of times, it thickened like a stew in the heat. The biggest problem with the Red, though, lay farther upstream.

The Red River was notorious for its rafts, which were naturally occurring logjams. Freeman saw his first one on the way to Natchitoches. It wasn't an especially large raft, only a couple of hundred yards in length, but it was big enough. "It consists of the trunks of large trees, lying in all directions," Freeman exclaimed, "and damming up the river for its whole width, from the bottom to about three feet higher than the surface of the water." A raft was formed when debris washed downstream, as a result of the Red's extremely erratic flooding; it would then snag on itself wherever the river slowed or narrowed. There was something alive in the stubborn perseverance of a raft. Logs shifted and floated away, they sank or disintegrated, and each time, it was only a matter of hours before new wood arrived and the components knit themselves together again. The rafts belonged in the river. On the way to Natchitoches, the men on the expedition laboriously untangled paths of clear water, just wide enough for the flatboats. They squeezed through and into clear water again. Above Natchitoches, though, rafts were far more serious.

Jefferson's original idea had been to send his expeditions on the rivers of the West because he regarded them as the easiest means of travel through wilderness. As each of the explorers learned, though, in the western part of the continent, the rivers *were* the wilderness, often the most rugged part of it. The smaller, slower rivers of the eastern seaboard were quiet canals by comparison with the tortured waterways of the West. Next to rivers like the gentlemanly Hudson and the placid Potomac, the rivers in the West were unrepentant brawlers. They sometimes changed season to season—even day to day—and not merely in personality or velocity but in direction and in course.

As hard as Clark worked on his map of the Missouri, it was actually a futile pursuit; without even a moment's warning, the Missouri often flopped itself into a new riverbed, finding the Mississippi in its own way. As Hunter and Dunbar learned, the Ouachita was beautiful but giddy, tripping down steps and letting itself get too wide in places, such that it became a slightly watery gravel pit. The Columbia was just a mean excuse for a river, presenting a new death threat every few miles; the Indians along its banks had learned to live with it, but that didn't make it any easier for Lewis and Clark. The most astounding, though, and certainly the most original, was the unkempt Red River with its rafts. They awaited Freeman, Custis, and Sparks.

Freeman was at the head of the most well-equipped and carefully staffed corps of all of Jefferson's expeditions. An American of 1806 would regard it as the most important of them all—the one with the most at stake, and the one most likely to affect the lives of the Americans of 1806 *in* 1806. Freeman's expedition was likely to prevent or start a war—a conflict that Americans both feared and craved.

In Natchitoches, Freeman had time—two weeks—to consider the wisdom of canceling the rest of the expedition. The river was descending into a streak of sludge—occasionally packed with tree trunks like toothpicks spilling out of a box. To say that Viana and his men were gunning for Freeman was more than just an expression. Freeman was a man of logic, and he had towering reasons to postpone the study of the natural history of the Red River until conditions were all-around more favorable. But it was 1806 and there was no choice but to go. A president, a nation, and a new territory couldn't be denied.

Meeting with the commanding officer at nearby Fort Claiborne, Freeman heard that Dearborn had sent updated orders. Despite all the turmoil, the message had nothing to do with canceling the expedition—quite the opposite. Another detachment of twenty soldiers had been detailed to fortify Freeman's party—first, "for the purpose of assisting the exploring party to ascend the river to the upper end of the Great Raft." The second part of the directive was that the extra soldiers "continue as far afterwards as might appear necessary to repel by force any opposition they might meet with."

The purpose of the expedition was apparently changing. At first, it was largely a scientific expedition, a benign means of claiming American rights to its newly acquired territory. After the roster grew to include twenty times more soldiers than scientists, though, it became in spirit a kind of flying wedge designed to keep Freeman and Custis safe until they could be deposited at their goal, the source of the Red River. No one expected the expedition to be peaceful anymore. It was something like lacrosse, except that Freeman was the ball and the other team used bullets. Jefferson, working through Dearborn, was playing for keeps in the same arena that Wilkinson had stirred two years before with his letter to his Spanish handlers. To paraphrase Wilkinson's most shocking assertion in terms of Jefferson's outlook for Freeman: the Spanish *are dead serious and ready to detach a sufficient body of chasseurs to intercept Captain Freeman and his party, who are on the Red River, and force them to retire or take them prisoners.* If attitudes were callous in Washington, the stakes were high, and the explorers the only means at hand to make a stand.

On June 1, Freeman was finished with final preparations for the trip. Custis wrote that day: "To morrow morning we leave this [town], with 7 boats, 40 men, three commissioned and four noncommissioned officers. It is expected that the Spaniards will endeavor to stop us. They are reinforcing at Nachidoches, 150 miles from this, for what purpose it is not known." There was nothing left to do but start for the upper Red River. The next day, at Nacogdoches, a Spanish lieutenant named Juan Ygnacio Ramón did the same.

Ramón marched under orders from Commandant Viana of the garrison at Nacogdoches. Incensed, Viana was adamant that Freeman had to be intercepted before he could meet with the Caddo, Comanche, or Pawnee tribes along the Red River. In his mind, powerful Indian nations held the key to any effort to wrest contested lands from the Spanish, and a meeting between them and the American interlopers had to be stopped at all costs. In fact, in the interest of showcasing tribal loyalty to His Catholic Majesty, Viana had originally made the decision to send an army of Indians to vanquish the planned Freeman expedition. He started his recruitment drive with two of the friendlier nations in East Texas—drawing a total of only seven warriors, who quit when they realized that they were the entire army. Viana quietly canceled the plan and then, once the trap was set and Freeman was on the way, he sent Ramón with two hundred forty mounted soldiers to quash American ambitions in the Southwest.

Twenty-One

FREEMAN AND A CERTAIN SUCCESS

The Red River rafts, for all their patterned chaos, were stunning to behold—the forest in abstract. Within five miles of leaving Natchitoches, Freeman and his forty-four men were stopped cold by one of them, the first of many leading to the logjam with a name: the Great Raft. The corpsmen were safe, as long as Ramón was on the western side of the Great Raft; it was one hundred fifty miles long.

Because of the Great Raft, the Red River had been regarded as impassable until Freeman came along. Early on, he could see how the river and its monumental idiosyncrasies had changed the culture of the region. "The labor incident to the formation of a passage though these small rafts," Freeman wrote, "is so great, that the navigation of this part of the river is never attempted; for it would require to be repeated everytime a passage was attempted."

The river had been clogged at the Great Raft for centuries, backing up with the trash of forests from as far away as Colorado. The water arriving from the west had to find somewhere to go, though, and so the Great Raft was bordered by the Great Swamp, which included not only swamps, but lakes, bayous, rivulets, and every other kind of wetland.

Perhaps the Red wasn't even a river over that span, except as a damp line between sections of flowing current. At the first of the rafts, Freeman wrote: "The wood lies so compact that large bushes, weeds and grass cover the surface." It was a floating island, but he found that the next raft they encountered was on its way to becoming something even better: a hardwood floor, as he marveled that the tree trunks "lie so close that the men could walk over it in any direction." Upriver, the rafts were even older and more compacted.

Jefferson, of course, would have been quite surprised to hear that Freeman and Custis could just as easily have walked up the Red River—on the Red River itself. The two of them might even have done so, except that they had seven boats in tow. After guiding the flotilla up a hard-won path through the second of the rafts, the leaders found a place to camp. The riverbanks were still elevated, although not as much as they'd been downstream; at least four feet high, they were lined with the tall grass known as cane. While Freeman and his men were resting, they heard a rustling in the trees, as though someone was coming. There was. The visitor, accompanied by a mule, was Lucas Talapoon, a resident of Natchitoches.

Sibley had recommended Talapoon as a translator and guide for the expedition, but his arrival must have aggravated Freeman. A couple of hours later, Sibley himself crashed through the trees with an informant—yet another dismaying sight. While Freeman and his men battled raw timber to move a couple of feet, people were scampering all over the land next to the river, rushing back and forth to Natchitoches as though it were an easy jaunt. It was, inasmuch as one didn't have to pick apart tree trunks as big as three feet wide and sixty feet long. Talapoon and Sibley carried an urgent message to Freeman. Spanish troops had been seen marching out of Nacogdoches toward the Red River. Viana was obviously well apprised of Freeman's movements. Freeman had no comment about the latest intelligence. He had long since accepted the reality of his position, or predicament. Even as he listened to the news, he placed his thoughts on the profusion of willows making a pair of soft, light-green walls along the riverbank. He had either developed a new admiration for trees that were vertical, or he simply couldn't involve himself in further fear talk about the Spanish soldiers.

On June 11, the expedition reached the outskirts of the Great Raft. One of the two guides accompanying Freeman was blunt about the prospect of continuing. "It was absolutely impractical," he said, according to Freeman, "to pass the great raft in boats of any kind; as neither Red nor White men had attempted it for 50 years before."

The news that would have helped Freeman was that Wilkinson was marching out of St. Louis with a force in defense of Orleans Territory in general and Natchitoches in particular. Unfortunately, it had yet to happen. Two months after Wilkinson received his orders from Dearborn to proceed without delay, he was still in St. Louis, apologizing to the president with what he called "sensible regret." It is hard to think what might be more pressing for a general than imminent invasion by a foreign power, but in Wilkinson's case, nothing was as simple as that. Owing to his longstanding relationship with Spain, he probably didn't have to get a letter from Dearborn to know what His Catholic Majesty's army was planning. As the summer of 1806 approached, he was also wary of Orleans Territory, because Burr was making his way there. Amid the usual tangle of truth and convenience that gave fiber to Wilkinson's excuses, he did have a problem that made all else irrelevant. His wife was gravely ill. Bedridden at their home in St. Louis, she was losing a battle with a disease that took her energy away by the day; it was apparently tuberculosis. The situation was unutterably sad. But it didn't mean that Wilkinson didn't have other, less sympathetic reasons for delaying his march to the south.

Wilkinson and Burr may have developed a serious plan for their own invasion, plausibly of Texas or even Orleans Territory, although the most likely relationship of all was that of teacher and pupil. Wilkinson had developed the art of extracting money from rich people and foreign governments in trade for some recipe of new information, old information, and misinformation. If Aaron Burr was trying to enter that profession on his own, then he was crowding Wilkinson's turf. In either case, Wilkinson was conspicuously staying away from Orleans Territory, including Natchitoches—which didn't help Freeman, at all.

Wilkinson had moved to send some soldiers to Natchitoches, but by the most circuitous route possible. In fact, within just three weeks of Pike's return from the exhausting Mississippi expedition, Wilkinson had engaged the lieutenant for an even longer exploration, to the Red River, but from the north, and then on to Natchitoches. Incredibly, he ordered Pike to leave in mid-July. His exact words in the official orders of June 24 were to "proceed without delay." When Jefferson had used those same words in ordering Wilkinson to Orleans Territory, the phrase equated to three months and counting. Pike was a simpler soul and he began his preparations within days. He had only one "pressing matter," which was to finish editing his official journal regarding the Mississippi trip for submission to Wilkinson.

Wilkinson sent the journal as a matter of course to Dearborn, who immediately recognized that while he and the president were waiting for Lewis and Clark to return, they had an appealing substitute in Pike. Dearborn rushed the journal to an editor friendly to the administration, thinking it could be published as a book. Pike didn't hear in advance about the plans to adopt him as one of Jefferson's men, though. He would leave St. Louis on July 15 in slightly insulting obscurity.

According to Wilkinson's orders, Pike was to provide a military escort for a large group of Grand Osages returning to their lands, which lay on the river named for them in what is now Missouri. Then, after tending to further diplomatic business with the Kansas, Pawnee, and Comanche Indian nations, he was to continue west on what might be described as a middle route, between that of Lewis and Clark across the north and Freeman in the south. Wilkinson based the second part of the orders on a stunning juxtaposition of the truth:

> As your Interview with the Cammanchees will probably lead you to the Head Branches of the Arkansaw, and Red Rivers you may find yourself approximate to the settlements of New Mexico, and therefore . . . keep clear of any Hunting or reconnoitring parties from that province, & to prevent alarm or offence because the affairs of Spain, & the United States appear to be on the point of amicable adjustment, and more over it is the desire of the President, to cultivate the Friendship & Harmonious Intercourse, of all the Nations of the Earth, & particularly our near neighbors the Spaniards.

Because Wilkinson seemed to be speaking about a different Spain and a different United States when he wrote that they were on the "point of amicable adjustment," the orders could easily raise the suspicion of an ulterior motive. In mid-1806, Wilkinson was having trouble manning the fort at St. Louis with even as many as thirty men. In fact, before Pike returned with his detachment from the Upper Mississippi River, only nine soldiers defended the city of St. Louis. For Wilkinson to deplete his guard again indicated that Pike's mission was important, yet it was a confusingly odd time to place such a high priority on moving a couple of dozen Grand Osages and on exploration farther west. The orders specified that whatever else Pike did, he should "descend the Red River accompanied by a party of the most respectable Cammanches to the post of Natchitoches and there receive further orders from me."

Natchitoches was the Nootka of 1806—the dot on the map on which continental ambitions focused. Wilkinson was sending Pike there from the north and west, rather than from America's strong side on the east, reflecting a strategy that would make Pike and his detachment available in Natchitoches, even while tightening a grip on the Red River. The fact that Wilkinson wanted Pike to travel with a cadre of Comanche dignitaries indicates the general's sensitivity to the inside game on the river—that is, the campaign for the loyalty of the Indian nations. Because Wilkinson's motivations in mid-1806 were shrouded, though, the question is whether he chose Pike as his most reliable officer, or his most gullible. If Wilkinson planned any action of his own, with or without Burr, he might have had reasons to position Pike's detachment along a western approach—or to move the zealous officer and a large group of soldiers out of the picture for several months. Another reason for the hastily arranged expedition was that Wilkinson knew perfectly well that whatever else happened in Spanish America, Jefferson's man wasn't finishing his trip on the Red River.

Jefferson's man—Freeman—was having his doubts, too, standing on top of the river at the outset of the Great Raft. His guide, François Louis Grappe, had offered an alternative to it, but Freeman was literal-minded. He listened as Grappe described the Great Swamp: a series of lakes and rivulets (or bayous, the slow-moving combination of the other two) which led all the way around the Great Raft, while running roughly parallel to it. At first, taking advantage of that route seemed like cheating—and Freeman would prefer one hundred fifty miles of raft clearing to that. President Jef-

ferson had appointed him "to ascend the Red River." To Freeman,
that indicated bluntly that he was supposed to ascend the Red River.

The bayou that Grappe suggested was actually more of a river
than the Red, having a stronger current. Freeman at least consented
to look at it. In fact, the barrier of the Great Raft had forced the
creation of a bypass for water coming downstream—and therefore,
for explorers going upstream. "This will in time be the principal
channel of the river," Freeman concluded on seeing the first of the
bayous, and with that, he abandoned the Great Raft for the bypass.
The expedition's seven boats slipped onto the bayou, and within
five miles they reached a lake that Freeman rejoiced to find was a
"beautiful sheet of water," with one shore rising forty feet to a forest
of hardwood trees. The two flatboats, surrounded by five pirogues,
glided easily around clumps of cypress trees. The lake represented
a gentle intermission for the expedition. The route out of the lake
led to a bayou and then another lake "and so on," as Freeman put
it, "through long crooked bayous, lakes and swamps, full of dead
standing timber."

Surrounded by water and barely searching out a glimpse of the
sun behind the vines and bushes, the men of the expedition were
deep in the swampland, increasingly cramped by plants, living and
dead. The boats were still moving, but the route eventually became
discouraging. Custis described the geography as "almost impenetrable Swamps & Lakes for more than 100 miles." It wasn't a place for
boats, which could barely squeeze between the rotting trunks. Freeman proceeded warily, in fear of a collision with one of the trees, so
weak and yet so heavy. He seemed reluctant to so much as look at a
tree, in fear that his gaze would tip it over and sink one of the boats.
At times, the water flowed quickly—in the anomaly of a fast-moving
swamp—and the crewmen had to tie the boats together, using ropes
to pull them one at a time against the current and past the tottering
trees. After more than a week of what Freeman called "incessant

fatigue, toil and danger, doubt and uncertainty," the expedition had a chance to stop and take an extended rest. In fact, they had no choice about it; the barges were surrounded in the gloom, wedged in by thick bushes and dead trees. The obvious course of action was to return to the White House and tell Jefferson that there was no such thing as the Red River, but instead, Freeman sent one of the guides in a canoe to the Caddo Indian village of Coashutta, about twenty miles ahead, to ask what to do.

THE CADDO CHIEF hadn't heard of the Freeman expedition in advance and yet he was awaiting it. The chief was Dehahuit, the young leader who had risen to become a strong influence in the region later occupied by the states of Louisiana, Oklahoma, and Texas. Dehahuit built a prosperous Caddo society that his neighbors actually asked to join, in loose confederation. Because the Osages were always at the ready to attack Caddo villages, he was forced to support a small fighting force, but, unlike many chiefs, he never considered himself a warrior. It was to his advantage. While the war-obsessed Indian nations around the country left themselves vulnerable to terms negotiated by Americans, Dehahuit was positioned as the arbiter between his warring neighbors: the Spanish and the Americans.

Dehahuit had been in a nearby village called Caddo Lake in mid-June when Ramón rode in, utterly lost. He'd intended to go to a different village, but he approached Dehahuit and brashly demanded to know whether the chief "loved the Americans." Ramón was outmatched when it came to the use of power. Dehahuit blandly said that "he loved all men; if the Spaniards had come to fight they must not spill blood on his land, as it was the command of his forefathers that white blood should not be spilled on their land." Ramón left, being in a hurry to find Freeman—and spill white blood—so De-

hahuit sent a messenger after him, making it clear that he intended
to help Freeman all that he could. Ramón had other problems, for
the moment; having gone to the wrong village and lost track of the
American expedition, he felt compelled to send a message to Viana,
asking what to do next.

Freeman and his crew, still waiting in the swamp, finally hacked
their way through the thick underbrush. Busting out of the weeds
and ultimately finding themselves once more on the Red River, they
began to rejoice. Then they met with the only sight that could possibly depress them after two weeks in a dreary swamp. It was Talapoon.

He happened to be sitting in a canoe, but that was practically
a prop. Yet again, he had scampered up from Natchitoches by
land . . . the easy route. For his part, Freeman contented himself
with the satisfaction of being the first person, and probably the last,
to take seven boats through the Great Swamp. Even if he weren't an
explorer, though, with a mandate to try the limits of possibility, he
would need the boats on the upper part of the Red River.

Talapoon had traveled upriver to arrange with Dehahuit to meet
Freeman at Coashutta. He was sitting in the canoe with a runner
sent by Dehahuit, relaying the urgent message "that about 300 Spanish Dragoons, with 4 or 500 Horses and Mules were encamped" in
the vicinity. He was referring to Ramón. Freeman and his flotilla
started upriver for Coashutta.

Above the Great Raft, the Red River was "broad & placid,"
according to Custis, "with high banks covered with lofty Cotton
trees." He was overwhelmed with the grace of the terrain, imagining
that if not for the rafts that stopped easy shipment of trade goods,
the upper part of the Red River "would become the Paradise of
America."

On June 26, the expedition arrived at Coashutta. "It stands on
the North side," Freeman wrote, "on a handsome bluff, about 30 feet
high, composed of sand stone rock, and washed by the river. This

little Village has been built within two or three years." Freeman awaited Dehahuit, who arrived on July 1 for the expected meeting. The two of them sat in the shade of a tree with their close associates, surrounded by young Indians. In the most equal encounter of the kind during the Jeffersonian exploration of the West, Freeman extended courtesy, much as he might have for the leader of any European nation. He didn't give a speech, he didn't simplify his comments into the childish or mythological, and he didn't use presents as punctuation. In the first, formal meeting, he and Dehahuit spoke about the future of the region; Dehahuit admitted that he wasn't used to such candor in his dealings with the Spanish. Over the course of two days, the conversation continued.

Dehahuit took a personal interest in Freeman and the others. Custis wrote down one of his comments:

> He said, he was glad we had undertaken to explore the River
> & again repeated that in making him acquainted with the
> object of the expedition we had given him much pleasure
> and wished us all possible success, that we were going where
> we might possibly be harassed by the Osage Indians who had
> always been the inveterate enemies of the Caddoes, that if we
> should kill any of them he & his people would dance for a
> month, but on the contrary if they should kill us he would,
> although his warriors are few, make it a common cause &
> avenge the deaths.

Dehahuit's pledge of loyalty was everything that Freeman—or Jefferson—could have wanted. On practical terms, though, Freeman couldn't even dream of being killed by an Osage. In his view of the Red River, he had to get past three hundred Spanish dragoons first, in order to give the Osages their chance. Ever polished, Dehahuit hadn't mentioned what he would do if it were the Spaniards who killed his new American friends. The meetings over, he left for his own thriving village, Kadohadacho, while on July 11, Freeman started again upstream. Dehahuit had directed several men to accompany him as guides.

Like Custis, Freeman was deeply impressed by the region. "The Valley of the Red river," he wrote, "is one of the richest and most beautiful imaginable. . . . It cannot be exceeded either in fertility or beauty, by any part of America or perhaps of the world. Through this valley, the Red River pursues a very winding course, in a bed varying from 200 to 250 yards in width." He went on with a detailed description in the exhilaration of discovering land just the way he loved it to be. In the vegetation, soil, drainage, and surroundings, he found nothing to criticize.

By that point, the expedition was navigating an area that was completely unknown to Americans, even Nolan, even Sibley. While Freeman took measurements, with help from Humphrey, Custis studied the plant and animal life as carefully as he could, considering how much of it there was. The personnel on the trip were relaxed, Freeman taking delight in many of the reactions of the crew and the Caddo guides. Nonetheless, no one could forget that Spanish dragoons were approaching, somewhere over the horizon. Camping on one particularly elegant prairie, Freeman thought it would make a nice place to be captured. He commented that "it was expected that the Spaniards would here have interrupted us."

The question in military offices to the south of the Red River was why it was taking Ramón so long to close in on Freeman. Ramón had failed to intercept Freeman's expedition in the village to which he had originally been ordered. Being reluctant to attack on U.S. soil, he'd sent a message to General Salcedo for clarification. Salcedo looked at the map of the Red River and made the convenient realization that all of the areas in question were, in fact, Spanish. Freeman was much farther west than Salcedo had ever envisioned, though, and he decided he couldn't trust the dithering Ramón. He ordered Lieutenant Colonel Simón de Herrera to chase down Freeman with an army of, incredibly enough, a thousand men. Herrera, forty-nine, had been an army officer since the age of fifteen. A staunch nationalist serving in the Provincias Internas of New Spain, he was ardently anti-American. By then, there was probably little that Salcedo didn't know about Freeman's expedition, including, for example, the fact that the force was composed of only forty-five men. Apparently, one thousand soldiers were still insufficient; Salcedo also directed Herrera to stop in Kadohadacho to absorb Ramón's three hundred mounted soldiers.

Herrera's force arrived in Kadohadacho on July 15, and the commander noticed that Dehahuit was flying the American flag. Herrera sternly informed the chief that since the village was located on Spanish territory, the tribe would either have to switch the flag or move. Dehahuit was considering his response when several of the soldiers preempted him, chopping down the flagpole. Moreover, they harangued Dehahuit for his loyalties, insisting that once they found Freeman and his men, they'd give them what they gave the flagpole and more specifically, "either kill them, or carry them off, prisoners in irons." Dehahuit was distressed by the threats and by the sheer anger of the men. He quietly selected his two fastest runners and directed them up the river to find Freeman.

In St. Louis on the same day, Pike was leaving on his second expedition, accompanied by much the same crew that had accompanied him up the Mississippi. "We sailed from the landing at Belle Fontaine, about 3 o'clock p.m. in two boats," Pike wrote. The boats set out on the Missouri, tracing the route of Lewis and Clark, although the ultimate goal was its tributary, the Osage River. Pike was joined on the expedition by Wilkinson's son, James Biddle Wilkinson. He was also a lieutenant, though subordinate to Pike on the expedition.

The party included fifty-one Osage and Pawnee Indians, who walked along onshore, guarded against assault by several of the soldiers. Stuck in the procession of boats and people, Pike, of course, wanted to go faster. He always did, but unfortunately, he couldn't employ his favorite technique of leaving everyone else behind while he scouted ahead. That part of the Missouri didn't need reconnaissance. By the third day, though, Pike had discovered a fun way to go faster: organizing races between the two boats. That was something he hadn't been able to do with only one barge on the Mississippi expedition. Two boats were a boon, and the races were almost constant, which is probably why, as they went along, more and more soldiers opted to walk with the Indians. Pike couldn't help noting in his journal that whichever boat he steered ended up winning.

As of July 1806, Jefferson's program of western exploration was at its fullest blossom. It hadn't unraveled neatly over the previous two and a half years, but the timing of its profusion was fortunate, nonetheless. The citizens of the new territories, especially Orleans, were more unsettled than ever. In the midst of his efforts to reopen negotiations with Spain over the border issue and that of the Floridas, a date was elusive and the diplomats were doing little but squabbling. The rumors of war in Orleans overlapped one another, there were so many. All of the rising problems would be assuaged by a closer bond between the old East and the new West—between the United States and its territories.

The expeditions fed the need for a more seamlessly fused East and West. They not only provided geographical data, but in the process, raised interest in the expanding map of the country. That map grew into a diploma of arrival for the regions covered, into which Americans could write themselves or their future. The image of soldiers on the Ouachita wading into freezing waters to *carry* their boat up the Chutes or of Zebulon Pike leaving his blood on the snow in order to reach the next Ojibwe village were imbued with the pain of all the men who kept going, no matter what. Every expedition with which Jefferson was associated threw sacrifice far, far down the route in the interest of introducing two parts of a country to each other. The men who made it through answered the question of how much the new lands were worth. Americans had no better way to tell the people of the West that they agreed than to raise Jefferson's explorers to the level of heroes.

Jefferson was aware, through Dearborn, that Pike had embarked on a second expedition. During the summer, his administration was managing the publication of Dunbar's journal. Of course, the expedition of Lewis and Clark was closest of all to Jefferson's heart—being the first and the longest, and involving two family friends. He was anxiously awaiting their return, but Freeman and his men were the explorers of the moment, and Jefferson knew well the serious danger they were in and for which he was responsible.

The runner that Dehahuit sent to the upper Red River arrived on July 26. Freeman listened to the details of the message regarding Herrera's tirade, as did the others in his party. "On receiving this intelligence," Freeman wrote, "the Indians were very much distressed and wished the party to return without seeing the Spaniards." Freeman didn't consider that possibility. He may have been a civilian, a professional man, a gentleman in every sense, and—according to at least a few who remembered him from the 31st parallel survey—a self-righteous goody-goody. Freeman may have been all of those things, but he wasn't afraid of thirteen hundred Spanish soldiers. "My instructions were to proceed until stopped by a superior force," he told the Indians, while immediately giving them a chance to return by themselves. "They said they would proceed with the party," he recalled, "but were certain none would ever go back."

The most important piece of information that the messengers brought was the actual location, a bluff two days distant, where the Spaniards would be waiting. Knowing that, Freeman's party wasn't surprised and couldn't be ambushed; they were actually able to plan for what the Spanish thought would be a sneak attack. Floating ever nearer to the bluff that had been designated and even espying evidence of the Spanish force every so often, Freeman was elaborately casual, giving no sign that anything extraordinary was about to happen. "The party continued to advance," he wrote, "until the usual time of dining, when the boats stopped and the men were directed to make their fires, and prepare for dinner as soon as possible." He happened to have chosen a spot in which, as he explained, "the Spanish guard was distinctly seen from hence, about half a mile further up."

Freeman and the other leaders had their dinner on the beach. Before long, they watched a group of Spanish horsemen riding along the crest of the riverbank on the other side and then saw the horses slide to a halt exactly opposite the American fires. The horsemen then turned around, obviously racing to report that the Americans had arrived. Less than a half hour later, Freeman wrote, "a large detachment of Horse, with four officers in front, advanced in a full gallop from the Spanish Camp along the beach towards us." Freeman and the officers immediately gave orders for thirty-two of the American soldiers to climb the riverbank and hide amid the brush, "ready to fire . . . and to keep up their fire in the most effectual manner possible." The rest were sentinels stationed on the beach. The Spanish horsemen numbered a hundred and fifty and were eventually joined by more than fifty foot soldiers. They started to cross the river, which was so shallow at that point that the horses' hooves easily touched the bottom.

The American sentinels on the beach hailed the Spanish horsemen with the order to stop. But the horses kept advancing, with all the concentrated yet exploding power of a cavalry charge. The sentinels shouted again and then cocked their firearms and "were in the act of presenting to fire." Fortunately, it took several long seconds to fire a bullet in those days. The horsemen stopped.

The Spanish officers, ignoring the Americans, ordered their men into position on the beach. Only then did they dismount. Viana himself had taken charge of the force and he led the Spanish officers slowly forward. Because the American troops were hidden in the bushes—guerrilla style—they intimidated the Spanish far in excess of their actual numbers. Captain Sparks was the first American to walk toward Viana and the others, meeting them halfway. Freeman immediately joined him.

Viana started by warning Freeman that if the expedition continued, his orders were to open fire.

Freeman replied, "The object of my expedition was, to explore the river to its source, under the instructions of the President of the U.S." He requested the objections in writing, but Viana refused, giving his word of honor instead. Freeman had done his duty.

The juncture had been reached at which Freeman's control over the situation would vanish with one more move, one more word. He agreed to leave the following day. Before turning to leave, however, he thought Viana said something in Spanish to one of his men about placing his soldiers on what had become the American side of the river. Freeman told his interpreter "that if a Spanish guard was placed near us they should be fired upon." He was offering battle to a force vastly superior. A moment went by and then Viana abandoned the idea. Freeman had done what a hundred diplomats had failed to do. Spain and America had a border, and it was the Red River.

The next day, July 30, the Americans packed up and started downriver. On one of the barges, Freeman opened his journal. He wrote down that the expedition had been a success.

Twenty-Two

MEN OF JEFFERSON

Late one summer night, Lewis and Clark were sitting up with a boatman who brought them news from home. The captains were along the Lower Missouri River, nearing the end of their long journey and complaining continually of the heat after such a long span in cooler parts of the north. Long past midnight, after chatting for hours, Clark had time to write in his journal that the boatman "informed us that we had been long Since given out by the people of the U S Generaly and almost forgotton, the President of the U. States had yet hopes of us."

Every so often, a report circulated in the nation's newspapers that the members of the Corps of Discovery had been killed by unnamed Indians. By no coincidence, Jefferson met such news by filing an update, however stale, about Lewis and Clark, with Congress. Both types of dubious information were so lightly published in newspapers around the country, though, that the boatman was right; the status of Lewis and Clark could be accurately described as "almost forgotten."

The last time that the captains had set foot in the United States proper was in May of 1804. Two years, four months, and a couple of days later, they were coming out of a time capsule and were no doubt relieved to learn that Jefferson had been reelected—and that he was still alive and the country was still bound together, as "U. States."

The return from the Pacific Ocean was on track to take only about six months, altogether, compared with travel time of fourteen months on the westward leg. Even at that, the homeward journey could have been shorter, except that the captains, to their credit, decided to explore the rivers of the eastern watershed of the Rocky Mountains, breaking up into smaller groups throughout most of the month of July and part of August across what is now Montana. Lewis had the duller assignment of retracing the trip on the Missouri River and retrieving supplies and specimens that had been stored there, while Clark took on the challenge of finding his way east on about five hundred miles of new terrain along the Yellowstone River. He traveled with the larger of the two parties, taking Sacajawea, since he would be navigating potentially dangerous Shoshone lands.

According to the plan, Lewis did make one side trip with three corpsmen in late July, following the northward Marias River. There was a fleeting hope that the Marias offered another route through the Rockies, but that didn't prove to be the case. Following a tributary creek (Two Medicine River) with only meager interest on July 27, Lewis and his men fell in with a band of eight men from the Blackfoot nation. Most of them were carrying bows and arrows, and pointed clubs known as eye-daggs. Only two had guns. Lewis gauged that his own detachment, fully armed, could dominate the Indians in a struggle, and so the whole group enjoyed a lively evening before the fire near the Blackfoots' shelter. As least one hopes they all enjoyed themselves, because the next morning, two of the Blackfoots were dead.

In the Blackfoot oral history, the Indians in the band were teenagers, as young as thirteen. They did have a good time with the corpsmen, even staging a race with them, betting on it and other games. The Blackfoots believed that they had won some guns and horses, and in the morning, awakening before the corpsmen, they started to take them.

In Lewis's account, the cool mountain air was having its well-known effect, making the explorers sleep deeply. The Indians, who were used to the bracing atmosphere, woke up early, and while the expedition's sentry was unawares, they crept around the sleeping corpsmen, stealing their guns. By the time Lewis came out of his deep slumber, the camp was a brawl, the Indians scurrying around, with the corpsmen trying to wrestle their weapons back. "R. [Reubin] Fields," Lewis wrote, was about fifty yards away and as an Indian "seized his gun [he] stabed the indian to the heart with his knife the fellow ran about 15 steps and fell dead." The members of the corps wanted permission to shoot the Blackfoot, but Lewis held them off, saying that the Indians weren't trying to kill the corpsmen. His remark was a small indication that the Blackfoot version, about a misunderstanding, may have held some truth. When the Indians persisted in taking the horses, though, Lewis considered it a crime tantamount to murder in the mountains:

> I called to them as I had done several times before that I
> would shoot them if they did not give me my horse and
> raised my gun, one of them jumped behind a rock and spoke
> to the other who turned around and stoped at the distance
> of 30 steps from me and I shot him through the belly, he fell
> to his knees and on his wright elbow from which position he
> partly raised himself up and fired at me, and turning himself
> about crawled in behind a rock which was a few feet from

him. He overshot me, being bearheaded I felt the wind of his bullet very distinctly.

Lewis's gunshot proved fatal. He had apparently panicked, since the Blackfoot had stopped approaching. As the others ran off with some of the horses, Lewis directed his corpsmen to beat a hasty escape to the Marias and on to the Missouri, before the tragedy escalated any further. About three weeks after surviving the gun battle with the Blackfoots, Lewis was shot by one of his own men. His first mistake was to go elk hunting dressed in brown leather. His second was to go hunting for anything with a man who "cannot see very well." That was Lewis's description of Peter Cruzette, his companion that day.

On the trail of an elk, the two had separated momentarily, when Lewis was shot in the backside. If Cruzette had been able to aim a little better, he might have put the ball through the chest or head of his target. Instead, the ball passed through one of Lewis's buttocks, grazing the other. He was infuriated. "Damn you," Lewis shouted to Cruzette, "you have shot me!" There was no response. Lewis called out several more times, without hearing anything. "I was now preswaded that it was an Indian that had shot me," Lewis wrote. Despite his condition, he hobbled as quickly as he could through the brush and back to the river, commanding his men there to prepare for attack. Lewis expected to be overwhelmed as he aimed his gun into the wilds, but was "determined . . . to sell my life as deerly as possible."

A search party gingerly returned to the hunting ground and brought back Cruzette, who expressed surprise on being told that he'd shot the captain. He further said he didn't hear any of Lewis's shouts, and perhaps he didn't; Cruzette had shot an elk and Lewis didn't hear that gunshot. No matter, Lewis didn't quite believe him on either point. He was convinced that Cruzette had heard the shouts but shrank away, ashamed at what he'd done. It was a cranky attitude on Lewis's part, but that was to be expected from a man lying uncomfortably in a pirogue, hoping his wounds weren't mortal and knowing that if they were, he hadn't sold his life for anything at all.

Clark and Lewis reconnoitered much as planned the next day, August 12. Lewis was still confined to a prone position, but his recovery would be steady. Reaching the Mandan villages two days later, the captains found that most of Fort Mandan had burned down in a prairie fire that had also destroyed parts of the nearby village. The loss of the fort didn't matter to Lewis or Clark, though. They'd planned only a short stay and were ready to leave after only three days. As usual, the Mandan villages represented a major juncture on the Missouri River, and so it was that the expedition lost a number of its members there. One good corpsman, an army private, received an early discharge so that he could immediately go back out west again as a fur trapper. Sacajawea also remained behind, along with her husband and toddler. Clark had become so fond of her child, whom he nicknamed "Pompie," that he couldn't leave without initiating plans to adopt him. The corps did receive one addition. A Mandan chief and his small family decided to accompany Lewis and Clark to St. Louis, traveling in two canoes lashed together.

By the fourth week of September, Lewis and Clark were on the Lower Missouri River, their expedition lurching toward St. Louis. With about two hundred fifty miles to go, every member of the crew was hungry, disheveled, and hot. Some were in worse trouble, suffering from eye damage caused by the reflection of the late-summer sun on the water. The captains faced a troubling problem: whether to pause and let the expedition's hunters find game or to press on, redoubling the effort to reach a European-American settlement. If they continued, their only food would be pawpaw, a kiwi-like fruit that grew profusely on the riverbank. They opted to push on, sheer excitement providing their energy.

On September 20, just when the sheer excitement was running even lower than food, the crew spotted cows grazing on the riverbank. There could be few signs of home more certain for a European-American than cows relaxing in a pasture. Had the animals looked back, they'd have seen a gaggle of seven canoes or pirogues, each carefully packed with bundles and handled by men who were very suddenly celebrating.

The men of the expedition wore buckskin head to toe, which was part of the reason they were overheated. Whenever they passed other boats, they did their best to trade for cloth shirts. The corpsmen didn't come home as unkempt mountain men, though. Whiskers weren't in style in Lewis and Clark's day, and indications are that the men were clean shaven, with their hair cut short or bound back. One change in appearance that they couldn't help was being deeply tanned in a way that was sure to draw notice as they reentered their own modern America.

By the time the corps approached St. Louis on September 22, they made sure that they weren't "almost forgotten," firing guns in the air as fanfare. By the time they pulled the canoes ashore for the very last time, they were surrounded by hundreds of people, a bit surprised and trying all at once to become part of the event.

A great many St. Louisans dashed to the post office, crowding into a line that formed there and writing notes as quickly as possible—just in time for an express postal shipment that was leaving that afternoon for the East. One man scrawled a message and sent it to a friend in Georgetown in the District of Columbia:

> Captains Lewis and Clark arrived here two hours since, having lost but one man of their party—they enjoy good health and are in high spirits. On their arrival we fired a salute of 17 guns—they have fully completed their tour to the Pacific. After penetrating to the source of the Missouri, they crossed the high mountains and descended Columbia

River, and in latitude 46 encamped for five months on the
Pacific ocean.

I have left the gentlemen for a moment to inform you
of their arrival. . . .

Two nights later, a formal dinner at a St. Louis inn honored
Lewis and Clark. They danced at a ball afterward. During the banquet, eighteen toasts were offered, and the number was a boast all
by itself. In that era, guests didn't make speeches: they boiled their
thoughts down to a single sentence—a toast—and the many to
which Lewis and Clark raised their glasses were reprinted widely.
The first of them all honored President Jefferson, "friend of science, the polar star of discovery, the philosopher and the patriot."
The toasts that followed closely on that one told the captains, while
they were still in a condition to hear, something about the region,
as well as the nation, to which they'd returned. One stressed with
perhaps too much emphasis the need for unity among the states
and territories. Soon after, the room rose to recite, "The territory
of Louisiana—freedom, without bloodshed, may her actions duly
appreciate the blessing." That remark pointedly differentiated Louisiana Territory from Orleans.

Even by express, the news that Lewis and Clark were safely in
St. Louis took most of a month to reach the eastern seaboard. By
late October, though, the captains were the talk of the big cities of
the East. Their story fanned out more slowly to the weekly or even
bi-weekly newspapers of the smaller towns. So it was that the tiny
New Hampshire Gazette in Portsmouth was headlining the break-
through in the West by reprinting a flash from Washington:

ARRIVAL OF CAPT's LEWIS AND CLARK
AT ST. LOUIS

This desirable and unexpected event took place on Tuesday,
the 22rd of September, about the hour of 10 o'clock in the

morning. On Monday evening, the news reached this place that capts. Lewis and Clark had arrived at the cantonment, near the mouth of the Missouri; and the great concourse of people that lined the back of the river at the time of their landing at this place the next day must be considered as a strong evidence of the respect entertained for those gentlemen for the danger and difficulties they must have encountered in their expedition of discovery.

In Washington, the return of Lewis and Clark was no longer merely a scientific or geographic achievement: it was a political reality. And better still, it was a reality that Jefferson's political detractors could sustain only in silent disgust—not with Lewis and Clark, but with the way that their return brought Jefferson back from the far corner in which he had parlayed his presidency. "A body of federalists conversing on our national government look like so many men who smell carion," wrote an editor in Connecticut, referring to the effect of the expedition's success. A Federalist paper in Boston tried to explain Jefferson's new position, in Lewis-and-Clark terms: "Like a boat descending a river," it observed, "the current sweeps him on, and he cries, what an excellent pilot am I, though he stirs neither hand, foot, not oar to get along!" There was a modicum of truth to that, much as Jefferson spoke of "quiet hands" in his administration's strategy, which turned events without being seen.

Had Lewis and Clark failed to return during that autumn (or at all), the story at the end of 1806 would have been Jefferson's inability to attain either West Florida or his version of the scope of Orleans. The reasonable question of how he could have made the Purchase without knowing its borders would have been the nation's dominant association with the word "Louisiana." Freeman's expedition—and Jefferson's irresponsible gamble in sending it—would only have highlighted the other motives of "the friend of science, the polar star of discovery."

Instead, Jefferson had his administration's favorite sons, Lewis and Clark, representing the best of the Louisiana Purchase, yet remaining innocent of the worst of it farther south. They brought home a Louisiana for the nation to love, of elk sunning themselves by splashing rivers, of mountains where the glistening snow never melted, and of Americans forging farther than any French, British, or Spanish explorer had even dared to try.

Jefferson responded to Lewis's first letter from St. Louis on October 20, with a very short note expressing "unspeakable joy" at the return of the expedition and "constant affection" for Lewis himself. Just two days later, he called his cabinet together to respond to matters less pleasant to the south, in the form of two crises that could no longer contain themselves: the Spanish incursion into Orleans and the rumors surrounding Burr, including accusations that Wilkinson, the presiding commander of the U.S. Army, was Burr's "Lieutenant or first in command." One reason for Jefferson to take the suspicions surrounding Wilkinson seriously was the general's otherwise inexplicable delay in leaving for Orleans, as ordered, in May—and June. As a result, Orleans was vulnerable, and so Jefferson ordered a strengthening of the troops through the use of state militias.

By then, Wilkinson was finally on his way to the Sabine River. Mrs. Wilkinson's condition had stabilized. His own situation had gone in the other direction. Writing to the capital from Natchez, he discouraged the use of the militias, promising to maintain Orleans Territory by peaceful means and not to use force until he had "penetrated the designs of the Spaniard." Or the designs of Burr. The only thing that was certain was that something had detained Wilkinson for four months in St. Louis.

During the first days of November, Wilkinson camped with a small army near the Sabine River and lost no time in suing for peace—before the war, instead of afterward. His proposal, the "Neutral Ground Agreement," formalized the previous notion of a buffer zone. It was advantageous to the Spanish in granting them use of the Sabine. Most previous estimates of the border, from the American point of view, had presumed that it stretched long past the Sabine and almost to Nacogdoches. Wilkinson ceded that detail in the name of a hasty agreement. He certainly received that, as the Spanish compliantly receded behind the new neutral zone. The northern border of Texas was left officially undefined.

The ease of the agreement led some observers to conclude that Wilkinson had cooperated with Burr only to the extent of earning a reward from the Spanish . . . for thwarting Burr.

On his way to New Orleans from the West, Wilkinson abruptly wrote to local officials in the city, accusing Burr of a conspiracy to separate the western states from the Union. "My God!" he exclaimed, "what a situation our country has reached. Let us save it if we can." Afterward, he made even stronger claims in two long, incendiary letters to Jefferson, dated November 10 and 12. By the time Wilkinson's exposés arrived in Washington, they didn't expose much. Newspapers were filled with fact and conjecture regarding Burr, and in mid-November, it would have been difficult to find the odd hermit who didn't know all about his apparent conspiracy.

On December 2, Jefferson sent his annual message to Congress, discussing Wilkinson's interaction on the Sabine River as though it were a military triumph, which it wasn't, and making mention of the conspiracy surrounding Burr, with the federal efforts to stop it. As the president was finally forced to address the serious problems staining the West, especially in Orleans Territory, he didn't offer the names of anyone involved: not Burr or Wilkinson, not the governors, military officers, conspirators, or informants. They had their place. He gave the nation the names only of its heroes:

> The expedition of Messrs. Lewis and Clarke, for exploring
> the river Missouri, and the best communication from that
> to the Pacific ocean, has had all of the success which could
> have been expected. They have traced the Missouri nearly

to its source, ascertained with accuracy the geography of that interesting communication across our continent, learned the character of the country, of its commerce, and inhabitants; and it is but justice to say that Messrs. Lewis and Clarke, and their brave companions, have by this arduous service deserved well of their country.

The attempt to explore the Red river, under the direction of Mr. Freeman, though conducted with a zeal and prudence meriting entire approbation, has not been equally successful, After proceeding up it about six hundred miles, nearly as far as the French settlements had extended which the country was in their possession, our geographers were obliged to return without completing their work.

Very useful additions have also been made to our knowledge of the Mississippi by Lieutenant Pike, who has ascended to its source, and whose journal and map, giving the details of the journey, will shortly be ready for communication to both houses of Congress. Those of Messrs. Lewis and Clarke, and Freeman, will require further time to be digested and prepared. These important surveys, in addition to those before possessed, furnish materials for commencing an accurate map of the Mississippi, and its western waters. Some principal rivers, however, remain still to be explored, toward which the authorization of Congress, by moderate appropriations, will be requisite.

Jefferson held forth the hope that the expeditions would continue. In fact, Freeman was still in the Natchez area, biding his time on the presumption that he would make another attempt at the Red River in the spring. Events discouraged others, if not Freeman, in that idea. When Wilkinson's Neutral Ground Agreement failed to address the Red River, the Spanish assumed that they still controlled it. Dunbar and Freeman drew the same conclusion. They quickly advised Dearborn that the Arkansas would be a worthwhile substitute, and Freeman continued to stay in Mississippi, waiting for his next chance to lead a federal expedition.

In their geographic work, Freeman, Custis, and Humphrey were far ahead of the pace of their times, as reflected by the fact that the full length of the Red wouldn't be explored for another forty-six years. Moreover, they had taken America into the West along the most disputed section of land related to the Louisiana Purchase. Unfortunately, the Freeman expedition was a reminder for Jefferson of a region misplayed by him, almost to the point of disaster for those who were part of it. After he characterized the expedition as a failure in his annual message to Congress, others presumed it to be so. He didn't emphasize it or even mention it again—saving himself the embarrassment of reliving his risky impetus and two months when the Red River of Texas was the worst place in the world for an American to be. All of the Jeffersonian explorers were courageous, but Freeman and Custis—a couple of civilians—faced more than just civilian hazards: wild animals, accidents, or violent weather. They also had to survive Spanish soldiers by the thousand. Freeman and Custis knew exactly what types of pawns they really were. They still thought it was necessary to occupy the land, however briefly; and perhaps it was.

After Freeman's return, Jefferson emphasized his explorers of the more pristine north, regularly including Pike with Lewis and Clark in his comments. It was an honor that would have pleased Pike. At the time, he was along the eastern Rocky Mountains in serious trouble.

Pike's primary assignment, after tending to business pertaining to several Indian nations, was to head south from what is now western Kansas. In that vein, Wilkinson had predicted that business with the Comanches would probably lead "to the Head Branches of the Arkansaw, and Red Rivers." Wilkinson then directed Pike to return east via the Red River and end his trip in Natchitoches. The headwaters of the Red and Arkansas Rivers are, in fact, four hundred miles apart, but in Wilkinson's almost offhand remark lay the start of Pike's troubles. His business didn't take him as far as any headwaters. If it had, the expedition would have been well equipped for that sort of route. And in that case, the summer clothes that he and his men wore might have been appropriate. Instead, Pike headed west, straight toward a Rocky Mountain winter. He and his men were clad in one layer of cotton clothing. They had no coats. Or even socks.

On November 11, 1806, Pike was along the Arkansas River in what is now the eastern part of Colorado. He had a decision to make: whether to continue west on the Arkansas River to look for those headwaters mentioned by Wilkinson or turn south to locate the Red River, which was to be his passage to Natchitoches. Never one to turn down any challenge, Pike looked to the source of the Arkansas. "Finding the impossibility of performing the voyage in the time proposed," he wrote in his journal, "I determined to spare no pains to accomplish every object even if it should oblige me to spend another winter in the desert."

The line of men on horses continued west, into the plains that lead to the Rockies. Nothing caught the wind, no trees or hillocks, no boulders or brambles, only the backs of the mounted soldiers, in their gauzy summer shirts. They wound their way into the mountains with the river, but soon found that it split into smaller creeks, any one of which could have been the source. Instead of calling that an interesting fact and then turning immediately south toward the Red River, Pike came to the conclusion that if he could survey the terrain from the top of a mountain, he could easily sort out the source of the river. Leaving most of the men behind in a hastily constructed shelter, he took three companions and set out for a blue-tinted mountain that appeared to be one day's march away, or about fifteen miles. Four days later—days spent climbing an intervening mountain and wading through waist-deep snow—Pike reassessed the situation. The mountain, he wrote, "now appeared at the distance of 15 or 16 miles from us, and as high again as what we had ascended." The blue-tinted mountain, apparently on wheels, seemed to remain a perpetual sixteen miles away and so Pike finally turned his back on it, the only thing on earth that ever made him give up.

On Christmas, Pike described a day in the life of his expedition:

> 800 miles from the frontiers of our country, in the most inclement season of the year; not one person clothed for the winter, many without blankets (having been obliged to cut them up for socks, etc.) and now laying down at night on the snow or wet ground; one side burning whilst the other was pierced with the cold wind . . . I will not speak of diet, as I conceive that to be beneath the serious consideration of a man on a voyage of such nature.

The soldiers often didn't eat anything at all for two days at a time, sometimes not for three. Moving around with fifteen men and more than two dozen pack horses, Pike found that getting out of the mountains wasn't as easy as simply going south, or any other direction. In fact, to his "great mortification" he spent most of December leading the expedition in a seventy-mile circle. So it was that by January 9, he had to admit that he "felt at considerable loss how to proceed."

The solution was Pike's usual one; he decided that he needed to lighten up and move more quickly, in order to locate the Red River. To that end, he left two men behind to care for the horses and most of the cargo while he set out on foot with the other members of the party. After marching seventy-eight miles in subzero weather, nine of the men had frostbitten feet. Pike left the corps to recuperate, as best they could with absolutely nothing to eat for the second day in a row. Pike and another man, a civilian named Dr. John Robinson, left to "hunt something to preserve existence." Failing to bring down the only animal they saw all day—a buffalo—they were too depressed to return to the camp and found some rocks in which to sleep: "sat up all night; from the intense cold it was impossible to sleep," Pike wrote, "Hungry and without cover." Lost, starving, freezing, and in some cases, very sick, the members of Pike's expedition had every reason to give up, but they had long since learned to keep their faith in Pike, their indomitable leader.

The next day, January 19, Pike was still staying away from the camp. That was on purpose, because he was planning where to die. On his fourth day without food, he was "extremely weak and faint," as he wrote, but he didn't want to go back to the frostbitten men, because he didn't want to see what he had done to them. A forest seemed like a good place to lie down and wait for the end to come. He and Robinson were making their way toward a stand of trees when they managed to kill a buffalo. With ample food for everyone, disaster was averted, but only temporarily. They were still lost, and a week later the full force of hunger, fatigue, and cold returned.

It was then that one of the men was heard to complain. He said that "it was more than human nature could bear, to march three days without sustenance, through snows three feet deep and carry burthens only fit for horses." When the outcry was over, Pike gathered all of the men together. With sober patience, Pike told them that he invariably expected more of himself than of anyone else. He then calmly discussed the predicament of the expedition, a rational assessment that he concluded by saying if there was one more grumble out of anyone, the punishment would be "instant death."

Because of the hardship that Pike's expedition endured from November to February, his notes didn't focus on nature or science.

And because he was entirely lost, he couldn't offer much in the way of geographical data. For those reasons, the latter part of Pike's travels, while extraordinary as a tale of sheer bravery, relate to survival, rather than exploration. Pike did well to keep the band moving, in a leapfrog pace dictated by the men who had to be left behind at any one time. Two groups had to stop at different points owing to frostbite, with some of the men even losing parts of their feet.

Finally, at the end of January, Pike pointed out the Red River. Jubilation naturally followed. Hoping to slip onto the river and through to Natchitoches, he excitedly sent some of his healthier men to gather their debilitated comrades, who had been left behind on the route. Some of those were still unable to travel, although that wasn't Pike's worst problem. The snow had started again, the ammunition was almost gone, and his best gun was broken, but nothing was insurmountable, as long as the Red River was finally beckoning, with a clear route to the safety—and heat—of Natchitoches.

But it wasn't the Red River. It was the Rio Grande.

The expedition had strayed into what is now the western half of Colorado, where the Rio Grande comes down from the mountains. Pike was in Spanish territory, a fact that he surely suspected and perhaps intended, though Jefferson would have argued that whichever river Pike had found, if he was north of a line determined by the Red and east of the headwaters of the Rio Grande, he was in the United States. Finding himself near a river connected with Spanish settlement, Pike was finally in the sphere to which he had been pointed by Wilkinson the year before. While Pike oversaw the construction of a small fortress and began to arrange for the retrieval of the men left behind, he gave Dr. Robinson permission to travel alone to Santa Fe, ostensibly to transact some financial business, the collection of a debt. With promises to return before Pike made his way east on the river (the supposed Red River), Dr. Robinson left on February 6.

At the end of February, a small detachment of soldiers approached the fortress, such as it was. There was no sense of confrontation, as in the clash between Viana and Freeman. With more pity than punishment, the soldiers took Pike into custody, convincing him to go willingly with them to Santa Fe.

Under Jefferson's aegis, exploration refreshed the republic, but only the most single-minded nationalist could root against the well-equipped Spanish detachment that rescued Pike's bedraggled men: emaciated and cold, some suffering serious health problems. Assisted by local villagers from a cosmopolitan mixture of Indian, French, and Spanish cultures, the detachment handed out blankets and warm clothes, carefully assisting those who couldn't walk. For all the jousting that Jefferson did with the Spanish for fifteen years, they were compassionate neighbors when they found an American lieutenant who needed help, far more than he would admit. One theory about the expedition holds that Pike, indeed, wanted to be captured (even sending Dr. Robinson to Santa Fe in order to accelerate the process), so that an enormous American force would have reason to storm into disputed territory to retrieve him. A paler version of that theory, which has more merit, holds that Pike wanted to be captured so that he could later report on Spanish military strength.

Pike and the members of the party were taken first to New Mexico and then to Chihuahua, a separate province of New Spain in what is now northern Mexico. They were held there in comfortable quarters on charges of trespassing. Most of the men, including Pike, were released in late spring. One private was killed in prison, in an altercation with one of the other American soldiers. The fatality was Thomas Miller, who had volunteered to accompany Pike on the last leg of the search for the source of the Mississippi. That was a very long year earlier.

———

THE SPANISH OFFICIALS made their point about Americans respecting Spanish territory, just as the Americans had made their
point, insinuating themselves into the West. No one wanted the
Pike arrest to escalate, least of all Jefferson, who interceded in the
negotiations over his release. When the Spanish official in charge
requested reimbursement of expenses and monies advanced to Pike,
he described Pike as a spy. Jefferson directed Madison to pay the
money, while stiffly insisting that the Spanish understand that "this
government has never employed a spy" and that Pike's mission was
solely to explore the Arkansas and Red Rivers. The Spanish replied
with a nearly complete list of Jefferson's explorers, all of whom, as
they calmly explained, were spies. Within a month, the prisoners
were escorted to Orleans Territory, and on June 22, 1807, Pike finally
reached Natchitoches. He was back in America, a free man again,
but it was only a bittersweet stop on the way back to St. Louis.

En route, Pike finally made it to the Red River, the dream he'd
harbored throughout the worst of his ordeal:

> My little excursion up the river was in order to establish the
> geography of the sources of the . . . Red River, as I well knew
> the indefatigable researches of doctor Hunter, Dunbar and
> Freeman, had left nothing unnoticed in the extent of their
> voyage up said river, I determined that its upper branches
> should be equally well explored.

It was not to be. If Pike's ordeal was over, so was his exploration
of the Southwest, a monumental effort that was, in many ways, the
embodiment of all Jeffersonian exploration. The motives of the expedition were not what they seemed to be. It was directed at the raw
overlap of the American-Spanish frontiers, no less than the equally
sensitive divide between American and Spanish diplomats. And it
was purposefully designed to apprise Spanish officials of the American presence in the West, irritating them almost, but not quite, to

the point of war. Pike's very persona displayed astonishing valor, worthy of that shown at other times by his fellow "*men* of Jefferson." The fact that his most dire circumstances were self-inflicted, due to poor judgment, was not representative of the other explorers, but then, his personal commitment to leadership was consistent with that of the others. Jefferson's captains in the West were far from the well-trained, perfectly prepared explorers of Carlos III's academy; those extremely admirable Spanish scientists and artists were practically bureaucrats in canoes compared to the individualistic men Jefferson convinced to go west for him. Pike's expedition in the West stands apart from the others, but only by way of exaggeration in almost every respect.

After leaving Natchitoches on June 22, Pike headed home to St. Louis. The next day, Dearborn sent a letter to Jefferson, letting him know that he had written to Dunbar and Freeman in Natchez, "informing them of the want of funds for prosicuting the exploring voyage up the Arkansas, and of your determination for suspending the expedition for the present years." With that, the magnificent era of Jeffersonian exploration was over.

The nation was changed for the efforts of less than a hundred crewmen and their six primary leaders. For the time being, the Red River held a quiet border. The Louisiana Territory belonged to Americans—not because money had been exchanged, but because those hundred men had gone a long way, so near to their own limits, in order to bring it home.

SOME OF THE leaders found that the hardest part of the job was returning home. John Evans had found that impossible fifteen years before. Dr. Hunter was glad to go back to his home life in Philadelphia, but he couldn't forget Louisiana, moving his family and businesses there in 1815. In addition to being known through the rest of his life as a "Man of Jefferson," he was credited with bringing the steam engine to Louisiana and proving its worth in industry. William Dunbar continued in the life he'd created, mirroring or even surpassing the aristocratic setting in which he'd grown up. Around Natchez, he was called, erroneously, "Sir William." Dunbar's role in Jefferson's explorations, both as leader and director, raised his reputation nationally, and he was also called—far more accurately—"the First Scientist of the South."

Zebulon Pike returned from incarceration in Mexico to learn that he was simultaneously regarded as a hero and lambasted as a traitor. The publicity surrounding his journey and ultimate capture had made him a romantic figure, while the whirlpool surrounding Aaron Burr had encompassed not only General Wilkinson, but Pike. Through the trials that ensued, no evidence was ever found that Pike was complicit in any of the plans laid by Burr, ranging from the capture of Texas to the purloining of the Louisiana Territory. (Burr and Wilkinson were acquitted of their changes, though not as irrefutably.) Pike's military career subsequently burgeoned, and he played a significant role in the War of 1812, helping to lead an attack on Toronto (then called York). He was killed in the battle, which the United States won. But he remained an idol in the first decades of the nineteenth century, revered as an American who did not even know how to quit. More famous than the man, however, is the one entity that bested his unflagging spirit and succeeded in making Zebulon Pike turn around: Pike's Peak, the "blue-tinted" mountain in Colorado.

Unlike Pike, William Clark and Meriwether Lewis were unsullied heroes when they returned from their expedition. Their observations of the natural world brought a swath of new species and habitats to light in the East; Lewis was especially detailed in his descriptions. Though his style was journalistic rather than scientific—as was that of Peter Custis, for example—his body of notes left a record of the West before the advent of American settlement that has been of ever-fresh value since. Unfortunately, the same could not be said for the navigational measurements that Lewis, with help from Clark, recorded during the journey. Dogged as Lewis was in making his observations under all conditions and despite calamities with the equipment, his figures were deemed useless by the West Point authority charged with translating them into recognizable coordinates. The latitudes could be calculated, but the longitudes were inaccessible. The fault was not Lewis's, nor did it lie with the stars. Even if he hadn't quite known what he was doing, he did it anyway, much to his credit. It was the Problem 4th, the method chosen by Patterson for Lewis, that proved impervious to later efforts of lining up the numbers Lewis supplied. Yet Lewis had not deviated from the observations required for the Problem 4th, even when alternates might easily have been added to the overall record. In that respect, the corps would have benefited from someone more experienced, such as Lieutenant Enoch Humphrey, the able mathematician who accompanied Freeman.

During the years after the expedition returned, Ellicott could have stepped in and almost certainly sorted out a way to obtain the longitudes, but he was feuding with the expert at West Point (whose job he long sought) and remained on the sidelines. Nor was Patterson officially consulted, and so all of the efforts Lewis made in celestial navigation came to nothing, at least until the last decades of the twentieth century, when investigators proved that he had indeed generated enough data for the calculation of the longitude. The fact that computers were used as much as they were in that effort may explain why the worthy mathematicians of 1807 decided to let Clark's dead reckoning suffice. And it more than did so, with help from an array of land-based devices, ranging from measuring chains to surveyor's equipment. Clark devoted much of his free time, especially at Fort Clatsop over the winter of 1805 to 1806, to drawing remarkably detailed maps of the immediate region covered by the corps.

Almost immediately upon returning from the expedition, Clark took his place as the first citizen of St. Louis, exhibiting a quiet dignity that lasted the rest of his life. No one in the city, nor the country, forgot the part he'd played in the nation's history; in that, he finally settled some of the score that had marred his older brother's life and had long damned his family's outlook. Clark had five children of his own with his first wife and three with his second. He maintained a personal tie to the expedition by raising Sacajawea's son, Jean-Baptiste, the toddler whom he liked to call "Pomp." Sacajawea fully supported the boy's growing up with Clark; she and her husband sometimes lived in St. Louis under Clark's aegis, and there is no doubt that Clark was genuinely fond of her.

Sacajawea died of an apparent fever at the Mandan villages in about 1812. Her story was resurrected about a hundred years later in several books, and she has since been regarded as an American treasure, perhaps not even as much for helping Lewis and Clark as for retaining her own blend of intelligence and compassion, despite being captured as a young girl.

William Clark filled government positions pertaining to the West, including that of superintendent of Indian affairs and governor of Missouri Territory when it was created in 1813. He also amassed a respectable fortune investing in businesses; as a hobby, he filled a museum room in his house with memorabilia from the expedition, as well as artifacts from the Indian cultures with which he worked.

Meriwether Lewis had an unsettled life after returning home, although his career resumed auspiciously enough when President Jefferson named him governor of Louisiana Territory in 1807 (in place of Wilkinson). Failed romances, a checkered record as governor, financial mistakes, and delays in completing his expedition journal for publication all led to the kind of despair or stagnation that wreaked havoc on Lewis's moods. While there were scattered reports suggesting that he eventually took to heavy drinking, it was evident that the comforts of America couldn't accommodate Meriwether Lewis. Jefferson loosened his bonds to him, but Clark never did, remaining loyal through all of his cocaptain's troubles.

Lewis was traveling to Washington from St. Louis in October 1809 to address his problems when he stopped at a farmhouse inn in western Tennessee and died under mysterious circumstances; at the time, it was presumed that the gunshots that killed him were self-inflicted. The fact that Lewis was capable of such a thing was reflected in Clark's response on hearing of his friend's death: "I fear O!" he lamented. "I fear the waight of his mind has overcome him." Even if Lewis was depressed, though, and even if he had suicidal thoughts, he still might have been murdered. If anyone at home wondered exactly what had happened to him, the answer—as in the case of the Swiss shoemaker who slipped overboard on Dr. Hunter's boat—never came. Lewis had assured his mother when he left Washington in 1803 that he'd be as safe in his travels as he was in the nation's capital. That hadn't proven to be the case, but the frontier had its mysteries and so did the people who were ardently drawn to it, and she probably knew that, even before he left.

The only irrefutable piece of evidence in the death of Lewis was contributed by Thomas Freeman, who was working in Natchez at the time. When word spread of Lewis's death, Freeman was directed to Tennessee to inventory Lewis's personal belongings. Jefferson subsequently asked him to deliver the effects to him at Monticello. The list that Freeman left was well organized, although there were reports that Lewis's papers were rearranged en route. Even without any comment on the circumstances of the tragedy, Freeman's account indicated that Lewis had been robbed (before or after his death) of most of his valuables.

Freeman had resumed his career as a surveyor immediately after his time on the Red River, reporting to Natchez to take the lead in tracing the Tennessee-Mississippi border. He wasn't widely celebrated, and many biographical sketches written during or after his lifetime neglected any mention of his exploration for the president. The Red River expedition was the least known for the same reason that it was the most urgent in its time; sailing west toward the guns, Freeman had been at play in the inside game of international politics. He reached the brink that all who were watching closely knew would be the strategic end of his expedition: the intercept by the Spanish. As a result, though, most other Americans erroneously concluded that he failed in his mission.

Freeman's career culminated with his appointment in 1810 as surveyor general for the lands south of Tennessee. In that capacity, he finally earned enough money to join those who had followed after him for decades: he bought vast tracts of land, as many as 8,480 acres in a single transaction. Freeman lived and worked near Natchez (in the territorial capital of Mississippi) until his death while on a trip to Huntsville, Alabama, in 1821. At a Fourth of July dinner in Natchez in 1818, the men in attendance were called on for toasts, and Freeman raised his glass to "the Boundaries of the U. States, from Baffin's Bay to Cape Horn." That being the entire Western Hemisphere, his toast was explosive and harmless at the same time, a bit of verbal fireworks for the holiday. It brought laughs all around the country when it was reprinted as news as far away as Boston. Freeman's toast was first raised in Natchez, though, where the Red River Expedition had started in an earlier era. There were those there who remembered, and when Thomas Freeman talked about borders, there must have been cheers.

In the last two years of his administration, Jefferson was distracted by the Burr trial. Even if he still had the inclination to organize expeditions, he no longer had the political influence in Congress to elicit funding. The Spanish-American relationship simmered just under the boiling point every day during Jefferson's eight years. The Spanish believed they belonged in the West. The Americans believed that they did. Jefferson couldn't move that particular border of wills, not even an inch. His presidency may have come to a brittle end, but the final years weren't lost.

The cold war never became a shooting war, for all of the tension and the many hopeful predictions that it would. Jefferson's expeditions and much-publicized explorers had been the masks of his conquest, the tools of diplomacy that allowed the stakes to rise without forcing a military response. In the last part of the twentieth century, the entry into space served the same purpose in a climate just as tense between the United States and the Soviet Union. Jefferson was no less aggressive than any other U.S. president, but he used the means he knew best and the ones he could control.

Jefferson's explorers unlocked the nineteenth century for a country that was then continually glancing backward toward the eighteenth. The nation had run a long way on the old lore: the victorious soldiers and sailors of the Revolution, the Spirit of '76, Ethan Allen, LaFayette, Daniel Boone of Kentucky. The explorers gave the first generation born after the Revolution its own reflection: new heroes, many of them only in their twenties, taking charge. Perhaps the fact that Jefferson's explorers were not the celebrities of science he'd once sought, but unassuming civilians and low-ranking army officers, made their accounts of the West ring true to other Americans. Those accounts represented science good enough to inspire pride, but never so arcane that they failed to tell the majority of Americans all that they wanted to know: what it was like out there.

The revered "wit of Hartford," Joel Barlow, had previously written patriotic poems about Christopher Columbus and George Washington. Columbus would have been 355 years old in 1806. Washington would have been a little younger, but in December of that year, Barlow wrote a poem about Meriwether Lewis. After each stanza was a refrain that ended with the phrase "the young hero's name." The nation loved the poem and the fact that it had a young hero. When Pike's journal of his Mississippi exploration was released in 1810, it brought him fame that eclipsed even that of Lewis and Clark for a time. Ceramicists and printmakers finally had new faces to produce en masse for the front halls of homes across America.

There was a time when being the first was enough, just going was the goal. The American seamen who visited the Northwest coast between Nootka and the Columbia River, for example, brought back scant information and no updated maps. They were only traders, not part of anything larger than their own enterprise. Lewis, Clark, Dunbar, Hunter, Freeman, and Pike set a different standard for bringing back, as Jefferson put it, "a basis of knowledge on which others may build." That obligation countered the tack on which America was gliding, some might say careening, in the Early Republic, of judging every endeavor on its profitability. Upon their return, there was a new ideal.

In 1809, Jefferson made his warmly anticipated return to his own property at Monticello, which he would continue to explore to the last week of his life. He had his land and it had its hero. In that, Jefferson left his own ideal.

Acknowledgments

Jefferson's America owes an enormous debt to those scholars who located and published the journals of individual explorers. Through the years, these editors have given readers the excitement of the West when it was entirely new to Americans. They also gave this book the treasure of firsthand accounts by those who were there.

The late Dr. John Francis McDermott published Hunter's journal for the American Philosophical Society in 1963. (The APS, still thriving after more than 250 years, has always served as a beacon for records pertaining to Jeffersonian exploration.) Dr. McDermott's extensive annotations of the Hunter journals are themselves a history of the frontier when it was moving toward and then past the Mississippi River. It was Jefferson himself who had Dunbar's journal transcribed and presented to the public for the first time. Dr. Trey Berry, Pam Beasley, and Jeanne Clements combined the two journals into one handsome volume, *The Forgotten Expedition*, published by Louisiana State University Press in 2006. Dr. Berry, now in the ranks of college presidents at Southern Arkansas University, has published a number of articles on the Dunbar-Hunter expedition, while Ms. Beasley is affiliated with Arkansas's state parks and Ms. Clements with its Museum of Natural Resources.

Dr. Donald Jackson (1919–1987) annotated the journals and letters of Zebulon Pike in a two-volume set, published by the University of Oklahoma Press in 1966. That work was invaluable to this book, as was Dr. Jackson's *The Letters of Lewis and Clark*, brought out by the University of Illinois Press in 1962. His books leave no stone unturned.

On the subject of Jefferson's Red River expedition, Dr. Dan Flores has contributed more than anyone to the scholarship that has lifted it recently from obscurity. His book *The Southern Counterpart to Lewis and Clark: The Freeman and Custis Expedition of 1806*, first published by the University of Oklahoma Press in 1984, presents the journals of Thomas Freeman and Peter Custis, along with a rich essay by Dr. Flores. He has since written other books on the West and its environment, including a narrative on the subject of coyotes in America.

The Lewis and Clark journals have been published in various forms for over two hundred years, but the edition produced by Dr. Gary Moulton, *The Definitive Journals of Lewis and Clark*, is the most enlightening. During a twenty-year effort, Dr. Moulton and his team presented the text with precision and meticulous annotation. The online edition, called the *Journals of the Lewis and Clark Expedition Online*, cited in the bibliography herein, has been growing in many ways, making the journals a living resource. Gary Dunham and Katherine Walter, codirectors of the online project since 2003, have led the University of Nebraska's effort to build on Dr. Moulton's work.

Anyone interested in the explorers featured in this book should go to the books named above for further reading.

I would like to thank Rich Schwantz of New Haven, Indiana, for his kindness in sending an early Hunter manuscript to me. I am also indebted to Jonathan Stafford of Colorado, both for the picture of Pike's Peak in wintertime that is featured, and for so graciously making it available. Mr. Thomas R. McKean supported this book in a very special way, by letting us feature the portrait of the Marquis d'Yrujo from his collection.

Notes

INTRODUCTION

1   **Audubon, the ornithologist** Howard Corning, ed., *Journal of John James Audubon Made During His Trip to New Orleans in 1820–1821* (Cambridge, MA: Business Historical Society, 1929), pp. 111–15.

2   **clamped down on the slave trade** Ira Berlin, *Many Thousands Gone: The First Two Centuries of Slavery in North America* (Cambridge, MA: Harvard University Belknap Press, 1998), p. 341.

2   **laws granting significant rights** Gilbert C. Din, *Spaniards, Planters, and Slaves: The Spanish Regulation of Slavery in Louisiana, 1763–1803* (College Station: Texas A&M University Press, 1999), pp. 132–36.

2   **his spirits were "very low"** Corning, *Journal of John James Audubon During His Trip to New Orleans in 1820–1821,* p. 114.

2   **"a letter to Doctor Hunter"** Ibid., p. 115.

2   **a special report to Congress** Thomas Jefferson, *The Limits and Bounds of Louisiana* (Philadelphia, 1806; repr. Boston: Houghton Mifflin, 1906), pp. 3–76.

2   **"Low in funds"** Corning, *Journal of John James Audubon During His Trip to New Orleans in 1820–1821*, p. 149. The coarse term "pissing" was partially concealed in the printed edition of the journal.

3   **"This *Physician*"** Ibid.

4   **"a person who to courage"** TJ to Caspar Wistar, February 28, 1803, in Paul Leicester Ford, ed., *The Works of Thomas Jefferson, Correspondence and Papers, 1803–1807* (New York: G. P. Putnam's Sons, 1904–05), vol. 9, p. 422.

4   **courses in the pure sciences** John F. Fulton, "The Impact of Science on American History," *Isis* 42, no. 3 (October 1951): 185–87.

4   **"this all devouring passion of gain"** William Dunbar, journal, January 1, 1779, in *Life, Letters and Papers of William Dunbar*, compiled by Mrs. Dunbar Rowland (Jackson: Press of the Mississippi Historical Society, 1930), p. 129.

5   **"Louisiana is the President's favorite Topic"** *Louisiana Under the Rule of Spain, France, and the United States,* edited by James Alexander Robertson (Cleveland: Arthur H. Clark, 1911), vol. 2, p. 23.

6   **"has elevated the president beyond Imagination"** Ibid.

CHAPTER ONE

7   **known among the Europeans as "Nootka"** Mark D. Kaplanoff, "Nootka Sound in 1789," *Pacific Northwest Quarterly* 65, no. 4 (October 1974): 162.

8   **had been the first European** William Ray Manning, *Nootka Sound Controversy* (Washington: Government Printing Office, 1905), p. 283.

9   **then serving as an aide** Kaplanoff, "Nootka Sound," p. 162.

9   **"cannot be confided in"** Frank T. Reuter, " 'Petty Spy' or Effective Diplomat: The Role of George Beckwith," *Journal of the Early Republic* 10, no. 4 (Winter 1990): 486.

9   **"shut up in the four walls"** TJ to Maria Cosway, September 8, 1795, in Founders Online, National Archives (http://founders.archives.gov/documents/Jefferson/01-28-02-0357).

11   **"Considerations on Louisiana"** TJ, "Considerations on Louisiana, 1790," July 12, 1790, in *Louisiana Under the Rule of Spain, France, and the United States,* edited by James Alexander Robertson (Cleveland: Arthur H. Clark, 1911), vol. 1, p. 265.

13   **Natchez, 268 miles north** U.S. Army Corps of Engineers, *Mississippi River Navigation* (Vicksburg: Mississippi River Commission, 1965), p. 3.

14 **2,665 Spanish subjects** Zenón Trudeau, "Report of Trudeau, 1791—and Census for 1794–5," in *The Spanish Regime in Missouri*, edited by Louis Houck (Chicago: R. R. Donnelly & Sons, 1909), vol. 1, p. 326.

14 **Nearly all of them** Zenón Trudeau, "Report Concerning the Settlements of the Spanish Illinois Country," January 15, 1798, in *Spanish Regime in Missouri* (1909), vol. 2, pp. 247–50.

14 **"ferocious men"** Barón de Carondelet to Marqués de Branciforte, June 7, 1796, in *Before Lewis and Clark: Documents Illustrating the History of the Missouri*, edited by A. P. Nasatir (Lincoln: University of Nebraska Press, 1990), vol. 1, p. 440.

14 **"opportunity of hunting out good Lands"** George Washington to William Crawford, September [17], 1767, in *The Papers of George Washington*, edited by W. W. Abbot and Dorothy Twohig (Charlottesville: University Press of Virginia, 1993), colonial series, vol. 8, p. 28.

15 **"hostile incursion"** Gilbert C. Din, "Spain's Immigration Policy in Louisiana and the American Penetration, 1792–1803," *Southwestern Historical Quarterly* 76, no. 3 (January 1973): 272.

15 **"A little bit of corn"** Barón de Carondelet to Marqués de Branciforte, June 7, 1796, in Nasatir, *Before Lewis and Clark: Documents Illustrating the History of the Missouri, 1785–1804*, vol. 1, p. 439.

15 **hunter named Jacques d'Eglise** Nasatir, "Introduction, Part III: The Precursors to Lewis and Clark," in *Before Lewis and Clark* (1990), vol. 1, p. 82.

16 **"an ignorant man"** Zenón Trudeau to Barón de Carondelet, October 20, 1792, ibid., pp. 160–61.

16 **"under the name of Mandan"** Ibid., p. 161.

16 **some had light-colored hair** Marshall T. Newman, "The Blond Mandan: A Critical Review of an Old Problem," *Southwestern Journal of Anthropology*, vol. 6, no. 3, pp. 255–56.

17 **"Assiniboines, Crees, Ojibwes"** Colin G. Calloway, *One Vast Winter Count: The Native American West* (Lincoln: University of Nebraska Press, 2003), p. 302.

17 **"the advantages that would come"** Jacques d'Eglise to Barón de Carondelet, June 19, 1794, in Nasatir, *Before Lewis and Clark*, vol. 1, p. 234.

17 **"they have saddles and bridles"** Zenón Trudeau to Barón de Carondelet, October 20, 1792, ibid., p. 161.

18 **Trudeau launched a trading company** Nasatir, "Introduction, Part III," in *Before Lewis and Clark* (1990), vol. 1, p. 82.

18   **having borrowed sixteen hundred pesos'** Trudeau to Barón de Caron-
      delet, June 8, 1794, ibid., p. 233.

18   **"husbands, fathers and brothers"** Jean Baptiste Truteau (attributed),
      "Remarks on the Manners of the Indians Living High Up on the Mis-
      souri," ibid., p. 258.

19   **Garreau left a debacle** J. D'Eglise to Barón de Carondelet, June 19,
      1794, ibid., p. 234.

19   **"running at full speed"** Truteau, "Remarks on the Manners," ibid.,
      p. 300.

19   **André Michaux** Rodney H. True, "François André Michaux," *Proceed-
      ings of the American Philosophical Society* 78, no 2 (December 10, 1937):
      314.

20   **With Jefferson's active assistance** Gilbert Chinard, "Jefferson and the
      American Philosophical Society," *Proceedings of the American Philosoph-
      ical Society* 87, no. 3 (July 14, 1943): 264, 266.

20   **raised a small advance** "Editorial Note: Jefferson and André Michaux's
      Proposed Western Expedition," *The Papers of Thomas Jefferson*, edited
      by John Catanzariti (Princeton: Princeton University Press, 1992),
      vol. 25, pp. 78–79.

20   **John Evans was a greenhorn** David Williams, "John Evans' Strange
      Journey: Part I, Following the Trail," *American Historical Review* 54,
      no. 2 (January, 1949): 278–81.

21   **The Welsh Indians** Ibid.; Thomas Stephens, *Madoc: An Essay on the
      Discovery of America by Madoc ap Owen Gwynedd in the Twelfth Century*
      (London: Longmans, Green and Co., 1893), pp. 50–73.

21   *"Ma proposition ayant été acceptée"* André Michaux and C. S. Sargent,
      "Portions of the Journal of André Michaux, Botanist. Written During
      His Travels in the United States and Canada, 1785–1796," *Proceedings of
      the American Philosophical Society* 26, no. 129 (January–July, 1889): 90.

22   **eighteen-year-old Meriwether Lewis** TJ, "Meriwether Lewis," in *The
      Writings of Thomas Jefferson*, edited by Andrew A. Lipscomb and Albert
      Ellery Bergh (Washington: Thomas Jefferson Memorial Association,
      1905), vol. 18, pp. 144–45.

22   **George Rogers Clark** James Alton James, *The Life of George Rogers
      Clark* (Chicago: University of Chicago Press, 1928), p. 420.

22   **"Col. Clark was nature's favorite"** John Reynolds, *The Pioneer History
      of Illinois* (Belleville, IL: N. A. Randall, 1852), p. 71.

23   **"On the basis of his success"** James Fisher, "A Forgotten Hero Remem-

bered, Revered and Revised: The Legacy and Ordeal of George Rogers Clark," *Indiana Magazine of History* 92, no. 2 (June 1996): 129.

24 **Harry Innes** "The First Judges of the Federal Courts," *American Journal of Legal History* 1, no. 1 (January 1957): 78.

24 **"the greatness of his mind"** TJ to Harry Innes, March 7, 1791, in Lipscomb and Bergh, *The Writings of Thomas Jefferson*, vol. 8, p. 135.

24 **Clark was yet again disgraced** Untitled news item, *Courier of New Hampshire* (Concord), June 5, 1794, p. 3.

25 **the Missouri River "failed."** "Evans Notes" (unpublished manuscript), E. G. Voorhis Memorial Collection, Missouri Historical Society, excerpted in David Williams, "John Evans' Strange Journey: Part II, Following the Trail," *American Historical Review* 54, no. 3: 514–15.

25 **There were no Paduca Indians** Frank R. Secoy, "The Identity of the 'Paduca': An Ethnohistorical Analysis," *American Anthropologist* 53 (1951): 525; John M. O'Shea and John Ludwickson, *Archaeology and Ethnohistory of the Omaha Indians: The Big Village Site* (Lincoln: University of Nebraska Press, 1992), p. 29.

CHAPTER TWO

26 **"First year, wheat"** TJ to George Washington, May 14, 1794, in *Thomas Jefferson's Garden Book*, annotated by Edwin Morris Betts (Philadelphia: American Philosophical Society, 1992), p. 218.

27 **"abandonment of them"** TJ to George Washington, May 14, 1794, in "Meriwether Lewis," in *The Writings of Thomas Jefferson*, edited by Andrew A. Lipscomb and Albert Ellery Bergh (Washington: Thomas Jefferson Memorial Association, 1905), vol. 9, p. 287.

27 **"a hill 500 f."** TJ to William Dunbar, January 12, 1801, Mrs. Dunbar Rowland, *Life, Letters and Papers of William Dunbar* (Jackson: Press of the Mississippi Historical Society, 1930), p. 112.

27 **To the north, the property followed** Sarah N. Randolph, comp., *The Domestic Life of Thomas Jefferson* (Charlottesville: University Press of Virginia, 1978), pp. 335–36.

27 **the hilltop took in three valleys** William Alexander Lambeth and Warren H. Manning, *Thomas Jefferson as an Architect and Designer of Landscapes* (1913; repr. Bedford, MA: Applewood Books, n.d.), p. 106.

28 **"Our own dear Monticello"** TJ to Mrs. Maria Cosway, October 12, 1786, in Lipscomb and Bergh, *Writings of Thomas Jefferson*, vol. 5, pp. 436–37.

28 **"knew the name of every tree"** Hamilton W. Pierson, *Jefferson at*

Monticello: The Private Life of Thomas Jefferson (New York: Charles Scribner, 1862), p. 43.

29   "an ardour which I scarcely" TJ to Ferdinando Fairfax, April 25, 1794, in Betts, *Thomas Jefferson's Garden Book*, p. 217.

29   "instead of writing ten" TJ to George Washington, April 25, 1794, ibid.

29   rows of peach trees TJ to John Taylor, Dec. 29, 1794, ibid., p. 220.

30   "In conformity with the Treaty" Barón de Carondelet to Branceforte, June 7, 1796, in *Before Lewis and Clark: Documents Illustrating the History of the Missouri, 1785–1804*, edited by A. P. Nasatir (Lincoln: University of Nebraska Press, 1990), vol. 1, p. 439.

31   "the award of 3,000 pesos" Ibid., p. 388n.

32   included four boats stuffed with goods Santiago Clamorgan and Anoine Reihle, "Report," July 8, 1795, *Before Lewis and Clark*, vol. 1, p. 358.

32   whose sole job it was John M. O'Shea and John Ludwickson, *Archaeology and Ethnohistory of the Omaha Indians: The Big Village Site* (Lincoln: University of Nebraska Press, 1992), pp. 18–19.

33   expert in the use of poison John Ludwickson, "Blackbird and Son: A Note Concerning Late-Eighteenth- and Early Nineteenth-Century Omaha Chieftainship," *Ethnohistory* 42, no. 1 (Winter 1995): 133.

34   in the care of independent traders Nasatir, *Before Lewis and Clark* (1990), vol. 1, pp. 89–92.

35   when he ran out of ink James MacKay to John Evans, January 28, 1796, ibid., vol. 2, p. 410. The last part of the second clause read: "In case you will be short of ink, use the powder, and for want of powder, in the summer you will surely find some fruit whose juice can replace both."

35   "The river," as he described it "History of John Evans's Journey in America" (Wales) *Greal, or Eurgrawn,* 1800, reprinted in Thomas Stephens, *Madoc* (London: Longmans, Green, 1893), p. 107.

36   Big John McDonnell Charles M Gates, ed., *Five Fur Traders of the Northwest* (St. Paul: Minneapolis Historical Society, 1965), p. 10.

36   Evans died in a dissipated state David Williams, "John Evans' Strange Journey: Part II, Following the Trail," *American Historical Review* 54, no. 2 (January, 1949): 528.

37   "Came into the Town of St. Louis" George Hunter, "Journal Kept by George Hunter of a Tour from Philad. to Kentuckey & the Illinois Country" (1796), original in the Hunter Papers, American Philosophical Society, reprinted in *The Western Journals of Dr. George Hunter*, edited by John Francis McDermott (Philadelphia: APS, 1963), p. 31.

37   **upon himself to go west in 1796** Ibid., p. 6.

38   **"I examined them with my spyglass"** Ibid., p. 21.

38   **"Lands of Gen. Washington"** Ibid., p. 22.

39   **a new plot to separate Trans-Appalachia** Thomas Marshall Green, *The Spanish Conspiracy: A Review of Spanish Movements in the West* (Cincinnati: Robert Clarke & Co., 1891), p. 353.

39   **"the farthest of our settlements"** McDermott, *Western Journals of George Hunter*, p. 31.

40   **"everything I hate"** TJ to James Madison, June 9, 1793, in Lipscomb and Bergh, *Writings of Thomas Jefferson*, vol. 9, p. 119.

42   **a surveyor named Thomas Freeman** Ralph E. Ehrenberg, "Mapping the Nation's Capital: The Surveyor's Office: 1791–1818," *Quarterly Journal of the Library of Congress* 36, no. 3 (Summer 1979): 290.

42   **One credited Freeman with** John DeButte to the Commissioners of the District of Columbia, March 16, 1794, Letters Received, Records of the Office of Public Buildings and Grounds, Record Group 42, National Archives, quoted in Ehrenberg, "Mapping the Nation's Capital," p. 290.

43   **"Mr. Strother is yet with me"** A. W. Putnam, *History of Middle Tennessee or Life and Times of Gen. James Robertson* (Tennessee Historical Commission, 1859), p. 583.

44   **important to many in the profession** "Proposals," advertisement, Charleston (South Carolina) *City Gazette and Daily Advertiser*, August 30, 1796, p. 4. Mention is also made of one of Freeman's other disputes over map sales in "Darby's Louisiana, &c.," *Niles Weekly Register*, November 22, 1817, p. 195.

44   **a street map of Washington** "A Plan of the City of Washington," advertisement, *Charleston City Gazette*, August 30, 1796, p. 4.

44   **"adjusting the Western limits"** Thomas Freeman to George Washington, April 13, 1796, Founders Online, National Archives (http://founders.archives.gov/documents/Washington/99-01-02-00435).

45   **"steady, sober and attentive to business"** Commissioners to George Washington, April 13, 1796, Applications for Office, 1789–1796, Library of Congress, George Washington Papers, series 7.

45   **Washington refused to be pressured** George Washington to Charles Carroll, May 1, 1796, in *The Writings of George Washington*, edited by John C. Fitzpatrick (Washington: U.S. Government Printing Office, 1939) vol. 37, pp. 29–30.

45   **the appointment in May 1796** George Washington to the Commissioners, May 30, 1796, ibid., p. 73.

CHAPTER THREE

46 **"worrying the Spaniards out"** Catharine Van Cortlandt Mathews, *Andrew Ellicott: His Life and Letters* (New York: Grafton Press, 1908), p. 157.

46 **"make a job out of his office"** John Francis Hamtramck Claiborne, *Mississippi as a Province, Territory and State* (Jackson, MS: Power & Barksdale, 1880), p. 172n.

48 **to take over the fur trade** Walter S. Dunn Jr., *Frontier Profit and Loss: The British Army and Fur Traders, 1760–1764* (Westport, CN: Greenwood Press, 1998), p. 4.

51 **"Men who do not own slaves"** William Dunbar, journal, January 1, 1779, in *Life, Letters and Papers of William Dunbar*, compiled by Mrs. Dunbar Rowland (Jackson: Press of the Mississippi Historical Society, 1930), p. 67.

53 **"disposed to be on good terms"** Claiborne, *Mississippi*, vol. 1, p. 197.

53 **"Ellicott landed here on the 10th"** Ibid., p. 144.

53 **Ellicott, reconsidering his own attitude** Andrew Ellicott to his wife, November 8, 1798, in Mathews, *Andrew Ellicott*, p. 160.

53 **"So far as their conduct"** "Deposition of Thomas Freeman," August 20, 1811, in James Wilkinson, *Memoirs of My Own Times* (Philadelphia: Abraham Small, 1816), vol. 2, pp. 646–47.

54 **he was warned by his friend** Claiborne, *Mississippi*, vol. 1, p. 207.

55 **"abuse of the spanish commissioner"** Mathews, *Andrew Ellicott*, p. 157.

55 **"He is not the man"** Stephen Minor to Porter Walker, August 24, 1799, in Claiborne, *Mississippi*, vol. 1, pp. 198–99n.

55 **suggesting that he could work** W. Dunbar, "Report of William Dunbar to the Spanish Government at the Conclusion of His Services in Locating and Surveying the Thirty-First Degree of Latitude," in Rowland, *Letters and Papers of William Dunbar*, p. 80.

55 **"A lover of science"** TJ to William Dunbar, June 24, 1799, *The Papers of Thomas Jefferson*, edited by Barbara B. Oberg (Princeton: Princeton University Press, 2004), vol. 31, p. 138.

56 **"a charming young man"** Barón de Carondelet to Thomas Power, April 23, 1797, in Daniel Clark, *Proofs of the Corruption of James Wilkinson* (Philadelphia: William Hall, 1809), p. 59.

56 **"less pleasing in practice"** Maurine T. Wilson and Jack Jackson, *Philip Nolan and Texas: Expeditions to the Unknown Land* (Waco: Texian Press, 1987), pp. 1–2.

56   **"Altho' his excentricities were many"** William Dunbar to TJ, August 22, 1801, *The Papers of Thomas Jefferson* (2004), vol. 31, p. 138.

57   **they saw the two regions very differently** Grand Pré to Barón de Carondelet, September 27, 1796, translated and printed in Lawrence Kinnaird and Lucia B. Kinnaird, "The Red River Valley in 1796," *Louisiana History: The Journal of the Louisiana Historical Association* 24, no. 2 (Spring 1983): 189–94.

57   **to define the borderlands** Patricia R. Lemée, "Tios and Tantes: Familial and Political Relationships of Natchitoches and the Spanish Colonial Frontier," *Southwestern Historical Quarterly* 101, no. 3 (January 1998): 341–42.

58   **"the facts you at present possess"** TJ to Philip Nolan, June 24, 1798, in *The Writings of Thomas Jefferson*, edited by Andrew A. Lipscomb and Albert Ellery Bergh (Washington: Thomas Jefferson Memorial Association, 1905), vol. 10, p. 55–56.

59   **"that extraordinary and enterprising man"** Daniel Clark to TJ, February 12, 1799, in "Concerning Philip Nolan," *Quarterly of the Texas State Historical Association* 7, no. 4 (April 1904): 309.

60   **"required their separation"** Wilkinson, *Memoirs*, p. 183.

60   **"I expeld him from the camp"** Mathews, *Ellicott*, p. 157.

60   **"When you look at the picture"** Ibid., p. 164.

61   **no mention at all of Thomas Freeman** Andrew Ellicott, *The Journal of Andrew Ellicott, Late Commissioner on Behalf of the United States During Part of the Year 1796, the Years 1797, 1798, 1799, and Part of the Year 1800* . . . (Philadelphia: Thomas Hobson, 1803), pp. 43–44.

61   **"Mr. Ellicott and the rest of us"** John Walker to unknown, June 1, 1800, in Claiborne, *Mississippi*, vol. 1, pp. 197–98.

62   **While aboard the boat, Ellicott** Ellicott to Dunbar, April 18, 1800, in Rowland, *Letters and Papers of William Dunbar*, p. 197.

62   **substantive package of research** "The Following Communications Were Received from President Jefferson," *Proceedings of the American Philosophical Society* 22, no. 119 (January 1801): 308.

62   **"a *monarchie masqué*"** TJ to Robert R. Livingston, December 14, 1800, in *Writings of Thomas Jefferson* (1905), vol. 10, p. 177.

63   **a man with *philosophical* pursuits** TJ to Dr. Hugh Williamson, January 10, 1801, in Lipscomb and Bergh, *Writings of Thomas Jefferson*, vol. 10, p. 190.

63   **"incest will all be openly taught"** "Burleigh," *Connecticut Courant*, September 20, 1800, reprinted in Charles O Lerche Jr., "Jefferson and

the Election of 1800: A Case Study in the Political Smear," *William and Mary Quarterly*, 3rd ser., 5, no. 4 (October 1948): 480.

63 **"sundry communications"** TJ to Caspar Wistar, December 16, 1800 (second letter), in *The Papers of Thomas Jefferson* (2005), p. 311.

63 **Dunbar was already a member** "Election of Members," January 17, 1800, reprinted in "Early Proceedings of the American Philosophical Society for the Promotion of Useful Knowledge," *Proceedings of the American Philosophical Society* 22, no. 119, pt. 3 (July 1885): 294.

64 **"under dilemma"** TJ to Andrew Ellicott, December 18, 1800, in Lipscomb and Bergh, *Writings of Thomas Jefferson*, vol. 19, p. 122.

64 **"Philosophical vedette"** TJ to Dunbar, January 12, 1801, Rowland, *Life, Letters and Papers of William Dunbar*, p. 111.

65 **"He is easy in his fortune"** TJ to Caspar Wistar, December 16, 1800 (first letter), in Oberg, *The Papers of Thomas Jefferson*, vol. 32, p. 311.

CHAPTER FOUR

66 **"A young, thriving, nation"** TJ to Robert Livingston, April 18, 1802, in *The Writings of Thomas Jefferson*, edited by Andrew A. Lipscomb and Albert Ellery Bergh (Washington: Thomas Jefferson Memorial Association, 1905), vol. 10, p. 314.

67 **pressure regarding religion was suspended** John Francis Bannon, "The Spaniards and Illinois Country, 1762–1800," *Journal of the Illinois State Historical Society (1908–1984)*, vol. 69, no. 2 (May 1976): 118.

67 **"the ambition of the Americans"** Instructions données au Citoyen Guillemardet, May 20–June 19, 1798, *Archives des Aff. Etr. MSS,* quoted in French Ensor Chadwick, *The Relations of the United States and Spain*: *Diplomacy* (New York: Charles Scribner's Sons, 1909), p. 43.

68 **"The appointment to the Presidency"** TJ to M. Lewis, February 23, 1801, *Letters of the Lewis and Clark Expedition*, edited by Donald Jackson (Urbana: University of Illinois Press, 1962), p. 2.

69 **She prepared the smoked hams** Hamilton Pierson, *The Private Life of Thomas Jefferson* (New York: Charles Scribner, 1862), p. 73.

69 **"of my neighborhood"** TJ to James Wilkinson, February 23, 1801, in Jackson, *Letters of the Lewis and Clark Expedition*, p. 1.

69 **"Barons of the Potomac"** Moncure Daniel Conway, *Barons of the Potomack and the Rappahannock* (New York: Grolier Club, 1912), pp. 151–52.

69 **"hypochondriac affections"** TJ to Paul Allen, August 18, 1813, in Jackson, *Letters of the Lewis and Clark Expedition*, pp. 591–92.

69 specifically as depression Ibid., p. 592.

70 "When only 8. Years of age" Ibid., p. 587.

72 "In selecting a private secretary" TJ to James Wilkinson, February 23, 1801, ibid., p. 1.

73 "to apprehend that Spain cedes Louisiana" TJ to James Monroe, May 26, 1801, in *The Papers of Thomas Jefferson*, edited by Barbara B. Oberg (Princeton: Princeton University Press, 2005), vol. 34, p. 186.

74 "His Catholic Majesty has been forthcoming" St. Cyr to Royal Court of Spain, July 22, 1802, author translation from original text, in Francis Paul Renaut, *La Question de la Louisiane, 1796–1806* (Paris: E. Champion, 1918), p. 70n.

75 "without a regular permission" William Dunbar to TJ, August 22, 1801, in Oberg, *The Papers of Thomas Jefferson*, vol. 31, p. 138.

76 "he appeared strongly attached" Andrew Ellicott to James Wilkinson, January 21, 1808, in Daniel Clark, *Proofs of the Corruption of Gen. James Wilkinson* (Philadelphia: Wm. Hall, Jun. and Geo. W. Pierie, 1809), p. 69.

76 "not provided myself with a passport" Winston De Ville and Jack Jackson, "Wilderness Apollo: Louis Badin's Immortalization of the Ouachita Militia's Confrontation with the Philip Nolan Expedition of 1800," *Southwestern Historical Quarterly* 92, no. 3 (January 1989): 454.

77 "They surrounded our camp" Ellis P. Bean, "Memoir," in Henderson K. Yoakum, *History of Texas: From Its First Settlement in 1685 to Its Annexation* (New York: Redfield, 1856), vol. 1, p. 407.

77 "eternal slavery" Zebulon Pike, untitled newspaper article, *Natchez Herald*, July 22, 1807, reprinted in *The Journals of Zebulon Montgomery Pike*, edited by Donald Jackson (Norman: University of Oklahoma Press, 1966), p. 255.

78 "Her pacific dispositions" TJ to Robert Livingston, April 18, 1802, ibid.

78 "on [the] globe one single spot" Ibid.

79 "You will be surprised" William Dunbar to Robt. Bird & Co., July 25, 1802, in *Life, Letters and Papers of William Dunbar*, compiled by Mrs. Dunbar Rowland (Jackson: Press of the Mississippi Historical Society, 1930), p. 116.

80 effectively closed the port Pierre Clément de Laussat to Duc Denis Descrés, April 18, 1803, in *Louisiana Under the Rule of Spain, France, and the United States*, edited by James Alexander Robertson (Cleveland: Arthur H. Clark, 1911), vol. 2, p. 30.

80 "The surplus produce of the West" W. C. C. Claiborne to James

Madison, January 28, 1803, in *Official Letter Books of W. C. C. Claiborne*, edited by Dunbar Rowland (Jackson, MS: State Department of Archives and History, 1917), vol. 1, p. 267.

80   **facing "docile" Spain** Chadwick, *Relations*, p. 51.

80   **"a measure of vigour"** Edward Thornton to Lord Hawkesbury, January 3, 1803, in Robertson, *Louisiana Under the Rule*, vol. 2, p. 15.

81   **government to prepare** Mary P. Adams, "Jefferson's Reaction to the Treaty of San Ildefonso," *Journal of Southern History* 21, no. 2 (May 1955): 174–82.

82   **amid unceasing talk of war** Ibid., p. 184.

CHAPTER FIVE

83   **"They pretend it is only"** TJ to George Rogers Clark, December 4, 1783, in *Letters of the Lewis and Clark Expedition*, edited by Donald Jackson (Urbana: University of Illinois Press, 1962), p. 654.

84   **The king actively committed** Iris H. W. Engstrand, *Spanish Scientists in the New World: Eighteenth-Century Expeditions* (Seattle: University of Washington Press, 1981), pp. 4–6.

84   **"character who to a compleat science"** TJ to Benjamin Smith Barton, in Jackson, *Letters of the Lewis and Clark Expedition*, p. 16.

85   **"a firmness & perseverance of purpose"** TJ to Paul Allen, August 18, 1813, ibid., p. 590.

85   **"From my ideas of Capt. Lewis"** Levi Lincoln to TJ, April 17, 1803, ibid, p. 35.

86   **Yrujo enjoyed finery** Richard Côté, *Strength and Honor: The Life of Dolley Madison* (Mt. Pleasant, SC: Corinthian Books, 2005), pp. 159–60.

86   **"explore the course of the Missouri"** Carlos Martínez de Yrujo to Pedro Cevallos, December 2, 1802, in *Letters of the Lewis and Clark Expedition* (1962), p. 4.

87   **"The President has been"** Ibid., pp. 4–5.

88   **two hundred bottles of champagne** John R. Hailman, *Jefferson on Wine* (Jackson: University Press of Mississippi, 2006), p. 271.

88   **out of his personal funds** TJ to Marquis de Yrujo, December 9, 1802, Library of Congress, Thomas Jefferson Papers at the Library of Congress, ser. 1, General Correspondence, 1651–1827, microfilm reel 027.

88   **"in favour of Great Britain"** Edward Thornton to Lord Hawkesbury, January 3, 1803, in *Louisiana Under the Rule of Spain, France, and the United States*, edited by James Alexander Robertson (Cleveland: Arthur H. Clark, 1911), vol. 2, p. 18.

89   **"but one sentiment throughout the Union"** James Madison to Charles
      Pinckney, January 10, 1803, in French Ensor Chadwick, *The Relations of
      the United States and Spain: Diplomacy* (New York: Charles Scribner's
      Sons, 1909), p. 53.

90   **"the second digit"** William Ewing Du Bois, *A Record of the Families of
      Robert Patterson (the Elder)* (Press of John C. Clark, 1847), p. 32n.

90   **There was a false story** TJ to M. Lewis, April 27, 1803, in *Letters of the
      Lewis and Clark Expedition* (1962), p. 44.

90   **"political business in the Mississippi country"** Untitled article, *Boston
      Columbian Centinel*, April 2, 1803, p. 2.

91   **"extraordinary agitation"** TJ, annual message to Congress, October 17,
      1803, in *The Writings of Thomas Jefferson*, edited by Andrew A. Lips-
      comb and Albert Ellery Bergh (Washington: Thomas Jefferson Memo-
      rial Association, 1905), vol. 3, p. 351.

91   **He sent communiqués** Arthur P. Whitaker, "The Retrocession of
      Louisiana in Spanish Policy," *American Historical Review* 39, no. 3
      (April 1934): 475–76; David A. Carson, "The Role of Congress in the
      Acquisition of the Louisiana Territory," *Louisiana History: The Journal
      of the Louisiana Historical Association* 26, no. 4 (Autumn 1985): 180.

91   **"what we believe a more certain"** TJ to William Dunbar, March 3,
      1803, in Lipscomb and Bergh, *Writings of Thomas Jefferson*, vol. 19,
      p. 131.

91   **"a perfect knowledge of the posts"** Albert Gallatin to TJ, April 13, 1803,
      in *The Writings of Albert Gallatin*, edited by Henry Adams (Philadel-
      phia: J. B. Lippincott & Co., 1879), vol. 1, p. 120.

92   **The relation is expressed** Richard S. Preston, "The Accuracy of the As-
      tronomical Observations of Lewis and Clark," *Proceedings of the Ameri-
      can Philosophical Society* 144, no. 2 (June 2000): 170–71.

93   **"having never been a practical astronomer"** TJ to Robert Patterson,
      November 16, 1805, in Jackson, *Letters of the Lewis and Clark Expedi-
      tion*, p. 270.

95   **"with his Jacob staff"** George R. Wilson, *Early Indiana Trails and Sur-
      veys* (Indianapolis: Indiana Historical Society, 1919), p. 418.

95   **grains of sand** Lola Cazier, *Surveys and Surveyors of the Public Domain,
      1785–1975* (Washington: U.S. Dept. of the Interior, Bureau of Land
      Management, 1976), p. 40.

95   **Freeman's Corner** George R. Wilson, "The First Public Land Surveys
      in Indiana: Freeman's Lines," *Indiana Magazine of History* 12, no. 1
      (March 1916): 9.

97   **"bend our whole views"** TJ to William Henry Harrison, February 27, 1803, in Lipscomb and Bergh, *Writings of Thomas Jefferson*, vol. 10, p. 371.

98   **up and down the Ohio River** Zebulon Butler, "Journal of General Butler," *The Olden Time* 2, no. 10 (October 1847): 495.

98   **his late father's estate** Reuben Gold Thwaites, "William Clark: Soldier, Explorer, Statesman," *Washington Historical Quarterly* 1, no. 4 (July 1907): 236.

CHAPTER SIX

101 **full shipping rights** Arthur P. Whitaker, "The Retrocession of Louisiana in Spanish Policy," *American Historical Review* 39, no. 3 (April 1934): 475–76.

102 **theater of war in North America** Barbé Marbois, *The History of Louisiana, Particularly of the Cession of That Colony to the United States* (Philadelphia: Carey & Lea, 1830), pp. 261–62.

102 **Another factor may well have been** David A. Carson, "The Role of Congress in the Acquisition of the Louisiana Territory," *Louisiana History*, vol. 26, no. 4, pp. 378–80.

102 **"by a reasonable and peaceable process"** TJ to John Bacon, April 30, 1803, in Thomas Jefferson Papers, LOC, Series 1: General Correspondence. 1651—1827 Microfilm Reel: 028.

103 **"You must know in the first"** Lewis to W. Clark, June 19, 1803, in *Letters of the Lewis and Clark Expedition*, edited by Donald Jackson (Urbana: University of Illinois Press, 1962), p. 59.

103 **the first to break the story** "Louisiana Ceded to the U. States," *New England Palladium* (Boston), June 27, 1803, p. 2.

103 **"I would not give one inch"** TJ to John Breckinridge, August 12, 1803, in *The Writings of Thomas Jefferson*, edited by Andrew A. Lipscomb and Albert Ellery Bergh (Washington: Thomas Jefferson Memorial Association, 1905), vol. 10, p. 409.

104 **just as safe in the wilderness** M. Lewis to Lucy Marks, July 2, 1803, in Jackson, *Letters of the Lewis and Clark Expedition*, p. 124.

105 **"so far and *all is well*"** M. Lewis to TJ, July 15, 1803, ibid., p. 110.

105 **fully prepared pioneers** Zadok Cramer, *The Navigator: Containing Directions for Navigating the Monongahela, Allegheny, Ohio and Mississippi Rivers* (Pittsburgh: Cramer & Spear, 1808); repr., selections edited by Joseph Arnold Foster (Claremont, CA: privately printed, 1951), p. 2.

105 **"which they call whisky"** M. Perrin du Lac, *Travels Through the Two Louisianas* (London: Richard Phillips, 1807), p. 36.

106 **the great ship was named the *Louisiana*** Sarah H. Kilkelly, *The History of Pittsburgh: Its Rise and Progress* (Pittsburgh: B. C. & Gordon Montgomery, 1906), pp. 122–31.

106 **Lewis believed him** Lewis to TJ, September 8, 1803, in Jackson, *Letters of the Lewis and Clark Expedition* (1962), p. 121.

106 **"what bloody teeth & fangs"** TJ to John Breckinridge, November 24, 1803, in Lipscomb and Bergh, *Writings of Thomas Jefferson*, p. 280.

106 **"It appears by the latest intelligence"** Untitled editorial, *Washington Federalist*, July 8, 1803, p. 2.

107 **"the alienation of Louisiana"** Marquis de Yrujo to Pedro Cevallos, August 3, 1803, *Louisiana Under the Rule of Spain, France, and the United States, 1785–1807*, vol. 1, trans. and edited by James Alexander Robertson (Cleveland: Arthur H. Clark Company, 1911), pp. 69–70.

107 **"a manifest violation"** Yrujo to James Madison, September 4, 1803, in Robertson, *Louisiana Under the Rule*, vol. 2, p. 78.

108 **"no doubt force must be used"** TJ to James Madison, September 14, 1803, in Paul Leicester Ford, *The Works of Thomas Jefferson, Correspondence and Papers, 1803–1807* (New York: G. P. Putnam's Sons, 1904–05), vol. 10, p. 30.

108 **"*Louisiana* is a foreign country"** "From the Balance," *New York Spectator,* September 9, 1803, p. 1.

109 **Louisiana is barely mentioned** *See*, for example, Altamira y Crevea, *Historia de España y de la civilización española* (Barcelona: J. Gili, 1909), 4 volumes.

109 **"an obscurity did not already exist"** Marbois, *The History of Louisiana* p. 286.

110 **questions about the Mississippi Valley** Thomas Maitland Marshall, *A History of the Western Boundary of the Louisiana Purchase, 1819–1841* (Berkeley: University of California Press, 1914), p. 10.

111 **"his usual custom he got drunk"** M. Lewis to TJ, September 8, 1803, in Jackson, *Letters of the Lewis and Clark Expedition*, pp. 121–22.

112 **In the frontier's inexact nomenclature** Mary Ann Sternberg, *Along the River Road: Past and Present on Louisiana's Historic Byway* (Baton Rouge: Louisiana State University Press, 2001), p. 51; Verne Huser, "On the Rivers with Lewis and Clark," *We Proceeded On*, vol. 29, no. 2 (May 2003): 18, 21.

112 **"the best sailors"** M. Lewis to TJ, September 13, 1803, in Jackson, *Letters of the Lewis and Clark Expedition*, pp. 124.

113 **"A schooner is just arrived"** "Important," *New York Commercial Advertiser*, October 24, 1803, p. 3.

113 **Jefferson's plan** TJ to Albert Gallatin, October 29, 1803, in Ford, *Works of Thomas Jefferson*, vol. 10, p. 45.

114 **"The object of your mission"** TJ to Meriwether Lewis, November 16, 1803, in Jackson, *Letters of the Lewis and Clark Expedition*, pp. 137–38.

CHAPTER SEVEN

115 **King Carlos IV was ready** French Ensor Chadwick, *The Relations of the United States and Spain: Diplomacy* (New York: Charles Scribner's Sons, 1909), p. 43.

116 **"It is painful to acknowledge"** El Marqués de Casa Calvo to Pedro Cavallos, March 30, 1804, in *Before Lewis and Clark: Documents Illustrating the History of the Missouri, 1785–1804*, edited by A. P. Nasatir (Lincoln: University of Nebraska Press, 1990), vol. 2, p. 728.

118 **just as obscure at the time** [Thomas Jefferson], *An Account of Louisiana, &c.* (Philadelphia: William Doane, 1803), p. 3.

119 **Born in New Jersey** William J. Backes, "General Zebulon M. Pike," *Somerset County Historical Quarterly* 8, no. 4 (October 1919): 241.

119 **"but of resolute spirit"** Henry Whiting, "Zebulon Montgomery Pike," *Library of American Biography*, 2nd ser., vol. 5 (Boston: Little, Brown & Co., 1864), p. 220.

121 **"his intention was to continue"** Carlos de Lassus to Casa Calvo, December 9, 1803, in Nasatir, *Before Lewis and Clark*, vol. 2, p. 719.

124 **Spain must keep control** Casa Calvo to Ceballos, January 13, 1804, in *Louisiana Under the Rule of Spain, France, and the United States*, edited by James Alexander Robertson (Cleveland: Arthur H. Clark, 1911), vol. 2, p. 162.

124 **preparations for a war** Yrujo to Cevallos, June 12, 1804, ibid., pp. 109–14.

124 **ordered to drop his plans** Yrujo to Cevallos, June 12, 1804, ibid., p. 128; Thomas Maitland Marshall, *A History of the Western Boundary of the Louisiana Purchase, 1819–1841* (Berkeley: University of California Press, 1914), p. 19.

124 **as "a nation of calculators"** Charles Pinckney to Madison, July 20, 1804, reprinted in Chadwick, *The Relations of the United States and Spain: Diplomacy*, pp. 74–75.

124 **Yrujo stormed into Madison's office** Ibid., pp. 70–71.

125 the "Emperor of Louisiana" "Miscellanies," Thomas's *Massachusetts Spy* (newspaper), April 11, 1804, p. 2.

125 Mitchell's congressional report Marshall, *History of the Western Boundary*, pp. 13–14.

126 "An expedition of discovery" Samuel L. Mitchell, "Exploration of Louisiana," in *Annals of Congress*, House of Representatives, 8th Congress, 1st session, pp. 1124–26.

127 "Congress will probably authorise me" TJ to Dunbar, March 13, 1804, Thomas Jefferson Papers at the Library of Congress, ser. 1, General Correspondence, 1651–1827, microfilm 030.

128 "Sir: Directions have been given" Henry Dearborn to Dunbar, April 4, 1804, in *Life, Letters and Papers of William Dunbar*, compiled by Mrs. Dunbar Rowland (Jackson: Press of the Mississippi Historical Society, 1930), p. 128.

128 didn't put Dunbar in a good mood William Dunbar to Henry Dearborn, May 13, 1804, ibid.

129 "the introduction of foreigners" Nemesio Salcedo to Pedro Cevallos, May 8, 1804, in Nasatir, *Before Lewis and Clark*, vol. 2, p. 729.

130 "this all devouring passion of gain" Dunbar to Henry Dearborn, May 13, 1804, in Rowland, *Letters and Papers of William Dunbar*, p. 128.

130 the big boat had twenty-two oars W. Clark, journal, May 13, 1804, in *The Journals of the Lewis and Clark Expedition* (University of Nebraska Press/University of Nebraska–Lincoln Libraries/Electronic Text Center, http://lewisandclarkjournals.unl.edu).

131 led by a chief named White Hair Louis F. Burns, *A History of the Osage People* (Tuscaloosa: University of Alabama, 2004), p. 54.

132 "to reach St. Charles this evening" Lewis, journal, May 20, 1804, ibid.

133 "It shall be the duty" Lewis, "Detachment Orders," May 26, 1804, ibid.

133 "we wer verry near loseing" W. Clark journal, May 24, 1804, ibid.

134 "every thing in prime order" W. Clark journal, July 30, 1804, ibid.

CHAPTER EIGHT

135 George Hunter was a busy man Hunter, autobiographical sketch, original in the Hunter Papers, American Philosophical Society, reprinted in *The Western Journals of Dr. George Hunter*, edited by John Francis McDermott (Philadelphia: APS, 1963), p. 87.

136 "fallen upon by Osage Indians" "Lexington, June 19," *Washington National Intelligencer*, July 4, 1804, p. 3.

137   **"with their boundless designs"** Vincente Folch, "Reflections on Louisiana," in *Louisiana Under the Rule of Spain, France and the United States*, edited by James Alexander Robertson (Cleveland: Arthur H. Clark, 1911), vol. 2, p. 334. The document was signed by Folch, the governor of West Florida, a Spanish territory, in order to protect Wilkinson's authorship.

137   **"may detach a sufficient body"** Ibid., p. 342.

137   **"astronomer, who is at this very"** Ibid., p. 338.

138   **"In the winter of 1776"** George Hunter, "Notes Collected by George Hunter Chemist, concerning some of his ancestors; for the information of his decendents.—" January 1, 1795, original in the Hunter Papers, APS, reprinted in McDermott, *Western Journals of Dr. George Hunter*.

139   **The business happened** Lu Ann De Cunzo, "An Historical Interpretation of William Birch's Print *High Street, from Ninth Street, Philadelphia*," *Pennsylvania History*, April 1983, p. 125.

140   **GEORGE HUNTER, CHEMIST** "George Hunter, Chemist," advertisement, *Philadelphia Gazette and Universal Daily Advertiser*, October 14, 1794, p. 3.

141   **Dunbar had finally agreed** William Dunbar to TJ, June 9, 1804, in *The Life, Letters and Papers of William Dunbar, 1749–1810*, compiled by Mrs. Dunbar Rowland (Jackson: Press of the Mississippi Historical Society, 1930), p. 134.

142   **"She is 50 feet long"** George Hunter to Henry Dearborn, June 14, 1804, in McDermott, *Western Journals of Dr. George Hunter*, p. 58.

142   **"reason to repent their imprudence"** George Hunter, "Journey to Explore Louisiana Begun May 27th 1804," ibid., p. 59.

143   **"almost naked"** Untitled article, *Farmer's Cabinet* (Amherst, New Hampshire), July 31, 1804, p. 3.

143   **The typical Grand Osage man** Christopher C. Dean, *Letters on the Chicakasaw and Osage Missions* (Boston: T. A. Marvin, 1831), p. 47.

143   **described the chiefs as "gigantic"** Untitled article, *Charleston* (South Carolina) *Courier*, July 7, 1804, p. 3.

143   **The Caddo, who lived** F. Todd Smith, "A Native Response to the Transfer of Louisiana: The Red River Caddos and Spain," *Louisiana History* 37, no. 2 (Spring 1996): 183.

144   **"Dr. Hunter of Philadelphia arrived"** Untitled article from *Kentucky Gazette*, reprinted in *Richmond* (Virginia) *Enquirer*, July 18, 1804, p. 2.

144   **"should we in the end"** William Dunbar to TJ, June 1, 1804, Thomas

Jefferson Papers at the Library of Congress, ser. 1, General Correspondence, 1651–1827, microfilm reel 030.

145 **"many important objects will present themselves"** William Dunbar to TJ, June 9, 1804, in Rowland, *Life, Letters and Papers of William Dunbar*, p. 133.

146 **he would pressure them to cede** Louis F. Burns, *A History of the Osage People* (Tuscaloosa: University of Alabama, 2004), p. 152.

146 **"by sending trusty persons to explore"** TJ to the Osages, July 16, 1804, in *Letters of the Lewis and Clark Expedition*, edited by Donald Jackson (Urbana: University of Illinois Press, 1962), pp. 201–2. For another view of the visit, by which the Grand Osage were hostages held lightly for the safety of Lewis and Clark, see "Osage Indians," Sag Harbor (New York) *Suffolk Gazette*, December 3, 1804, p. 1.

147 **"Reflecting on this awful event"** McDermott, *Western Journals of Dr. George Hunter*, p. 61.

CHAPTER NINE

149 **"it has now much abated"** Thomas Rodney to Cesar A. Rodney, July 27, 1804, in *Pennsylvania Magazine of History and Biography* 64 (1920): 47.

150 **"This will delay our final departure"** George Hunter to Henry Dearborn, July 31, 1804, in *The Western Journals of Dr. George Hunter*, edited by John Francis McDermott (Philadelphia: APS, 1963), p. 62.

150 **"Abutifull Breeze"** W. Clark, journal, July 27, 1804, in *The Journals of the Lewis and Clark Expedition* (University of Nebraska Press/University of Nebraska–Lincoln Libraries/Electronic Text Center, http://lewisand clarkjournals.unl.edu).

150 **"found the Misquitors"** W. Clark, journal, July 27, 1804, ibid.

151 **La Liberté hadn't returned** Joseph Whitehouse, journal, July 29, 1804, ibid.

151 **"This is a singular anamal"** Lewis, journal entry, July 30, 1804, ibid.

152 **"This being my birth day"** W. Clark, journal entry, August 1, 1804, ibid.

152 **"thay fired meney Guns"** Charles Floyd, journal entry, August 2, 1803, ibid.

153 **"they all use paint"** Joseph Whitehouse, journal entry, August 2, 1804, ibid.

153 **"the Council was held"** Floyd, journal entry, August 3, 1804, ibid.

154 **Blackbird died** John Ludwickson, "Blackbird and Son: A Note Concerning Late-Eighteenth- and Early Nineteenth-Century Omaha Chieftainship," *Ethnohistory* 42, no. 1 (Winter 1995): 141.

156 **"I went to the hunt Buffalow"** W. Clark, journal, August 19, 1804, in *Journals of the Lewis and Clark Expedition*, http://lewisandclarkjournals .unl.edu.

158 **"Having but very indifferent workman"** Hunter, *Western Journals* (1963), p. 63.

158 **Spanish would immediately arrest any Americans** William Dunbar to TJ, August 18, 1804, in *The Life, Letters and Papers of William Dunbar*, compiled by Mrs. Dunbar Rowland (Jackson: Press of the Mississippi Historical Society, 1930), p. 140.

158 **"conclude to suspend this"** TJ to William Dunbar, July 17, 1804, Founders Online, National Archives (http://founders.archives.gov/ documents/Jefferson/99-01-02-0091).

160 **"a mass of information"** William Dunbar to TJ, August 18, 1804, in *Life, Letters and Papers of William Dunbar* (1930), p. 140.

160 **"Although it is almost eight months"** [Juan Manuel de Salcedo] to Pedro Cevallos, August 20, 1804, in *Before Lewis and Clark: Documents Illustrating the History of the Missouri, 1785–1804*, edited by A. P. Nasatir (Lincoln: University of Nebraska Press, 1990), vol. 2, p. 749.

CHAPTER TEN

163 **"There is never a moment"** TJ to Philip Mazzei, July 18, 1804, in *The Writings of Thomas Jefferson*, edited by Andrew A. Lipscomb and Albert Ellery Bergh (Washington: Thomas Jefferson Memorial Association, 1905), vol. 11, p. 38.

163 **amiable Scotsman** Margaret Bayard Smith, *The First Forty Years of Washington Society* (New York: Charles Scribner's Sons, 1906), pp. 394–95.

164 **political observers were confident** "Constitutional Amendment Ratified," *Boston Democrat*, August 22, 1804, p. 2.

164 **had not, as his enemies predicted** "Mr. Jefferson," *Richmond* (Virginia) *Enquirer*, December 3, 1805, p. 3.

164 **A year after the announcement** "Communication No. 2," *Litchfield* (Connecticut) *Monitor*, August 10, 1804, p. 1.

164 **"Except for Salt Mountains"** "Retrospect," *Alexandria* (Virginia) *Daily Advertiser*, September 28, 1804, p. 2.

164 **"while so much of the public money"** Untitled article, *Salem* (Massachusetts) *Gazette*, September 4, 1804, p. 3.

164   **"We wanted free navigation"** "Reasons—No. VIII," New York *Commercial Advertiser*, September 11, 1804, p. 2.

165   **"Mr. Jefferson and his friends"** Untitled article ["Mr. Jefferson"], Philadelphia *United States Gazette*, August 28, 1804, p. 2.

165   **"A perfect Eden"** "Reasons—No. VIII," New York *Commercial Advertiser*, September 11, 1804, p. 2.

165   **"subterfuges, evasions, and subtleties"** Marqués de Casa Yrujo to Cevallos, June 12, 1804, in *Louisiana Under the Rule of France, Spain, and the United States, 1785–1807*, edited by James Alexander Robertson (Cleveland: Arthur H. Clark, 1911), vol. 2, pp. 134–35.

165   **continuing loyalty to His Catholic Majesty** Casa Calvo, letter to the editor, July 7, 1804, *New Orleans Gazette*, reprinted in "Discontent in Louisiana," *Richmond* (Virginia) *Enquirer*, August 25, 1804, p. 2.

167   **"the Americans had no right"** Charles Pinckney to James Madison, July 20, 1804, in *The Papers of James Madison*, Secretary of State Series, edited by David B. Mattern, J. C. A. Stagg, Ellen J. Barber, et al. (Charlottesville: University of Virginia Press, 2005), vol. 7, pp. 487–88.

168   **"the necessity of exacting satisfaction"** Périchon de Vandeuil to Talleyrand, August 6, 1804, in French Ensor Chadwick, *The Relations of the United States and Spain: Diplomacy* (New York: Charles Scribner's Sons, 1909), pp. 75–76.

169   **"Major Ellis from a tour"** George Hunter, journal entry, September 19, 1804, original in the Hunter Papers, American Philosophical Society, reprinted in *The Western Journals of Dr. George Hunter*, edited by John Francis McDermott (Philadelphia: APS, 1963), p. 66.

169   **Someone who knew Ellis** Thomas Rodney to Cesar A. Rodney, October 20, 1804, Simon Gratz, "Thomas Rodney," in *Pennsylvania Magazine of History and Biography* 44 (1920): 62.

169   **"The rumor prevails"** William Dunbar to TJ, October 14, 1804, in *Life, Letters and Papers of William Dunbar*, compiled by Mrs. Dunbar Rowland (Jackson: Press of the Mississippi Historical Society, 1930), p. 141.

170   **a "large Canoe"** George Hunter, miscellaneous notes, in McDermott, *Western Journals of Dr. George Hunter*, p. 71.

172   **"Mr. Dunbar's excellent Circle of Reflection"** Ibid., p. 83n.

CHAPTER ELEVEN

176   **"Soldiers do not exert themselves"** William Dunbar, October 18, 1804, in "Journal of a Voyage Commencing at St. Catherine's Landing," in

Documents Relating to the Purchase and Exploration of Louisiana (Boston: Houghton Mifflin, 1904), p. 9.

177 **"having uttered repeated expressions"** Meriwether Lewis, "Details for the Court Martial," October 13, 1804, in *The Journals of the Lewis and Clark Expedition* (University of Nebraska Press/University of Nebraska–Lincoln Libraries/Electronic Text Center, http://lewisandclarkjournals .unl.edu).

177 **"discarded from the perminent"** Ibid.

177 **the number was officially reduced** Byron Fanwell, *Encyclopedia of Land Warfare* (New York: Norton, 2001), p. 307.

177 **"observed that examples"** Clark, journal, October 14, 1804, in *Journals of the Lewis and Clark Expedition*, http://lewisandclarkjournals.unl.edu.

178 **"Having given the Soldiers"** William Dunbar, October 21, 1804, in "Journal," *Documents Relating to the Purchase* (1904), p. 10.

181 **"We took him into the boat"** Hunter journal [October 1804], in *The Forgotten Expedition: 1804–1805*, edited by Trey Berry, Pam Beasley, and Jeanne Clements (Baton Rouge: Louisiana State University Press, 2006), p. 13.

182 **"covered frame of rough"** William Dunbar, October 21, 1804, in "Journal," *Documents Relating to the Purchase* (1904), p. 13.

182 **"How happy the contrast"** Ibid., p. 13

183 **bustling cities surrounded by plantations** E. G. Swem, "A Letter from New Madrid, 1789," *The Mississippi Valley Historical Review*, vol. 5, no. 3 (December, 1918): 343–46.

183 **"100 feet broad"** George Hunter, official report, in *The Western Journals of Dr. George Hunter*, edited by John Francis McDermott (Philadelphia: APS, 1963), pp. 82n–83n.

184 **"If one may judge"** George Hunter, October 23, 1804 in McDermott, *Western Journals of Dr. George Hunter*, p. 82.

184 **"Made slow advancement"** Dunbar journal, October 24, 1804, in *Documents Relating to the Purchase and Exploration of Louisiana*, p. 20.

186 **"The twining vines entangle"** Ibid., pp. 21–22.

188 **"The day being fine"** Dunbar journal, October 26, 1804, ibid., p. 25.

188 **"jaded or unwilling to work"** Hunter journal [October 1804], in Berry, Beasley, and Clements, *The Forgotten Expedition: 1804–1805*, p. 27.

189 **"to try to force the boat thro"** George Hunter, October 26, 1804, in McDermott, *Western Journals of Dr. George Hunter*, p. 84.

CHAPTER TWELVE

191   **evidence of a raid** Joseph Whitehouse, journal, September 27, 1804, *The Journals of the Lewis and Clark Expedition* (University of Nebraska Press/University of Nebraska–Lincoln Libraries/Electronic Text Center, http://lewisandclarkjournals.unl.edu).

192   **A third was located** Douglas R. Parks, *Traditional Narratives of the Arikara Indians: Stories of Alfred Morsette* (Lincoln: University of Nebraska Press, 1991), p. 10.

192   **"Their language is So"** W. Clark journal, October 12, 1804, *Journals of the Lewis and Clark Expedition*, http://lewisandclarkjournals.unl.edu.

193   **called Mother Corn** Hand, oral history, "The Origin of the Arikara," in George A. Dorsey, *Traditions of the Arikara* (Washington: Carnegie Institution, 1904), p. 22.

193   **their diet and whole way of life** Hand, oral history, Ibid., pp. 12–13.

193   **one of their chiefs north** Ibid., October 10 and 12, 1804.

193   **named Ar-ketarna-Shar** W. Clark journal, October 10 and 12, 1804, *Journals of the Lewis and Clark Expedition*, http://lewisandclarkjournals .unl.edu.

193   **"a custom Similar to the Sioux"** W. Clark journal, October 12, 1804, ibid.

194   **the women as "our squaw"** Patrick Gass journal, October 15, 1804, ibid.

194   **"carressing our men"** W. Clark journal, October 15, 1804, ibid.

194   **strength, knowledge, or power** James P. Ronda, *Lewis and Clark Among the Indians* (Lincoln: University of Nebraska Press, 1988), pp. 63–64.

195   **"a great many of the natives"** Patrick Gass journal, October 25, 1804, *Journals of the Lewis and Clark Expedition*, http://lewisandclarkjournals .unl.edu.

197   **stop bothering to call him** Aaron Burr to Theodosia Burr Alston, November 17, 1804, Matthew L. Davis, *Memoirs of Aaron Burr with Miscellaneous Selections from His Correspondence*, volume 2 (New York: Harper & Brothers, 1837), p. 351.

197   **"The subject in dispute"** Aaron Burr to Theodosia Burr Alston, November 17, 1804, in Davis, *Memoirs of Aaron Burr*, vol. 2, p. 352.

197   **concerted effort to visit Florida** Aaron Burr to Theodosia Burr Alston, September 26, 1804, *Memoirs of Aaron Burr*, vol. 2, p. 342.

198   **the Marquis de LaFayette** TJ to Marie-Joseph-Paul-Yves-Roch-Gilbert du Motier, marquis de Lafayette, February 14, 1806, Founders Online, National Archives (http://founders.archives.gov/documents/ Jefferson/99-01-02-3238).

198 **"form of government thus provided"** TJ Annual Message to Congress, November 8, 1804, in *The Writings of Thomas Jefferson*, edited by Andrew A. Lipscomb and Albert Ellery Bergh (Washington: Thomas Jefferson Memorial Association, 1905), vol. 3, p. 368.

199 **"due state of organization"** Ibid.

CHAPTER THIRTEEN

200 **"I then got a runner"** Hunter journal, October 26, 1804, in *The Forgotten Expedition: 1804–1805*, edited by Trey Berry, Pam Beasley, and Jeanne Clements (Baton Rouge: Louisiana State University Press, 2006), p. 27.

201 **"to my entire satisfaction"** Dunbar journal, October 27, 1804, in "Journal of a Voyage Commencing at St. Catherine's Landing," in *Documents Relating to the Purchase and Exploration of Louisiana* (Boston: Houghton Mifflin, 1904), p. 27.

201 **"From the experience we have had"** Dunbar journal, October 31, 1804, ibid., p. 31–32.

203 **"restless before the Speech"** Lewis journal, October 29, 1804, *The Journals of the Lewis and Clark Expedition* (University of Nebraska Press/ University of Nebraska–Lincoln Libraries/Electronic Text Center, http://lewisandclarkjournals.unl.edu).

203 **area known as the Mandan villages** Frank H. Stewart, "Mandan and Hidatsa Villages in the Eighteenth and Nineteenth Centuries," *Plains Anthropologist* 19, no. 66, pt. 1 (November 1974): 296.

203 **confused the Minitari with another tribe** Allan R. Taylor, "The Many Names of the White Clay People," *International Journal of American Linguistics* 49, no. 4 (October 1983): 429–32.

205 **"This we are disposed to do"** Lewis to Charles Chaboillez, October 31, 1804, in *Letters of the Lewis and Clark Expedition*, edited by Donald Jackson (Urbana: University of Illinois Press, 1962), vol. 1, p. 214.

205 **"The Chronometer ran down"** Lewis, journal, October 29, 1804, *Journals of the Lewis and Clark Expedition*, http://lewisandclarkjournals.unl .edu.

206 **known as equal altitudes** Richard S. Preston, "The Accuracy of the Astronomical Observations of Lewis and Clark," *Proceedings of the American Philosophical Society* 144, no. 2 (June 2000): 171.

208 **"some of them often grumbling"** Hunter journal, November 4, 1804, in Berry et al., *Forgotten Expedition*, p. 40.

209 **"a man acquainted"** Hunter journal, November 13, 1804, ibid., p. 53.

210 "it was supposed at the Post" William Dunbar, October 18, 1904, in
     "Journal," in *Documents Relating to the Purchase*, p. 80.

212 a teller of tall tales Hunter journal, November 22, 1804, in *Western
     Journals of Dr. George Hunter*, edited by John Francis McDermott (Phil-
     adelphia: APS, 1963), pp. 95–96.

212 "Doctor Hunter was employed in the cabin" Dunbar journal, *Docu-
     ments Relating to the Purchase*, pp. 61–62.

213 "by the motion of the boat" Hunter journal, November 18, 1804, in
     McDermott, *Western Journals of Dr. George Hunter*, p. 96.

CHAPTER FOURTEEN

215 "The river continues to run" Hunter journal, November 27, 1804, in
     Western Journals of Dr. George Hunter, edited by John Francis McDer-
     mott (Philadelphia: APS, 1963), p. 97.

215 The ledges weren't clean Arthur H. DeRosier, *William Dunbar: Scien-
     tific Pioneer of the Old Southwest* (Lexington: University Press of Ken-
     tucky, 2007), p. 144.

217 The Chutes consisted of an uneven Hunter journal [December 4,
     1804] and Dunbar journal, December 4, 1804, in *The Forgotten Expedi-
     tion: The Louisiana Purchase Journals of Dunbar and Hunter*, edited by
     Trey Berry, Pam Beasley, and Jeanne Clements (Baton Rouge: Louisi-
     ana State University Press, 2006), pp. 97–98.

217 "The water tho' extremely rapid" Dunbar journal, December 3, 1804,
     ibid., p. 96.

220 At a temperature of 145 degrees Hunter journal, December 11, 1804,
     ibid., p. 114.

220 from the Indians Thomas Rodney to Cesar A. Rodney, October 20,
     1804, in Simon Gratz, "Thomas Rodney," *Pennsylvania Magazine of
     History and Biography* 44 (1920): 63.

220 "a voyage of trouble and retardment" William Dunbar to TJ, Novem-
     ber 9, 1804, in Thomas Jefferson Papers at the Library of Congress, ser.
     1, General Correspondence, 1651–1827, microfilm reel 031.

221 Jefferson and Clinton won "Presidential Election," *New York Morning
     Chronicle*, December 29, 1804, p. 2.

221 impeachment proceedings "The Vice President," *Albany Centinel*, No-
     vember 13, 1804, p. 3.

221 as many in Congress noted Ibid.

221 "the natural color of whose hands" Untitled article, *Washington Feder-
     alist*, November 7, 1804, p. 3.

221 **currying favor** Jonathan Daniels, *The Devil's Backbone: The Story of the Natchez Trace* (New York: McGraw-Hill, 1962), p. 139.

222 **Jefferson's tacit absolution of Burr** "Dr. Joseph Browne," *New York Morning Chronicle*, March 25, 1805, p. 2.

222 **"his magnificent uniform"** James Ripley Jacobs, *Tarnished Warrior* (New York: Macmillan, 1938), p. 213.

223 *This is a truth* "Gen. James Wilkinson," *Farmer's Weekly Museum*, March 30, 1805, p. 3.

224 **"how strongly the sympathy"** James Wilkinson, *Memoirs of My Own Times* (Philadelphia: Abraham Small, 1816), vol. 2, p. 271.

228 **"Decr. 30th, 1804, Sunday"** Hunter journal, *Western Journals of Dr. George Hunter*, pp. 108–9.

CHAPTER FIFTEEN

231 **"a shortcut home to his family"** Hunter journal, January 19, 1805, in *The Western Journals of Dr. George Hunter*, edited by John Francis Mc-Dermott (Philadelphia: APS, 1963), p. 113.

231 **a formal home such as Dunbar's** C. Lucy Brightwell, *Scenes in the Life of Alexander Wilson, the Ornithologist* (London: Sampson Low, Son and Co., 1861), p. 137; Alexander Wilson, diary entry, May 23, 1810, in *The Poems and Literary Prose of Alexander Wilson*, edited by Alexander B. Grosart (Paisley, Scotland: A. Gardner, 1876), vol. 1, pp. 221.

232 **"We arrived at Mr. Dunbar's"** Hunter journal, February 3, 1805, ibid., p. 116.

232 **"are indeed a great natural Curiosity"** William Dunbar to TJ [February 1805], in *Life, Letters and Papers of William Dunbar*, compiled by Mrs. Dunbar Rowland (Jackson: Press of the Mississippi Historical Society, 1930), p. 142.

234 **"which of the two powers"** TJ to Marie-Joseph-Paul-Yves-Roch-Gilbert du Motier, marquis de Lafayette, February 14, 1806, Founders Online, National Archives (http://founders.archives.gov/documents/Jefferson/99-01-02-3238).

236 **"considered by the republicans"** James Elliot, "Letter II," Randolph, VT, *Vermont Weekly Wanderer*, May 27, 1805, p. 1.

236 **"The great irregularities and delays"** William Dunbar to TJ, February 15, 1805, Jefferson Papers, microfilm reel.

237 **the finest address heard** Untitled article, *Washington Federalist*, March 13, 1805, p. 3.

237 **"waged against federalism"** TJ to Dr. George Logan, May 11, 1805, LOC.

238 **"Your letters of the 2d"** TJ to William Dunbar, March 14, 1805, Founders Online, National Archives (http://founders.archives.gov/documents/Jefferson/99-01-02-1387).

239 **four thousand seedlings** Thomas Main to TJ, March 10, 1807, in *Thomas Jefferson's Garden Book*, annotated by Edwin Morris Betts (Philadelphia: American Philosophical Society, 1992), p. 342.

239 **when it came to hedge thorns** "Hedges," *National Intelligencer and Washington Advertiser*, July 24, 1805, p. 2.

240 **Sacajawea was described** H. M. Brackenridge, *Journal of a Voyage up the River Missouri, Performed in Eighteen Hundred and Eleven*, edited by Reuben Gold Thwaites, vol. 6 (Cleveland: Arthur H. Clark Company, 1904), pp. 32–33.

240 **an 1802 hunting/exploration trek led** "Introduction, Part III: The Precursors to Lewis and Clark," in *Before Lewis and Clark: Documents Illustrating the History of the Missouri, 1785–1804*, edited by A. P. Nasatir (Lincoln: University of Nebraska Press, 1990), vol. 1, p. 110.

240 **"among the most happy"** Lewis journal, April 7, 1805, in *The Journals of the Lewis and Clark Expedition* (University of Nebraska Press/University of Nebraska–Lincoln Libraries/Electronic Text Center, http://lewisandclarkjournals.unl.edu).

246 **"Your observations on the difficulty"** TJ to William Dunbar, May 25, 1805, in *The Writings of Thomas Jefferson*, edited by Andrew A. Lipscomb and Albert Ellery Bergh (Washington: Thomas Jefferson Memorial Association, 1905), vol. 11, pp. 74–75.

CHAPTER SIXTEEN

250 **pyramid arose "as if by magic"** "The Arrival of Gen. Wilkinson at St. Louis," *National Intelligencer and Washington Advertiser*, Washington, DC, September 13, 1805, p. 2.

250 **the source of the Mississippi River** James Wilkinson to Pike, July 30, 1805, in Donald Jackson, *The Journals of Zebulon Montgomery Pike* (Norman: University of Oklahoma Press, 1966), vol. 1, p. 3.

252 **"Our relations to Spain"** James Wilkinson to Henry Dearborn, July 27, 1805, ibid., p. 229.

253 **scouting the Philadelphia shops** TJ to Freeman, November 16, 1805, in Thomas Jefferson Papers at the Library of Congress, ser. 1, General Correspondence, 1651–1827, microfilm reel 034.

254 **"Capt. Lewis who has been sent"** TJ to William Jarvis, July 6, 1805, ibid., microfilm reel 034.

255 **Pike, born in New Jersey** Henry Whiting, "Zebulon Montgomery Pike," *Library of American Biography* (Boston: Little, Brown, 1864), 2nd ser., vol. 5, p. 220.

256 **Pike's article** Zebulon Pike, "Pike's Memorandum on Louisiana," *Medical Repository*, 2nd hexade, vol. 4 (1804): 409–11.

257 **"You will proceed to"** James Wilkinson to Zebulon Pike, July 30, 1805, in *The Journals of Zebulon Montgomery Pike*, edited by Jackson, vol. 1, p. 3.

258 **he lost another dog** Ibid., p. 16.

259 **"a boat came up"** *Black Hawk: An Autobiography*, edited by Donald Dean Jackson (Urbana: University of Illinois Press, 1955), p. 52.

259 **Saukenuk was home to four thousand** Julia Mills Dunn, "Saukenuk," *Transactions of the Illinois State Historical Society*, 1902, p.133.

260 **"he would reach the very"** Editor's note in *The Journals of Pike*, edited by Jackson, vol. 1, p. 14n.

261 **including the Mdewakanton** Frederick Webb Hodge, *Handbook of American Indians North of Mexico, A-M* (Washington: Government Printing Office, 1912), Part 1, p. 826.

261 **"100,000 Acres for a Song"** Pike to James Wilkinson, September 23, 1805, in Jackson, *Journals of Zebulon Pike*, vol. 1, p. 238.

262 **"an impressive display of sentiment"** Pike journal, September 17, 1805, ibid., pp. 33–34.

262 **"thought they were getting a bargain"** Gary C. Anderson, *Kinsmen of Another Kind: Dakota-White Relations in the Upper Mississippi Valley* (Lincoln: University of Nebraska Press, 1984), p. 82.

262 **"In the morning"** Pike journal, September 24, 1805, in Jackson, *The Journals of Zebulon Pike*, vol. 1, p. 39.

263 **"that his face was"** Pike journal, September 25, 1805, ibid., p. 40.

264 **"A wonderful exhibition"** Pike journal, September 17, 1805, ibid., p. 34.

CHAPTER SEVENTEEN

266 **he came upon a recumbent buck** Pike journal, November 2, 1805, in *The Journals of Zebulon Montgomery Pike*, edited by Donald Jackson (Norman: University of Oklahoma Press, 1966), vol. 1, p. 53.

267 **"he is a much abler Soldier"** James Wilkinson to Henry Dearborn, November 26, 1805, ibid., p. 249.

269 **Most of the men were bloodied** Lewis journal, June 22, 1805, in *The Journals of the Lewis and Clark Expedition* (University of Nebraska Press/University of Nebraska–Lincoln Libraries/Electronic Text Center, http://lewisandclarkjournals.unl.edu).

270 **he'd have fewer men** Roy E. Appleman, *Lewis and Clark: Historic Places Associated with Their Transcontinental Exploration* (St. Louis: Lewis & Clark Trail Heritage Foundation, 1993), pp. 146–47.

270 **"We arrose very early"** M. Lewis, July 15, 1805, in *Journals of the Lewis and Clark Expedition*, http://lewisandclarkjournals.unl.edu.

270 **"These mountains appear to be"** Joseph Whitehouse, July 17, 1805, ibid.

270 **"It appears as if"** Lewis, July 18, 1805, ibid.

270 **The Dearborn River** Salish–Pend d'Oreille Culture Committee, *The Salish People and the Lewis and Clark Expedition* (2005), p. 49.

272 **"Both Capt. C and myself"** M. Lewis. July 28, 1805, in *Journals of the Lewis and Clark Expedition*, http://lewisandclarkjournals.unl.edu.

274 **"the most distant fountain"** M. Lewis, August 12, 1805, ibid.

274 **Geologists later determined** John E. Thorson, *River of Promise, River of Peril* (Lawrence: University of Kansas Press, 1994), p. 13.

276 **including her brother** Robert R. Archibald, "Legacy of the Lewis and Clark Expedition," *History News* 60, no. 2: 21.

276 **"This day I completed"** Lewis, August 18, 1805, in *Journals of the Lewis and Clark Expedition*, http://lewisandclarkjournals.unl.edu.

277 **"The road was excessively dangerous"** Lewis, September 19, 1805, ibid.

277 **"One of our horses fell backwards"** Whitehouse, September 19, 1805, ibid.

278 **His health wasn't as strong** Ronald V. Loge, "Illness at Three Forks: Captain William Clark and the First Recorded Case of Colorado Tick Fever," *Montana: The Magazine of Western History* 50, no. 2 (Summer 2000): 13–14. Dr. Loge suggests that Clark probably contracted a form of tick fever at Three Forks.

278 **corps had enough to eat** Allen V. Pinkham and Steven R. Evans, *Lewis and Clark Among the Nez Perce: Strangers in the Land of the Nimiipuu* (Norman: University of Oklahoma Press, 2013), p. 21.

279 **"This business"** Pike journal, September 27, 1805, in Jackson, *Journals of Zebulon Montgomery Pike*, vol. 1, p. 41.

279 **"Finding ourselves devoid of munitions"** Phil Carson, *Across the Northern Frontier: Spanish Explorations in Colorado* (Boulder: Johnson Books, 1998), p. 168.

280 **"When we arose in the morning"** Pike journal, October 16, 1805, in Jackson, *Journals of Zebulon Montgomery Pike*, vol. 1, p. 48.

CHAPTER EIGHTEEN

281 **important piece of correspondence** Thomas Freeman to TJ, November 10, 1805, in The Thomas Jefferson Papers at the Library of Congress, ser. 1, General Correspondence, 1651–1827, microfilm reel 034.

282 **"Not withstanding the disagreeable"** William Clark journal entry, November 9, 1805, in *The Journals of the Lewis and Clark Expedition* (University of Nebraska Press/University of Nebraska–Lincoln Libraries/Electronic Text Center, http://lewisandclarkjournals.unl.edu).

283 **found the Wishram "troublesome"** Joseph Whitehouse, journal, October 22, 1805, ibid.

283 **"waves tossed them about at will"** W. Clark journal entry, November 12, 1805, ibid.

283 **"the best canoe navigators I ever saw"** W. Clark journal entry, November 11, 1805, *Journals of the Lewis and Clark Expedition*, http://lewisandclarkjournals.unl.edu.

286 **If the United States purchased West Florida** French Ensor Chadwick, *The Relations of the United States and Spain: Diplomacy* (New York: Charles Scribner's Sons, 1909), p. 94.

286 **Writing to his friend** Thomas Freeman to John McKee, 1805, in Dan Flores, *Southern Counterpart to Lewis and Clark: The Freeman and Custis Expedition of 1806* (Norman: University of Oklahoma Press, 1984), p. 53.

286 **"These expeditions are so laborious"** TJ to Count de Volney, February 11, 1806, *Letters of the Lewis and Clark Expedition*, edited by Donald Jackson (Urbana: University of Illinois Press, 1962), p. 291.

288 **"found it necessary, at length"** TJ, annual message to Congress, December 3, 1805, in *The Writings of Thomas Jefferson*, edited by Andrew A. Lipscomb and Albert Ellery Bergh (Washington: Thomas Jefferson Memorial Association, 1905), vol. 3, p. 384.

288 **"made Signs that he got"** W. Clark journal, November 11, 1805, *Journals of the Lewis and Clark Expedition*, http://lewisandclarkjournals.unl.edu.

289 **"Mr. Haley"** W. Clark journal, November 6, 1805, ibid.

289 **"see the passific ocean"** John Ordway journal, November 18, 1805, ibid.

290 **"communication with the waters"** TJ to Lewis, June 20, 1803, Thomas Jefferson Papers at the Library of Congress, ser. 1, General Correspondence, 1651–1827, microfilm reel 028.

290 **"A handsom view of the ocean"** Ordway journal, November 18, 1805,

Journals of the Lewis and Clark Expedition, http://lewisandclarkjournals .unl.edu.

290 **"Men appear much Satisfied"** Clark journal, November 18, 1805, ibid.

291 **in the style of men's top hats** Lewis, January 19, 1806, ibid.

291 **"Two of the Clatsops"** Lewis, January 18, 1806, ibid.

291 **"our party from necessaty"** Lewis, January 3, 1806, ibid.

292 **George H. Monk** Letter to Roderick McKenzie, April 18, 1807, in Gordon Charles Davidson, *The North West Company* (Berkeley: University of California Press, 1918), p. 240n.

295 **cold, wet feet so long** Pike journal, February 4, 1806, in *The Journals of Zebulon Montgomery Pike*, edited by Donald Jackson (Norman: University of Oklahoma Press, 1966), vol. 1, p. 89.

CHAPTER NINETEEN

297 **"on the accomplishment of my voyage"** Pike journal, February 1, 1806, in *The Journals of Zebulon Montgomery Pike*, edited by Donald Jackson (Norman: University of Oklahoma Press, 1966), vol. 1, p. 87.

298 **"with distinguished politeness and Hospitality"** Ibid., p. 88.

301 **"and paid the 15 millions"** Untitled article, *Washington Federalist*, February 18, 1806, p. 1.

301 **submitted a packet to Congress** TJ, "Expedition of Lewis and Clarke," submitted February 19, 1806, *Annals of Congress*, 9th Congress, Appendix, pp. 1036–38.

301 **The packet included** *Travels in the Interior Parts of America, Communicating Discoveries Made in exploring the Missouri, Red River and Washita*, edited by Thomas Jefferson (London: Richard Phillips, 1807), pp. 4–40. The same book was published in America in 1806.

303 **"My young Warriors"** Pike journal, February 24, 1806, in Jackson, *The Journals of Zebulon Montgomery Pike*, vol. 1, p. 97.

305 **"The rain Seased"** John Ordway journal, March 23, 1806, *The Journals of the Lewis and Clark Expedition* (University of Nebraska Press/ University of Nebraska–Lincoln Libraries/Electronic Text Center, http://lewisandclarkjournals.unl.edu).

306 **"But on a Second reflection"** Clark journal, April 2, 1806, ibid.

307 **"I am extremely glad"** Dunbar to TJ, March 17, 1806, in *Life, Letters and Papers of William Dunbar*, compiled by Mrs. Dunbar Rowland (Jackson: Press of the Mississippi Historical Society, 1930), p. 330.

310 **Melgares mustered four hundred soldiers** Phil Carson, *Across the*

Northern Frontier: Spanish Explorations in Colorado (Boulder: Johnson Books, 1998), p. 169.

310 **Melgares would be waiting** Thomas Maitland Marshall, *A History of the Western Boundary of the Louisiana Purchase, 1819–1841* (Berkeley: University of California Press, 1914), p. 25.

310 **"superior skill in throwing the Ball"** Pike journal, April 20, 1806, in Jackson, *Journals of Zebulon Montgomery Pike*, vol. 1, pp. 125–26.

311 **"a subaltern with but twenty men"** Pike journal, March 13, 1806, ibid., p. 103.

311 **alcohol had distorted** Pike journal, April 2, 1806, ibid., p. 130.

312 **"Mr. Freeman with his party"** Dunbar to TJ, May 6, 1806, in Rowland, *Life, Letters and Papers of William Dunbar*, p. 194.

312 **"Arrived about 12 Oclock"** Pike journal, April 30, 1806, in Jackson, *The Journals of Zebulon Montgomery Pike*, vol. 1, p. 131.

312 **"we left Fort Adams"** Custis journal, n.d., in Dan Flores, *Southern Counterpart to Lewis and Clark: The Freeman and Custis Expedition of 1806* (Norman: University of Oklahoma Press, 1984), p. 103.

313 **a proclamation from the Spanish king** Marshall, *History of the Western Boundary*, p. 44.

CHAPTER TWENTY

314 **"Pike returned a few days ago"** "Excerpt of a letter from a man to his father in Pittsburgh," *New York Gazette*, June 12, 1806, p. 2.

315 **"a flighty, rattle-headed fellow"** James Ripley Jacobs, *Tarnished Warrior* (New York: Macmillan, 1938), p. 101.

316 **didn't leave for his spring vacation** TJ to Jacob Crowninshield, May 13, 1806 in Paul Leicester Ford, *The Works of Thomas Jefferson, Correspondence and Papers, 1803–1807* (New York: G. P. Putnam's Sons, 1904–05), vol. 10, p. 265.

316 **"a long peace with Spain"** TJ to Elizabeth Trist, April 27, 1806, quoted in *Thomas Jefferson's Garden Book*, annotated by Edwin Morris Betts (Philadelphia: American Philosophical Society, 1992), pp. 310–11.

317 **"According to our latest dispatches"** TJ to W. C. C. Claiborne, April 27, 1806, in Ford, *The Works of Thomas Jefferson: Correspondence and Papers, 1803–1807*, vol. 10, p. 253.

317 **"advanced in considerable force"** TJ, annual message to Congress, December 2, 1806, in *The Writings of Thomas Jefferson*, edited by Andrew A. Lipscomb and Albert Ellery Bergh (Washington: Thomas Jefferson Memorial Association, 1905), vol. 3, p. 416.

317 **"recent information received from New Orleans"** Henry Dearborn to James Wilkinson, May 6, 1806, Thomas Jefferson Papers at the Library of Congress, ser. 1, General Correspondence, 1651–1827, microfilm reel 035.

318 **"I was able to get from Washington"** TJ to Jacob Crowninshield, May 13, 1806, ibid.

319 **"meanders of the red river"** Freeman journal, in Dan Flores, *Southern Counterpart to Lewis and Clark: The Freeman and Custis Expedition of 1806* (Norman: University of Oklahoma Press, 1984), p. 119.

319 **"Owing to Mr. Freemans"** Custis journal, ibid., p. 103.

319 **"a shrub growing in great abundance"** Custis journal, n.d., ibid., p. 109.

321 **Caddo was actually the language** F. Todd Smith, "A Native Response to the Transfer of Louisiana: The Red River Caddos and Spain," *Louisiana History* 37, no. 2 (Spring 1996): 165.

322 **new Kadohadacho chief named Dehahuit** F. Todd Smith, "The Kadohadacho Indians and the Louisiana-Texas Frontier, 1803–1815," *Southwestern Historical Quarterly* 95, no. 2 (October 1991): 180–83.

322 **some additional nations** W. C. C. Claiborne to TJ, July 14, 1805, in *The Letter Books of W. C. C. Claiborne* (Jackson, MS: State Department of Archives and History, 1917), vol. 3, pp. 124–25.

322 **Dehahuit may well have been** John Sibley to William Eustis, January 30, 1810, in Julia Kathryn Garrett, "Dr. John Sibley and the Louisiana-Texas Frontier, 1803–1814," *The Southwestern Historical Quarterly*, vol. 47, no. 4 (April 1944): 389.

323 **"the trunks of large trees"** Freeman journal, in Flores, *Southern Counterpart to Lewis and Clark*, p. 127.

325 **"for the purpose of assisting"** Ibid., p. 123.

325 **"To morrow morning we leave"** Custis journal, ibid., p. 125.

CHAPTER TWENTY-ONE

327 **"The labor incident"** Thomas Freeman journal for June 9, 1806, in Dan Flores, *Southwest Counterpart to Lewis and Clark: The Freeman and Custis Expedition of 1806* (Norman: University of Oklahoma Press, 1984), pp. 133–34.

328 **"The wood lies so compact"** Thomas Freeman journal for June 2, 1806, in Flores, *Southwest Counterpart*, p. 127.

328 **"lie so close that the men"** Thomas Freeman journal for June 8, 1806, ibid., p. 131.

329 "It was absolutely impractical" Thomas Freeman journal for June 11, 1806, ibid., p. 134.

329 "sensible regret" James Wilkinson to Henry Dearborn, August 2, 1806, in *The Journals of Zebulon Montgomery Pike*, edited by Donald Jackson (Norman: University of Oklahoma Press, 1966), vol. 2, p. 128.

330 "proceed without delay" Wilkinson to Pike, June 24, 1806, ibid., vol. 1, p. 285.

330 could be published as a book *The Expeditions of Zebulon Montgomery Pike*, edited by Elliott Coues (New York: Harper, 1895), p. xxxiv.

331 "As your Interview" James Wilkinson to Zebulon Pike, June 24, 1806, in *Letters of the Lewis and Clark Expedition*, edited by Donald Jackson (Urbana: University of Illinois Press, 1962), vol. 1, p. 286.

333 "in time be the principal channel" Thomas Freeman journal for June 11, 1806, in Flores, *Southwest Counterpart*, p. 135.

333 "almost impenetrable Swamps" Peter Custis, journal undated, ibid., p. 154.

333 "incessant fatigue, toil and danger" Thomas Freeman journal, July 1, 1806, ibid., p. 143.

334 Dehahuit was positioned as the arbiter Timothy K. Perttula, Dayna Bowker Lee, and Rabert Cast, "The First People of the Red River: The Caddo Before and After Freeman and Custis," in *Freeman and Custis Expedition of 1806: Two Hundred Years Later*, edited by Laurence M. Hardy (Shreveport: Louisiana State University Press, 2008), p. 90.

334 "he loved all men" Thomas Freeman journal, July 1. 1806, in Flores, *Southwest Counterpart*, p. 146.

335 It was Talapoon Thomas Freeman journal, July 1. 1806, in Flores, *Southwest Counterpart*, pp. 145–46.

335 "about 300 Spanish Dragoons" Thomas Freeman journal, July 1. 1806, ibid., p. 146.

335 "the Paradise of America" Peter Custis, journal undated, ibid., p. 154.

335 "It stands on the North side" Thomas Freeman journal, July 1. 1806, ibid., p 149.

336 "He said, he was glad" Peter Custis, journal undated, Flores, *Southwest Counterpart*, p. 164.

337 "The Valley of the Red river" Thomas Freeman journal, July 1. 1806, ibid., p. 175.

337 "it was expected" Ibid., p. 181.

338 "kill them, or carry them off" Foster Todd Smith, *From Dominance to*

Disappearance: The Indians of Texas and the Near Southwest (Lincoln: University Press of Nebraska, 2005), p. 86.

338 **"We sailed from the landing"** Zebulon Pike journal, July 15, 1806, in Jackson, *The Journals of Zebulon Montgomery Pike*, vol. 1, pp. 290–91.

340 **Jefferson was aware** Henry Dearborn to Pike, February 24, 1808, ibid., vol. 2, pp. 300–301.

340 **"On receiving this intelligence,"** Thomas Freeman journal, July 26, 1806, in Flores, *Southwest Counterpart*, p. 192.

341 **"The party continued to advance"** Ibid., p. 199.

341 **"a large detachment"** Ibid., p. 202.

342 **"The object of my expedition"** Ibid., p. 204.

342 **"that if a Spanish guard"** Ibid., pp. 205–6.

342 **the expedition had been a success** Ibid., p. 206.

CHAPTER TWENTY-TWO

343 **the boatman "informed us"** W. Clark journal, September 17, 1806, *The Journals of the Lewis and Clark Expedition* (University of Nebraska Press/University of Nebraska–Lincoln Libraries/Electronic Text Center, http://lewisandclarkjournals.unl.edu).

343 **with Congress** TJ, "Expedition of Lewis and Clarke," February 19, 1806, in *Annals of Congress*, 9th Congress, Appendix, pp. 1036–37.

344 **taking Sacajawea** Harold P. Howard, *Sacajawea* (Norman: University of Oklahoma Press, 1971), p. 112.

345 **Blackfoot believed that they had won** "Untelling the Big Lie: The Murder of Two Blackfeet by Lewis & Clark Party," *Indian Country*, July 27, 2013.

345 **"I called to them"** M. Lewis journal, July 27, 1806, in *Journals of the Lewis and Clark Expedition*, http://lewisandclarkjournals.unl.edu.

346 **"you have shot me!"** M. Lewis journal, August 11, 1806, ibid.

347 **initiating plans to adopt him** W. Clark journal, August 17, 1806, ibid.

348 **deeply tanned** Robert John Moore Jr. and Michael Haynes, *Lewis & Clark, Tailor Made, Trail Worn: Army Life, Clothing & Weapons of the Corps of Discovery* (Helena, MT: Farcountry Press, 2003), p. 65.

348 **"Captains Lewis and Clark arrived here"** "Extract of a letter from St. Louis, to a gentleman in Georgetown," September 22, 1806, *Alexandria* (Virginia) *Daily Advertiser*, October 27, 1806, p. 3; see also "Extract of a letter from St. Louis, upper Louisiana dated September 23, 1806," *New York Herald*, October 29, 1806, p. 2; "We stop the press," *South Carolina Gazette*, November 15, 1806.

349   "The territory of Louisiana" "Arrival of Capts. Lewis and Clark at St. Louis," *New Hampshire Gazette*, December 2, 1806, p. 2.

349   ARRIVAL OF CAPT's LEWIS AND CLARK "ARRIVAL OF CAPT's," *Portsmouth* (New Hampshire) *Gazette*, December 2, 1806, p. 2.

350   "A body of federalists" Untitled article, *The Witness* (Litchfield, Connecticut), December 3, 1806, p. 3.

350   "Like a boat descending a river" Untitled article, *Boston Repertory*, November 21, 1806, p. 2.

351   "Lieutenant or first in command" TJ, "Notes on a Cabinet Meeting," October 22, 1806, in *The Writings of Thomas Jefferson*, edited by Andrew A. Lipscomb and Albert Ellery Bergh (Washington: Thomas Jefferson Memorial Association, 1905), vol. 1, p. 458–59.

351   "penetrated the designs of the Spaniard" Wilkinson to Dearborn, September 8, 1806, quoted in Thomas Maitland Marshall, *A History of the Western Boundary of the Louisiana Purchase, 1819–1841* (Berkeley: University of California Press, 1914), p. 29.

352   "what a situation our country" James Wilkinson to Colonel Cushing, November 7, 1806, in James Wilkinson, *Burr's Conspiracy Exposed; and General Wilkinson Vindicated Against the Slanders of His Enemies on That Occasion* (Washington City: Published for the author, 1811), p. 61.

352   sent his annual message to Congress TJ, annual message to Congress, December 2, 1806, in *Writings of Thomas Jefferson*, edited by Lipscomb and Bergh, vol. 3, p. 414.

352   "The expedition of Messrs. Lewis" TJ, ibid., p. 13.

353   Freeman was still in the Natchez Frances C. Roberts, "Thomas Freeman—Surveyor of the Old Southwest," *Alabama Review* 60, no. 3 (July 1987): 222–23.

355   one layer of cotton clothing Pike journal, December 3, 1806, in *The Journals of Zebulon Montgomery Pike*, edited by Donald Jackson (Norman: University of Oklahoma, 1966), vol. 1, p. 353.

355   "another winter in the desert" Pike journal, November 11, 1806, ibid., p. 344.

356   Pike finally turned his back Pike journal, November 27, 1806, ibid., p. 351.

356   "800 miles from the frontiers" Pike journal, December 25, 1806, ibid., p. 361.

356   "felt at considerable loss" Pike journal, January 9, 1807, ibid., p. 367.

357   "sat up all night" Pike journal, January 18, 1807, ibid., p. 369.

357 **planning where to die** Pike journal, January 19, 1806, ibid., p. 369.

357 **"more than human nature could bear"** Pike journal, January 24, 1807, ibid., pp. 371–72.

360 **"this government has never employed a spy"** TJ to James Madison, August 30, 1807, in *The Writings of Thomas Jefferson*, edited by Andrew A. Lipscomb and Albert Ellery Bergh (Washington: Thomas Jefferson Memorial Association, 1905), vol. 11, p. 347.

360 **"My little excursion up the river"** Pike journal, December 24, 1806, ibid., p. 361.

361 **"the want of funds"** Henry Dearborn to TJ, June 23, 1807, National Archives.

361 **moving his family and businesses** Miriam L. Luke, "The Genealogy and Career of Dr. George Hunter," typescript (Covington, IN: 1979, Allen County Public Library, Fort Wayne, IN), p. 7.

362 **bringing the steam engine to Louisiana** Oliver Evans, "Observations on Steam Engines," *The Agricultural Museum*, May 22, 1811, p. 361.

362 **"Sir William"** Franklin LaFayette Riley, *Sir William Dunbar, The Pioneer Scientist of Mississippi* (Oxford: Mississippi Historical Society, 1899), p. 85; Mary D. Hudgins, "William Dunbar, History Maker," *Arkansas Historical Quarterly* 1, no. 4 (December 1942): 331.

363 **investigators proved that he** Richard S. Preston, "The Accuracy of the Astronomical Observations of Lewis and Clark," *Proceedings of the American Philosophical Society* 144, no. 2 (June 2000): 178–87. Robert Bergantino of Butte, Montana, was instrumental in casting new light on Lewis and Clark's navigational work. See Bob Bergantino and Ginette Abdo, "Lewis and Clark in Montana: A Geologic Perspective," Montana Bureau of Mines and Geology, accessed on the Internet: mbmg.mtech.edu/gmr/lewis_clark/L&C.pdf.

365 **died under mysterious circumstances** Alexander Wilson to Alexander Lawson, May 18, 1810, in *The Poems and Literary Prose of Alexander Wilson*, edited by Alexander B. Grosart (Paisley, Scotland: A. Gardner, 1876), vol. 1, pp. 209–10.

365 **"I fear O!"** William Clark to Jonathan Clark, October 28, 1809, in James J. Holmberg, *Dear Brother: Letters of William Clark to Jonathan Clark* (New Haven: Yale University Press, 2002), p. 216.

365 **The list that Freeman left** *Letters of the Lewis and Clark Expedition*, edited by Donald Jackson (Urbana: University of Illinois Press, 1962), vol. 1, p. 470.

366 **Freeman's career culminated with his appointment** Silas Dinsmoor,

MD, "Silas Dinsmoor," in Peter J. Hamilton, *Colonial Mobile* (Cambridge, MA: Houghton Mifflin Company, 1910), p. 558. Dr. Dinsmoor's profile of his grandfather, Freeman's deputy.

366 **"the Boundaries of the U. States"** Untitled article, *New England Palladium*, August 7, 1818, p. 2.

367 **Barlow wrote a poem** Joel Barlow, "Of the Discoveries of Captain Lewis," *Washington National Intelligencer*, January 16, 1807, p. 3.

Selected Bibliography

BOOKS

Bancroft, Hubert Howe. *History of Arizona and New Mexico: 1530–1888*. San Francisco: History Book Company, 1889.

Bennett, Hugh Hammond. *Thomas Jefferson, Soil Conservationist*. Washington, DC: U.S. Department of Agriculture, Soil Conservation Service, 1944.

Berry, Trey, Pam Beasley, and Jeanne Clements, eds. *The Forgotten Expedition: 1804–1805*. Baton Rouge: Louisiana State University Press, 2006.

Betts, Edwin Morris, ann. *Thomas Jefferson's Garden Book, 1766–1824*. Philadelphia: American Philosophical Society, 1992.

Betts, Edwin M., and Hazlehurst Bolton Perkins. *Thomas Jefferson's Flower Garden at Monticello*, 3rd ed. Charlottesville: University of Virginia Press for the Thomas Jefferson Memorial Foundation, 1986.

Cazier, Lola. *Surveys and Surveyors of the Public Domain, 1785–1975*. Washingon, DC: U.S. Dept. of the Interior, Bureau of Land Management, 1976.

Chadwick, French Ensor. *The Relations of the United States and Spain: Diplomacy.* New York: Charles Scribner's Sons, 1909.

Claiborne, John Francis Hamtramck. *Mississippi, as a Province, Territory and State. Vol. 1.* Jackson, MS: Power & Barksdale, 1880.

DeRosier, Arthur H. *William Dunbar: Scientific Pioneer of the Old Southwest.* Lexington: University Press of Kentucky, 2007.

Engstrand, Iris H. W. *Spanish Scientists in the New World: The Eighteenth-Century Expeditions.* Seattle: University of Washington Press, 1981.

Flores, Dan Louie, ed. *Southern Counterpart to Lewis and Clark: The Freeman and Custis Expedition of 1806.* Norman: University of Oklahoma Press, 1984.

Hardy, Laurence M., ed. *Freeman and Custis Red River Expedition of 1806: Two Hundred Years Later.* Shreveport: Louisiana State University, 2008.

Houck, Louis, ed. *The Spanish Regime in Missouri.* 2 vols. Chicago: R.R. Donnelley, 1909.

Jackson, Donald, ed. *The Journals of Zebulon Montgomery Pike.* 2 vols. Norman: University of Oklahoma Press, 1966.

———. *Letters of the Lewis and Clark Expedition, with Related Documents, 1783–1854.* Urbana: University of Illinois Press, 1962.

Jefferson, Thomas, ed. *Travels in the Interior Parts of America.* London: Richard Phillips, 1807.

Jefferson, Thomas, and William Dunbar. *Documents Relating to the Purchase and Exploration of Louisiana.* Boston: Houghton Mifflin, 1904.

Lambeth, William Alexander, and Warren Manning. *Thomas Jefferson as an Architect and Designer of Landscapes.* Bedford, MA: Applewood Books, 1913.

Loomis, Noel M. and Nasatir, Abraham P. *Pedro Vial and the Roads to Santa Fe.* Norman: University of Oklahoma, 1967.

Marshall, Thomas Maitland. *A History of the Western Boundary of the Louisiana Purchase, 1819–1841.* Berkeley: University of California Press, 1912.

Mathews, Catharine Van Cortlandt. *Andrew Ellicott: His Life and Letters.* New York: Grafton Press, 1908.

McDermott, John Francis, ed. *The Western Journals of Dr. George Hunter 1796–1805.* Philadelphia: American Philosophical Society, 1963.

Michaux, André, *Journal of André Michaux*. Cleveland: A. H. Clark, 1904.

Moulton, Gary. *The Definitive Journals of Lewis and Clark*. 7 vols. Lincoln: University of Nebraska Press, 2002.

Nasatir, A. P., ed. *Before Lewis and Clark: Documents Illustrating the History of the Missouri 1785–1804*. 2 vols. Lincoln: University of Nebraska Press, 1990.

Perrin Du Lac, Marie. *Travels Through the Two Louisianas*. London: Richard Phillips, 1807.

Randolph, Sarah N., comp. *The Domestic Life of Thomas Jefferson*. Charlottesville: Published for the Jefferson Memorial Foundation by the University Press of Virginia, 1978.

Riley, Franklin LaFayette. *Sir William Dunbar, The Pioneer Scientist of Mississippi*. Oxford: Mississippi Historical Society, 1899.

Robertson, James Alexander, ed. *Louisiana Under the Rule of Spain, France, and the United States, 1785–1807*. 2 vols. Cleveland: Arthur H. Clark, 1911.

Rowland, Mrs. Dunbar, comp. *Life, Letters and Papers of William Dunbar*. Jackson: Press of the Mississippi Historical Society, 1930.

Rowland, Dunbar, ed. *Official Letter Books of W. C. C. Claiborne, 1801–1816*. 3 vols. Jackson: State Department of History and Archives, 1917.

Sibley, Dr. John. *A Report from Natchitoches in 1807*. New York: Museum of the American Indian, 1922.

Smith, Ben A., and James W. Vining. *American Geographers, 1784–1812*. Westport, CT: Praeger, 2003.

Stephens, Thomas. *Madoc: An Essay on the Discovery of America by Madoc Ap Owen Gwynedd in the Twelfth Century*. London: Longmans, Green, 1893.

Wilkinson, James. *Memoirs of My Own Times*. 3 vols. Philadelphia: Abraham Small, 1816.

INTERNET RESOURCE

University of Nebraska Press/University of Nebraska–Lincoln Libraries/ Electronic Text Center. *The Journals of the Lewis and Clark Expedition*. http://lewisandclarkjournals.unl.edu.

ARTICLES

Adams, Mary P. "Jefferson's Reaction to the Treaty of San Ildefonso." *The Journal of Southern History* 21, no. 2 (May 1955): 173–88.

Bannon, John Francis. "The Spaniards and the Illinois Country, 1762–1800." *Journal of the Illinois State Historical Society (1908–1984)* 69, no. 2 (May 1976): 110–18.

Berry, Trey. "The Expedition of William Dunbar and George Hunter Along the Ouachita River, 1804–1805." *Arkansas Historical Quarterly* 62, no. 4 (Winter 2003): 386–403.

Bradley, Jared T. "W. C. C. Claiborne and Spain: Foreign Affairs under Jefferson and Madison." *Louisiana History* 12, no. 4 (Autumn 1971): 297–314.

Cox, Isaac Joslin. "Hispanic-American Phases of the 'Burr Conspiracy.'" *Hispanic American Historical Review* 12, no. 2 (May 1932): 145–75.

———. "The Freeman Red River Expedition." *Proceedings of the American Philosophical Society* 92, no. 2 (May 1948): 115–19.

———. "The Pan-American Policy of Jefferson and Wilkinson." *The Mississippi Valley Historical Review* 1, no. 2 (September 1914): 212–39.

Danisi, Thomas C., and W. Raymond Wood. "Lewis and Clark's Route Map: James MacKay's Map of the Missouri River." *Western Historical Quarterly* 35, no. 1 (Spring 2004): 53–72.

Din, Gilbert C. "Spain's Immigration Policy in Louisiana and the American Penetration, 1792–1803." *Southwestern Historical Quarterly* 76, no. 3 (January 1973): 255–76.

Fisher, James. "A Forgotten Hero Remembered, Revered and Revised: The Legacy and Ordeal of George Rogers Clark." *Indiana Magazine of History* 92, no. 2 (June 1996): 109–32.

Hamilton, William B. "The Southwestern Frontier, 1795–1817: An Essay in Social History." *The Journal of Southern History* 10, no. 4 (November 1944): 389–403.

Hollon, W. Eugene. "Zebulon Montgomery Pike and the Wilkinson-Burr Conspiracy." *Proceedings of the American Philosophical Society* 91, no. 5 (December 1947): 447–56.

LaVere, David. "Between Kinship and Capitalism: French and Spanish Rivalry in the Colonial Louisiana-Texas Indian Trade." *Journal of Southern History* 64, no. 2 (May 1998): 197–218.

Lemée, Patricia R. "Tios and Tantes: Familial and Political Relationships of Natchitoches and the Spanish Colonial Frontier." *Southwestern Historical Quarterly* 101, no. 3 (January 1998): 341–58.

Ludwickson, John. "Blackbird and Son: A Note Concerning Late-Eighteenth-and Early Nineteenth-Century Omaha Chieftainship." *Ethnohistory* 42, no. 1 (Winter 1995): 133–49.

Preston, Richard S. "The Accuracy of the Astronomical Observations of Lewis and Clark." *Proceedings of the American Philosophical Society* 144, no. 2 (June 2000): 168–91.

Quinn, C. Edward. "A Zoologist's View of the Lewis and Clark Expedition." *American Zoologist* 26, no. 2 (1986): 299–306.

Roberts, Frances C. "Thomas Freeman—Surveyor of the Old Southwest." *Alabama Review* 40, no. 3 (July 1987): 216–30.

Shepherd, William R. "Wilkinson and the Beginnings of Spanish Conspiracy." *The American Historical Review* 9, no. 3 (April 1904): 490–506.

Smith, F. Todd. "A Native Response to the Transfer of Louisiana: The Red River Caddos and Spain, 1762–1803." *Louisiana History* 37, no. 2 (Spring 1996): 163–85.

———. "The Kadohadacho Indians and the Louisiana-Texas Frontier, 1803–1815." *Southwestern Historical Quarterly* 95, no. 2 (October 1991): 177–204.

Williams, David. "John Evans' Strange Journey: Part I, The Welsh Indians." *American Historical Review* 54, no. 2 (January 1949): 277–95.

———. "John Evans' Strange Journey: Part II, Following the Trail." *American Historical Review* 54, no. 3 (April 1949): 508–29.

Wilson, George R. "The First Public Land Surveys in Indiana: Freeman's Lines." *Indiana Magazine of History* 12, no. 1 (March 1916): 1–33.

Wilson, M. L. "Thomas Jefferson—Farmer." *Proceedings of the American Philosophical Society* 87, no. 3 (July 1943): 216–22.

Young, Raymond A. "Pinckney's Treaty—A New Perspective." *Hispanic American Historical Review* 43, no. 4 (November 1963): 526–35.

Index

Note: Page numbers in *italics* refer to maps.